ALL IN IT TOGETHER

Also by Alwyn Turner

Crisis? What Crisis? Britain in the 1970s

Rejoice! Rejoice! Britain in the 1980s

A Classless Society: Britain in the 1990s

The Last Post: Music, Remembrance and the Great War

The Biba Experience

The Man Who Invented the Daleks:
The Strange Worlds of Terry Nation

Halfway to Paradise: The Birth of British Rock

My Generation: The Glory Years of British Rock

Glam Rock: Dandies in the Underworld

Portmeirion (contributing editor)

The History of British Military Bands (three volumes)

Tribute: A Salute to the British Armed
Forces of the Second World War

ALL IN IT TOGETHER

England in the Early 21st Century

ALWYN TURNER

P

PROFILE BOOKS

First published in Great Britain in 2021 by
Profile Books Ltd
29 Cloth Fair
London
ECIA 7JQ

www.profilebooks.com

1 3 5 7 9 10 8 6 4 2

Typeset in Sabon by MacGuru Ltd
Printed and bound in Great Britain by
Clays Ltd, Elcograf S.p.A.

A CIP catalogue record for this book is available from the British Library.

ISBN 978 1 78816 672 0
eISBN 978 1 78283 786 2
Audio ISBN 978 1 78283 847 0

FSC
www.fsc.org
MIX
Paper from
responsible sources
FSC® C018072

For Thamasin

Contents

Prologue: Faith

I

Manchester City fans of a certain vintage – those who remembered the late-1960s team of Colin Bell, Franny Lee and Mike Summerbee – would no doubt have disagreed, but Maine Road stadium in Moss Side was not a place where you'd normally expect to witness a miracle. Let alone one that heralded the return of the messiah. Yet there it was: a column of sunlight falling through a moonless night sky, illuminating just Maine Road itself, while all around remained in darkness. 'It's daylight!' exclaimed the television news reports. 'It's daylight inside the stadium and it's night outside. There's no explanation for the light. This isn't a hoax.'

And then a gawky, cheaply dressed Mancunian appeared on the screens. 'This is the work of God, and I'm his son,' he announced. 'God in human form.'

Russell T. Davies's drama *The Second Coming* (2003) told the story of Steve Baxter, played by Christopher Eccleston, an ordinary, if awkward, man with three O levels (he failed French). He works at EasyRent Video in Salford, before he's suddenly struck by a blinding revelation that he is the son of God, a new messiah come to save humanity. Having grabbed the attention of the media with the Maine Road Miracle, he makes his first address to the world. 'You are becoming gods,' he tells his audience. 'You've unravelled DNA. You're five years away from building your own people. And at the same time you're cultivating bacteria strong enough to kill every living thing.' Then his voice changes, challenging now, taunting: 'Do you think you're ready for that much power? You lot? You lot? You cheeky bastards!'

The point of the drama is that this is not a delusion. Steve really is the son of God. And he's confused, disorientated. His head is filled with the whole of Creation, but he's also a normal bloke, and he can't see what he's supposed to do with this level of consciousness. His coming will reveal to humanity the Third Testament, but how? All he knows is that he won't be the one writing it.

It takes an old schoolfriend, Judy, to figure it out. He must die. Just like last time, he must voluntarily give his life for humanity. But this time it's going to be final. 'When you die, you're not ascending to paradise,' she says. 'You're dying properly and for ever, taking the whole thing with you. God and heaven and hell – all dead. The end of this world and the start of a new one, without religion on our backs.' She tells him that the dinner she's cooked for him is full of rat poison, and, recognising the truth of her words, he eats it anyway.

This, it transpires, is the Third Testament. It's the 'death of God', the emergence of humanity into a new evolutionary phase, without the need for the crutch of religion. As Judy puts it, 'As soon as we get rid of God, that's when we grow up.'

The new millennium was not celebrated in Britain as a Christian event. A thousand years earlier, there had been fears among the faithful that the end was nigh; this time there was an entirely secular panic that a programming glitch – known as Y2K or the millennium bug – might damage the world's computers.* The official Millennium Experience, at the Dome in Greenwich, South London, did have a gallery called the Faith Zone (one of fourteen such zones), but the show was careful not to overdo the Christianity. The central values of modern society were deemed to be inclusion, diversity and tolerance, so it was important to celebrate all the mainstream religions practised in the country.

The same thinking was evident when Churches Together in England, an organisation that represented the main Christian denominations, issued a prayer for the occasion. Titled the Millennium Resolution, it mentioned neither God nor Jesus, as if this were the faith that dare not speak its name. Churches Together also took the opportunity to offer a 'general confession' for the sins committed by Christians individually and collectively; the general secretary explained that 'there have been two thousand very positive years of Christianity, but there has also been a flip side'.[1]

The Second Coming, in other words, reflected the fact that Britain was now a post-Christian country, even if it was reluctant

---

* It didn't. Hundreds of billions of dollars were spent on preventive measures that worked. In some quarters, though, Y2K became a symbol of scaremongering. 'We will look back and wonder what all the fuss was about,' said Conservative MP Bernard Jenkin when asked in 2018 about the economic consequences of Britain leaving the European Union. 'A bit like the millennium bug. Remember all the experts on the millennium bug?' (*Today*, BBC Radio 4, 6 August 2018)

to admit such a thing. In 2001, for the first time in 150 years, the census asked people to identify their religion, if any. Eight million people in England and Wales said they had no religion, and by 2011 this had risen to 14 million. But that was still only a quarter of the population.* Over the same period, those identifying as Christian fell by 4 million, from 72 to 59 per cent, with greatest representation among the old and in the north of England. Despite the decline, this was still a long way clear of the second largest faith group, Muslims, who had nearly doubled in number to 2.7 million, just under 5 per cent.†

On the other hand, there remained a residual respect for the churches. When the polling organisation MORI asked people in 2003 who they trusted to tell the truth, 71 per cent expressed faith in the clergy, comparable to the support enjoyed by judges, though a little way behind doctors and teachers. (Politicians and journalists came in last, each with an 18 per cent showing, unchanged in two decades.)[2] Fifteen years on, in 2018, priests had slipped a little in public estimation, but were still trusted by 62 per cent – which was more than pollsters themselves.[3]

And culturally the old faith remained. In large parts of the country the popular image of the Church of England still persisted: a snug, carol-service and sweet-sherry image. It could be seen in the way that the most popular television comedies – the ones that attracted the big audiences if not always the critics – still included the reassuringly familiar touchstone of the vicar. A 2004 BBC series *Britain's Best Sitcom* invited viewers' votes, and Richard Curtis's old-fashioned entertainment *The Vicar of*

---

* The least religious place was Norwich, where 42.5 per cent reported having no religion.

† In Scotland, where the question was phrased slightly differently, the direction of travel was the same: in 2011, 54 per cent were Christian, 37 per cent had no religion, just 1.4 per cent were Muslim.

Dibley (1994) came third,* infuriating many better-informed folk, from Ally Ross, the *Sun*'s TV reviewer, to Ricky Gervais, whose own show *The Office* (2001) came twenty-fifth. ('There are certainly ten better sitcoms than *The Office*,' Gervais conceded. 'It's just that *Vicar of Dibley* is not one of them.')[4] What seemed to be the final episode of *Dibley* was broadcast on the first day of the millennium, but the show was briefly revived at Christmas in 2004 and again in 2006; on the latter occasion, it attracted over 13 million viewers, the highest rated programme on Christmas Day.

That same day, the long-running *My Family* (2000) introduced Kevin, the local vicar, who became a recurrent character. And six years on from that, in 2012, the highest-rated Christmas Day show was a special of *Mrs Brown's Boys* (2011), getting shrieks of laughter from the studio audience when a Catholic priest walks in to find a middle-aged woman in what looks like a compromising position, a comic misunderstanding that would have been recognisable forty years earlier. The critically acclaimed sitcom *Rev* (2010), with its gentle, human portrayal of an inner-city parish, couldn't compete with those shows for viewing figures, but did win a BAFTA. So too did *Gavin & Stacey* (2007), which eventually reached a mass audience when it transferred from BBC Three to BBC One; its vicar, Father Chris, was characteristic of the mildly eccentric type, a purveyor of left-field metaphor: 'We've all got a different relationship with God, just like we've all got a different relationship with sandwiches.'

The best-loved comedian of the time, Peter Kay, was brought up a Catholic, but now espoused a vague spirituality unencumbered by doctrinal or organisational baggage. 'I think Jesus was just an ordinary person, like me and you,' he wrote in his best-selling autobiography, *The Sound of Laughter* (2006), adding, 'I believe in a God of some kind, in some sort of higher being.

---

* *Only Fools and Horses* and *Blackadder* came in first and second places.

Personally I find it very comforting.'[5] The editor of comedy website chortle.co.uk said of Peter Kay, 'His stock in trade is a cosy world of things we can all relate to, and I suppose a belief in God is part of that cosy world.'[6]

Cosy, comforting … These were not attributes associated with metropolitan liberals, a tribe whose distance from the rest of the country inspired a thousand newspaper columns (most of them written by metropolitan liberals). Nick Hornby's novel *How to Be Good* (2001) told the story of a typical modern couple in north London. Katie is a GP, a decent middle-class type, tormented by guilt that she's failing in her relationships with her parents, her children and her husband. He, on the other hand, is tormented by rage at a society in which there's a diminishing demand for mediocre men with humanities degrees. In another place and another class, he'd 'be angry about poofs and communists', but his professed left-wing politics deny him even this satisfaction. So instead he rants against trivial targets at dinner parties and in a column for the local paper (he's billed as 'The Angriest Man in Holloway'), and he works on a novel – 'facetious, unkind, full of itself' – that will never be published. Then he has a Damascene moment on the road to Finsbury Park, and falls under the influence of a spiritual guru and faith healer, a young man who took too much Ecstasy in his former incarnation as a club DJ. Meanwhile, Katie visits an Anglican church, but finds no answers to her confusion, only 'woolly-minded nonsense'.[7]

Elsewhere, woolly-minded nonsense remained perfectly sufficient. 'Can you imagine a world without God, Mum?' asks Eva Beaver, a librarian from Leicester in Sue Townsend's *The Woman Who Went to Bed for a Year* (2012), and her mother reflects: 'We'd all be at each other's throats, wouldn't we? As it is, we tick along nicely.' But that's just in England, protests Eva; what about everywhere else? 'Well they're mostly heathens, aren't they? They have their own way of carrying on.'[8]

*

In the real world, many Christians felt a little aggrieved that their faith did not seem to warrant the same sensitivity accorded to others. It was not a new complaint, but it gained fresh currency whenever incidents of what appeared to be anti-Christian prejudice were reported: the case, for example, of Nadia Eweida, a 55-year-old check-in worker at Heathrow Airport, dismissed from her job with British Airways in 2006 for wearing a small cross around her neck.* The offence was felt by some as an attack not simply on religion but on their culture. 'Was I on holiday when this became not a Christian country?' asked comedian Roy Chubby Brown. 'What does BA stand for? Bastard Atheists?'

Meanwhile the churches seemed to outsiders as if they were wrestling constantly, and a little obsessively, with sexual morals. In 2003, the Church of England named the Reverend Jeffrey John the new suffragan bishop of Reading, an announcement greeted with some dismay by traditionalists, when it emerged that he 'had been in a gay relationship for decades'.[9] The appointment was denounced by archbishops from around the world – Sydney, Nigeria, the West Indies, the Congo – with the latter warning of a possible schism, the emergence of an 'Anglican Communion for the western people and another for the south'.[10]

The Church's official position, thrashed out in the previous decade, was a characteristic compromise. Gay sexual relationships might sometimes be tolerated – if disapproved of – in the laity, but homosexual clergy were obliged to live celibate lives, and that had not always been the case with the Reverend John, even if it was now. ('The relationship has not been sexually expressed for years,' he said. 'This is not unusual, even in heterosexual relationships.')[11] Eventually, John was persuaded to turn down the appointment, to avoid damage 'to the unity of the Church',[12]

---

* Eweida lost her claim for compensation against BA, but in 2013 won a case against the British government in the European Court of Human Rights, where it was ruled that her right to religious freedom had not been protected.

and his friend Rowan Williams, the archbishop of Canterbury, said he'd been distressed by the 'appalling prejudice and abuse' on display.[13] 'I don't understand why God hates poofs so much,' puzzles Colin, an unemployed alcoholic in *Rev*, and the Reverend Adam Smallbone has to correct him: 'He doesn't, Colin. God loves poofs. He loves us all.'*

More seriously, the Catholic Church was enmired in a series of scandals concerning the sexual abuse of children, and though the worst stories came from elsewhere, dozens of British priests were defrocked in the first two decades of the new century. Mention of the Church was now frequently accompanied by reference to child abuse, and this became a standard line for comedians and others to take. As Steve tries to come to terms with his mission in *The Second Coming*, a priest tells him, 'It won't be easy getting people to listen. Some of us have been trying for years.' To which he retorts, 'And some of you have been shagging choir boys.'

Not everyone, however, saw this as being the biggest issue when it came to religion. 'I suspect that most of the sexual abuse priests are accused of is comparatively mild,' reflected Richard Dawkins; 'a little bit of fondling perhaps, and a young child might scarcely notice it.' Much more worrying, he suggested, was the 'brain washing' of the young: 'The Roman Catholic Church is one of the forces of evil in the world because of the powerful influences it has over the minds of children.'[14]

Dawkins was professor for the public understanding of science at Oxford University, a post created especially for him in 1995 with a reported £1.5 million endowment from Charles Simonyi, the man who gave us Microsoft Word. 'What I do best is promote an understanding of the poetry of science and an aesthetic appreciation of the wonders of life and the universe,' Dawkins said,[15] though as far as the public were concerned, he was known not for celebrating wonders but for condemning miracles. His

---

* In 2014 *Coronation Street* introduced Billy Mayhew, a gay vicar.

seemed an austere position – he was scathing of Peter Kay's word 'comforting' – and one that allowed little room for fantasy. 'It is anti-scientific,' he said of the world of fairy tales. 'Looking back to my own childhood, the fact that so many of the stories I read allowed the possibility of frogs turning into princes – whether that has a sort of insidious effect on rationality, I'm not sure.'[16]

His early books on evolutionary biology had brought unexpected fame, but real stardom came with the publication of *The God Delusion* (2006), a huge hit that within 8 years had been translated into 35 languages with 3 million sales. He became the media's favourite celebrity atheist: apple-cheeked and Anglican in appearance, earnest in manner, and married to *Doctor Who* actress Lalla Ward. Dawkins's book was famous enough that it could be used as shorthand in the TV drama *Apparitions* (2008) to show that a young man who owns a copy is 'a very committed atheist'. (Unusually, the atheism in this case turns out to be a case of demonic possession, and the services of an exorcist are required to stop the afflicted man raping his own daughter.)

The success of *The God Delusion* made Dawkins the front-runner of the so-called Four Horsemen of Atheism, ahead of Sam Harris, riding *The End of Faith* (2004), Daniel Dennett on *Breaking the Spell* (2006), and Christopher Hitchens, bringing up the rear with *God Is Not Great* (2007). Other runners and riders in Britain included philosopher A. C. Grayling with *The Good Book: A Humanist Bible* (2011) and polymath Jonathan Miller, whose television series *Atheism: A Rough History of Disbelief* (2004) opened with him in New York City on the Staten Island ferry; the gap in the skyline where the World Trade Center had once stood was, he said, 'a forceful reminder of the potentially destructive power of the three great monotheistic religions that have dominated the world, in one way or another, for nearly two thousand years'.

Whether this New Atheism, as it was named, with its onslaught on faith, changed hearts and minds was uncertain. Most of the country seemed content to ignore its contribution to public debate. It was striking, for example, that fiction in the early years of the century was dominated by global brands that centred on magic, myth and the pseudo-religious: J. K. Rowling's Harry Potter series (1997) and, from America, the Robert Langdon novels of Dan Brown (2000) and Stephanie Meyer's *Twilight* saga (2005).* Each achieved worldwide sales of over 100 million – five times that in the case of Harry Potter – and spun off into movie series that were box-office hits. All of which suggested that the public still had a taste for fantasy.

The Four Horsemen couldn't keep pace with such runaway successes. They did make an impact, though. 'It has been a good year for atheists,' conceded a leader in *The Times* on Christmas Eve 2007,[17] at a time when Borders bookstores were running a special promotion; every copy of *The God Delusion* came with a free anti-Christmas card bearing the message: 'O Come All Ye Faithless'.[18] The newspaper went on to list the words used by Dawkins to describe believers: 'malevolent ... vicious, sado-masochistic and repellent ... dodgy, perniciously delusional ... sanctimoniously hypocritical ... cockeyed'. Such aggressive and mocking language might be appropriate for America – with its culture wars over abortion and creationism, its fundamentalists, televangelists and presidential prayer meetings – but it felt terribly strident in Britain, where the public persona of the archbishop of Canterbury was that of an absent-minded academic, not a snake-handling preacher of fire and brimstone.

For the New Atheists, the stakes were high. 'Reason and a respect for evidence are the source of our progress, our safeguard against fundamentalists and those who profit from obscuring the

---

* *Twilight* also inspired – via fan fiction – another publishing sensation, the *Fifty Shades* trilogy (2011) by the British writer E. L. James, which depicted a sadomasochistic relationship and made mainstream the vocabulary of fetishism: butt plugs, nipple clamps and safe words.

truth,' insisted Dawkins. 'We live in dangerous times when super-stition is gaining ground and rational science is under attack.'[19] But it wasn't obvious that the solution was abuse. The tone of public debate was not noticeably raised by having an Oxford professor describe religion as 'An organised licence to be accept-ably stupid,'[20] or hearing him denounce the Pope as being 'either stupid, ignorant or dim'.[21]

Nor did any of this assist the public understanding of science, which remained sketchy at best. The most famous scientist in the world, perhaps the most famous since Albert Einstein, was Stephen Hawking, who founded the Centre for Theoretical Cos-mology at Cambridge in 2007. His status was such that he could appear as himself on top-rated shows such as *Star Trek: The Next Generation, The Simpsons* and *The Big Bang Theory*.* And when the BBC broadcast its series *100 Greatest Britons* (2002), Hawking was voted into twenty-fifth position, one place higher than William Tyndale, translator of the Bible into English.

It was not his thinking that made him famous, though, so much as his personal story, the motor neurone disease that meant his presence was that of a frail, schoolboyish figure in a wheelchair, slyly smiling as his words were intoned in a computer-generated and much imitated voice.† Eddie Redmayne won an Oscar for his portrayal of Hawking in *The Theory of Everything* (2014), beating Benedict Cumberbatch, nominated for playing computer pioneer Alan Turing in *The Imitation Game* (2014), another British scien-tist who was primarily known for the adversity he faced.

Beyond the human interest, it was debatable how much of Hawking's work was comprehensible to non-scientists; *A Brief History of Time* (1988) sold over 10 million copies, but was widely

---

* Richard Dawkins also appeared in *The Simpsons* and in *Doctor Who*.
† 'He's not a genius, he's pretentious,' said Ricky Gervais. 'Born in Oxford and talks in that fake American accent.' (*Out of England*, 2008)

reputed to be the biggest-selling partially read book of modern times. Scientific thought had become so abstruse, so technical and rarefied, that most laypeople could do little more than nod along to mention of, say, the many-worlds theory of quantum mechanics. There was no evidence offered for this conjecture, though some took it on trust, just as the theology of the Trinity could be taken on trust. Similarly, Brian Cox – former pop star turned academic and popular scientist – could be seen on the quiz show *QI*, outlining Richard Feynman's theory that there was only one electron in the entire universe that 'keeps moving backwards and forwards through time'. It was 'a legitimate view,' said Professor Cox, although it sounded rather less plausible than the existence of a creator god.

There was a huge and growing chasm between scientific research and the public understanding of that research.* So when the Human Genome Project announced in 2003 that it had completed its work on sequencing the DNA found in human beings, no one doubted the scale of the achievement. But the popular perception of DNA remained fixed in the sensationalist realms of designer babies, Frankenstein food and fictional murder inquiries. Indeed, the inexorable rise of detective novels and dramas was based on forensics, the one branch of science that still promised absolute truth in this uncertain world. ('The days of tracing criminals from their fingerprints were long gone,' observed Leigh Russell's DI Geraldine Steel.[22])

Even when it came to experiment, a leap of faith appeared to be required. Cern's Large Hadron Collider (LHC), buried in a seventeen-mile-long circular tunnel near Geneva, was the biggest machine humanity had ever built. Serious broadcasters and newspapers regularly ran pieces on the project, excitedly explaining

---

* A 2009 sketch in *The Armstrong & Miller Show* had a modern layman transported back to the mid-nineteenth century and struggling to explain to Michael Faraday what $E=mc^2$ actually meant.

that particles would be fired at each other at very nearly the speed of light, thereby recreating conditions immediately after the Big Bang. Quite what this meant passed the understanding of many, but it looked beautiful on television and presumably was worth the billions spent on its construction. Beyond that lay mystery, except that it was something to do with the Higgs boson, which – to the intense irritation of physicists – had been nicknamed the God Particle. And that sounded sexy and exciting and dangerous, hinting that scientists were playing at God with unforeseeable consequences.

In the days leading up to the LHC being switched on in September 2008, newspapers provided a running commentary on what might, we were told, be the end of the world. 'Some experts fear it could create a huge black hole that swallows the planet and wipes out mankind,' warned the *Sun*, though it also quoted a German biochemist, Otto Rössler, who thought we were okay for at least four years; thereafter, the prognosis was not so good: 'The weather will change completely, wiping out life. There will be a biblical Armageddon.'[23]

These scares weren't really taken seriously.* It was all so remote. Phrases like 'the Big Bang' and 'subatomic particles' were familiar from popular science and sci-fi, but the phenomena to which they referred couldn't easily be visualised or comprehended, so the supposed doomsday dangers of the LHC were treated as a bit of jokey fun. The Higgs boson was 'abhorrent to nature', argued some scientists, and the public was satisfyingly thrilled to hear it.[24]

But even if the idea of the world ending on 10 September 2008

---

* The sketch show *That Mitchell and Webb Look* had a parody of religious broadcasting, with a genial host, Donny Cosy, visiting Cern: 'Roland and the other boffins here at the Large Hadron Collider are up to something rather exciting. Because they're trying to blow up the universe. Which I have to say, Roland, to a layman like me sounds like a terrible idea.'

didn't really take hold, it did fit into the established public perception of how science was reported. It felt as if a para-religion was emerging, complete with priests and promises and the power over life and death, just as Steve Baxter had said in *The Second Coming*. And though the LHC might not kill us, there were plenty of other predictions of plague and pestilence to chill the blood.

In March 2003 the World Health Organisation issued an emergency warning about a condition called severe acute respiratory syndrome (SARS), a coronavirus that was frequently fatal. There had been an outbreak of the disease in China, spreading to Vietnam, but it was the arrival of an infected person in Frankfurt that provoked the panic. 'SARS is now a worldwide health threat,' said a WHO spokesperson. 'It's moving at the speed of a jet. It's bad.'[25] The most serious outbreak in the West came in Ontario, Canada, where there were over 250 cases; the mayor of Toronto tried to calm nerves – 'This isn't a city in the grip of fear and panic,' he said – but it didn't help that his name was Mel Lastman, as if he'd stepped out of a post-apocalyptic film.[26]

A couple of days later, the first suspected case was reported in Britain ('Killer jet bug is here', shuddered the headlines)[27] and Sir Liam Donaldson, the chief medical officer of England, was soon advising British people not to travel to Hong Kong or Guangdong. The *Daily Express* consulted Dr Patrick Dixon, founder of the AIDS charity ACET, who said that 'on current trends there could be a billion cases within sixty weeks', and concluded, 'This is a far more serious epidemic potentially than AIDS.'[28] *The Economist*, on the other hand, was suggesting that the fears were exaggerated: 'Only 4 per cent of those laid low by SARS have died so far.' But if there really were a billion cases, that still represented 40 million dead. And there was little comfort in the magazine pointing out that there were worse things: 'Ebola fever can kill 90 per cent of those infected.'[29]

There were also worries that the outbreak could tip the world into recession, though the impact in Britain at least was restricted to very particular businesses: British Airways blamed SARS for a drop in bookings, Chinese restaurants in Glasgow said turnover was down by 40 per cent, and there was a fall in the share price of media group Informa, which specialised in trade shows and international conferences. There were calls for Britain to adopt strong measures, including the screening of all air passengers entering the country, but Donaldson was unmoved: 'We can't close our borders to the rest of the world.'[30]

The crisis was short-lived, and in mid-2003 the WHO announced that SARS had been contained. It had left its mark, however, for the panic had raised fears of a pandemic to rival the 100 million killed by Spanish Flu in 1918–20, and that image was not easily forgotten.

It returned in the form of another threat from Asia, this time a deadly strain of avian flu (H5N1), which was transmitted between birds but could kill humans who handled infected animals. By October 2004, when the first avian case was identified in Britain – a parrot that was being held in quarantine – there were 61 known human fatalities in the Far East, but the real fear was that the virus would mutate into a strain that could be transmitted human-to-human. Sir Liam Donaldson was back in the news, warning that a pandemic in the UK could see the deaths of 50,000 people, while Professor Neil Ferguson of Imperial College, London said that globally there could be '100 million deaths or more', adding, 'The 1918 scenario is within what people should be planning for.'[31] Websites did a good trade in the antiviral drug Tamiflu and in disposable masks and gloves, but again the mass deaths that were feared did not follow. Nor did they with the swine flu (H1N1) pandemic of 2009, when Donaldson warned that the 'best case scenario' was 3,100 deaths in Britain, the worst 65,000;[32] there were fewer than 500 fatalities.

Even when the public health predictions were not so doom-laden, they still seemed designed to make our flesh creep. In the wake of an unfounded story linking the MMR vaccine to autism, there was a downturn in vaccination, and dire consequences were feared. 'We are facing a real prospect of outbreaks of measles,' warned Dr George Kassianos of the Royal College of General Practitioners in 2002. 'We are going to start to see dead babies.'[33] It was a frightening prospect that happily didn't materialise. Over the following ten years, there were just eight deaths from measles in England and Wales, compared to eighteen in the preceding ten years, while the number of notified cases halved.[34]

By the time of that warning, however, the medical profession's treatment of dead babies had itself become a scandal. It emerged in 1999 that the Bristol Royal Infirmary was, without asking parents, retaining the hearts of infants who had died there. The practice was not unique to that institution. An inquiry into the Alder Hey Children's Hospital in Liverpool reported in 2001 that over 100,000 body parts, including whole corpses, were being kept there. The collection dated back to the 1940s and had been properly acquired – that is, with parental consent – up until the appointment of Professor Dick van Veltzen, a Dutch pathologist, in 1988. He had 'ordered the unethical and illegal retention of every organ in every case', had falsified records and had lied to parents; the report concluded that he 'must never be allowed to practise again'.[35] The public were shocked by the revelations. In his novel *Scaredy Cat* (2002), Mark Billingham drily summarised the impact of the scandal: 'Rates of organ donation had dropped dramatically. Transplant numbers were down. Pathologists had trouble making new friends.'[36]

The year after the Alder Hey report, another inquiry concluded that Dr Harold Shipman, a genial-looking GP in Hyde, Greater Manchester who'd been convicted in 2000 of murdering 15 of his patients, had actually killed more than 200. The exact total would never be definitively known, but it was sufficient to establish him as the most prolific known serial killer in the world.*

---

* Shipman committed suicide in prison in 2004. The home secretary, David

And then there was the 2008 investigation into the abnormally high death rate in Stafford Hospital …

There had always been a market for predictions of disaster, of course. What was impressive now was the number of available options: from Prince Charles warning in 2003 that nanotechnology might reduce the world to grey goo, through to a fashionable belief (based on a misunderstanding of the Maya Long Count calendar) that the world would end on 21 December 2012. However absurd, they all fed into a sense of catastrophe, that things were going wrong, even that the end times might soon be upon us. We thought we were post-Christian, yet still the turning of the millennium proved to be an unsettling time.

The greatest expression of that was the idea of climate change caused by the production of greenhouse gases. Scientists had been warning of this for decades, and even politicians (with Margaret Thatcher in the first wave) had been raising it since the 1980s. It hadn't been as big back then, though, because the fear of nuclear destruction still seemed the most likely cause of Armageddon. But the end of the cold war meant nuclear weapons were less pressing an issue, and climate change emerged as the ultimate nightmare. 'There is little doubt that we are on the tip of the sixth great wave of extinction in the history of life on Earth,' said Robert May, former chief scientific adviser to the government, in 2001; 'caused not by external crisis but by us.'[37] We might have got rid of God, but we had instead taken on ourselves responsibility for the destruction of the planet by flame and flood.*

In this precarious, threatened world, science and medicine seemed to offer little reassurance, scant hope for the future. Which

---

Blunkett, said it made him 'feel like opening a bottle'. (*The Blunkett Tapes* p. 575)

* 'It's too late to stop global warming now,' the teenage Jake tells his parents in a 2008 episode of sitcom *Outnumbered*. 'Your generation's completely ruined the world for our generation.'

was perhaps why we liked to see our scientists as human beings; it provided a measure of comfort. As did those oddball vicars who still turned up in family sitcoms.

II

This is an account of England in the first decade and half of the twenty-first century, a time when faith was sometimes in short supply. Objectively, materially, life was good for most people. As the millennium dawned, Britain was halfway through the longest period of uninterrupted economic growth it had ever known. That ended abruptly in 2008 with the worst recession since the war, but more widely there was a deepening sense of anxiety and insecurity. There seemed so little of substance that could be relied upon. Because if religion and science were found wanting, so too were many of the institutions that were supposed to bind society together.

Politicians, bankers and journalists have seldom ranked high in the public estimation, but they used to be seen as a necessary nuisance, and there was an acceptance, albeit grudging, of their professional competence. That attitude didn't survive – respectively – the expenses scandal, the financial crash and the revelations about phone hacking. Meanwhile, the BBC was hurt by a succession of stories, from the behaviour of its highest-paid presenter, Jonathan Ross, to the misrepresentation of the Queen. Nor did the Corporation emerge unscathed from the discovery that the ugly rumours about Jimmy Savile were based on even uglier fact.

And in the wake of Savile's exposure came the pursuit of historic child abuse, further tarnishing the memory of a shared culture that had already been condemned as politically incorrect. The past was 'problematic', to use a fashionable term. It was not to be trusted, not even yesterday's television, let alone a formerly proud history shaped by imperialism. The repudiation of recent times was found even within left-wing institutions: for too long, said TUC official Frances O'Grady* in 1998, the trade union movement had been 'male, pale and stale'.[38]

In these sensitive, slightly nervous times, as the crimes of the past were called to account, there grew a suspicion of power itself. Again it could be seen in the trade unions, the historical image of which was now fixed on the crushing of the 1984–5 miners' strike rather than the victories of the 1970s, the days when unions could bring down governments. Being defeated was akin to being oppressed, and that had a moral status that power did not.

In fact, power, as symbolised by the nation's political structures, seemed unsure of itself. The point of the first-past-the-post electoral system used for Westminster was that it produced stable, majority government, yet two of the three elections held in 2010–17 resulted in hung parliaments. Internationally, the European Union did little to endear itself to the people, while the United Nations suffered a damaging blow to its authority when it was sidelined in the build-up to the invasion of Iraq; three of the permanent members of the Security Council opposed the action, so America and Britain acted alone. That war was the single most controversial government policy in these years, damaging further the standing of politics, and it remained the subject of dispute throughout. There was a plethora of inquiries and reports into various aspects of the conflict – including those by Lord Hutton (reporting 2004), Lord Butler (2004) and Sir John Chilcot (2016) – but although facts and details came to light, few minds were changed, and at times it felt as if the country had little interest in things like facts and details.

Most importantly of all, the United Kingdom was beginning to lose a sense of itself as a country. There was increasing talk of

---

* Fifteen years later, O'Grady became the first woman to become general secretary of the TUC.

the four constituent nations, and their paths were unmistakably diverging, so that it was becoming hard to speak of the UK as a single entity. It was now apparent that devolution in the 1990s had begun a process, not completed it. The major separation was between England and Scotland, with a surge of nationalism in the latter, raising the possibility that the tricentenary of the 1707 Act of Union might be followed in short order by its repeal. Nationalism intensified in England too, but it was a more troubled enterprise. The problem lay in the disproportionate numbers. England was home to nearly 85 per cent of the UK's population, and it had always been the overwhelmingly powerful figure in this curious partnership.

The Scots could define themselves as being different to the English and thereby take the role of the plucky underdog (the kind the English prided themselves on backing), but England could not reciprocate without looking arrogant and bullying. Which it often did. There was a standard joke that tennis player Andy Murray was seen as British when he was winning, and Scottish when he was losing.* Further, England was more multicultural – in addition to being more multiracial – than its neighbours, and the big cities, London in particular, were drifting ever further from the rest of the country. Instead, English nationalism, primarily manifest outside those big cities, increasingly identified itself in opposition to the EU. That tendency, moving remorselessly from Euroscepticism to Brexit, dragged the rest of the UK along in its wake. Because, despite the differences, the Union – and England's dominance of it – remained intact.

The dominance was such that it was difficult to separate out a distinctly English culture or heritage. There had previously been

---

* It would have been so much easier if Tim Henman, who was definitely English, had been the first British man to win Wimbledon since Fred Perry in 1936. But it was Murray who beat Novak Djokovic in straight sets in the 2013 final.

no need to do so, and the dividing lines between England, Britain, Great Britain and the United Kingdom had long been cheerfully blurred. The two great creation myths of modern Britain, for example, were shared across the islands: first, the stand against the Nazis in 1940, and then the Swinging Sixties – unimaginable without the presence of Sean Connery, Mary Quant, George Best. Similarly, those institutions that could still inspire loyalty, affection and respect were held in common: the monarchy, the armed forces, the NHS. England didn't even have its own national anthem, and used 'God Save the Queen' at international football matches,* where others had 'Flower of Scotland' or 'Hen Wlad Fy Nhadau'. (Northern Ireland also used 'God Save the Queen', though in other sports it opted for 'Londonderry Air'.)

For many years, England hadn't had its own flag either, but in recent times – spurred on by the Euro 96 football tournament – there had been a widespread adoption of the St George Cross. Widespread, but not universal. Displaying this symbol outside the context of a sporting occasion was the kind of thing that respectable people didn't do; it was a coarse working-class practice that implied rather too much English nationalism. When Labour's shadow attorney general, Emily Thornberry, visited the Medway constituency of Rochester and Strood for a 2014 by-election campaign, she tweeted a picture of a white van parked outside a house bedecked in St George flags, with a simple message: 'Image from #Rochester.' Everyone knew what she meant, which was why she had to resign from the shadow cabinet. 'We are hugely in favour

---

* Indeed, for much of this time, the England national football team didn't even have an English manager. The so-called Golden Generation were coached by Sven-Göran Eriksson (2001–06) and Fabio Capello (2008–12), and still didn't get beyond the quarter-finals of a major tournament. Elsewhere, though, England did win the Rugby World Cup in 2003 and a great Ashes series in 2005, making stars of Jonny Wilkinson and Andrew Flintoff respectively.

in the Labour Party of people expressing pride in their national identity and national symbols,' said historian turned Labour MP Tristram Hunt,[39] but no one imagined for a moment that he had a St George flag flying from *his* house.

So although the following pages focus on England, on its attempt to define who and what it was, the story is necessarily entwined with that of the country more widely. The government, the television programmes, most of the newspapers – they were all UK-wide. They were also, as it happens, all largely based in England and mostly in London.

This is not an insider's account. It is set in the public domain, not in the corridors of power in Westminster, Whitehall or the City of London. Its focus is on how events played out before our eyes on-screen and in print, the stories that shaped our sense of who we were and who we wished to be. It dwells quite happily in the margins; figures such as Robert Kilroy-Silk and Ann Cryer loom larger than do some chancellors and foreign secretaries. On the other hand, popular culture, whether in the form of *Life on Mars* or the bakery chain Greggs, matters more than the winners of the Booker or Turner Prizes.

In fact, popular culture matters a great deal, because it was often where battles were fought. Certainly they were no longer being fought in crowded town-hall meetings or on the picket lines. The decline in party membership and in the numbers of trade unionists meant that there was now less participation in politics than there had been a generation ago. Instead, politics had become almost a spectator sport, one in which the dwindling ranks of those who cared took ever more tribal positions in support not just of parties, but of factions within parties.

In his novel *The Lord's Day* (2007), Michael Dobbs observed that 'for better or worse, history is usually written by the media'.[40] No historian could countenance such heresy, but it is certainly true that, in modern times, history is made by the media. Not just the news media, though; perceptions are shaped by entertainment as well as current-affairs shows, and stand-up comedians are often more influential than broadsheet commentators.

This was particularly so in this period, when the media itself was in transition. We were seeing the dawn of the Information Age, trying to adjust to a technological revolution led by the World Wide Web, a development that bid fair to eclipse even the invention of printing. In this early phase, the new media remained dependent on older forms – newspapers, television – but the balance of power was shifting. So too was advertising revenue. The result was a decline in standards of news coverage, a rise in short-lived stories penned by fewer and fewer journalists. Not everything that was reported in the media (and not everything that's repeated here) was 'true', and much of it was trivial, but as Gordon Brown sadly observed, 'The power of myth in politics can be stronger than reality.'[41] Or, in Tony Blair's words: 'the mood trumps the policy every time'.[42]

Consequently, fictional portrayals of Blair – and there were many of them – were taken as seriously as the reality of the man himself. Perhaps more so, since he was so remote in these years. Like Steve Baxter in *The Second Coming*, he became a messianic figure, convinced that we were on the cusp of momentous change. 'Today, humankind has the science and technology to destroy itself or to provide prosperity to all,' Blair told the Labour Party conference in 2001. 'Yet science can't make that choice for us. Only the moral power of a world acting as a community, can.'[43] He later reflected that when he wrote the speech, 'I felt we were on the eve of a mighty decision about the world's future.'[44]

1

Peace and War

I

The new Queen Elizabeth Hospital in Birmingham opened in 2010. Designed by BDP architects, it was a striking structure. Three hollowed-oval towers, gleaming white-panelled cliffs punctuated by glass, rose nine storeys high above the sprawling semi-detached suburbs of Edgbaston, 'like a row of noughts'[1] in one account, or, alternatively, 'like a mighty white spaceship'.[2] It was the first new hospital in the city since the war, a set of standing stones that memorialised the Labour Party's commitment to the National Health Service.

'This hospital is a legacy for the future,' said the chief

executive of the University Hospitals Birmingham NHS Foundation Trust.[3] Which presumably was why it was here, in April 2010, that prime minister Gordon Brown launched his manifesto for the forthcoming general election, claiming, 'We are in the future business.'[4]

But these were difficult times. After sixteen years of continuous growth, the economy had been hit hard by the worldwide crash of 2008, and the Conservative opposition was telling anyone who'd listen that Britain had been left vulnerable by Labour profligacy; the government, it was alleged, had failed to fix the roof while the sun was shining. Brown was determined to reject the charge. 'Look at what we together have built,' he declared, gesturing to the foyer of the Queen Elizabeth. 'We didn't just fix the roof. We built an entire hospital.'[5]

But why was he here at all? he was asked. These were NHS premises and political activity was prohibited in such places. He was within his rights, though. The hospital was not open yet, still two months away from being handed over to the trust, and it remained at this stage the property of construction firm Balfour Beatty. They were building the facility, under the private finance initiative (PFI), at a reported cost of £627 million, but they were to be suitably recompensed: the trust was committed to 35 years of mortgage repayments that would – so the *Birmingham Mail* informed its readers – bring the final cost to the public purse up to an estimated £2.58 billion.[6] Many had questioned the wisdom of such deals, the way they saddled the NHS with huge debts for generations to come, but such cavilling wasn't on Brown's agenda. Here was an achievement to be trumpeted.

And perhaps too, here was a chance to lay a ghost. Because nine years earlier, the previous prime minister, Tony Blair, had visited the original Queen Elizabeth Hospital, which had stood nearby, on land donated by the chocolate firm Cadbury, and things had not gone smoothly at all ...

*

That day, in May 2001, also saw the unveiling of a general election manifesto, this time at the International Convention Centre in Centenary Square, after which Blair made the three-mile trip to the Queen Elizabeth for a photo opportunity to emphasise Labour's promise to the public services. In earlier times, a manifesto launch would have been a London affair, but Birmingham had been chosen 'to reconnect with grass-roots voters and show commitment to the West Midlands'.[7] The visit shouldn't have been too controversial. There was a closure threat hanging over the hospital's heart transplant unit, which meant that Blair would be met by a small group of protestors, shouting 'Have a heart,' but that sort of thing was inevitable and unlikely to attract the attention of the national media.

What was not expected was that, as he tried to enter the building, the prime minister would be buttonholed by one of those grass-roots voters with whom he was supposed to be reconnecting.

Sharron Storer was a 38-year-old postmistress, whose partner, Keith Sedgwick, had a form of blood cancer and was being treated at the Queen Elizabeth. She was furious with the state of the hospital and berated Blair with her complaints. 'It is absolutely appalling,' she said. 'I hope you are going to have a look at it and find out how terrible it really is.' Sedgwick had recently been admitted, but with no specialist bed available, had spent the first 24 hours in casualty. Visibly thrown by her diatribe, Blair apologised and said that the government was trying to improve things, but Storer was scathing: 'You just walk around, making yourself known. You don't actually do anything to help anybody.' He suggested they go inside where they could talk out of camera shot, but she was in no mood for his emollience. 'There is nothing to talk about because you still won't do anything,' she concluded and stormed off, pushing past him.[8]

'His smile was the thing that triggered me,' she said later. 'I saw him coming towards me, with that look he has as if everything is perfect with the country, and suddenly I felt this surge of anger.'[9]

She'd backed Labour in 1997, but said she wouldn't be voting at all this time. 'The staff have been remarkable,' she insisted, 'the doctors could not have done enough for Keith. I blame the government for not giving them the funding they need.'[10]

'In general I agree with her,' Blair reflected a couple of days afterwards. 'Despite the progress we've made there is a lot of frustration like hers out there when things go wrong.' He asked for more time: 'We can't change years upon years of neglect to the NHS just like that.'[11]

It was the kind of encounter that politicians dread, 'one of those impossible situations where you just couldn't win', as Education Secretary David Blunkett put it.[12] Blair was perfectly courteous, but it looked very bad and the incident threatened to blow the manifesto launch off the headlines. In the event, it didn't lead the news bulletins that evening, but only because of more sensational developments elsewhere. That afternoon the deputy prime minister, John Prescott, had been out and about in Rhyl, north Wales, when he was struck on the back of the neck by an egg thrown by a local farmer. Prescott – a decent amateur boxer in his youth – turned, hit his assailant with a straight left, and was shaping to follow with a right hook, before being restrained by stewards. Footage of a cabinet minister doling out rough justice on the streets was a genuine novelty, and it grabbed most of the media attention.

The episode outside the Queen Elizabeth Hospital, however, was ultimately more indicative of the mood of the nation. 'For once, politicians had to listen to an ordinary person,' Sharron Storer told the press. 'I'm heartily glad if I gave him an experience he won't forget.'[13] She didn't have any demands to make of Blair, no questions to ask or solutions to propose, save that she wanted him to live up to her hopes of improvement. She wished to articulate her dissatisfaction, not to hear explanations or justifications or even policies.

She hardly gave him a chance to say a word, but in truth there was nothing he could say. The fact that Keith Sedgwick, in his weakened condition, had been left standing in a corridor for half an hour before even a chair could be found, let alone a bed, was surely a question for hospital administrators rather than the prime minister. But it illustrated a wider trend. The public's disenchantment with politicians and their ability to effect real change was growing, yet so too was the range of things for which politicians were held responsible. For most of the country the NHS was an article of faith, its doctors and nurses beyond reproach; therefore, if one's experience was negative, it must be the fault of someone else, almost certainly that of the government.

For Blair, the incident illustrated how the media had become obsessed with 'the celebration of the protest', more interested, he said, in the one heckler than the 999 supporters.[14] But this wasn't quite right, because not all heckles were equal. If a protest were to gain traction, it had to resonate with a wider public mood. It also required the heckler to be of good character. Five weeks after his meeting with Sharron Storer, Blair was again the target of a disgruntled user of the NHS. 'Oi! Blair, you tosser! Like to see you waiting here for six hours,' shouted a 48-year-old outpatient who was waiting to be seen at the Royal London Hospital. But this was Martin Wright, a long-standing East End anarchist, who was at the time reading a copy of the newspaper *Class War*, the front cover of which had a picture of Blair and Tory leader William Hague under the headline: 'Same old shit'.[15] Consequently, he rated far less press attention than Sharron Storer, who looked like exactly the kind of voter that New Labour needed onside.

The one certain conclusion that came out of that day in Birmingham was that the experiment of reconnecting with grass-roots voters hadn't got off to a flying start. Prescott expressed his frustration about the egg-throwing to his colleagues, saying 'it was bloody ridiculous that we had to take all this shit from people just because we were politicians'.[16] He had a point, but he was out of step with the times. The nine years between the visits of Blair and Brown to the Queen Elizabeth Hospital were going to see an ever-widening gulf between government and governed.

If public services hadn't seen the improvements expected by the electorate in the four years since Tony Blair and Labour had come to power in 1997, that was partly because the government was paying off the debt accumulated during the recession earlier that decade. There had, however, been achievements in that first term. Most notably, there had been a redistribution of income through the introduction of the minimum wage and an expansion of means-tested benefits. At a time of economic growth, the biggest beneficiaries proportionally had been the poorest.

This redistributive agenda, though, wasn't much proclaimed, firstly because the tax and benefits system had become so convoluted that it was difficult to communicate the changes, and secondly because it all smacked too much of old-style Labour for a prime minister who was nervous of his party's past. 'When I talk proudly of what we've done for the poor,' reflected cabinet minister Robin Cook, 'I feel vaguely uneasy as if I've somehow gone off-message.'[17] In any event, it lacked the big vision that Blair sought. 'We did some terrific things,' he said privately of his first term; 'but a national minimum wage does not transform the country.'[18] He wanted to make history and, thus far, had failed to do so. When, on the first day of the new millennium, the *Daily Mirror* published a list of the thousand most important people of the previous thousand years, he was at a lowly 950.[19] Of course, he'd been in office less than three years, so perhaps it was to be seen as a compliment that he was included at all – except that one place ahead of him was Neil Kinnock, which looked like a calculated insult.*

---

* Other British politicians who made the list were: Churchill (47); Attlee (56); Disraeli (191); Gladstone (269); Thatcher (285); Walpole (305); Lloyd George

According to John Prescott, Blair felt he'd underachieved: 'he was of the opinion that he had wasted the first term and wanted the second to bring about fundamental changes in the delivery of public services'.[20] The public too was unimpressed, as Blair's polling adviser Philip Gould reported in July 2000. 'We quickly seem to have grown out of touch,' he wrote in a confidential memo that was immediately leaked to the press.[21] 'We are out-flanked on patriotism and crime. We have been assailed for spin and broken promises. Perhaps worst of all, the New Labour brand has been badly contaminated. It is the object of constant criticism and, worse, ridicule.'* This was why Sharron Storer's complaints resonated so loudly.

However inauspicious the start of the 2001 election campaign, though, the outcome was always a foregone conclusion. 'The question was not so much whether we would win, but by how much,' reflected Peter Mandelson. 'Would the margin be too narrow, the turnout so low, to constitute a convincing endorsement.'[22] The majority was indeed down, but not by much: from 179 in 1997 to 167 this time, with 5 fewer Labour MPs (and 6 fewer Labour women). There was no great wave of enthusiasm. 'I've got to decide,' observed satirist John Bird, 'whether I'm more disappointed that Labour didn't do this time what it said it would do, or more hopeful that it will do next time what it said it would do last time.'[23] Blair saw it differently: 'We won, and handsomely,' he boasted.[24]

As for the Tories, they'd written their own chances off even before the election had been called. 'For many voters and most of

---

(336); Heath (655); Balfour (678); Profumo (822); Douglas-Home (854); Callaghan (856); Chamberlain (857); Macmillan (866); Powell (919); Astor (954). Nye Bevan was included twice, at 149 and at 700, which may give an accurate impression of the rigour with which the list was compiled.

* In 2002 Bournemouth Council experimented with putting up billboards of various celebrities in the hope that the public would stick used chewing gum to the posters rather than dropping it on the pavement. Among those pictured were Jeffrey Archer, Jeremy Beadle and Tony Blair.

the media, the Conservative Party is a lost cause'[25] – that was the verdict in January 2001 of Nigel Hatislow, the Conservative candidate for Birmingham Edgbaston, home of the Queen Elizabeth Hospital. Michael Spicer, incoming chairman of the backbench 1922 Committee, was even more downbeat, fearing the loss of another 60 or 70 seats. 'We may even lose our position as the official opposition,' he despaired in his diary.[26]

In the event, it wasn't that bad, but it was still awful, worse even than in 1997, since it made clear that last time had been no isolated accident. Then, the Tories had won just 165 seats, all of them in England. Now they returned to Westminster still with 165 English MPs, augmented by a single representative from Scotland. There was a small swing from Labour to Tory of 1.8 per cent, but fewer people actually voted Conservative than last time; over the course of two elections, nearly 5.75 million votes had been lost by the party. So uninspired were the faithful that only 55 per cent of *Daily Mail* readers turned out for the Tories.[27] Four years on from John Major's humiliation, this was all they'd managed to achieve. In an episode of *My Family* that year, geeky younger son Michael was the Conservative candidate in the school elections. 'You can't be standing as a Tory!' remonstrates his father, and he replies, 'Why not? What have you got against persecuted minorities?'

None of it felt like much of an event. There was none of the sense of occasion that had been present in 1997. That was to be expected, and understandably election-night television viewing figures were down by about a quarter. More concerning was the fact that voter turnout fell by 12 points, even though 1997 itself had set a post-war record low. With an extra 500,000 on the electoral roll, some 5 million fewer actually voted. Spike Milligan had once joked, 'One day the don't knows will get in, and then where will we be?' Wherever it was, we were now there. For the first time since the exceptional election of 1918,* more people absented

---

* The 1918 general election was the first to have voting on a single day, and

themselves than voted for the victorious party. The incumbent government was returned despite failing to attract the support of even a quarter of registered voters.

When the Labour MPs reassembled in Westminster, there was no sense of jubilation. 'I should have been elated,' observed David Blunkett, now home secretary. 'But I was not.'[28] At the first meeting of the new Parliamentary Labour Party, 'the mood was decidedly downbeat', according to junior minister Chris Mullin,[29] while Tony Blair felt that 'the PLP were in truculent mood'.[30] He was 'pissed off that three weeks after delivering another massive majority, he was surrounded by so much anger and sullenness'.[31]

If backbenchers were ungrateful to the leader who'd just won a second majority, the same was even more true of his neighbour in Downing Street. Gordon Brown had served through the first term as chancellor of the exchequer, but not with any display of grace. He believed that a deal had been done back in 1994, shortly after the death of Labour leader John Smith, whereby Blair would run for the leadership and then, in due course, hand over the reins to Brown. With no apparent sign of such a transfer of power, and with Blair denying that there was a commitment, the dispute drove a wedge between the two men who had worked so closely together for over a decade, and who, along with Peter Mandelson, had launched the New Labour brand.

Somewhat in the manner of a Hanoverian Prince of Wales, Brown set up a rival court to prepare for the eventual succession. Even during the election campaign, the sniping from the sidelines had continued. 'He's out of control,' Blair grumbled to Mandelson. 'He's been out of control for weeks.'[32] Immediately after the

---

was held a month after the Armistice. The electorate had more than doubled, following the Representation of the People Act earlier that year, and many of the newly enfranchised men were still abroad in uniform.

victory, Brown resumed his haranguing of the prime minister, demanding to know when he'd be stepping down. 'Tony quite often complained to me about how badly Gordon was behaving towards him,' foreign secretary Jack Straw wrote later, although he felt the solution was in Blair's own hands: 'Tony didn't have to keep the guy there as chancellor. As long as he did, he'd be a problem.'[33]

Blair did contemplate the idea of moving Brown to the Foreign Office after the election, but concluded that the offer would be rejected: 'I'm sure he'd just resign, make trouble and bide his time.'[34] The problem was that Brown enjoyed great support in the party and, if he had returned to the backbenches, would undoubtedly have become a focus for rebellion. 'He is not liked, even if he is admired,' was Robin Cook's assessment of Brown,[35] but while that might have been true of cabinet colleagues, the party membership was more enthusiastic, feeling that the chancellor had the movement in his heart and his guts, in a way that Blair simply did not. 'I believe that at every point in our history Labour needs not just a programme but a soul,' Brown declared in his speech to the 2003 conference, and everyone got the point.[36] Many activists shared the hopes of writer John O'Farrell: 'When Gordon was prime minister, then we'd see some real change.'[37]

If Blair was reluctant to take Brown on by moving him from the Exchequer, Brown was equally unwilling to strike directly at Blair, to challenge him openly in a contest. With neither man prepared to take a decisive step, the two circled each other warily, and the atmosphere grew tenser and more damaging with every passing month.

The most enduring fictional portrait of this government came in the sitcom *The Thick of It* (2005), which depicted a headline-obsessed world of insecure politicians, dysfunctional advisers and incompetent civil servants. At the centre was the government's chief spin doctor, Malcom Tucker, a character based on Blair's former director of communications, Alastair Campbell,* but one also in the great tradition of British sitcoms, a foul-mouthed blend of Basil Fawlty, Norman Stanley Fletcher and Edmund Blackadder: 'You cannot fuck me. I am unfuckable. I have never been fucked and if you fucking try and fuck me, you'll find my fucking arse'll grow fucking fangs and snap your fucking cock off.'

Beyond the heroic levels of swearing, the show was chiefly notable for the political class's dislike of the people they are supposed to serve. 'They're from a different fucking species,' marvels cabinet minister Hugh Abbot of the public. 'You know, with their T-shirts and weird trousers and tabards. Why do they wear clothes with writing on? And why are they so fucking fat?' His opposition shadow, Peter Mannion, feels much the same: 'This is the trouble with the public, they're fucking horrible!' Never is there any sense of actually achieving anything for the country, or of a coherent vision or belief, just a need to stay in motion, lest a moment of reflection reveal the futility of it all. 'This can't go on. This is fucking suicide,' says Tucker, but somehow it does.

Real life was sometimes even more absurd. The split at the top of Labour was replicated in feuds and fights between the respective courts, sometimes to the point of self-parody. In 2001 the *Mail on Sunday* reported that Mandelson had been in touch with 'a witch doctor and priest in the Candomblé cult, a mystical Brazilian sect that worships African gods', and had asked the man to cast a spell on his bitter rival Charlie Whelan, who was Brown's spin doctor. 'I am not asking you to do anything bad with him but let him disappear from politics,' Mandelson was said to have requested.[38] 'Perhaps he could go to another country and not have contact with England ever again.'†

---

* Campbell had stepped down as Tony Blair's chief adviser in 2003, having worked with him since 1994.

† 'It was the moment when I realised that he'd actually gone completely bonkers,' reflected Mandelson's former researcher Derek Draper.

And still the feuding continued. Eventually, a new deal was done between Blair and Brown over dinner in John Prescott's apartment in November 2003. 'It was at that meeting that Tony promised to go by the next election,' recorded Prescott.[39] Details of the dinner were not made public until January 2005, when *Sunday Telegraph* journalist Robert Peston published his book *Brown's Britain*, written with the chancellor's cooperation. By that stage, Blair had already reneged on his promise (if there had been such a thing), announcing in September 2004 that he would seek a third term. Brown's response, as reported by Peston, was damning because it chimed with a growing sentiment in the country: 'There is nothing that you could ever say to me now that I could ever believe.'[40]

Aware that the electorate had been left unsatisfied by Blair's first term, Labour's manifesto for 2001 was centred on public spending. And there was an immediate change of priorities, so that while the final budget before the election saw £49 billion allocated to repaying the national debt, the one afterwards increased borrowing by £30 billion. The second term saw substantial growth in key public-sector areas; there were 22,000 extra doctors in England and Wales, 53,000 more nurses, 25,000 more teachers and an additional 16,000 police officers.* Not all the money, however, resulted in improved performance. Much of the new NHS funding was spent on a deal for GPs, rewarding them handsomely for meeting targets that were mostly being met already. As with many PFI deals, the government found itself outwitted in negotiations, in this instance by the British Medical Association, with the result that British GPs became the highest paid in Europe.

Nor was all the domestic policy popular. In 1998 Labour had

---

* Control of health, education and policing in Scotland and Northern Ireland was devolved to the national institutions. The Government of Wales Act 2006 later devolved powers to Cardiff.

abolished the principle of free university education – established by Harold Macmillan's Conservative government in 1962 – by introducing tuition fees of £1,000 a year. Some of the elite universities argued that this was too low, and that there should be what was then called a 'top-up' fee, enabling individual institutions to charge up to £3,000 a year. The 2001 manifesto unequivocally set its face against the idea: 'We will not introduce "top-up" fees and have legislated to prevent them.'

There was, therefore, some disquiet when the government announced in 2003 that it would be bringing forward a bill to introduce precisely these charges. 'We had the manifesto commitment not to allow top-up fees,' wrote Blair in his memoirs, 'but frankly it would have been absurd to postpone the decisions necessary for the country because of it.'[41] It confirmed the public's sense that manifesto promises counted for nothing.*

The Higher Education Act, introducing the £3,000 top-up fees, passed by the skin of its teeth in January 2004, the government securing a majority of just five, after a huge Labour rebellion. It was also noted that the legislation had passed only with the support of Scottish MPs, representing constituencies that would not be affected by its provisions. In the last year of the old century, William Hague had deployed the slogan 'English votes on English laws', warning of a 'ticking timebomb beneath the British constitution',[42] and if there was no explosion with tuition fees, there was the sense that another stick of dynamite had been added.

University tuition fees were just one element of Blair's reforms of the public sector. Increased funding was not by itself the answer, he believed; there needed also to be structural change.

---

* Some politicians resented the attention given to the issue. 'If there is one thing that really pisses me off, it's middle-class whingers going on about fucking tuition fees,' Labour MP Stephen Pound told a constituent during the 2001 election. 'If that's your attitude you can shove your vote up your arse.' (*Scotsman* 4 June 2001)

The key was to decentralise decision-making away from national and local government, particularly in health and education, creating self-governing foundation hospitals and academy schools, whose managers would have more financial independence and be empowered to bring in outside expertise. Standards would rise in these institutions and, since people would be given greater choice over where to be treated and where to send their children, others would be obliged to raise their game to compete.

His proposals didn't meet with universal approval in the Labour movement. 'The public services must not be reduced to the language of customer service,' warned Patricia Hewitt, the trade and industry secretary. 'You can't deliver health care or education as if you're delivering pizzas.'[43] In private, there were even more powerful voices of opposition. 'They are following Tory policies,' was Brown's verdict,[44] while Blair complained, 'What I want to do is being blocked by Gordon.'[45]

The reforms did make progress, but it was a long, painful business, failing initially to win over many of those expected to run the new system. In March 2005 the education secretary, Ruth Kelly, was jeered by head teachers at a conference. At the same time a poll commissioned by *Pulse*, the magazine for GPs, revealed anger in the medical profession at the government's policies on the NHS, with support for Labour in free fall: just 11 per cent of doctors said they'd vote for the government, down 19 points since 2001, while the Conservatives and Liberal Democrats were now the favoured options at 30 and 29 per cent respectively. Nor were the public convinced. In a straw poll on GMTV, over half the 11,000 callers said that the NHS had got worse under New Labour.[46] And Philip Gould's focus groups were showing that the party also had a problem 'with its core support, the C2 and D voters; the working-class heartland voters who use public services a lot'.[47]

Blair's own verdict on that second term was not markedly different from his evaluation of the first, and showed the same exasperation at the pace of change: 'we made a radical increase in public spending to cure the underinvestment of the Thatcher years, but it was not an end in itself'.[48]

If the New Labour project was fraying at the edges, the Conservative Party was in tatters. By lunchtime on the day after the election defeat, William Hague had resigned as leader. It had been a thankless task, taking over from John Major after the rout of 1997, but some had seen him as the Tory answer to Tony Blair, a young, energetic politician with wit and charm. To the public, however, he just lacked any sense of weight. Blair was the youngest prime minister of the twentieth century, but Hague was eight years younger even than that – just 36 when he took over. In later years, he would shrug off the experience. 'I've never really regretted becoming the leader of the Conservative Party,' he'd say. 'Someone had to do the night shift.'[49]

His one legacy was to change the system for choosing his successor. Previously, only MPs had voted in leadership elections; the new process charged MPs with whittling down the list of job applicants to two candidates, who would then take their case to the members of the party for a final verdict. Though it sounded plausible, the first try-out was not a resounding success.

Hague's shadow chancellor, Michael Portillo, was immediately installed by bookies as the odds-on favourite to succeed,[50] but he'd made too many enemies in the parliamentary party with his perceived arrogance and factionalism, and he failed to make the final shortlist of two. Instead, Conservative members were offered a choice between Ken Clarke – an MP since 1970, who'd served in government under three prime ministers, and been health secretary, education secretary, home secretary and chancellor – and Iain Duncan Smith, with just nine years in the Commons and no ministerial experience at all. Clarke was a well-known and popular figure, a decent public speaker and a persuasive communicator. Duncan Smith was none of these things; he was so little known that the historian and journalist Francis Wheen, to whom he bore a physical resemblance, reported that even Conservative MPs would sometimes mistake the two of them.[51]

'Presented like this,' acknowledged an editorial in the *Daily Telegraph*, 'the choice would appear to be what the Americans call a "no brainer".'[52] The Tory membership thought otherwise. There were around 300,000 registered party members and they were perhaps a little set in their ways, with an average age of over sixty. 'It's like that stairlift commercial with Thora Hird,' marvelled one of Duncan Smith's team after a meeting in Solihull. 'Perhaps we should give away a free carriage clock.'[53]

No such inducements were necessary. The Conservative Party, still soaked in remorse from the assassination of Margaret Thatcher more than a decade earlier, had abandoned all normal rules of politics and was emotionally committed to her last crusade: tilting at the windmills of the European Union. Clarke was out of step, an enthusiast for the EU and all its works, while Duncan Smith had consistently opposed John Major on the Maastricht Treaty, voting against his own government 11 times and abstaining on 47 other occasions. Further, although the Tories had never had a Catholic as leader, he was a former Scots Guards officer and his traditional values played well; as Robin Cook noted, 'He holds all the Tory prejudices.'[54]

At the London hustings, a poster was displayed of Clarke sharing a pro-European platform with Blair, with the legend 'Lest we forget'; and at the same meeting, there was a standing ovation for Duncan Smith when he boasted of how many times he'd rebelled. The contest was, said MP Nicholas Soames, 'the physical incarnation of the split that has poisoned our party'.[55] And in that contest, the words of Thatcher carried great weight: 'I simply do not understand how Ken Clarke could lead today's Conservative Party to anything other than disaster.'[56]

The result was a victory for Duncan Smith with a clear majority of three to two among the quarter-million voters. As Clarke later put it, 'the Conservative Party had gone mad'.[57] Pro-European Tories were horrified. The new leader, said Chris Patten, former party chairman turned European commissioner, was 'an uglier Hague, without the charm or parliamentary talent',[58] and within hours David Curry MP was passing on whispers to the press: 'People are already saying that in eighteen months IDS will be out.'[59] Winnie Ewing of the Scottish National Party suggested that IDS stood for the Tories being In Dire Straits,[60] while some of his parliamentary colleagues adopted the franker formulation In Deep Shit.[61]

A bad situation swiftly became worse. Duncan Smith spent his first year trying to get away from the issue of Europe, pushing instead the message of 'compassionate Conservatism'. The intention was sound, and he was more thoughtful than he was given credit for; in what journalist Peter Oborne called 'potentially the most interesting speech by a Tory leader for two decades',[62] he talked of a visit to the run-down Easterhouse suburb of Glasgow and outlined his thoughts on welfare reform. But no one much was listening.

He made little impact in the Commons, the one arena where Hague had been impressive, and less in the country, where the public never warmed to him or even much noticed him. He was the first Tory leader in 130 years who didn't get a waxwork effigy in Madame Tussaud's. 'He is not in the papers very much and you never hear his name,' explained a spokesperson. 'We are not sure if our visitors will recognise him.'[63] When he published a novel, *The Devil's Tune* (2003),* it reportedly shifted fewer than a hundred copies,[64] and his publisher said they were hoping for

---

* 'I wanted to be a novelist when I was growing up,' he told the press. 'But then I wanted to be a concert pianist too.' (*Evening Standard* 25 February 2003) He wasn't the only Tory MP with such aspirations: Ann Widdecombe had two novels to her name already and Boris Johnson was to publish his first in 2004.

American sales, because 'they haven't heard of him there'.[65] Above all, he lacked the respect of his colleagues. Left to themselves, they would not have elected him, but they had not been left to themselves, and his authority – such as it was – derived from the membership not the MPs. His weak hand on the tiller ensured there was the constant threat of mutiny from those supporting his rivals: Portillo, Clarke, David Davis, John Redwood and others.

By the end of 2002, there were fears that the party's decline might become terminal. Asked about the possibility, Margaret Thatcher was almost reassuring: 'The Tory party will last. I don't know about Iain Duncan Smith, because we all die, but the party doesn't.'[66] Chris Patten agreed: 'I don't think the party will die, but I do think that it will continue to live on a drip until it pulls itself together.'[67] Even Duncan Smith's own director of strategy, the 31-year-old Dominic Cummings, was in despair: 'for many people, just about the only thing less popular than the euro is the Tory Party'.[68]

That at least hinted at the one solid achievement of Duncan Smith's leadership: Britain's failure to adopt the European single currency. In the eyes of its supporters, the euro was the big test of whether the country was serious about the EU and truly wanted to be a player on the global stage. An advert in the *Financial Times* – signed by a hundred business leaders from James Dyson to Christopher Haskins, representing companies from Kettner's Restaurant to Rentokil – warned of 'a serious threat to our future prosperity and to our influence in the world' if Britain didn't join the single currency.[69] 'Of course we can "survive" outside the euro,' said Patten. 'But we will lose our place, lose influence, lose the sense of really mattering.'[70] As Robin Cook put it, 'we will just drift to the margins'.[71]

Blair, who wanted to matter and didn't like the margins, was keen and had promised a referendum on the issue, which was expected to dominate his second term. The timing of any such vote, though, was largely in the hands of Gordon Brown, who was noticeably less enthusiastic. His decision on whether to join, he said, would be driven by economic considerations, but essentially this was a political question. With Ken Clarke as Conservative leader, a referendum would have been easier to win and might have provoked a Tory split; now, it was the one thing capable of uniting the party behind Duncan Smith. The risk was too great, the outcome too uncertain, so the opportunity to demonstrate – in Blair's words – that 'the future of my country lies in being at the heart of Europe'[72] slipped away.* Duncan Smith's finest moment was something that didn't happen.

Two phrases survived from his sorry incumbency. At the 2002 Conservative conference, the chairwoman of the party, Theresa May, decided to tell the members some home truths. 'You know what they call us?' she asked the faithful as they snoozed gently after lunch in Bournemouth. 'The nasty party.'[73] It was hardly an original expression, having been used in the days of both Major[74] and Hague[75] and become commonplace in recent times, but still it was May who was remembered for saying it. And her speech became the best-known statement of those Tory modernisers seeking to adjust to Blair's Britain. 'There's a way to go before we can return to government,' she warned. 'Our base is too narrow and so, occasionally, are our sympathies.' And, she pointed out, 'Twice we went to the country unchanged, unrepentant, just plain unattractive. And twice we got slaughtered.'[76] No one believed that Duncan Smith was either changed or repentant.

The other phrase was Duncan Smith's own. At that same conference, he tried to dismiss the charge that he was an ineffectual leader. 'Never underestimate the determination of a quiet man,' he warned unconvincingly.[77] A year later, as rumours of a leadership challenge swirled around him, he returned to the theme: 'The quiet man is here to stay and he's turning up the volume.'[78]

---

* The only two countries that were offered a referendum on the single currency – Denmark (2000) and Sweden (2003) – both voted against.

He wasn't and he didn't. A month later he lost his job, dismissed by the parliamentary party, who'd had enough and had decided to put aside their differences in favour of a compromise caretaker, the former home secretary Michael Howard.* 'I will lead this party from its centre,' Howard declared.[79] There was no need to consult the membership, since there was only one candidate, so the old system was in effect restored; it was left to the MPs to choose. And it worked. The feeling was that the Tories had rediscovered their ruthless streak; facing destruction at the polls, they'd acted swiftly and efficiently. As one of Howard's supporters, backbench MP David Cameron, later wrote, 'there was a sense that the grown-ups and the professionals were back in charge'.[80]

The experiment with party democracy had failed, because the members – riding their pet hobby horses – had chosen the wrong man: someone who spoke to them but not to the public, someone whose concerns failed to resonate with the country, someone who knew nothing of government but much about principled rebellion. The Conservatives, at least, resolved not to repeat the mistake.

Perhaps they should have known, because the omens for this new system hadn't been good. The very first ballot of MPs had required a rerun, since two candidates had come joint bottom and the rules allowed for only one to be eliminated. It was the 'Fight of the Living Dead,' jeered the *Daily Mirror*. 'They can't even agree who comes last.'[81] And then the announcement of the members' choice, scheduled for 12 September 2001, had to be delayed by 24 hours because on that day there was only one story in town.†

---

* Michael Howard didn't write novels, but his wife, Sandra, did, starting with *Glass Houses* (2006).

† Even then, the election of Duncan Smith didn't make it to the front page of the *Daily Telegraph*.

II

The Boeing 767 passenger plane hit the North Tower of the World Trade Center in New York City at 1.46 p.m. British time, on Tuesday 11 September 2001. By the time a second plane hit the South Tower at 2.03 p.m. pictures were being carried live on the BBC News channel. An hour later, with a third plane now reported to have hit the Pentagon, Tony Blair was telling the TUC conference in Brighton that these were terrorist attacks, the work of 'fanatics utterly indifferent to the sanctity of life'.[82]

'From that moment on,' wrote Jack Straw, 'foreign and defence policy dominated Tony's premiership.'[83] There was the sense of a mission. Under attack from Gordon Brown, with MPs reluctant to endorse his public-sector reforms and with a cooling of public enthusiasm, Blair had been looking a beleaguered figure at home. 'I feel a lack of allies,' he told Peter Mandelson. 'I feel isolated – in government, from the Lib Dems, from individual supporters who were with me in 1997.'[84] Among the successes of Blair's first term had been the military actions in Kosovo in 1999, freeing the province from Serbia, and in Sierra Leone in 2000, helping end a vicious civil war. These were the early fruits of the 'new doctrine of international community' that he proclaimed in 1999, arguing that the principle of non-interference in the affairs of other states needed to be 'qualified', that there were times when it was right to be 'actively involved in other people's conflicts'.[85] Now was the time for that doctrine to find full expression. The 9/11 attacks gave him a purpose, one that was to define his entire political career and to transform British politics.

The first response, in those early hours when it was feared that there were up to 10,000 deaths, perhaps 500 of them British,* was solidarity with Britain's most important ally. 'We stand shoulder

---

* The final count showed 2,977 dead, the vast majority of them American. Of the other 90 nations who lost citizens, the UK was the worst affected with 67 fatalities, the highest British death toll in a terrorist attack since the war.

to shoulder with our American friends,' Blair said.[86] Four weeks later, as he addressed the Labour conference in a speech broadcast live in the US, there was the political vision. 'Out of the shadow of this evil should emerge lasting good,' he said: 'hope amongst all nations of a new beginning where we seek to resolve differences in a calm and ordered way; greater understanding between nations and between faiths; and above all justice and prosperity for the poor and dispossessed.'[87] This was the best tribute we could pay the victims. 'The kaleidoscope has been shaken,' he concluded. 'The pieces are in flux. Soon they will settle again. Before they do, let us reorder this world around us.'

The image wasn't entirely new. In 1988, as he surveyed Mikhail Gorbachev's reforms in what was then the Soviet Union, Blair had written in the same vein: 'The last few months have seen the kaleidoscope of international politics shaken dramatically and resettle in patterns of a new and unforeseen kind.'[88] The difference this time was that he could help shape the reordering of the world.

The presidential election campaign of George W. Bush in 2000 was greatly enjoyed by British commentators and comedians, mocking the way he mangled the English language. Even Bush looked a little bemused by what was coming out of his mouth, though the phrases that emerged were oddly memorable. He'd talk about cherishing the family because that was 'where wings take dream'; he'd worry about how 'more and more of our imports come from overseas'; and he'd wonder: 'will the highways on the internet become more few?'[89] Some believed that he was deliberately hamming up the malapropisms and misspeaking to appear folksy, others that they were evidence of a dyslexic brain, but mostly the British just laughed.* Bush was so ignorant that he

---

* A 2003 episode of the TV series *Jonathan Creek* included a character who made ventriloquist dummies. He makes one of Bush and when asked why

couldn't name the leaders of Pakistan, India and Chechnya, and what was worse – for neither could most of those laughing – he let himself be tricked into revealing his lack of knowledge in a television interview.

When he was nonetheless elected, taking office in January 2001, it was seen as evidence of how dumb America had become. But since the new president appeared to embody what the *Independent* called 'the ignorant isolationism of mainstream Republicans',[90] most in Britain could conclude that he probably wouldn't matter much.

In reality, of course, Bush was not the fool he was made out to be,* but he did have a serious lack of foreign-policy experience, his political career having been restricted to six years as governor of Texas. Now, with 9/11, he faced his first and sternest test, but his path was perfectly clear. America had been attacked on a scale not seen since Pearl Harbor, and responsibility had been fixed on the al-Qaeda network, founded and headed by Osama bin Laden. Therefore the American president – whoever that might have been – was going to hit back hard at al-Qaeda, which had, since the mid-1990s, been based in those parts of Afghanistan controlled by the Taliban, an extremist Muslim movement. When the Taliban refused a demand to hand over bin Laden, retaliation was inevitable; America would strike Afghanistan, whether alone or with the backing of the rest of the world. 'I don't care what the international lawyers say,' declared Bush. 'We're going to kick some ass.'[91]

The fact that America did not act alone was due to Blair more than anyone. Determined that the international community should take a stand against rogue states, he threw himself

---

its mouth doesn't move, turns it upside down, explaining, 'He doesn't talk through his mouth.'

* 'He is not as stupid as you think,' Blair told Ken Clarke, who remained unconvinced. (Clarke, *Kind of Blue* p. 421)

into the role of coalition builder, travelling 40,000 miles in the 8 weeks after 9/11 to hold 54 meetings with foreign leaders. He was, said the *New York Times*, 'America's closest ally', while the *Wall Street Journal* called him 'America's chief foreign ambassador'.[92] He found widespread international support for the action against Afghanistan, although few countries beyond Britain were prepared to add military assistance.

Bombing started on 7 October 2001, while special forces were sent to assist the Northern Alliance, a coalition of anti-Taliban forces inside Afghanistan. After the initial attacks, it seemed for a couple of weeks as if the military operation on the ground was stalling, and the news was dominated by the humanitarian consequences of the bombing. British public opinion, which had been strongly in support of the campaign, faltered a little, with women and older people in particular beginning to turn against the war, though even here there was still majority backing. And then the Northern Alliance made sudden, rapid progress, and the capital Kabul fell some five weeks after the start of hostilities. By mid-December, the Taliban and al-Qaeda had been driven out of power, even if many of their members – including bin Laden – had escaped to the remote fastness of the Tora Bora mountains.

That closed the first phase of operations, but no one thought it was genuinely the end. This was always going to be a difficult project in territory that had proved troublesome for everyone from Alexander the Great and Genghis Khan to the British empire* and the Soviet Union. Continued armed resistance seemed certain, and the prospect of peace and stability was made less likely still because years of civil war meant there was no infrastructure to

---

* The historical parallel was drawn by the TV drama *Sherlock* (2010), a modern-day take on Arthur Conan Doyle's original, which opened with Dr Watson having nightmares about his time as an army doctor in Afghanistan. His nineteenth-century predecessor had been wounded at the Battle of Maiwand in the Second Anglo-Afghan War in 1880.

support the building of a new state. Nonetheless, few at the time would have predicted that in February 2018 the conflict would overtake Vietnam to become the longest-running war in American history. Britain, meanwhile, had withdrawn the last of its combat troops in 2014, after 13 years and more than 450 British deaths.

Had the UK's involvement in the War on Terror, as America designated its response to 9/11, been restricted to Afghanistan, it would – despite the lengthy engagement – have had little purchase on the popular imagination. But there was also Iraq. Indeed there had always been Iraq. In 1996, while he was in opposition and Bill Clinton in the White House, Tony Blair had supported the American bombing of the country, and two years later had sent in British planes to join USAF attacks, his first experience of ordering military action.

Similarly, Blair's first meeting with President Bush, seven months before 9/11, was held against the backdrop of a new wave of American and British bombing in Iraq. After the meeting, Blair said that Britain and America would use 'whatever means were needed' to stop the government of Saddam Hussein 'from developing nuclear, chemical and biological weapons'. Quite what that would entail was not spelled out, though Bush's adviser Richard Perle – who had also served under Ronald Reagan – was clear that the bombings were just the start. There was a new resolution in the White House, and regime change was on the agenda. 'Clinton paid lip service to removing Saddam from office,'* said Perle. 'The Bush administration recognises that this is the only way to resolve the problem. Mr Bush expects the UK to be part of that resolution.'[93] The events of 9/11 provided the opportunity, and in their first telephone conversation after the attacks, Bush told Blair his targets were, first, bin Laden and then 'other countries, including

---

* The Iraq Liberation Act of 1998 had stated regime change as official US policy.

Iraq, and other countries not even linked to OBL'.[94]

The international negotiations in the eighteen months between that call and the onset of hostilities on 19 March 2003 resembled at times an intricate dance routine choreographed on the spur of the moment by its principals, with a supporting cast of weapons inspectors, dodgy dossiers and UN resolutions. The ending was clear enough, though. War was coming. Not just another bombing campaign, but a full-scale invasion of Iraq. Blair's role was to be a loyal ally though not too much so: 'Britain has got to be a partner, not a poodle,'* he said.[95] It was a difficult act to pull off, even for a politician with his skills as a communicator, and through the long build-up to the war, he increasingly lost support at home.

He faced three key questions: Why? Why now? On whose authority? The aim, he said, was simply to remove Iraq's stockpiles of weapons of mass destruction (WMD). If Saddam Hussein complied with this demand, then there would be no need for military action. In order to demonstrate the urgency, Blair took the unprecedented step of publishing intelligence information, which he presented to the House of Commons in September 2002: a 'fifty-page dossier, detailing the history of Iraq's weapons of mass destruction programme, its breach of United Nations resolutions, and its attempts to rebuild that illegal programme'.

The most startling disclosure was that Iraq 'has existing and active military plans for the use of chemical and biological weapons, which could be activated within forty-five minutes'.[96] That claim was based on an uncorroborated, single source who was, in Robin Cook's words, 'reporting hearsay from another uncorroborated, single source'.[97] But it grabbed enough attention to be repeated in the reports of every newspaper, most sensationally in the *Sun*'s headline: 'Brits 45 mins from doom'. The paper

---

* That image was already in common currency: 'left-winger Jeremy Corbyn accused the government of being America's poodle', the *Daily Mirror* had reported after the earlier bombing of Iraq. (19 February 2001)

warned that 'British servicemen and tourists in Cyprus could be annihilated by germ warfare missiles,' which 'could thud into the Mediterranean island within forty-five minutes of tyrant Saddam Hussein ordering an attack', spreading 'death and destruction through warheads carrying anthrax, mustard gas, sarin or ricin'.[98] Even if one took the dossier as gospel, this was a complete misreading of the information provided, conflating two separate claims,* though no one in government saw fit to say so. Blair later conceded that 'in retrospect' he should have corrected the reporting.[99]

But this wasn't the dodgy dossier. That was a second one in February 2003, a nineteen-page document this time. It was, Blair's spokesman Alastair Campbell later claimed, merely 'a briefing paper compiled for the Sunday papers',[100] but it was a little more significant than that; it was released to delegates at the United Nations, and when American secretary of state Colin Powell spoke to the UN, he made explicit reference to 'the fine paper that the United Kingdom distributed yesterday, which describes in exquisite detail Iraqi deception activities'.[101]

It was unfortunate, therefore, that this dossier was swiftly discovered to contain large chunks plagiarised without acknowledgement from other sources, including an academic article by an Iraqi–American researcher, Ibrahim al-Marashi, who pointed out that some of his evidence was several years old. 'I'll be more sceptical of any British intelligence I read in future,' he said.[102] The government insisted this didn't invalidate the essential truth of the dossier. It did, however, undermine the idea that the material had come from reliable intelligence sources. And those working in intelligence were not impressed. The document was full of 'silly errors', one said.[103] 'You cannot just cherry-pick evidence that suits your case and ignore the rest,' said another; 'it is a cardinal

---

* The dossier said the regime had 'constructed a new engine test stand for the development of missiles capable of reaching UK bases in Cyprus', but this was not related to the 45 minutes.

rule of intelligence.'[104] An official at the foreign office later admitted, 'It had not been fact-checked.'[105]

And still there was the question of why now. What had changed to make this action so urgently necessary? The only obvious reason was that it was America's wish. Long after the event, Blair continued to insist that, even as military forces were gathering in the Middle East, war was not a done deal. 'Only one person decides,' he wrote. 'I knew at that moment that George had not decided.'[106] And, on behalf of Britain, Blair waited for the decision to be made.

The other reason for pursuing this now was the hope of momentum, that the coalition of opinion built to support the invasion of Afghanistan might hold together for Iraq. It did not. The United Nations Security Council passed Resolution 1441, calling on Iraq to cooperate with the UN weapons inspection team or else 'face serious consequences', but those consequences were not spelled out. Britain made strenuous and sincere efforts to get a second resolution, explicitly authorising military force, accepted, but when it became clear that France and Russia were going to veto such a proposal, attempts were abandoned. And so when America attacked Iraq, it did so without UN backing, and with substantial military assistance from Britain alone.

Nor was there great support among the British people. Unlike the invasion of Afghanistan, this was not easy to see as a just war, and there was serious political opposition, including from the Liberal Democrats, whose leader, Charles Kennedy, was taunted as 'Charlie Chamberlain' by Tory MPs.[107] In February 2003, there was a Commons vote on a motion declaring the case for military action 'as yet unproven'. Blair had anticipated 50 Labour back-benchers defying the whip; it turned out to be 122, joined by the Lib Dems and by 13 Tories (including Ken Clarke) rejecting their party's official position of support. On a similar motion the following month, the numbers had increased: 217 MPs were now against war, including 189 Labour backbenchers.

Among the rebels on the latter occasion was Robin Cook, which made the parliamentary opposition look a good deal more serious. Cook was Labour's most effective debater – 'probably the most brilliant parliamentarian of our times,' said Prescott, 'but he was well aware of it'[108] – and in a less image-obsessed age could reasonably have aspired to the top job ('apparently I am too ugly to be the next Labour leader' was his own summary[109]). He had served as foreign secretary in Blair's first term and now resigned from cabinet because he disagreed with the invasion. He'd seen the intelligence briefings and rejected the government's central argument: 'Iraq probably has no weapons of mass destruction in the commonly understood sense of the term.' The British people, he concluded, 'do not doubt that Saddam is a brutal dictator, but they are not persuaded that he is a clear and present danger to Britain'. And he felt unable to give his backing to 'a war that has neither international agreement nor domestic support'.[110]

Opinion polls that January confirmed Cook's assessment of public opinion. One showed 47 per cent against war, 30 per cent in support, with a growing shift against the government. Another suggested that just 9 per cent would be in favour if there were no UN mandate, and indicated that 71 per cent of social groups C2DE believed Blair put his support for Bush above their own interests. That feeling was amplified in a third poll, which showed that 63 per cent didn't trust Blair.[111] Once hostilities commenced, there would be a swing to support British troops, but never in modern times had Britain gone to war with such half-hearted public endorsement.

The overwhelming response of the British public to the 9/11 attacks was sympathy with America, but even at the outset there was some dissent. A special, unscheduled episode of BBC One's *Question Time* was broadcast live (rather than pre-recorded as was the normal practice) two days after the atrocities, and aroused considerable controversy. Labour MP Tam Dalyell, a veteran of anti-war campaigns, warned against military action: 'If there's massive retaliation, sure as nuts, it'll happen again.' Another panellist, the *Independent* columnist Yasmin Alibhai-Brown, said that Americans were only now realising that 'many people really, truly detest them around the world'. Some of the audience joined in, denouncing the country's foreign policy, and when one person spoke in defence of America, he was booed. Also on the panel was Philip Lader, recently retired as American ambassador to Britain, who was close to tears at some of the comments: 'I find it hurtful that anyone could suggest the majority of the world despises the United States.'

Over 2,000 complaints were reported to have been received, but the sentiments were not confined to the studio audience. Chelsea Clinton, daughter of the former US president, arrived at Oxford to study for a masters degree that autumn and was struck by how hostile the atmosphere was: 'Every day I encounter some sort of anti-American feeling. Sometimes, it's from other students, sometimes it's from a newspaper columnist, sometimes it's from peace demonstrators.'[112] On the left, it was America's perceived warmongering and its support for Israel that attracted condemnation; on the right, there were memories of American backing for Irish terrorism, as former Tory minister Virginia Bottomley later reflected: 'I thought 9/11 was a horrific event, but the American reaction was in total contrast to how they had responded to the IRA over the years.'[113] It was an uncomfortable truth, rarely articulated in public, that for many British people, news of 9/11 was received with a gut-level 'They had it coming.'

A week after the bombing of Afghanistan started, a demonstration in London attracted over 20,000 protestors, not all of whom were the usual suspects. 'Old men in Islamic dress marched with former Greenham women and dreadlocked anti-capitalists who booed when they passed McDonald's,' reported the *Independent on Sunday*.[114] There were contingents from other major cities, where a level of activism was expected, but also coaches arriving from less noted centres of protest: Guildford, High Wycombe, St Albans, Woking.

When the international focus switched from Afghanistan to Iraq, opposition grew and so did the protests. Churches, mosques and temples mobilised, as did trade unions and colleges, while many non-aligned individuals from housing estates, suburbs and villages turned out for what was often their first experience of political protest. 'Alongside veteran peace campaigners, trade unionists and anti-globalisation activists will be pensioners, lawyers, bankers and middle-class housewives with their children,' noted the *Birmingham Mail* on the eve of the biggest demonstration of all.[115]

That came on Saturday, 15 February 2003 in a coordinated programme of some 800 marches in 60 countries around the world, from Australia, Bangladesh and Indonesia to Russia, Spain and South Africa, bringing out tens of millions of people. There were a million on the streets of Rome, 500,000 in Berlin; there were 200,000 in Damascus, 10,000 in the Canary Islands, and 80 on Orkney. And in London an estimated 2 million staged the largest political gathering in British history.

'Are they all lefties?' asked the *Daily Telegraph* in advance of the demonstration, and gave its own answer: 'Pretty much, though not exclusively.'[116] That, however, was not most people's experience of the march. 'The Socialist Workers marched next to posh Jane, who brought her own bottle of port because she remembered how cold she'd been on the Countryside March,' reported the *Sunday Herald*. 'It was the most ethnically and socially diverse march Britain has ever seen. There were Peruvians and Pakistanis, Nigerians and Norwegians. In Parliament Square an Ali G lookalike danced to dub reggae on his ghetto blaster while a wan young Christian stood next to him holding a home-made crucifix.'[117] Playwright Alan Bennett was there, the first time he'd been on a demonstration since Suez in 1956 (and even then he hadn't intended to be involved). 'There seems no structure to it, ahead of us some SWP banners,' he noted in his diary; 'beside them the Surrey Heath Liberal Democrats. Scattered among the more seasoned marchers are many unlikely figures, two women in front of us in fur hats and bootees looking as if they're just off to the WI.'[118]

The demonstrators represented a new mood in the country. 'The nineties are looking like an innocent decade, and who would have thought that at the time?' wrote Ian McEwan in *Saturday* (2005), a novel set on that day. 'Now we breathe a different air.'[119] David Blunkett, who wasn't present, described the protest as 'frighteningly intimidatory, and people so bellicose'.[120] He was wrong. There would be real anger to come, but the tone of the march was light; many of the participants had never even chanted a slogan before, and didn't do so now, instead simply marvelling at the multitudes that filled central London. 'They were ordinary people in their everyday clothes, from every walk of life and every age group in Britain,' wrote Robin Cook. The irony, he reflected, was that many were the people Blair had courted for the last decade: 'he is destroying the new base that he almost single-handedly built for Labour among the new middle classes'.[121]

Robin Cook's last words before he resigned were to Alastair Campbell: 'I really hope it doesn't all end horribly for you all.'[122] In fact, Iraq turned out worse than anyone had anticipated, as Tony Blair admitted: 'never did I guess the nightmare that unfolded'.[123]

After a period of bombing (which had started in the summer of 2002), the invasion itself was relatively straightforward. Within three weeks Baghdad had fallen, and on 1 May 2003, the end of combat operations was declared by George Bush, standing on an aircraft carrier, in front of a banner proclaiming 'Mission Accomplished'. But the immediate aftermath saw the virtual collapse of society in Iraq. Much of the water, sewage and electrical infrastructure had been heavily damaged in the bombing, and in the absence of a police force, the streets became the territory of armed mobs. There was widespread looting, not only of shops but of hospitals and of the Iraq Museum, one of the world's great storehouses of antiquities. A year on from Bush's announcement, Chris Mullin wrote in his diary, 'In Iraq the Lords of Chaos rule. Every night our television screens are filled with images of hooded gunmen rampaging at will.'[124] Local insurgent groups filled the vacuum, as well as 'external forces', to use Blair's unironic words: 'Iraq became for them, and by their choice, the field of battle.'[125]

The ramifications of the invasion for the country, the region and the world would take decades to play out. For Britain, which kept troops in Iraq until May 2011, there was the immediate human cost of 179 dead service personnel* and the certainty of future terrorism.† And there was too a huge political cost, not just to Blair himself but to the relationship between politicians and people.

The issue was the missing WMD. Because it turned out that Robin Cook had been correct, and Iraq had no such weapons. As this became increasingly clear, Downing Street grew impatient that the media were still harping on about the subject. Alastair Campbell complained that 'no matter how much we said there were other priorities now, the public were being told as a matter of fact that we had done wrong'.[126] The only line that could be taken was to try to move the goalposts. 'It's not crucially important,' said Jack Straw of the WMD question.[127] But it was important, as Blair acknowledged: 'It was, after all, the *casus belli*.'[128]

Blair had been so insistent on the matter, so clear that this was

---

* Estimates of the total number of deaths directly attributable to the invasion and occupation of Iraq have varied widely. The Iraq Body Count project recorded around 125,000 dead in the first ten years, while accepting that this was a minimum figure and the real number was probably much higher.
† Asked in February 2003 whether military action against Iraq would leave Britain more or less vulnerable to terrorism, Eliza Manningham-Buller, the director general of MI5, didn't hesitate: 'More – it will radicalise a new generation of young Arabs.' (Mullin, *A View from the Foothills* p. 366)

why Britain was going to war, that when the weapons were not found, many felt they'd been tricked. A poll at the end of May 2003 showed 63 per cent saying Blair had misled them, with 27 per cent believing that he had deliberately lied.[129] The perception was reinforced that month by the BBC journalist Andrew Gilligan, with a story that the first dossier had been rewritten – 'sexed up' was the expression – on the instructions of Downing Street, because the evidence had been so thin. He quoted an intelligence source: 'The classic example was the statement that weapons of mass destruction could be ready for use within forty-five minutes.'[130] In the ensuing row between the BBC and Alastair Campbell – the person said to have ordered the rewrite – the source was identified by Downing Street as Dr David Kelly, a biological weapons expert who knew Iraq well; he'd been to the country 39 times as a weapons inspector for the UN, doing such valuable work that the director of the UN team nominated him for a Nobel Peace Prize.*

When Campbell appeared in front of the foreign affairs committee of the Commons in June 2003, he said he was shocked at the suggestion that the government would 'sex up a dossier as a way of trying to convince the public' to go to war. 'Are we really so cynical that we think the prime minister, any prime minister, is going to make prior decisions to send British forces into conflict and would not rather actually avoid doing that?'[131]

By now many did think precisely that, and some of the attacks became very bitter indeed. Paul Starling, Welsh political editor of the *Daily Mirror*, went far beyond Iraq in his assault: 'Politics since 1997 has been the most rotten in modern British history, worse than the drift and sleaze of the Major years and worse even than the in-yer-face selfishness and destruction of the Thatcher years,' he wrote. 'Mr Blair has systematically targeted truth.'[132]

---

* The fallout from the government's fight with the BBC eventually saw the resignation of Gavyn Davies and Greg Dyke, the Corporation's chairman and director general, and of Andrew Gilligan.

Meanwhile, there was a barrage of criticism from the kind of people who were regarded – in a newly fashionable term – as national treasures, those who had been around long enough that they were part of the fixtures and fittings.* 'They lied through their teeth, they lied, lied, lied,' said agony aunt Claire Rayner, 72. 'I thought it was gangster capitalism,' offered broadcaster John Peel, 63, adding, 'Did Tony Blair mislead the country? I suspect he did.' And actor Sean Connery, 72, similarly disapproved of the entire venture: 'It's like taking a hammer to kill a fly.' 'Why do they never trust us with the truth?' asked Keith Waterhouse, 74, the nearest thing Fleet Street had to a national treasure. 'Why does Tony Blair believe we have the mentality of a bunch of kids?' Most authoritative was Labour's elder statesman Denis Healey, 85: 'All the evidence I have seen suggests they twisted the evidence on weapons of mass destruction.'[133]

Rising above such squabbles, Blair flew to Washington, where he addressed both houses of Congress, an honour granted to just three previous prime ministers: Winston Churchill, Clement Attlee and Margaret Thatcher. He was received with multiple standing ovations – three of them before he'd said a word – and with a respect and a courtesy that was seldom in evidence at home these days. That speech, on 17 July 2003, was final confirmation that he was now one of the world's leading statesmen, and that even America wished to pay tribute. And on the same day, Dr David Kelly went for a walk in the woods near his Oxfordshire home, took a handful of painkillers and slit his wrist.

Blair was on a plane to Tokyo when he heard the news of Kelly's death. He was greeted by the press at the airport, and 'that cunt Jonathan Oliver' (in Alastair Campbell's words[134]) from the

---

* A poll in 2011 produced the following top ten of 'Britain's greatest national treasures': David Attenborough, Stephen Fry, Sean Connery, Paul McCartney, Stephen Hawking, Bobby Charlton, J. K. Rowling, Judi Dench, Tom Jones, Richard Attenborough. (*i* 25 November 2011)

Mail on Sunday shouted out, 'Have you got blood on your hands, prime minister?'[135] That set the media tone. Sky's political editor, Adam Boulton, reflected, 'if Alastair Campbell hadn't started his war against the BBC, then Dr Kelly would still be alive today', while the *Daily Mail* front page had photos of Blair, Campbell and defence secretary Geoff Hoon, with the headline: 'Proud of yourselves?'[136] The *Daily Mirror*'s headline was: 'Spun to death – Iraq expert driven to tragic "suicide"'.[137] And those inverted commas were devastating. As the former Labour MP Tony Benn wrote in his diary, 'Of course immediately the question is: did Kelly commit suicide or was he murdered?'[138] That was indeed the first response of a great many people. Most then dismissed just as quickly the idea that the British state had killed a civil servant to stop him causing political embarrassment, but the fact that such a thing had even been considered was far from reassuring.*

Perceptions of Blair never really recovered. 'Up until then, we'd been sceptical about the Iraq war,' says a character in Jonathan Coe's novel *Number 11* (2015), reflecting on Kelly's death. 'But the day he died it became absolutely clear: the whole thing stank. Suicide or murder, it didn't really matter. A good man had died, and it was the lies surrounding the war that had killed him.' The consequence, she concludes, was that 'None of us could pretend any longer that we were being governed by honourable people.'[139]

On the eve of the invasion, Blair had appealed for the public's trust: 'in the end people have just got to make up their minds whether they believe me or not, I'm afraid'.[140] Many had now done so, and the nickname 'Tony Bliar' – first used by Tories in 1999[141] – became ubiquitous.† A poll in early 2004 had more

---

* An opinion poll in 2010 showed 20 per cent believing Kelly committed suicide; 24 per cent saying he didn't, with the rest undecided. (*Daily Mail* 16 August 2010)

† Robert Mugabe, president of Zimbabwe, had earlier offered the more elegant formulation 'Tony B. Liar'. (*Guardian* 7 March 2002)

than half saying the prime minister had lied to take the country to war,[142] while the party's own research concluded, 'Levels of dissatisfaction and cynicism are approaching those of the Major years'.[143] For the politically non-partisan, it felt worse than that. In the mid-1990s there had at least been an attractive alternative to the Tories in the shape of New Labour, but if Blair's party were now seen to be similarly untrustworthy, then there was no hope for the country.

Blair continued to argue that the world was a better place for the removal of a tyrant (Saddam was hanged in December 2006 after a trial in an Iraqi court),* and there was one undeniably positive development, when Libya began dismantling its WMD programmes at the end of 2003. 'A little bit of fear about what America might do was no bad thing,' reflected Blair, who played a pivotal role in the Libyan negotiations.[144]

But in terms of domestic politics, he had an almost impossible hand to play, largely because there had been no obvious benefit to Britain. For America, the strikes against Afghanistan and Iraq were presented as retaliation and also as pre-emptive self-defence; successive administrations could point to the fact that there was no repeat of 9/11. Bush was selling homeland security. Whereas Blair's liberal interventionism offered no element of self-interest: it was expensive, it cost the lives of serving men and women, and it put the country at risk of terrorist reprisals. It could actually be seen as unpatriotic.

It also damaged relations with the European Union. While there were some – Spain's José Maria Aznar, Italy's Silvio Berlusconi – who joined Britain in supporting the Iraq war, others did not, most notably Jacques Chirac in France and Gerhard Schröder in Germany. The American defence secretary, Donald Rumsfeld,

---

* The *Sun* marked the occasion with a game of hangman, illustrated with a gallows and a picture of Saddam in eight pieces: 'Cut out and play our fun noose game,' it invited.

could afford to dismiss them as 'old Europe',[145] but Britain's distance from the other two big EU nations merely confirmed what was apparent from its failure to join the euro: the UK was still semi-detached from its neighbours, and would likely always be so, torn between Europe and the English-speaking world.

Blair believed that even his opponents 'admired the fact I counted, was a big player, was a world not just a national leader'. The British people, he insisted, 'prefer their prime ministers to stand tall internationally'.[146] He had, however, perhaps misjudged the mood of the nation. People had voted Labour not in order to police the world, but to repair the crumbling fabric of their own country. Increased spending on public services was not yet producing the promised results, and here was the prime minister more concerned with the global stage. This perception of misplaced priorities became far stronger as the bloody saga of Iraq wore on, but it was there early on. 'What is the difference between God and Tony Blair?' wrote journalist Matthew D'Ancona in January 2002. 'Answer: God is everywhere, but Tony Blair is everywhere except Britain.'[147]

And it mattered more somehow because it was Blair. It was getting difficult now to remember, but he had started his premiership on a wave of extraordinary goodwill directed specifically at him. 'I discovered not just admiration but adoration for Blair,' wrote the BBC political correspondent Nicholas Jones, reporting on the crowds during the 1997 campaign. 'I had to force myself to remember that they were talking not about a pop star but a politician.'[148] Much of the personal affection had drained away over the first five years, but Iraq finished off whatever was left.

'The British people, whom I genuinely adored,' wrote Blair in his memoirs, 'had ceased loving and were not going to start again.'[149] The former US president Bill Clinton, who had always been close to Blair, put it best in July 2003: 'People are falling out of love with Tony because they think he's fallen out of love with them. He's a statesman, and that's great, but their world is here and now and they are paying him to sort out their world.'[150]

2

Left and Right

I

The millennium did not start well for the political establishment in
Europe. In February 2000 Austria got a coalition government that
included the far-right Freedom Party, led by Jörg Haider, a controversial politician opposed to Islam, immigration and the European
Union. Over the next two years, there were further electoral successes
for right-wing populists across the continent: Silvio Berlusconi's
Forza Italia, the Danish People's Party, Vlaams Blok in Belgium
and the Pim Fortuyn List in the Netherlands, even though Fortuyn
himself ('a gay, bald bigot spitting venom at Muslims', according to
the *People*)[1] was murdered during the election campaign.

Meanwhile in France, Jean-Marie Le Pen of the Front National made it through to the second-round run-off in the French presidential elections, though he was then beaten heavily by Jacques Chirac. And Helmut Schmidt, the grand old man of German politics, held out little hope for his country either. 'We are stuck with a multicultural society and we can't cope with it,' he said. 'Nor do Germans want to do that. To a great extent they are racist deep down.'[2]

None of this sat well with the EU dream of a united continent. There was a widespread sense of dissatisfaction. Mainstream parties were still in office, but seemed to be failing to meet the hopes and expectations of their electorates, so that people were beginning to look to the fringes. In Britain, where first past the post handicapped new parties, the phenomenon was less obvious, but there were still concerns. 'I find it difficult to be optimistic about the future of parliamentary democracy,' wrote Robin Cook in his diary in 2001, 'unless we recognise that our present political culture is destroying trust not just in government but in our democratic process.' There was a danger, he believed, that there might develop 'a vacuum which will be occupied by extremist political movements with simple destructive solutions'.[3]

There were already signs of such movements to both left and right of the Westminster parties. And although their impact was marginal at the time, they would come to shape the politics of the following decade.

Contrary to popular perception, the British left had not been killed by the twin onslaught of Margaret Thatcher and Tony Blair. Those few in the Labour Party who called themselves socialists were seldom seen in public any more, but they were still there, dug in for a long winter, refusing to compromise their principles. 'We've all been working for a Labour victory,' John McDonnell, the former deputy leader of the Greater London Council, had said in 1986. 'But not unity at any price. Not unity at the price of a coalition with the right in the Labour Party.'[4] In Westminster, the flame was kept flickering by the Campaign Group of MPs, whose *éminence grise*, until his retirement from the Commons in 2001, was ex-cabinet minister Tony Benn.

Beyond Parliament, there were shadowy groups that occasionally flitted into view, such as the masked anti-capitalists who ran riot in London on May Day 2000, decorating Winston Churchill's statue with a grass Mohican. These were the likes of Reclaim the Streets – a 'non-hierarchical, leaderless, openly organised, public group', according to their website[5] – and they were deplored by the orthodox left. 'Lacking a coherent long-term class strategy, they lashed out angrily at visible symbols of capitalism,' sniffed Ken Livingstone, who'd been McDonnell's old boss at the GLC.[6]

And somehow there survived a tangle of Marxist groups, whose small and declining membership still retained an influence in the trade union movement. Around the turn of the century there emerged a new generation of general secretaries: Mark Serwotka of the civil service union the PCSU (elected in 2000), Jeremy Dear of the National Union of Journalists (2001), Matt Wrack of the Fire Brigade Union (2005), railwaymen Mick Rix and Bob Crow at ASLEF (1998) and the RMT (2002) respectively. All had political affiliations beyond the Labour Party.* Crow had been a member of the Communist Party of Great Britain, and then of the Socialist Labour Party (led by Arthur Scargill, lifetime president of the miners' union), with Rix also a member of the latter group. From the Trotskyist section of the left, Wrack was in the Socialist Party† and Dear a supporter of Socialist Appeal

---

* Readers not fully up to speed with the factionalism of the British far left are advised not to expend too much effort in trying to differentiate between the various groups mentioned in this and succeeding paragraphs.
† Officially it was named the Socialist Party of England and Wales, to distinguish it from its sister organisation in Scotland, but the full title was seldom used – possibly because SPEW was not the happiest of acronyms.

(both groups born of the Militant Tendency), while Serwotka had been expelled from Labour for his membership of another group, Socialist Organiser.

The history of such sects was not rich in electoral success. Even at the high point of Militant's infiltration of Labour in the 1980s, it had only secured three MPs, and none at all when sailing under its own colours. Elsewhere, the Socialist Workers Party (SWP) – the Marxist group despised by all other Marxist groups for not being rigorous enough in its theory and for having the most members – had never managed to get a councillor, let alone an MP, elected. The obvious answer to their perpetual impotence was for the various far-left groups to come together as a single bloc, but that had long proved impossible, given the deep doctrinal differences, however imperceptible these were to the outsider. There was also the reluctance of often elderly male leaders to surrender their authority: better to be the only fish in a puddle than lose oneself in even the smallest of ponds.

Nonetheless, an attempt was made, and in the 1990s a new coalition, the Socialist Alliance, was forged with the aim of contesting elections. It started with the Socialist Party and Workers' Liberty (formerly Socialist Organiser), and later picked up the International Socialist Group, the Revolutionary Democratic Group, Workers Power and, most importantly, the SWP. The only really significant absentee was the Socialist Labour Party, which remained aloof, with Arthur Scargill denouncing the Socialist Alliance in time-honoured fashion as 'splitters'.[7]

Despite that echo of past spats, there was something of a new mood in evidence on the far left. The collapse of the Soviet Union had been a massive blow, but also an opportunity. The internecine struggles between the various brands of Marxism, Leninism, Trotskyism, Maoism, Hoxhaism and so on didn't seem quite so important in a reduced world where a communist could look only to Cuba or to Venezuela, with its newly elected president Hugo Chávez. Perhaps it was time to bury the ice pick. Dave Nellist of the Socialist Party, chair of the Socialist Alliance and a man who had implausibly shared an office with Tony Blair, when they'd first arrived as Labour MPs in Westminster, suggested that disputes weren't as bitter as once they had been. 'If we have differences over what happened to Russia in 1973, or the next six years of the economic plan,' he shrugged, 'now we talk about it over a pint.'[8]

What brought many together was the London mayoralty campaign in 2000. The obvious Labour candidate was Ken Livingstone, so when the party rigged the selection process to exclude him, he announced that he'd stand as an independent instead, and thousands on the left, both inside and outside Labour, flocked to his cause. In national politics, Livingstone meant little, but memories of the GLC – abolished by Thatcher in 1986 – gave him a status in London, and his grass-roots campaign saw him elected at the expense of the official Labour candidate, Frank Dobson, and of the Conservative Steven Norris.

Some of the groups and individuals supporting him also fielded candidates for the London Assembly, which was having its first elections the same day. Under the name of the London Socialist Alliance, they got just 3 per cent of the constituency vote, but the campaign demonstrated that left groups outside the Labour Party could work together electorally, and the experience invigorated the Socialist Alliance.

The new group sold itself on broad policy, rather than doctrine. 'The consensus between the major political parties,' said the national chair, Liz Davies, 'has meant that those who support public ownership, who are against the scapegoating of asylum seekers, against the murderous bombing of Afghanistan and against New Labour's punitive criminal justice agenda are unrepresented and have no one to vote for.'[9] The Socialist Alliance had been formed to fill this gap, but progress was not immediately apparent: in the 2001 general election it fielded 98 candidates, who averaged just over 500 votes each. Together with the Scottish Socialist Party, the Socialist Labour Party and various others, however, the far-left vote (excluding Northern Ireland) was just shy of 200,000, way in advance of the British National Party, and double the size of the support registered in 1997. There were possibilities here, if unity could be maintained and extended, and if Tony Blair continued to lead Labour from the centre, driving socialists out of the party.

There were also cultural possibilities, for Blair's government was losing much of the support it had once enjoyed from the left-inclined celebrities of art and entertainment. 'Luvvies for Labour' they'd been nicknamed in the 1990s, but now they were departing in such droves that John O'Farrell suggested they form a support group, Luvvies Labour's Lost.[10] Some – playwright Harold Pinter, actor Ricky Tomlinson, journalist John Pilger and lawyers Imran Khan, Louise Christian and Gareth Peirce – lent their names to the Socialist Alliance, while radical film-maker Ken Loach directed an election broadcast for the grouping. There was support too from the comedy wing of the left: Jeremy Hardy, Linda Smith, Mark Steel, Mark Thomas. And of the new union leaders, Bob Crow, Mark Serwotka and Matt Wrack also came out for the Socialist Alliance.*

Despite the abstruseness of the Marxist sects, with their theoretical journals and summer schools, the far left's public message was a simple one, amounting to little more than a them-and-us creed, as espoused by Bob Crow: 'My view is that there are two classes of people out there, those that go to work and those who own the means of production.'[11] A similar approach to international affairs saw a division between the West (principally Britain, America and Israel) and the rest. In normal circumstances, none of it would have amounted to very much. The Socialist Alliance attracted little media attention and when it was mentioned in the

---

* Mick Rix did not; he had left Scargill's group and rejoined Labour by this point, though the fact that his dog was named Che suggested that he wasn't a natural supporter of the Blairite project.

press, was generally dismissed as 'extremist', 'ultra-left', 'Trotskyist'.[12] The whole enterprise was inherently unstable, and there were already signs of splits, most notably when the Socialist Party walked out. But then normal circumstances ended, and the far left suddenly took on a much greater significance with the outbreak of war.

Salma Yaqoob, the daughter of Pakistani immigrants, was born in Bradford in 1971, but grew up in Birmingham. After graduating from Aston University, she remained in the city, working as a psychotherapist and married to a GP. She was thirty when she was reported in the local press as saying, 'Muslims in Birmingham were a "besieged community" and had become victims of abuse and suspicion since the atrocities of September 11.'[13] She spoke from her own experience; a few days after the al-Qaeda attacks in 2001, a man had spat at her in the street. 'I was just so shocked I was shaking with fear,' she said. 'It's so humiliating.' She had never been involved in politics before, but now she joined a group opposing a military response to the attacks, and her life was never the same again. 'I feel like a character in the film *The Matrix*, who moves between a world that is comfortable but an illusion, and reality, which is much worse. I cannot choose to return to the way I was before I woke up.'[14]

Yaqoob became one of the most media-friendly faces of the anti-war movement – by 2010, the *Guardian* was calling her 'the most prominent Muslim woman in British public life'[15] – but she was far from alone. Muslims and British Asians across the country felt under threat in the heated atmosphere of the time, and many of them wanted to register their opinion.

One place which allowed them to do so was a political campaign, launched a couple of weeks after 9/11 and named the Stop the War Coalition. It was, at the outset, a leftist initiative, bringing in Labour veterans – Tony Benn was president, John McDonnell vice-chair – as well as union leaders, including Crow, Rix and

Serwotka. As political attention shifted from Afghanistan to Iraq, however, Stop the War broadened to include many of the smaller mainstream parties; the Liberal Democrats, Scottish National Party, Plaid Cymru and Greens all affiliated, as did the Muslim Association of Britain. There were also non-aligned individuals, including many who were new to activism or British Muslims or both. And this time the range of celebrity supporters was more A-list: actress Emma Thompson, singer Damon Albarn, architect Lord Rogers, entrepreneur Anita Roddick.* More impressive still, a national newspaper, the *Daily Mirror*, supported the movement, paying £10,000 to hire a big screen for the demonstration in February 2003.†

It was the most significant campaign of its kind since the Anti-Nazi League and Rock Against Racism in the late 1970s. And like those initiatives, it relied heavily on the organisational experience of the Socialist Workers Party. A leading member of the SWP, Lindsey German, became the convenor of Stop the War, and she and other members also served on the steering committee. So too did veteran figures from the left, such as Arthur Scargill, Tariq Ali and Mike Marqusee, and Labour MP Jeremy Corbyn.

---

* Glenda Jackson, Oscar-winning actress turned Labour MP, was unimpressed by the presence of celebrities. 'I didn't notice any at the Countryside Alliance march and that didn't exactly lack for publicity,' she sniffed (*The Times* 31 January 2003), though to be fair, reports of the huge Liberty and Livelihood march in 2002 – protesting against the proposed ban on hunting with hounds – did mention a sprinkling of stars, including Anthony Andrews, Melvyn Bragg, Rory Bremner, Willie Carson, Jim Davidson, Clarissa Dickson-Wright, Julian Fellowes, Ranulph Fiennes, Frederick Forsyth, Edward Fox, Zac Goldsmith, Max Hastings, Vinnie Jones, Allan Lamb, John McCririck, Elle Macpherson, John Mortimer, Nicholas Parsons, Diana Rigg, Anne Robinson and Anthony Worrall-Thompson.
† Under its editor Piers Morgan, the *Daily Mirror* took an anti-war position. In May 2004 he was sacked after publishing fake photos purporting to show British soldiers abusing Iraqi prisoners.

George Kerevan, an ex-Trotskyist now in the SNP, cast an amused eye over the leadership: 'I note seven separate Marxist grouplets are formally represented, plus their numerous front bodies.'[16] The Socialist Party said that the leadership was 'overwhelmingly drawn from left-wing organisations', and added that it had three members itself on the steering committee 'but does not have any of the inner-core of officers'.[17]

All of which meant that the press could talk about the 'hard-left bias'[18] and 'the hard left make-up of the steering committee'.[19] When, though, *The Times* suggested that Stop the War was merely a front for the Socialist Alliance, it was a step too far. The chair of the Coalition, Andrew Murray, wrote indignantly to the paper: 'The overwhelming majority of the committee (myself included) have no involvement with the Socialist Alliance,' he insisted.[20] Indeed not. He was, however, a leading member of the Communist Party of Britain,* and he knew how important Stop the War was to the far left. 'It has the greatest political potential of any [campaign] I have encountered,' he reported back to his party executive. 'We need now to entrench the party in the mass anti-war movement at every level.'[21]

The broad base of this popular front ensured a huge turnout for the early rallies, including that of February 2003. But once hostilities started, when the invasion of Iraq was a fait accompli and the campaign had self-evidently failed, there was a dwindling of activism. The non-aligned began to fall away, and Stop the War increasingly became a forum for Marxists and Muslims. It was a combination of these groups that launched a political party in January 2004 with the intention of fielding candidates in elections. The new party was called Respect, and it was built on an implausible coalition of the Socialist Workers Party with some other left groups, and the Muslim Association of Britain (MAB)

---

* Not to be confused with the Communist Party of Great Britain, from whom they split in 1988, taking with them the daily newspaper, the *Morning Star*.

– effectively a relaunch of Socialist Alliance, but now with added Islam. And there was one other crucial component: George Galloway MP.

Born into a working-class Catholic family in Dundee in 1954, George Galloway had joined the Labour Party in his teens and made an early impression, becoming the youngest ever chair of the Scottish Labour Party at just 26. Elected to Parliament in 1987 (his victory in Glasgow Hillhead ended Roy Jenkins's Commons career), he courted publicity with his extravagant persona. He was a lifelong teetotaller, but apart from that he could have passed for a recently retired footballer: tanned, with a silvery moustache, fat cigars and Italian suits, as well as a 'reputation as a ladies' man'.[22] He was happy behind the wheel of his red Mercedes convertible ('I don't feel as manly, somehow, being driven'[23]), he described John Lennon's song 'Imagine' as 'the ultimate socialist anthem',[24] and he named his favourite actor as Jack Nicholson. Inevitably, he was nicknamed 'Gorgeous George'.

He was also one of the most fluent speakers in British politics – 'the best natural orator in the House', according to Liberal Democrat Vince Cable[25] – and he relished the role of left-wing hero. Accordingly, he peppered his conversation with quotes from Lenin and Ho Chi Minh, and with regrets for the fall of the Soviet Union ('the biggest catastrophe of my life'), and said his ultimate hero was Che Guevara ('a person with poetry in his soul').[26] He'd been committed to the Palestinian cause since he was twenty, and a quarter-century later, looking out across the river Jordan towards the West Bank, he recalled his fantasies of liberating the land from Israel: 'I used to dream I would be part of the force that would wade ashore, Kalashnikov in hand, and return it to its rightful owners.'[27]

He specialised in international affairs, and had impressive contacts in all the right places; he was on friendly terms with Gerry Adams, Yasser Arafat and Fidel Castro (who was 'cool not cruel'[28]). Most famously, he visited Saddam Hussein in 1994, ending their televised meeting with: 'Sir, I salute your courage, your strength, your indefatigability.'[29] That had been in the days of John Smith's leadership of Labour, and he'd almost had the whip withdrawn in consequence.

He'd opposed war with Iraq in 1991, and he did so again in 2003. So vociferous was he that he was expelled from Labour later that year for bringing the party into disrepute. The charges stated that he had 'incited Arabs to fight British troops' and 'incited British troops to defy orders',[30] but the truth was that he'd become an embarrassment to the leadership. There were plenty of Labour MPs speaking against the war in Iraq, but none with the flamboyant eloquence of Galloway, nor with his platform: he wrote a column in the Scottish *Mail on Sunday* for seven years. 'They will rue this day,' he vowed as he was thrown out of Labour,[31] and he stalked off to hatch his plans for a new party.

Galloway was no political soulmate of the SWP – 'George has always hated and despised Trotskyites,' pointed out erstwhile comrade Diane Abbott[32] – but there was nowhere else much to go. And the creation of Respect did give him some status. In return, he offered himself: a big-name draw and an actual MP, things of which the far left had been dreaming for decades. He and Salma Yaqoob were the public faces of the party, while its foot soldiers were drawn from the SWP and the MAB.

There were doubts about the wisdom of this initiative. Some in the Stop the War Coalition advocated non-involvement in electoral politics altogether. The advice from Workers Power was for socialists to spoil their vote and 'write Troops Out of Iraq on your ballot paper'.[33] (Even Tony Benn lost patience at this point: 'Really, the squabbles of the left are very boring.'[34]) Others feared that Respect would eclipse the broader anti-war movement: Mick Rix of ASLEF resigned from the steering committee of Stop the War, and other union leaders were said to think the organisation was 'lurching into sectarianism'.[35] From outside the Coalition, journalist Nick Cohen warned in newspaper columns and in his book *What's Left?* (2007) against the joining together of 'white far left and brown religious right'. The SWP were 'playing identity politics by trying to build support on the back of Muslim grievance', he wrote, in a way that abandoned socialist principles of class and offered British Muslims only separation from mainstream society.[36]

In any event, Respect was surely not destined to last, so conflicting were the agendas of the two strands feeding into it. On the one side, there was Abdul Khaliq Mian, Respect's parliamentary candidate in East Ham, London: 'I don't think of it as a radical party.'[37] And on the other, there was Lindsey German, candidate for neighbouring West Ham and a revolutionary communist for over thirty years, who presumably thought it was at least a little bit radical. There was a calculated trade-off here for the far left. Opinion polls showed British Muslims deserting Labour in droves, with support having halved since 2001,[38] which raised the prospect of new recruits. But there was little appetite for socialism red in tooth and claw, and so compromises had to be made. In 2001 the Socialist Alliance had called, in true Trotskyist fashion, for the nationalisation of 150 companies; the Respect manifesto in 2005 spoke only of nationalising public transport and the arms industry.

The first photograph in that manifesto illustrated the oddity of the enterprise, showing Mian and German awkwardly smiling at the camera alongside two other candidates. One was Oliur Rahman, who had become Respect's first councillor when he won a 2004 by-election in Tower Hamlets at the age of 23, and was now contesting the parliamentary seat of Poplar and Canning Town. The other was George Galloway. And after the 2005 election, he was still the party's only MP, though he'd swapped his Glasgow constituency for Bethnal Green and Bow in the East End of London, where 40 per cent of voters were Muslim.

His election as a Respect candidate in a solid Labour seat

rightly captured the headlines, and, as far as most people were concerned, he was the be-all and end-all of the party. The International Bolshevik Tendency probably called it right: Respect became 'little more than a vehicle for Galloway's political views and relentless self-promotion'.[39] On the upside, that meant the party had a larger presence in the public arena than it would otherwise have managed, with, for example, his annual appearance on BBC One's *Question Time*. On the downside, that exposure also included the three weeks in January 2006 that Galloway spent as a house-mate on the reality television series *Celebrity Big Brother*.

He entered into the spirit of the show with gusto and was roundly ridiculed by media and public alike. The image of him robot-dancing in a tight red leotard was widely reproduced, as was his performance as a cat, licking imaginary milk from the cupped hands of actress Rula Lenska. To his credit, he took the derision with as much style as anyone could have managed; when he started hosting a radio phone-in programme on TalkSport later that year ('The Mother of All Talk Shows'),* he used the music from 1960s cartoon series *Top Cat* as the theme tune. Still, it was a bit undignified for an elected MP, let alone for the man who'd once said, 'I would have loved to have been foreign secretary.'[40]

The *Big Brother* appearance, wrote Tony Benn in his diary, was 'so humiliating'. That, at least, was his instinctive response, but he was later able to rationalise it all, and find a positive political angle. Galloway might have made a fool of himself, 'but when you come to think of it, he hasn't lied to Parliament, he hasn't sent soldiers to their deaths, he hasn't authorised the rendition of people through British airports to be tortured'.[41]

Again, in normal circumstances none of this would have meant a great deal to political life. For the most part the far left remained

---

* A title derived from Saddam Hussein's warning to American-led coalition forces in 1991 that they faced 'the mother of all battles'.

out of sight of the media and was not taken seriously. Despite the disputes over Iraq, despite the dysfunctional squabble at its head, Labour was still the party of Blair and roses, and no one really imagined that the spectre of Bennism might return to haunt the corridors of power.

Indeed Tony Benn himself, no longer in Parliament, was now toothless enough to be considered a national treasure. He worked up a live show, in which he sat in an armchair, with a flask of tea next to him on an occasional table, and chatted about his life and politics; it sold out theatres the length of the land, from Berwick to Eastbourne. Back in 1974, Kingsley Amis had called him 'the most dangerous figure in British politics today',[42] and he'd been the target of regular death threats; nowadays even hate mail was a rare treat. 'Dear Arsehole,' read one anonymous letter from Tring in Hertfordshire. 'It's time you buggered off and lived with Saddam Hussein, or die [*sic*] like your ghastly dead wife.' And Benn's cheerful reaction – 'So at least I haven't sold out' – reflected why he was so loved, now that he was nowhere near power.[43]

There was no reason to assume that any of it really mattered to the mainstream. Yet this sequence of joint campaigns – Ken Livingstone's mayoralty, the Socialist Alliance, the Stop the War Coalition, Respect – built closer connections between the various Marxist splinters than had ever existed before. It also built links between the far left and the Labour left – the likes of Jeremy Corbyn, John McDonnell and Diane Abbott. And that became important when Corbyn, then the chair of Stop the War, stood for the leadership of the Labour Party in 2015. Because what was striking about his campaign, and his early appointments after he unexpectedly won, was how ecumenical he was in choosing comrades.

So, for example, Socialist Action had been a junior partner in Respect, and went on to supply Corbyn's chief of staff, Simon Fletcher, and an economic adviser, John Ross, both of whom had done the same jobs for Livingstone when he was mayor. Andrew

Murray, former chair of Stop the War, left the Communist Party of Britain to become special political adviser to the new Labour leader. Corbyn's press officer in the 2015 race was Carmel Brown, who had been a spokeswoman for Stop the War on Merseyside and a member of Respect; indeed, her eight-year-old daughter Hope was said to have coined the party name.[44] Elsewhere, his most significant supporters in the media were Paul Mason, formerly of the BBC, Channel 4 and Workers Power, and Owen Jones of the *Guardian*, who admired Galloway's style of politicking: 'You don't have to like him; but, if you want to change the world, you do have to learn from him.'[45] Supportive union leaders included Mark Serwotka and Matt Wrack, as well as Len McCluskey, general secretary of Unite the Union since 2010, who had worked closely with Militant in Liverpool in the 1980s.

The fervour generated by the 2015 leadership bid drew on the earlier campaigns. 'This is like Stop the War with bells on,' enthused Carmel Brown.[46] But there was something else going on here as well. 'This is not just about a bunch of youngsters getting involved,' said Kat Fletcher, who organised the volunteers and was herself a former member of Workers' Liberty. 'We're seeing people coming back to the party, or seeing people who've been dormant for a decade or two.'[47]

II

A long time ago, even before George Galloway was elected to Parliament, Robert Kilroy-Silk had also been a Labour MP. More than that, he'd been a potential star of the party, an articulate, attractive and committed advocate of working-class politics. Fighting his way out of childhood poverty in Birmingham, he'd studied at the London School of Economics and then become a politics lecturer at Liverpool University. 'Socialism is not dead, just dormant,' he wrote in *Socialism since Marx* (1973), as he denounced a capitalist system that 'enriches the few at the expense of the many'.[48] Elected to Parliament for Harold Wilson's old constituency Ormskirk in February 1974, he gave a televised interview as he drove to London to take his seat, predicting that he'd be prime minister within fifteen years.

Once in Westminster, he campaigned for unfashionable causes, particularly for prisoners, chairing the all-party penal affairs group as well as Labour's civil liberties group, and he waited for promotion. The times, however, were against him. Labour's defeat in 1979 meant that, just when he might have hoped for a first government appointment, he was instead stuck on the opposition benches, watching Margaret Thatcher go on and on, and itching with restless ambition. 'I want power,' he said. 'I don't make any bones about it.'[49] The frustration was compounded when his constituency was redrawn as Knowsley North and he found himself battling with the local Trotskyists of the Militant Tendency. He didn't fit in with the parliamentary left either; in 1985 he got into a scuffle with Jeremy Corbyn, although he insisted that reports of fisticuffs were exaggerated. 'I didn't really hit him,' said Kilroy-Silk. 'If I had, he'd have stayed down.'[50]

In 1986, in his mid-forties prime, he lost patience with it all and threw in his hand, leaving Parliament to become host of a daytime talk show, *Day to Day* (later renamed *Kilroy*), on BBC television. It was a format imported from America: a small studio audience containing some invited guests alongside members of the public, with the host roaming around as they all discussed emotional issues and topics from the day's news. Kilroy-Silk turned out to be good at it, developing the persona of a stern but sympathetic tribune of the people.

At one point in 1997, there was excited talk of a move to Hollywood. 'He's set to become the new Oprah Winfrey after signing a money-spinning deal,' frothed the *Sunday Mirror*,[51] but that very same week he attracted less-welcome press when he interviewed a self-confessed, though disguised and anonymous, paedophile on air. The man was arrested as he left the studio – the police having been tipped off by an audience member using a mobile phone – and the BBC was forced to apologise. It wasn't clear whether the Corporation's regret was greater still on learning that the man was a hoaxer who'd made up the whole story. Nor was it clear whether it was because of this incident that the supposed American deal fell through, but certainly there was no more talk of Hollywood.

Instead, he stayed just where he was, the presenter of *Kilroy*, a permanent fixture in the schedules, while younger rivals – Vanessa Feltz, John Stapleton, Trisha Goddard – rose, and sometimes fell, around him. He was getting good ratings, but somehow it never took him any further. And as the years passed he seemed increasingly disengaged, bored, struggling to keep himself amused. 'You are talking about a Hegelian idea of thesis and antithesis combined with a Millite theory of liberty,' he told a white witch who was a guest on the show. 'Everybody can see that.'[52] He was still 'the king of daytime telly', according to the *Sun*,[53] but this was a man who'd wanted to be prime minister.

'TV is just a job to me,' he admitted. 'I'm paid an awful lot of money, which is why I continue to do it.'[54] And the material compensation was indeed impressive: a handsome salary from the Kilroy Television Company, which made his show, was topped up by income from Kilroy Executive Cars, which had the contract for bringing the guests to the studio. Altogether, the accounts for him and his wife in 2002 showed earnings of £1.2 million in 'presenters and consultancy fees'.[55] And he had what the tabloids liked to call a lifestyle to match: a villa in Marbella 'set in 100 acres of beautiful countryside'[56] and a manor house once owned by rock star Ozzy Osbourne in Buckinghamshire, complete with deer park, three aviaries and a nye of oriental pheasants. As he said, 'I've been poor, very poor, and I would never want to go back.'[57]

Even so, it clearly irked him that he was so peripheral to the public debate. In 2001 he got a national newspaper column, but it was only in the less-than-influential *Sunday Express*.* His attempt to break into prime-time television that year came in the form of a quiz show, *Shafted*, which was so unpopular that it was pulled after four episodes, 'taken off the air because it was affecting the viewing figures for *Cold Feet*, which followed it'.[58] Memories of his political career had faded, and he was now known primarily for his impressive tan, which rivalled that of another daytime presenter, antiques dealer David 'cheap as chips' Dickinson.

In January 2004, with his career still stuck in the 9 a.m. slot, the 61-year-old Robert Kilroy-Silk returned to the front pages in a blaze of outrage. The offence was caused by a *Sunday Express* column in which he addressed concerns that the War on Terror was 'destroying the Arab world'.[59] Even if we were so doing, he argued, why should we care? 'After all, the Arab countries are not exactly shining examples of civilisation, are they?' Arabs might loathe Westerners, but equally the West had no love for 'suicide bombers, limb-amputators, women repressors'. And he added that, while there were 'thousands of asylum seekers' from the Arab world 'living happily in this country on social security', there was 'not one single British asylum seeker in any Arab country'.†

He did have some history of surviving provocative comments – he'd once got into trouble for calling Ireland 'a land of peasants, priests and pixies'[60] – but this time it was felt he'd gone too far. The BBC cancelled his show, issuing a statement that 'these comments do not reflect the views of the BBC'[61] (as if anyone really thought they might), and Trevor Phillips, chair of the Commission

---

* At the time, the *Sunday Express* was the sixth biggest-selling Sunday title, behind the *News of the World*, *Mail on Sunday*, *Sunday Mirror*, *People* and *Sunday Times*.

† This latter thought was not unique to Kilroy-Silk. 'There's a simple test of a country,' wrote Tony Blair: 'are people trying to get into it or get out of it?' (Blair, *A Journey* p. 365)

for Racial Equality, asked the police to investigate. They did so but, six months later, the Crown Prosecution Service decided not to bring any charges.

Kilroy-Silk had not been quiet in the interim. The loss of income was deeply unwelcome, but perhaps the controversy over his comments was the nudge that his life needed, a prompt by fate that there was still time for one last tilt at politics. Four months after his show was axed, he was making news again, announced as a UKIP candidate for the East Midlands in the forthcoming elections to the European Parliament.

The UK Independence Party had been founded in 1993 by Alan Sked, a lecturer in international history at the London School of Economics (after Kilroy-Silk's time) and an erstwhile parliamentary candidate for the Liberal Party. It was, by any standards, a quixotic endeavour. The long struggle to ratify the Maastricht Treaty had exposed deep divisions in the Conservative Party over the European Union, but the idea of actually leaving the EU – which was UKIP's avowed intent – was not on the agenda of any serious politician. This new group looked like another of those which eked out a herbivorous existence in the scrubland just this side of the Monster Raving lunatic fringe, something akin to the continuity Liberal Party perhaps, or the yogic-flying, transcendentally meditating Natural Law Party.

In the elections to the European Parliament in June 1994, UKIP came ninth (tenth if the various independents were counted as a single block), gaining just 1 per cent of the vote. Nonetheless, it fielded enough candidates to ensure it got an election broadcast on television – five minutes of Sked talking to the camera – and attracted a little press attention. 'I love Europe,' Sked explained. 'I just don't want to be under some federalist super-state.' He was at pains to stress that this was not a racist enterprise, 'that party members are not British nationalists and do not want to bring the empire back'.[62] But Britain's future, like its past, did not lie with its continental neighbours. 'The truth is, politically and economically, we do not fit in to Europe,' he said. 'Our traditions are different.'[63]

Much the same argument was put forward in October 1994 by the former chancellor of the exchequer Norman Lamont. Speaking to a fringe meeting at the Tory conference, he suggested that Britain was so out of tune with the EU that the time might come when we would decide to leave, or when others might make that decision for us. 'The unthinkable is no longer incredible,' read the headline to an article by the *Independent*'s Andrew Marr: 'for the first time in a generation, the idea of withdrawal from the European Union is being aired by mainstream politicians'.[64] The following month, the billionaire businessman James Goldsmith announced the creation of the Referendum Party, dedicated to fighting the next election on the single issue of a vote on Britain's relationship to the EU.

So it was that, a mere fourteen months on from its launch, UKIP no longer looked quite so isolated, its cause now being adopted by others. That did little to raise the party's profile, though, outgunned by Goldsmith's enormous spending power. In the 1997 general election, it came tenth, its 193 candidates averaging a shade under 550 votes each, barely a third of those recorded by the 547 candidates of the Referendum Party. A couple of months after that poll, however, James Goldsmith died, and his party subsequently dissolved itself, removing the principal rival.

Meanwhile, UKIP was coming under new management. Shortly after the election, Sked was replaced as leader by Michael Holmes, a 59-year-old retired businessman who'd made his fortune publishing free local newspapers. Alongside Holmes was his most significant backer, a vigorous young commodities broker named Nigel Farage, who quickly emerged as the most media-friendly figure at the top of the party – in 2000, he would be UKIP's first representative on *Question Time*. The takeover of the leadership, Farage later wrote, was not ideological but organisational. Sked, 'a metropolitan theoretician',[65] was just not up to the job: 'Even those who liked him and admired his intellect conceded that he could not run a piss-up in a brewery.'[66] Challenged by this new faction, Sked abandoned not only the leadership, but also the party he had himself created, claiming subsequently, 'They are racist and have been infected by the far right.'[67]

If UKIP had looked like a sideshow before, the internal row seemed destined to finish off any possibility that it might ever amount to something. The EU, however, had other ideas.

Up until now, Great Britain (but not Northern Ireland) had used its traditional first-past-the-post system for elections to the European Parliament; the constituencies were far bigger than those represented at Westminster, but the principle remained the same. That changed with the EU's insistence that all countries use some form of proportional representation, in response to which the UK adopted a regional list system in time for the 1999 election. The result was that – on a record low turnout of just 24 per cent* – three minor parties saw MEPs elected for the first time: Plaid Cymru, the Green Party and, ironically, UKIP. Freed from the made-in-Britain shackles of first past the post, UKIP quadrupled their vote, came fourth in the poll and secured three seats courtesy of the EU that they opposed so vehemently.

The party's elected representatives were Nigel Farage, Michael Holmes and another retired businessman, Jeffrey Titford, whose family had run funeral parlours on the east coast of England (it was said that his great-grandfather had buried the Duke of Wellington). He'd once been a Tory councillor, and in 1997 had won nearly 5,000 votes for the Referendum Party in Harwich, before a brief sojourn in the far-right New Britain party. His presence was the fruit of Michael Holmes's endeavours to bring in candidates from James Goldsmith's now-disbanded outfit.

Whether this was a good move was a moot point. From

---

* A record low for any country in a European Parliament election.

Holmes's perspective, it did nothing to ease 'the bitterness and the infighting' that still consumed UKIP.[68] Within six months of that electoral breakthrough in 1999, he and Farage had fallen out. Writs were issued, office locks were changed, and factions fought for control. In January 2000, Holmes resigned as leader, and two months after that left the party altogether, echoing the complaint made by Sked: UKIP 'had been infiltrated by extremists'.[69] In just seven years of existence, the party had lost both its first two leaders. It was starting to look like carelessness.*

In the ensuing power struggle, Titford was voted in as leader, and 200 leading members voted with their feet, issuing a joint resignation statement that the party was now 'condemned to the far right'.[70] One supporter said UKIP had '8,000 members and 9,000 egos';[71] another talked of Nigel Farage's 'double-dealing, backstabbing, disloyalty and treachery'.[72]

And so the party blundered on, repeatedly tripping up on the shoelaces it seemed unable to tie. The 2001 general election saw it win 1.5 per cent of the vote, up from the 0.3 per cent achieved in 1997, but still a long way from the potential it saw for itself; a 2001 party broadcast announced, in a prescient foreshadowing of figures to come, 'A recent opinion poll revealed that 52 per cent of people in Britain believe we should leave the EU altogether.'[73]

During his brief tenure as leader, Michael Holmes described UKIP members as 'a bunch of mavericks'.[74] That was one of the kinder descriptions. Earlier, a party spokesperson had acknowledged that they were seen as being 'nutty as fruitcakes',[75] while Nigel Farage suggested they were 'bumbling amateurs'.[76] Chris Huhne, a Liberal Democrat MEP, was happy to set the record straight in 2001: 'They're not fascists, they're not corrupt and they're

---

* Holmes stood down as an MEP in 2002, replaced by UKIP's Graham Booth, who made his maiden speech in the Old Devonian language, an obscure branch of Celtic that died out in the medieval era.

not morons,' he said. 'Some of their members are headbangers, though.'[77] One of Huhne's colleagues, Chris Davies, went with 'nutters'.[78] Later, as the next European elections approached in 2004, an internal Conservative Party briefing paper was leaked to the press, giving the Tory lines of attack on UKIP; according to the fourteen-page document, the party was 'full of cranks and political gadflies'.[79]

UKIP professed themselves delighted with the latter description, and commissioned a range of ties adorned with the image of a gadfly. The phrase was also used in the title of the first full-length account of the party, Mark Daniel's *Cranks and Gadflies* (2005). In fact, Daniel went further than the title, describing the membership as 'idiots, paranoiacs and conspiracy theorists' as well as 'traders, whores and vagabonds'. This was strong stuff, all the more so when it transpired that the author, under his real name Mark Fitzgeorge-Parker, was also UKIP's press officer and had been a parliamentary candidate. Perhaps he embodied the point he was making: a louche, 51-year-old, alcoholic hack writer who'd been educated at Ampleforth, Cambridge and HM Prison Ashwell, he was 'a libertine, as opposed to a libertarian', according to Nigel Farage,[80] whose autobiography he ghosted.*

The public image of the party was that it was overwhelmingly male, white, middle class and elderly. Asked about this in 2004, Farage laughed off at least one of the claims: 'Oh no, I wouldn't say we were too male.'[81] But the handful of celebrity backers in the early days did rather give the impression of a party of opinionated old buffers in an upmarket country club, moaning about the modern world: retired racing driver Stirling Moss, TV astronomer

---

* Some of the autobiography reads more like Daniel than Farage: 'I approve of Jesus. He seems a decent sort who liked his wine and the company of riff-raff, knew when to pick up the whip and set about him, and displayed exemplary manners with that girl caught enjoying a little light relief.' (Farage, *Flying Free* p. 113)

Patrick Moore, explorer Ranulph Fiennes, actors Leo McKern, Edward Fox and Joan Collins.

This was not a party of London, where its candidate in the first mayoral election in 2000, Damian Hockney, had only come eighth, despite being, in the words of *The Times*, 'UKIP's most flamboyant member'.[82] (Elsewhere, the *Guardian* reported that he was an enthusiast for cosmetic surgery: 'He has had nips and tucks galore, plus liposuction and a nose job, and recently admitted to wanting a "buttock implant" to make him look sexier in jeans.')[83] Even so, the London mayoralty attracted a lot of media attention, and it was felt that a celebrity candidate was needed for the 2004 election.

UKIP's choice was Frank Maloney, a boxing promoter described by the British press as a 'tough guy'[84] and by his American rival Don King as a 'mental midget'.[85] He adopted the novel approach of insulting large parts of the city he was seeking to represent:[86] Whitechapel, he said, was 'a ghetto' these days – 'barely anyone speaks English and to look around you would think you are in a different country' – and he wasn't going to be campaigning in Camden Town at all, because 'there are too many gays' there.* A decade on, Maloney asked to be henceforth known as Kellie, having resolved her longstanding questions over gender identity.

Maloney's distaste for homosexuals ('I don't think they do a lot for society')[87] was hardly unusual in the socially conservative ranks of UKIP, but it was not universal. One of the more striking figures in the early years was Nikki Sinclaire, a national-executive member who had been the party's secretary and came out as a lesbian in 2004. 'There are gay people who feel that this country has been sold down the river to the EU and I'm one of them,' she told the papers.[88] She was also 6 feet 4 inches tall, and 'said that

---

* Maloney came fourth, with 115,666 first-preference votes, 6.2 per cent of the electorate.

because of her height and sexuality she was often forced to deny being a transsexual'.[89] It was not until much later, when she published her autobiography, *Never Give Up* (2013), that she revealed she had indeed had sex reassignment surgery at the age of 23. She was finally elected to the European Parliament for UKIP in 2009 (though she was no longer in the party), which meant, disclosed the *Sun* with some excitement, that UKIP had given us 'Britain's first transsexual parliamentarian'.[90]

Some of the judgements on UKIP politicians and members were overly harsh. They were not all, in Matthew Parris's words, 'nutcases, fruitcakes and "Cry God for Harry, England and St George" merchants'.[91] But there was no doubt that the party had a particular appeal for misfits and monomaniacs, those who didn't get much of a hearing in mainstream parties. It was hard to know whether the arrival of sacked talk-show host Robert Kilroy-Silk, just in time to get elected to the European Parliament in 2004, raised or lowered the tone of the party. What it certainly did was intensify the infighting.

There were two major battles for UKIP. The first was to avoid the taint of racism. It was a time when the extreme right was becoming noisy again, having virtually disappeared from British politics after the losses suffered by the National Front in the 1979 general election. In 1999 the British National Party elected a new leader, Nick Griffin, a 40-year-old veteran of the far right, who began to reposition the party, ditching its neo-Nazi associations to create a more electorally acceptable image, emphasising culture rather than race, talking about Europe and crime as well as immigration. He'd studied law at Cambridge, and was the most respectable and palatable far-right leader in Britain since Oswald Mosley.

Griffin sought common ground with UKIP. An editorial in the BNP's magazine *Spearhead* in 2000 tried to get the ball rolling: 'If the power of the Establishment is to be challenged, the streams of popular protest represented by the UKIP and the BNP will have to come together.'[92] At the time, UKIP was getting around eight votes for each one that Griffin's party could muster, so it was clearly in the latter's interests to cosy up; just as it was clearly in UKIP's interests to spurn their advances, infuriated by jibes that they were simply 'BNP in blazers'.[93] On Nigel Farage's initiative, the publicist Max Clifford was hired – at a cost of £100,000 for six months – to polish up the party image and to distance it from extremists. Nonetheless, the BNP continued to grow under Griffin's leadership: in the 2004 European and 2005 Westminster elections, it was outpolled only one to three by UKIP.

The second battlefront was within the party itself, a dispute over quite what the objective of the organisation was. Ultimately, of course, it was withdrawal from Europe, but how was such a thing to be achieved? Some saw UKIP as a fully fledged party in its own right, working to a continuation of the Thatcherite agenda: low taxes, small state, patriotic, tough on crime and immigration. For others it was essentially a single-issue pressure group. Among the latter was Tory peer Malcolm Pearson, who had the Conservative whip withdrawn when he came out in support of UKIP in the 2004 European elections, and who would later switch parties and become its leader. His argument was simple: 'The only party which might save our democracy, our right to govern ourselves, from the corrupt octopus in Brussels is the Conservatives. But the only people at the moment who can make the Conservative leadership see sense are UKIP.'[94]

Meanwhile, although the disputes continued, the party was beginning to look more stable. It was again under new leadership, Jeffrey Titford having been succeeded by Roger Knapman in 2002. With a decade in Parliament as a Tory MP under his belt and a couple of years as a government whip, Knapman – uncharismatic as he was – had the kind of solid experience not previously seen at the top of UKIP. 'Very grown up,' was Farage's verdict, 'far more politically astute than anyone else in the party.'[95]

Knapman was leader when Robert Kilroy-Silk joined, promising to speak up for ordinary folk. 'They are fed up with being lied to,' Kilroy declared. 'They are fed up with being patronised by the metropolitan political elite.'[96] His arrival generated much publicity, enabling UKIP to overtake the Liberal Democrats, first in the opinion polls and then at the ballot box. In the Euro-elections of June 2004, the party came third, having gained an additional 2 million votes, and won 12 seats in the European Parliament. It was the big story of the poll.

Less noted at the time was the fact that in European elections, where proportional representation gave a broader choice, England was – like the rest of the kingdom – becoming a multi-party state. A decade earlier, there was a 40-point gap between the first- and fourth-placed parties; now that was down to 12 per cent. Traditional loyalties were splintering. Veteran Marxist Ken Coates noted that UKIP was getting a lot of support in the old coalfield areas, and agreed with Tony Benn's perception that the party was 'appealing to the disillusioned working class'.[97] Iain Duncan Smith had a different perspective: 'The UKIP vote would not have been so high if I had been leader [of the Conservative Party] because Eurosceptics would have trusted me.'[98]

Among the dozen UKIP MEPs (all white, all male), the dominant figures were Nigel Farage and Robert Kilroy-Silk. Both were committed to the idea of converting UKIP into an electoral vehicle, though few believed it would be sturdy enough to carry both their egos. 'I told Nigel that there was only one person Kilroy-Silk was interested in,' warned Max Clifford.[99] Sure enough, within a week of their election triumph, the two men were reported to have had 'differences'.[100]

As far as the media were concerned, Kilroy-Silk was 'UKIP's star turn',[101] its leader-in-waiting. But he didn't wish to wait. The man who'd once called on socialists to act with 'a tint of arrogance'[102] was now 62 and impatient. At the party conference in October 2004, he set out his stall in a typically assured performance. There had been talk of not fielding candidates against Eurosceptic Tory MPs, but he was having none of it. 'The Conservative Party is dying,' he declared. 'Why would you want to give it the kiss of life? What we have to do is kill it. That is our destiny.'[103] He could be quite sinister at times.

The next day, the wind in his sails, he made his move. He told the media that Roger Knapman had promised to step down as leader after the European elections, and had reneged on that commitment. But a general election was expected the following May, and it was essential that a change be made now, so that he, Kilroy, could turn UKIP into an 'effective electoral fighting force'.[104] This was his *carpe diem* moment. 'What everybody tells me they want is for the current leader to accept the inevitable and to stand down,' he declared. 'I have been told by every senior member of the party that they would like me to be leader. I am told there is a vast majority of the party who would like that to happen.'[105]

He was exaggerating. The membership was far from convinced by the new kid on the block. 'Kilroy must prove himself,' said one scathingly.[106] 'He's only a minor celebrity after all.'* The 'senior members' didn't seem impressed either. Farage, who now saw Kilroy as 'a mini-Mosley',[107] said a contest 'would set us back years', and Jeffrey Titford – the only former leader still in the party, and therefore its de facto elder statesman – shook his head sadly: 'It's a terrible thing, ego, isn't it?'[108] Knapman denied saying he'd step down and insisted that he was staying.

Kilroy-Silk responded by resigning the UKIP whip in the European Parliament and by trying to force a vote of no confidence in Knapman, but the attempted coup failed to take off. His image wasn't helped when a demonstrator threw a bucket of slurry over him, shouting, 'This is in the name of Islam.'† In January

---

* Maybe they'd been dazzled by the latest luminary to join the UKIP cause: Jamaican-born chef Rustie Lee, another star of daytime television.
† 'Kilroy-Silk dung over' was the unsympathetic headline in the *Daily Mirror*.

2005, a year on from the *Sunday Express* column that cost him his BBC job, he announced that he'd left UKIP altogether. Just eight months before, Knapman had welcomed him into the party: 'He is hugely respected as a journalist and broadcaster, and firm in his views.'[109] Now, the still-incumbent leader was less than distraught: 'He's gone, we wanted him to go, it only remains to break open the champagne.'[110]

The renegade immediately launched his own party, Veritas, named after the Roman goddess of truth. 'Unlike the old parties, we shall be honest, open and straight,' Kilroy-Silk told the press.[111] He persuaded some former colleagues to defect from UKIP, including the 'flamboyant' Damian Hockney, who was now a member of the London Assembly, but it still looked like a one-horse carriage, and was nicknamed Vanitas. Like UKIP in 1993, it was a quixotic endeavour; unlike UKIP, it never became anything else. In the 2005 general election, Veritas got 40,000 votes to the BNP's 193,000, while UKIP – still under Knapman – topped 600,000. Apart from anything else, Kilroy-Silk lost the slogan war; Veritas was 'the straight-talking party', while UKIP had a much more powerful demand: 'We want our country back.'[112]*

By July 2005, Robert Kilroy-Silk had resigned from the leadership of his own party, less than six months after launching it. He stayed on as an MEP until 2009, but took time out to appear in the eighth series of the reality television show *I'm a Celebrity ... Get Me Out of Here!* He was the first of the twelve contestants to be voted off the show.

Twelve years an MP, five as an MEP, Kilroy-Silk never did make it to high office. He spent a year as part of Labour's shadow team on

---

(7 December 2004) On *Have I Got News for You*, Paul Merton suggested, 'When the shit hit the tan.'

* This wasn't entirely new. 'I will give you back your country,' William Hague had told the Tory conference in 1999.

home affairs in 1984–85, and that was as close as he came. Given a different set of circumstances, however, he could have played the role he clearly felt had been promised him by Fate. For a brief moment, with UKIP riding high in the months around the 2004 European elections, it seemed that he might be capable of becoming a major political figure, an insurrectionary who could kick over the traces, shake up the establishment in a way that no UKIP leader had yet managed. And then it all crumbled to dust in his hands.

Kilroy-Silk's strange eight-month affair with UKIP was seen at the time to have done serious damage to the party. Certainly membership and donations fell with his departure, but in retrospect what it revealed was that there was a new toughness to the outfit. It still suffered self-inflicted wounds, of course, whether from MEP Godfrey Bloom opening his mouth wide enough to fit in both feet, or Ashley Mote, elected in 2004, serving a nine-month jail sentence for benefit fraud while still remaining an MEP. But it had proved strong enough to survive Kilroy-Silk's attack from within.

'We have to be policy-based, not personality-based,' said Roger Knapman in 2004.[113] He was wrong. UKIP was to transform British politics, but faced with the British electoral system, it could do so only on the strength of personality. Just not Kilroy's.

Robert Kilroy-Silk and George Galloway had a great deal in common, probably more than either would like to admit. Both were working-class grammar-school boys of Irish Catholic stock who had been useful boxers in their youth; both became Labour MPs who dreamed of high office and ended up on reality TV; both were powerful orators, earned more from the media than from politics and had a taste for the good life, though Galloway's holiday home was in Portugal, not Spain. They were divisive figures who alienated many of those who should have been colleagues – 'I would be lying if I said I didn't have enemies,' admitted Galloway[114] – and they left Labour for new parties that then split.

Kilroy-Silk's 1988 comment on left-wing MPs (including Gallo-way), that they were 'out to prove their political machismo',[115] applied equally to both. They had the same strengths, accompanied by the same weaknesses: good-looking but vain; articulate yet drawn to cheap provocation; serious and lacking a sense of humour. And, as so often with men of frustrated destiny (David Owen, Jeffrey Archer), there was with both of them the sense that a snarl lay just beneath the surface charm.

For all their failings, they almost looked and sounded as if they could be credible populist leaders, articulating the anger of the people. Yet somehow they didn't quite convince. Perhaps they were simply too early. In the first years of the twenty-first century, there might have been public dissatisfaction with mainstream politics, but the economy was still growing and living standards still rising. The British people were not yet ready for new parties and flamboyant demagogues.

3

Past and Present

I

'People are afraid of being proud of being English. I'm not.'[1] It wasn't a sentiment one expected to hear from a Hell's Angel, but 49-year-old Alan Fisher, aka Snob of the London Chapter of the Angels, had just been asked to lead a contingent of bikers down the Mall, in a pageant to mark the Golden Jubilee of Her Majesty the Queen. And he was bursting with patriotic pride.

Golden jubilees are as rare as hen's teeth. So when, in June 2002, Elizabeth II became the first monarch since Victoria in 1887 to achieve fifty years on the throne, the occasion clearly had to be marked. There was nervousness, however, in palace and political circles. It was just ten years since the Queen's *annus horribilis* had ended with the Windsor Castle fire, provoking a furious public outcry about tax; five years since the death of Princess Diana had dragged the monarchy to a post-war nadir. There had been serious efforts to improve the image of the royal family more recently, but the public response to the Jubilee was not certain. And for the Queen personally, 2002 had already been a difficult year, with the deaths of her mother and her only sibling.

The solution was for the monarchy to demonstrate its embrace of multiculturalism, made possible by the Queen's close commitment to the Commonwealth and by Prince Charles's inclusive support of spirituality and faiths. The Jubilee, it was decided, should celebrate modern Britain in all its diversity.

Back in 1977, the Silver Jubilee had been marked most famously by street parties. The average age of Britons was then 34, so most of the population could remember the Queen's accession at a time of rationing, austerity and killer fogs, with the country still struggling to emerge from the Second World War and with much of the empire still intact. There was then a stronger sense of community, built on a shared culture, and street parties were the obvious expression of that spirit of local allegiance. Now such events were deemed outdated by national organisers, and there were only a third of the number in 2002.

There were, however, a great many other celebrations around the country over the extended four-day bank-holiday weekend, from Eastbourne, where some of the more patriotic holidaymakers went in for 'a St George's suntan – smearing a cross on their chests in sun block before taking the rays',[2] to Croft-on-Tees, North Yorkshire, where the first prize in the fancy-dress competition went to a woman dressed as Compo from the sitcom *Last of the Summer Wine*, complete with ferrets in her pockets. Birmingham prided itself on 'the biggest gay and lesbian celebration of the Queen's Golden Jubilee anywhere in the country',[3] and at a party in the appropriately named Jubilee Street, Whitechapel in London's East End, changes were noted from 1977. 'If you'd said the word samosa to me during the Silver Jubilee, I wouldn't have known what you meant,' reflected a 61-year-old woman, wearing a plastic Union Jack apron. 'But this time round, it's important to make this day special for all members of this community. We can hark back to the good old days as much as we like, but things have to move on.'[4]

The centrepiece, of course, was also in London, a few miles to the west. If community spirit was weaker now, there was instead a growing appetite for communal experience on a grand scale, and over the course of two days the Mall was packed with hundreds of thousands of well-wishers having a rowdy, good-natured party. When nothing else was happening, they entertained themselves with impromptu singalongs – 'Land of Hope and Glory', 'Maybe It's Because I'm a Londoner', 'You'll Never Walk Alone' – but official events were also staged. For lovers of ceremonial, there was a regal procession from Buckingham Palace to a service in St Paul's Cathedral, with lashings of pomp and circumstance; the Queen was in the Gold State Coach, last used in 1977, drawn by eight white horses, while her children Charles and Anne rode alongside, resplendent in their military uniforms, escorted by the Household Cavalry.

And at the other end of the cultural spectrum, there was that pageant featuring the Hell's Angels contingent, alongside a fleet of double-decker buses and another of yellow AA vans, together with a motley assortment of old police cars, ambulances and fire engines. There were also floats, eclectic to the point of eccentricity, intended to represent the last 50 years. There was a 10-foot-wide plate of chips and peas, accompanied by a giant tomato-ketchup bottle. There was a red telephone box and an avocado-coloured bathroom suite. There was an art float, including work by Gilbert and George, Francis Bacon and Antony Gormley, and a celebrity float with real-life stars: actors Maureen Lipman and William Roache, TV chef

Keith Floyd, broadcaster Jimmy Savile. Eliciting the biggest cheers of all, there was a float representing the 1966 World Cup, with Bobby Moore's granddaughter on board. And then there were the people chosen to populate this mad parade: Chelsea pensioners, the Tiller Girls, hula-hula dancers, thousands of gospel singers, a Dalek, people dressed as mosques, groups from the Notting Hill Carnival, children from every Commonwealth nation. Later, there was a fly-past by the Red Arrows and by Concorde.*

All of it was held together by a joyful, celebratory atmosphere. The Queen looked genuinely thrilled and touched by the size of the crowds and by the display of love and respect for her role in the nation's life. She had a permanent smile on her face. It was even there when she slipped in her earplugs and went out to join the 12,000 people who'd won tickets for a pop concert in the garden of Buckingham Palace. The line-up included some younger faces – Atomic Kitten, Mis-Teeq, S Club 7, Will Young – as well as the national treasures of British music: Dame Shirley Bassey, Sir Cliff Richard, Sir Paul McCartney, Sir Elton John, as well as Tom Jones, Ray Davies and Rod Stewart, whose knighthoods came later (as did that of compère Lenny Henry). Around a million were said to have watched on the giant screens erected in London and other cities, which the night before had shown England's opening match in the World Cup, a 1–1 draw with Sweden. There was a global television audience of 200 million.

Also on the bill was the former Black Sabbath singer, Ozzy Osbourne. The Queen was said to have been 'closely involved'[5] in inviting him, which seemed implausible; more convincing was the 'senior royal source' quoted as saying, 'I don't know who Ozzy Osbourne is, but please don't quote me on that.'[6] Although he was in his fifties, Ozzy still liked to call himself the Prince of Darkness, and the media still liked to indulge him, pretending

---

* Concorde was to be taken out of service the following year, having never regained its former status after the 2000 crash.

that his inclusion added a note of danger to the proceedings. Not invited were the Sex Pistols, who had provided the cultural opposition in 1977, with their much-banned single 'God Save the Queen'. Now, singer John Lydon dismissed Ozzy as a 'dismal, tired, worn-out drug addict'[7] and announced that his own band was reuniting for some money-spinning gigs off the back of the Jubilee. And that too, in its own idiosyncratic, punk way, was a tribute to the Queen.

If the whole occasion didn't last in the public consciousness as strongly as did 1977, it was a big hit at the time, an affirmation of a new image of Britain, blending pageantry and tradition with modernity and inclusion. In 1897, Victoria's Diamond Jubilee had seen London's greatest-ever parade, as all the colonies and dominions of the empire came to kneel in tribute to the woman who ruled a quarter of the world. Now the same nations were dancing, not kneeling, and Britain felt rather pleased with its modern, diverse identity. Bill Deedes – more than a decade older than the Queen herself, and a veteran of war, cabinet and *Daily Telegraph* – wrote, 'Of all the royal pageants I have seen in the past seventy years, this one came closer to the life of our nation than any before it.'[8]

Britain's relationship with its past, and particularly with its empire, was a subject that politicians could never quite shake off. As opposition leader, Tony Blair had fought hard against the accusation of Labour being anti-patriotic; election adverts in 1997 included images of the Union flag and the British bulldog, with 'Nimrod' and 'Land of Hope and Glory' on the soundtrack, and one of Blair's speeches included the line 'I am proud of the British empire' (excised after strong protests from Robin Cook).[9] Initially it had worked. When Blair declared of Labour, 'We are patriots,'[10] the public largely believed him. There were undoubtedly some on the left who did not share his sentiment, who were actually rather ashamed of their country and its history, but they were on the disregarded fringes of the party.

It wasn't always easy, however, to juggle respect for the past with realpolitik. While the bicentenary of the Battle of Trafalgar in 2005 could hardly be ignored – it was Britain's greatest naval victory – it was important not to offend the French, who were such close friends these days. The solution was elegantly diplomatic: a re-enactment of the encounter, but rather than being between the UK and France, it was contested by the Red and Blue teams.

More complicated was the bicentenary of the abolition of the slave trade in 2007. In advance of the occasion, the government set up a committee, jointly chaired by John Prescott (whose Hull constituency had once been represented by abolitionist William Wilberforce)* and Baroness Amos, the first black woman to serve as a cabinet minister. This was to be a celebration of one of the great pieces of reforming legislation in British history, with a range of cultural events: 'museum exhibitions, theatrical productions and music festivals'.[11] There was also a much less welcome consideration: the question of whether to say sorry for British involvement in the slave trade.

It was a contentious issue. Liverpool City Council had apologised in 1999 for the city's part in the transatlantic trade, but Business West – which represented firms in Bristol – dismissed the idea of an apology as 'balderdash'.[12] Now, in the build-up to the anniversary, it was speculated that the prime minister might formally apologise on behalf of the nation. There was a potential pitfall here. In America, demands were growing for reparations to be paid for slavery, either by the nation or by businesses, and similar calls were starting to be heard in Britain; in a Channel 4 documentary *The Empire Pays Back* (2005), Robert Beckford of Birmingham University calculated that Britain owed the

---

* Relieved of duties on 'the night shift', William Hague continued his rehabilitation with a much praised biography of William Wilberforce (2007), following on from an earlier work on Pitt the Younger.

descendants of slaves £7.5 trillion, at the time just shy of six years' worth of national GDP.*

This was the danger for the government. If Tony Blair did apologise for the empire's involvement in the pre-1807 trade, and for the continuation of colonial slavery through to abolition in 1833, it might imply a liability under law, and would embolden campaigners. 'It is the fear of reparations which has prevented Western nations from holding up their hands,' said David Fleming, a museum director in Liverpool.[13]

Fleming was then unveiling plans for what would become the International Slavery Museum, which opened in 2007 and was the most substantial legacy of the commemorations. Other cities also marked the occasion. The Museum of London Docklands, which was housed in nineteenth-century sugar warehouses, opened a new gallery: London, Sugar, Slavery. Birmingham took the opportunity to clean and repair its long-neglected statue of Joseph Sturge, founder of Anti-Slavery International, the world's oldest human rights organisation (a new left hand was also added to the statue, the original having fallen off in 1875). And in Bristol there was a campaign to rename the Colston Hall, a concert venue called after eighteenth-century slave trader and MP Edward Colston; the proposed new name was Abolition 200, though that didn't come to fruition, and it would be another ten years before the City Council agreed that Colston's name should be dropped.[†]

As the anniversary approached, a piece appeared under Blair's name in the *New Nation*, voicing regret if not quite apology. The bicentennial, he wrote, was a chance 'to express our deep sorrow that it ever happened, that it ever could have happened and to rejoice at the different and better times we live in today'.

---

* The activist group Ligali felt this understated the case: '£7.5 trillion barely scratches the surface of the debt Britain owes to Africa'. (Ligali.org, 'The Empire Pays Back', 15 August 2005)
† The Colston Hall was finally renamed Bristol Beacon in 2020.

Michael Eboda, editor of the *New Nation*, professed himself content: 'It's pretty much as close to an apology as he can give ... I am pleased with it.'[14] The columnist Yasmin Alibhai-Brown, normally a critic of Blair's government ('They trash, bleed and loot Iraq, never apologise, and still grab control of its future'),[15] was ecstatic. 'This morning has broken like the first dawn,' she wrote. 'The self-righteous leader who never says sorry has proffered fulsome contrition.'[16] Some were still dissatisfied, among them Ken Livingstone, who criticised the lack of explicit apology. He got a chance to make amends at a ceremony to mark Annual Slavery Memorial Day: 'As mayor, I offer an apology on behalf of London and its institutions for their role in the transatlantic slave trade.'[17] It was an emotional moment. Livingstone's voice was faltering, he had tears in his eyes, and twice he had to be comforted by veteran Civil Rights campaigner the Reverend Jesse Jackson.

By then, however, the prime minister *had* apologised, in unscripted comments that didn't attract much attention. Asked at a press conference in March 2007 why he hadn't said sorry, he replied, 'Well actually I have said it. We are sorry, and I say it again now.'[18]

Beyond the slave trade was the wider question of how Britain should remember its empire and therefore how it could define itself today. For Blair, the legacy of imperialism was the country's ability 'to punch above our weight', in the common political expression. 'We do not have an empire,' Blair said in India in January 2002. 'We are not a superpower. But we do have a role.' That role was as 'a pivotal player and a force for good' based on 'our history, our geography, our language, the unique set of links with the United States, Europe, the Commonwealth, our position within the United Nations and NATO, the skill and reputation of our armed forces, our contribution to debt and development issues'.[19]

This was still in the days when Blair's liberal interventionism had yet to be discredited in the eyes of the public. No one then dreamed that Afghanistan would become such a long-term commitment, and the invasion of Iraq was still more than a year away. By the time Blair left office, the global role he espoused seemed much less attractive.

The Conservative Party largely shared his vision and supported his decisions to go to war, but didn't mention the empire as much as he did. Indeed, they were trying hard to neutralise any lingering whiff of imperialist nostalgia. This was, in large part, what the whole 'nasty party' debate was about – the attempt to shed the media stereotype of Tory members 'still rooted in the post-war psychology of the 1950s when women knew their place, homosexuality did not officially exist, there were few British blacks and Britain still wallowed under an illusion it had a glorious Empire'.[20] UKIP got a thicker coat of tar from the same brush – 'doddering old duffers in pith helmets harking back to the days of Empire through pink gin-stained spectacles'[21] – but actually they too seldom mentioned imperial glories.*

Further to the left, and increasingly in academic circles, the imperial legacy had centred in the last few decades on a charge sheet alleging brutality, exploitation and racism. Allied to that was the claim that crimes such as the Opium Wars, the Bengal Famine and the suppression of the Mau Mau were forgotten for political reasons, because so little had changed. As Seumas Milne saw it in 2005: 'Those who write colonial cruelty out of twentieth-century history want to legitimise the new imperialism,† now bogged down in a vicious colonial war in Iraq.'[22]

---

* UKIP's 2010 election manifesto, however, did say history teaching should 'reflect the greater levels of trade by Arab slave traders (including the seizing of English citizens for slaves from the south-west), the role of African tribes in the trade and Wilberforce's world-leading abolition campaign'.

† Margaret Hodge, a minister previously seen as a Blair loyalist, later described Iraq as an act of 'moral imperialism'. (*Evening Standard* 17 November 2006)

It wasn't entirely clear, however, against whom the historical charges should be brought, unless it were everyone who was white and British and had therefore been born with a share of collective guilt. Nor was it clear what could be done about it, since this secular version of original sin came without the hope of redemption attached to its Christian prototype. The aim was simply to strip away the cosy, whitewashing illusions, exposing the shocking truths that lay behind cherished national myths, so that Britons – especially the English – might learn there was nothing special about their country save for the enormity of its crimes.

It was not a doctrine that offered a great deal of hope, and it didn't attract a great many adherents either, since, like the New Atheism – with which it had considerable overlap – it felt a little chilly. Historian and future Labour MP Tristram Hunt complained that 'history on television is in danger of telling comforting stories about ourselves to ourselves, rather than confronting the past'.[23] But for many people, there was no great wish to confront, and being comforted was rather welcome. Anti-empire thinking did, however, have a wide circulation, spread through those two great liberal institutions, the state education system and the national broadcaster, sometimes in partnership. In his book *Empire: How Britain Made the Modern World* (2003), historian Niall Ferguson quoted an extract from the BBC website aimed at schoolchildren: 'The Empire came to greatness by killing lots of people less sharply armed than themselves and stealing their countries, although their methods later changed: killing lots of people with machine-guns came to prominence.'[24] The message gradually permeated national culture, even if the details were hazy; the words 'empire' and 'slavery' were so commonly entwined that Cecil Rhodes could be described in a front-page article in the *Sunday Times* as a 'slave owner', even though he was born twenty years after the abolition of slavery in the empire.[25]

Those who berated Britain's past did so in the name of social justice, essentially a moral position. But since the morality came from leftist politics rather than religion, it offered an intriguing break with its antecedents. In earlier times, reformers – from William Wilberforce to Mary Whitehouse – believed that the nation had taken a wrong turn and needed to be redirected to the path of righteousness; there had been a better time to which we could return. Now, for the new breed of moral campaigners, the past was a contaminated country, the suppressed memory of which was poisoning the present. This rejection of the old world became a cultural commonplace, promoted by commissioners of television shows. It wasn't always aggressively hectoring, however; indeed, it was often delivered in a mollifying tone, and it turned up in some odd forms.

By the time television became popular in mid-1950s Britain, the golden age of detective fiction was dead, but the medium couldn't help revisiting the scene of the crime. The great survivors kept on going – Agatha Christie's *Poirot* and *Marple* both ran on ITV until 2013 – and were now joined by newly written detective shows set in the past. We revisited Britain in the 1940s in *Foyle's War* (2002), the 50s in *Jericho* (2005), *Father Brown* (2013)* and *Grantchester* (2014), the 60s in *Inspector George Gently* (2007) and *Endeavour* (2012), the 70s in *Life on Mars* (2006), and the 80s in *Ashes to Ashes* (2008). The recent past was also disinterred by cold-case teams in *Waking the Dead* (2000) and *New Tricks* (2003).

The central character in these historical series was essentially modern – literally in the case of the time travellers in *Life on Mars* and *Ashes to Ashes*, by character and inclination in the others – and they shared our assumed liberal outlook. They were here to tell us what was meet and right, to reassure us that our values were superior, and to take a defiant stand against the sins of yesterday's

---

* The name and character of Father Brown were retained from the G. K. Chesterton creation, but little else; there were new stories and it was relocated from the golden age to a post-war Cotswolds village.

Britain.* We should give ourselves a contented, self-satisfied pat on the back.

'Where's that brother of yours?' a white Englishman asks a man of Pakistani heritage in *Grantchester*. The jokey reply – 'He's like the railways. Always delayed!' – is met with arrogant contempt: 'Well, maybe your railways. Nothing wrong with ours.' Racism, both casual and organised, is endemic in these shows. So too is class snobbery. 'Alan Archer is the prime example of the folly of Rab Butler in trying to educate the lower classes,' shudders Lady Livinia Pryde in *Father Brown*. 'He was permitted to march off to a left-wing university, from which he returned with ideas above his station.'

There's also prejudice against homosexual men and against women generally. In *Inspector George Gently*, Sergeant Bacchus is opposed to women in CID: 'What is the point in training them up, right? They just go off and have bairns. That's why we don't have any female detectives.' Gently, our representative in 1960s Newcastle,† has to put him right: 'Well then, maybe it's time that we did.' This is, incidentally, in an episode centring on callous company directors covering up a scandal about asbestos and dead employees. Big business is not to be trusted either.

There are still more dangers. 'Are you familiar with the term "paedophile"?' a woman asks Gently. 'It's usually a father, or an uncle, or a father and an uncle – they tend to hunt in packs. It's never dealt with. Never.' Gently is investigating historic abuse at a children's care home, a storyline that also turns up in episodes of *Dalziel and Pascoe* and *Endeavour*. Even in 1940, while engaged

---

* The same was true of *Garrow's Law* (2009), in which the great barrister William Garrow was depicted as a man of twenty-first-century sensibilities but in Georgian London.

† This version of Gently bore little relation to the character originally created by novelist Alan Hunter in a series of novels that ran from 1955 to 1999, and was set in Norfolk.

in a moral fight against fascism, the Britain of *Foyle's War* is knee-deep in looters, profiteers, Nazi sympathisers and collaborators.

Life on Mars and its spin-off *Ashes to Ashes* fitted the same pattern but took a more light-hearted approach, since they bounced ideas off a shared memory of yesterday's television as much as yesterday's reality. In each series, a police officer from the present day is whisked back to join the detective squad of DCI Gene Hunt, first in Manchester in the 1970s, then in London in the 80s. In both cases, they are horrified at what they encounter.

The men in the squad are boorish, beery chain-smokers with a disrespectful attitude towards women in terms of both sex and work: 'Never mind, son, plenty more slags in the sea,' Hunt consoles one of his team who's had an unsuccessful date.* Nor are they any sounder on gay rights; this is Hunt's description of a suspect: 'Stephen Warren is a bum bandit. Do you understand? A poof. A fairy. A queer. A queen. Fudge packer. Uphill gardener. Fruit-picking sodomite.' And Ray Carling – the most boneheaded of them all – can't believe the changing times when a black officer joins the team: 'First women, now a coloured. What's going to be next, dwarves?'

It was assumed that viewers would disapprove in an enlightened way, but they could also enjoy the naughty thrill of being allowed to witness such things being played for laughs. 'Gene Hunt verbalises what people are frightened to say in case they're labelled misogynistic, racist or homophobic,' said actor Philip Glenister.[26] And since this was the BBC in the twenty-first century, we knew we were in safe hands really; the potential offence would never get too outrageous, the extremes of racial and sexual language and behaviour would be studiously avoided, and there'd be a strong moral message to take away from the show.

---

* *'Life on Mars* was just the tip of a sexist iceberg,' reflects a retired policewoman in Kate Atkinson's 2010 novel *Started Early, Took My Dog*. (p. 219)

There was a similarly ambivalent approach to the robust cop-pering on display. When the press demand results after a fatal hammer attack, Hunt's solution is simple: 'We pull in someone from the "we don't like you" list, we put their dabs on the hammer, charge them, whip it past the beak. There's loads of scum out there deserve another spell inside.' Challenged by his modern counterpart, he's unrepentant: 'The world's getting tougher, and the police have to match it. The people want the job done, they don't want to know how.' The viewers at home could tut while still dreaming wistfully of the days when villains actually got nicked. And then got punished.

There was also something appealing about the idea of public servants who haven't heard of risk-assessment forms. Ray Carling's commitment to social justice may be lamentable, but when a woman is trapped in a burning building in an episode of *Ashes to Ashes*, he doesn't hesitate before rushing in to rescue her.

In 2007, three years before this episode was screened, there had been much disquiet over an incident in Wigan in which a ten-year-old boy had drowned trying to rescue his younger sister who'd fallen in a pond. The girl was saved by a couple of anglers, but there was criticism of two community support officers who had attended the scene but didn't dive in. Criticism, that is, from the press but not from their superiors. 'It would have been inappropriate for PCSOs to enter the pond,' ran the official police statement. 'They are not trained in water rescue.'[27] It transpired that this was standard procedure for police officers, who were 'no longer required to be trained in swimming or lifesaving', and were advised not to go into water.[28]

The fire brigade had similar instructions. Earlier that same year, a firefighter had rescued a woman from drowning in the river Tay. 'I was in the water for eight minutes and it was heart-stoppingly cold, but we saved her,' he said afterwards. He was then warned that he faced an investigation for disregarding regu-lations.[29] 'We now have the utterly ludicrous situation of brave men and women working in the emergency and rescue services being actively discouraged from helping the public and saving lives,' wrote broadcaster Lorraine Kelly in the *Sun*.[30] By comparison, Gene Hunt and his Neanderthals seemed quite an attractive alternative.

There was nothing new about reinventing the past in the fiction of the present. The height of empire had also been the heyday of the historical novel, from Scott and Dickens to Stevenson and Conan Doyle. Even so, this new television format was striking. And now, as ever, the work spoke more of today than yesterday, sometimes unwittingly so, and sometimes deliberately, because there's fun to be had in anachronistic satire. In an episode of *Ashes to Ashes* set on the eve of the 1983 election, a policewoman declares her political allegiance: 'Labour is the only party that believes in equality and socialist principles. Always has done and always will. They would never have gone into a pointless war like the Falklands.' 'Actually, Shaz,' our time-travelling representative of Blair's Britain starts to explain, but then thinks better of it: 'Never mind …'

II

One of the oddities of the period detective shows was that, despite their subject matter, no one ever drew attention to the remarkably low incidence of violent crime, as compared to the present. The annual homicide rate for England and Wales in the 1950s averaged 7.5 deaths per million population; by the 2000s, despite the huge medical advances in the interim, enabling lives to be saved that would once have been lost, this had risen to 14.3, nearly double. There were now nearly 750 homicides a year.

Given such numbers, most murder victims now attracted little more than local news coverage, but there were those who commanded national attention. One such was Jane Longhurst, a 31-year-old special needs teacher from Brighton, East Sussex, killed in 2003 by a man obsessed with strangulation. They had been engaged, he said, in erotic asphyxiation; it was a consensual sex game that had gone wrong. There was no evidence for such a claim, and the jury found him guilty, but the case had ramifications. The prosecution made great play of the fact that the killer was 'a frequent viewer of violent pornography on the internet' and had visited 'sites such as Necrobabes, Violent Pleasure, and Deathbyasphyxia'.[31] Immediately after the conviction, there were calls for tighter con- trols of what was available online: 'Killed by the internet,' ran the headline in the *Daily Mirror*,[32] while the *Sun* offered 'Web of evil'.[33] The murderer's violent fantasies predated his access to the internet – he said he was 'practising asphyxial sex' by the end of the 1980s[34] – so clearly were not caused by it, but the headlines chimed with an inclination towards censorship in government circles.

The legislation that emerged, Section 63 of the Criminal Justice and Immigration Act 2008, banned extreme pornographic images, which were defined as material depicting necrophilia, bes- tiality, and acts which threatened life or which would be likely to result 'in serious injury to a person's anus, breasts or genitals'. For those concerned about artistic freedom (the status, for example, of Rubens's 1602 masterpiece *Leda and the Swan*), pornography was also defined: imagery 'produced solely or principally for the purpose of sexual arousal'.*

Few regretted the lost access to Necrobabes, but an impor- tant principle was abandoned in the process. Previous obscenity legislation had been concerned with possession for sale or distri- bution, so that a distinction was made between public sale and

---

* The emphasis here was on imagery, but in 2009, for the first time in over 30 years, a prosecution was brought against a fictional text under Section 4 of the Obscene Publications Act; the case, against the author of an online story *Girls (Scream) Aloud*, was subsequently abandoned.

private ownership. But now that separation had been removed, and possession alone outlawed. And possession, it turned out, included images stored on the memory of a computer or mobile phone, regardless of how they had got there, whether downloaded from a forbidden website or attached to an unsolicited email.

The extreme-porn legislation was a key shift in the relationship between the state and the individual, an erosion of the privacy of the citizen. It was also in keeping with a trend in government that had first been discerned in the 1980s and had been growing ever since: a tendency to tell people how to conduct their personal lives.

In opposition, for example, New Labour proposed a minister for public health, whose task, explained shadow health secretary Chris Smith, would be to 'co-ordinate action to improve the nation's health and reduce inequalities'.[35] Some of this turned out to be public health in the sense that it was generally understood – making provision for the feared epidemics of SARS and bird flu – but much of it seemed to be more about badgering people to change their habits. The priorities, concluded writer John Mortimer, were misguided: 'The absurdity of a government that allows thousands to become infected and die from superbugs in filthy NHS hospitals, and then worries about how much wine we drink at supper in our own homes, should be obvious.'[36]

In a benign form, there was the campaign led by the Health Education Authority urging us to eat at least five portions of fruit and vegetables a day, in order to stave off disease and to counter the so-called obesity epidemic. The figure of five portions had no scientific basis, and other countries differed – Canada recommended seven, France ten – but five, according to the NHS, was 'chosen by public health campaigners because it was seen as an achievable target for most people'.[37] Even then, there was considerable confusion over what counted in the calculation; it was 2003 before tinned spaghetti was officially declared not a vegetable.

Yet the nation's waistline continued to expand. In 1997 the

NHS health survey for England found that 62 per of men and 53 per cent of women were overweight, with one in five classed as obese. Twenty years on, despite all the lectures, those figures had actually risen, to 67 and 62 per cent, with obesity up to one in three. Some suggested that the cause might lie elsewhere, that permitting supermarkets to acquire an ever-more-dominant share of retailing might be encouraging the consumption of unhealthy, unnatural, manufactured food, where profit margins were higher than they were on fruit and veg.

Similarly, it turned out that relaxing restrictions on gambling and pub-opening hours led to some people struggling to deal with the impulse to bet and to drink. No amount of nagging people to 'Be Gamble Aware' and to 'Drink Responsibly' could compensate for the ensuing social problems. 'And what's binge-drinking, anyway?' asks a character in Peter Robinson's novel *Friend of the Devil* (2007). 'Five or more drinks in a row, three or more times a month. That's how the so-called experts define it. But you tell me which one of us has never done that.'[38]

Government campaigns on diet, drink and betting were advisory of course, even if accompanied by threats that the NHS might refuse operations for the obese. The ban on smoking in enclosed public places, on the other hand, was statutory, taking effect in Scotland in 2006 and the rest of the UK the following year, with disputed results: the Scottish government claimed that heart attacks fell by 17 per cent as a result of the prohibition, while a Bath University study reported that in England there was a fall of just 2.3 per cent.[39] Meanwhile, in an unintended consequence, Gedling Council in Nottinghamshire reported an 80 per cent fall in car crime: there were now so many people hanging around in public places, smoking outside pubs, offices and shops,* that opportunistic thefts had virtually ceased.

---

* There was a brief phase when these pavement clusters of smokers were known as snoutcasts, a word coined by the comic *Viz*.

Less welcome developments included the precipitate decline in numbers going to pubs, bingo halls and working-men's clubs. 'Is the smoking ban a war on the working class?' wondered a correspondent to the *Liverpool Echo*, and she may have had a point.[40] As John Reid, then the health secretary, had noted a couple of years earlier, the war against tobacco was 'an obsession of the learned middle class'.[41] Labour backbencher Diane Abbott saw a political problem here: 'Under New Labour, the party has gone from speaking for the white working class to speaking at them – whether about junk food or the smoking ban.'[42]

Allied to this wish to correct our behaviour was a growing taste for surveillance. The Regulation of Investigatory Powers Act 2000 was intended to combat terrorism and paedophilia, but of the 151 local authorities who responded to a Freedom of Information request in 2008, nearly half admitted they were using the act for much less serious offences. Secret cameras had been installed to catch people who put their bins out on the wrong night, or who lied about their address to get their children into a better school. Dog fouling, fly-tipping and misuse of disabled parking-spaces were also targeted. 'Snooping appears to have become the favourite pastime in town halls up and down the land,' said Shami Chakrabarti of the pressure group Liberty.[43] None of this sat well with a country that had long harboured contempt for petty bureaucrats. Nor did the government's attempt to introduce identity cards prove popular, and the proposal was so watered down by the time it passed into law in 2006 that hardly anyone noticed it before it was repealed four years later.

Conversely, the public seemed happy enough to surrender information to commercial firms. A character in Peter Berry's TV thriller *The Last Enemy* (2008) spells out how much of our privacy we've already given up to databases and to companies eager to get to know us: 'All the important information, information you can sell: your income, your diet, how much alcohol you consume, what books you read, how much your house is worth, your last three addresses, who you phone, who phones you, where you travel to, who travels with you, where your children go to school ...'

As the boundary between public and private dissolved, it seemed that an Englishman's home was no longer his castle, not even if he were the prime minister himself. In 2005 the *Mail on Sunday* serialised the memoirs of former Labour spin doctor Lance Price. This included an account of the night of the Welsh Assembly elections in 1999, when it looked for a while as though Labour might not win. Tony Blair, wrote Price, was furious, railing against the 'fucking Welsh'.[44] Downing Street insisted that the phrase be removed from the published book, but by then a complaint had been lodged with the North Wales Police and an inquiry launched into whether this had been a racist incident.

'There is almost no way we could not investigate what is being reported,' pronounced the chief constable, Richard Brunstrom. 'It is not trivial.'[45] It was, though. It was really very trivial indeed. It was a man shouting at the telly in the privacy of his own home. So although no charges were brought, and although it took a heart of stone not to laugh at a prime minister being hoist by his own petard, it still seemed a little disturbing. 'The government has given us laws and I think they are good laws,' said Brunstrom. 'We have to balance resources but we have definitely put more effort into hate crime.'*

The police had also become concerned with what people said on the media. In 2001 broadcaster Anne Robinson joked about the Welsh on the BBC television show *Room 101*. 'I've never taken to them,' she said. 'What are they for?' As Wales's greatest living

---

* Lance Price's first novel, *Time and Fate* (2005), gently guyed the Blair government's tendency to interfere, with talk of the Emergency Powers Must Give Your Name and ID Number When You Answer the Phone Act, and the Anti-Terrorist Put Your Hand Up Before You Go to the Loo Bill.

writer Jan Morris pointed out, this was merely Robinson acting out her 'carefully nurtured persona as a curmudgeonly old bag',[46] but she was still questioned by the police, as was the BBC's director general Greg Dyke, before it was announced that no charges would be brought. The Broadcasting Standards Commission said her comments 'came close to the boundaries of acceptability', before concluding that the programme wasn't actually racist.[47]

The open expression of racism had long been socially unacceptable, and in the new century homophobia went a long way to matching its pariah status. In the 1980s, the right had chosen homosexuality as the battleground in its war against liberalism, and the scale of its loss was now becoming clear. In 2000 the age of consent for gay men was lowered to sixteen, the ban on homosexuality in the armed forces was lifted, and – in Scotland – Section 28 of the Local Government Act 1988 was repealed.* In 2001 the Criminal Injuries Compensation Authority recognised the rights of gay partners, in 2002 same-sex couples were allowed to adopt, and in 2005 the first civil partnerships of gay couples were solemnised.

These legislative changes were initially opposed by the Tories under Iain Duncan Smith, but Michael Howard, in his first speech as leader, said the party 'must understand how Britain has changed in the last twenty years'[48] and offered free votes on the later bills. There was broad support in the country, but there were still some who believed homosexual practices were sinful, and it was they who attracted the attention of the police. Both the Catholic writer Lynette Burrows in December 2005 and Sir Iqbal Sacranie of the Muslim Council of Britain the following month were investigated for religiously orthodox comments made on BBC radio, much to the distress of the Corporation, which hurriedly distanced itself: 'In a live radio show it sometimes happens that challenging and

---

* Section 28, which banned local authorities from 'promoting homosexuality', was repealed in the rest of the UK in 2003.

unpleasant opinions are expressed.'[49] Again, no charges were brought, since no actual crime had been committed, but the police said it was obliged to speak to people if a 'homophobic incident' was reported. 'It is all about reassuring the community,' explained a spokesperson.[50]

Not everyone was reassured by this new role of the police as custodians of public manners, however. There seemed to be an element of mission creep. What had been heralded as tolerance of diversity seemed now more akin to enforcement of orthodoxy. Some also wondered where the limits lay. The Crime and Disorder Act 1998 had introduced the concept of hate crime into British law, so that an offence of assault, say, or criminal damage, would attract a longer sentence if it were motivated by religious or racial hatred. In 2003 this was extended to include hatred based on a victim's disability or perceived sexual orientation. These were the groups recognised in law, but then police forces around the country began suggesting their own categories against whom hate might be recorded: in Manchester, it was youth subcultures such as goths, punks and emos;[51] in Gloucestershire the homeless;[52] in London the elderly and redheads.[53] By the time the Law Commission began to consider in 2018 whether to include misogyny and misandry as well,[54] there was literally not a person in the country who wasn't at risk of being hated. And 'hate crime' was increasingly used as though the hate itself were the crime, rather than the aggravating factor in an offence.

The development attracting greatest controversy was a proposal to introduce an offence of incitement to religious hatred. Among those objecting were comedian Rowan Atkinson, cartoonist Gerald Scarfe and theatre director Nicholas Hytner, who argued that the measure would, in the words of the writers' pressure group English PEN, 'gravely undermine both freedom of speech and Britain's longstanding climate of tolerance'.[55] The government insisted that the intention was not to restrict the discussion of religion itself: 'It is hatred against people rather than hatred of ideas that we are trying to prohibit.'[56] Nonetheless, the legislation was defeated twice in the Lords, and an attempt to revive it was lost only because it ran out of time before the 2005 election.

It was a temporary reprieve. In its manifesto, Labour promised to pursue the question, making it an election issue. 'What will Michael Howard do for British Muslims?' asked minister Mike O'Brien provocatively in *Muslim Weekly*.[57] 'Will he promote legislation to protect you from religious hatred?'* And in 2006 the Racial and Religious Hatred Act was passed into law. It had, however, been amended – again in the Lords – so that it now referred only to 'threatening' words or behaviour, rather than the original 'threatening, abusive or insulting', and so that evidence of intent had also to be proved.†

Something was changing here, something serious enough to trouble more than just the usual tabloid suspects. *Guardian* columnist Polly Toynbee argued that the religious hatred legislation shifted 'the cultural balance away from free speech towards a sanctimonious right to feel offended'.[58] And novelist Salman Rushdie, who knew about religious censorship, was on the same page. 'Everybody needs to get thicker skins,' he said. 'There is this culture of offence, as though offending someone is the worst thing anyone can do.'[59]

There was, however, no reduction in the levels of offence being taken. Precisely the opposite. And this was the cause of some confusion and unease, since it implied that, despite the evident

---

* 'Will his foreign policy aim to help Palestine?' O'Brien further nudged. The previous year, Ian McCartney, chair of the Labour Party, had called shadow chancellor Oliver Letwin – who was, like Howard, Jewish – a '21st-century Fagin'. McCartney was shocked that anyone might think this was anti-Semitic: 'I have fought racism all my life,' he protested. (*Sunday Times* 29 February 2004)

† The new legislation led to the abolition in 2008 of the common-law offences of blasphemy and blasphemous libel, which had given special protection to Christianity.

progress that had been made, the sins of the past continued into the present. The messages were so mixed. Did the multicultural celebrations of the Golden Jubilee reflect the true values of modern Britain? Or had there actually been no real advance since the dark days depicted in the period detective shows?

Those in authority appeared to believe the latter. No matter how much we prided ourselves on being more tolerant than previous generations, there was a fear in polite society that we were not to be trusted, that the old evils still lay within us. Constant vigilance was required, and government, councils and police felt obliged to monitor what had once been private behaviour. The principle of inclusion demanded the practice of intrusion.*

The official position had been clear a generation ago, when Margaret Thatcher eulogised 'a British empire that took both freedom and the rule of law to countries that would never have known it otherwise'.[60] Now there was a government shaped, at least in part, by the anti-racism and anti-imperialism championed by the left in the 1980s, and it was no longer certain what it believed. Speaking in Tanzania in 2005, Gordon Brown said that 'the days of Britain having to apologise for its colonial history are over'.[61] He pleased neither those who felt a greater apology was necessary, nor those who resented apologising at all.

The impression given was that all this history stuff was an irritation, a distraction from the shiny modernism of New Labour. But the unfortunate echoes remained. In January 2002, a world away from the mountainous wastes of Afghanistan where British troops were battling insurgents, Tony Blair took down a copy of Rudyard Kipling's novel *Kim* (1901) from the shelves at Chequers, hoping to understand better Britain's painful history in the region.[62]

---

* 'Paradox works well and mists up the windows, which is handy,' says the cynical young historian Irwin in Alan Bennett's play *The History Boys* (2004): '"The loss of liberty is the price we pay for freedom" type thing.'

*

On 7 July 2005, Islamic suicide bombers detonated bombs on three Underground trains and a bus in London, killing themselves and 52 members of the public, and injuring hundreds more. Most of those who died were British, but such was the nature of London that eighteen other countries also suffered fatalities. It was the worst terrorist attack in England since the Second World War. The most haunting images came that afternoon, pictures of a sombre, subdued city, full of people walking home in the absence of public transport. 'There was no panic,' wrote David Lodge in his novel *Deaf Sentence* (2009), 'but a stoic, phlegmatic, Blitz-like mood on the streets.'[63]

Two weeks later, a second wave of bombings on public transport in London was mercifully thwarted when the detonators failed on four devices and a fifth was discarded. There were further terrorist attacks to come, and more plots that were stopped before they could reach fruition.

Some had feared that such events would provoke a violent backlash against Muslims, but it did not materialise. The day before the bombs, London had been awarded the right to host the 2012 Olympic Games, beating the favourite, Paris, largely by selling itself on its ethnic diversity and mutual tolerance. '7 Million Londoners: 1 London,' was the slogan promoted by mayor Ken Livingstone in response to the attack. And that attitude prevailed. A study in 2010 showed that 90 per cent of Muslims in London* said they felt British, compared with just 45 per cent of those in Paris who felt French.[64]

---

* The same was true of Leicester, the other British city sampled in the study.

4

Class and Underclass

I.

Bernard Manning, the country's most controversial comedian, died in June 2007 at the age of 76. He'd been a huge star in the early 1970s, a time when comics – those on ITV, at any rate – were expected to be working class in their culture and conservative in their politics. But then everything changed. The rise of alternative comedy, combined with a reawakening of the dormant Oxbridge tradition, brought to the fore a new generation of entertainers, men and women who had left university at the start of the long Tory government: educated, metropolitan, left-leaning, mostly middle class, with a strong distaste for Margaret Thatcher.*

They also disapproved of Bernard Manning. It became axiomatic that comedy – even when not overtly political – should spurn caricatures of groups designated as oppressed: women, homosexuals, ethnic minorities. Manning was attacked for doing precisely that. He was the incarnation of all that was unacceptable. As the tide turned, he found himself stranded, the television work drifting away, though audiences, ageing with him, still kept coming to his gigs. The *Guardian*'s obituary captured the confused relationship between the veteran comic and the new liberal establishment of popular culture: 'Seen as a public face of intolerance, this member of a minority group – the socially deprived northerner – was in turn despised and even hated.'[1]

He was not quite the last of the breed, however. Just a month before Manning's death, Channel 4 had screened a documentary on the one man still practising the tradition of conservative, working-class, northern comedy. 'He's been playing live to over 150,000 people a year for over three decades,' it opened, 'selling over forty million quid's worth of tapes and DVDs.' And, for the first time in his 62 years, albeit accompanied by a disapproving voice-over, Roy Chubby Brown – 'Britain's Rudest Comic,' as he was billed – had his moment on television.

Born in 1945 in Grangetown, a steel town on the outskirts of Middlesbrough, the boy then known as Royston Vasey was brought up – in the loosest sense – by his father, after his mother left home when he was eight. He waited till he was fourteen before he also

---

* This is the generation of Robert Bathurst, Jo Brand, Ade Edmondson, Ben Elton, Julian Clary, Harry Enfield, Dawn French, Stephen Fry, Jeremy Hardy, Hattie Hayridge, Hugh Laurie, Rik Mayall, Paul Merton, Jennifer Saunders, Jan Ravens, Tony Slattery, Mark Steel, Emma Thompson, Sandy Toksvig, Paul Whitehouse. All twenty of these were born within five years of each other, in 1957–61, and all but two (Merton and Steel) went to university.

left, sometimes sleeping rough, sometimes finding accommodation in borstals, the merchant navy or prison. Eventually, he became an entertainer on the northern club circuit, adopting his new name as part of a double act, Alcock and Brown, and keeping it when he went solo. He found his style when Bernard Manning told him after a gig that 'I needed to "smut up" my act a bit,'[2] and he swiftly became known as the bluest of blue comics, extremely crude in both subject matter and language.

Coming on stage to an enthusiastic audience chant of 'You fat bastard!' Roy Chubby Brown was a skittle-shaped, bespectacled figure wearing a garish patchworked suit, topped with 1930s flying helmet and goggles, a legacy of the Alcock and Brown days. He'd greet the audience – 'Ey-oop, cunts!' – and then for the next ninety minutes he'd deliver a mix of one-liners and stories, interspersed with a few songs and a lot of put-downs to hecklers. His material centred on sex. It was full of women who were up for it and women who were not, men who were frustrated or cuckolded or who had fantasies way out of their league; above all, it centred on his own grubbily implausible exploits and failures. Like the suit, the act was a vulgar, bastardised reminiscence of Max Miller half a century earlier, delivered with foul-mouthed glee.

He wasn't welcome on television, apart from his *Top of the Pops* appearance in 1995, duetting with the band Smokie on 'Living Next Door to Alice (Who the F*** Is Alice?)'.* But he built a sizeable audience with a stream of audio cassettes (*Thick as Shit, Fucked If I Know, Kiss My Arse*), and then, with *From Inside the Helmet* (1990), switched to live videos and ultimately DVDs. They emerged every November and did very good festive business: in the run-up to Christmas 2009, his *Too Fat to Be Gay*

---

* There was also a 2010 cameo appearance as Mayor Larry Vaughan in the television comedy *The League of Gentlemen*, set in a fictitious town named after him, Royston Vasey. It was his only acting role.

was reported to be outselling *Hello Wembley!*, the latest Michael McIntyre release.

The two men could not have been further apart, in terms of style, appeal, even geography. As its title suggested, McIntyre's DVD had been recorded during his record-breaking six-night stint at the Wembley Arena, London, while Brown's was filmed at the Civic Hall, Wolverhampton. His heartlands were not London and the south-east; over the course of the decade he also filmed in Billingham, Birmingham (twice), Blackpool, Glasgow, Manchester, Newcastle upon Tyne, Northampton and Stoke-on-Trent. He wasn't to be found on the festival circuit of Edinburgh, Montreal and Melbourne.

His live audience was mostly male, almost exclusively white, rarely sober. They were considerably younger than him, and they were working class. 'I entertain lorry drivers, road sweepers and people like that,' he said. 'Fitters, welders.' You were more likely to encounter lagered-up lads on a stag weekend than students on a gap year. The video market, though, may have been a little broader, judging by a *Reader's Digest* poll in 2004[3] in which the magazine's aspirational readers judged Brown to be the seventh-funniest comedian of all time.*

Amid the filth, there were occasional dips into politics. 'I was a Labour man all my life,' he reflected in an interview. 'My father was a Labour man. We're not posh people, we're off council estates.'[4] He still lived in Middlesbrough and tried to stay true to his roots. His response to the death of Margaret Thatcher in 2013, for example, was to put ten minutes of abuse into his act: 'Where I'm from, everybody hated her.'[5]

There was also a strong vein of insulting foreign countries. His 2003 show saw him explaining that, as far as he personally was concerned, he didn't want to stand shoulder to shoulder with the Americans; instead he invited them to 'Fuck off! Fuck, fuck, fuck,

---

* The list was topped by Tommy Cooper.

fuck off!' The audience appreciation was almost as big as that for his castigation of France, a routine that included a song for the French president: 'Jacques Chirac, you big sack of cack'.*

Nevertheless there was little sign of bellicose jingoism. The same show saw him suggest that the best Christmas present for Tony Blair would be a one-piece jigsaw, 'cos he's a thick cunt'. A couple of years later, he snorted derision at Blair's liberal interventionism. 'So what has Iraqi freedom meant to you, then?' he challenged his audience. 'Is your petrol cheaper? Does your lager taste better? Are you getting more pussy than you can handle?' Behind the typically earthy set of priorities, there lay a distinct lack of interest in 'punching above our weight'. And he was clear where he stood on Afghanistan and Iraq. 'Tony Blair should be hung,' he said in an interview. 'He got us into a war that we should not have been involved in. There's 285 mothers in this country who lost their sons because of him.'[6]

So there he was in the new century, a working-class man in his sixties, swearing like a trooper, speaking out against war, and yet Roy Chubby Brown was in no danger of becoming a national treasure. In fact he was attracting ever more controversy. Like Bernard Manning, he was simply not acceptable in polite society. Many of the medium-sized theatres in the country were owned by local councils, and there were some – particularly Labour administrations – who didn't like the idea of him being on their property. He was banned at various times from civic venues in, among others, Ashfield, Bradford, Cambridge, Cardiff, Egremont, Hamilton, Ipswich, Leeds, Leicester, Llandudno, Oldham, even his home town of Middlesbrough.

---

* 'Audiences don't like the French. When I take the mick out of them, people applaud,' confirmed the Cornish comedian Jethro. He later joined UKIP: 'The British have got a lot to be proud of, and it's not right that we're expected to lose our traditions.' (*Sun* 2 December 2000)

The problem, explained one council leader, was that Brown's act was 'highly offensive',[7] trampling all over those demarcation lines about sexist, racist and homophobic content. He disagreed. 'I'm not a racist, or a sexist; I'm a humorist.'[8] But the vocabulary alone – with its poofters, Pakis and cunts – was enough to see him condemned. And a great many of the jokes were indeed sexist, even misogynistic. Then again, in the sexual encounters he described, men seldom emerged with any more credit or dignity than did women. And his absurd physicality tended to undercut any sense of reality, so that even when the imagery of the jokes was violent, it was meant to be a cartoon violence. 'Chubby is a simple character,' was his own assessment. 'He means no harm, and those people who realise this love him whether they are male or female.'[9]

To the charge of homophobia, he had a simple answer. 'Phobia means you're frightened of something,' he said. 'I am. I'm frightened of a cock up the arse.' Yet when he told gags about the likes of Elton John and Michael Barrymore, the real target tended to be the star, not the sexuality. The fact that they were gay was merely used as a stick with which to beat them; as with his jokes about Madonna or Michael Jackson, it was wealthy, powerful figures who were being ridiculed. Indeed, Brown's obsession with sex, his Rabelaisian celebration of the physical, sometimes spilled over into an implied, if vague, tolerance of other sexualities, an immoral equivalence. 'I'm a pussy man,' he declared. 'I like minges, motts, fannies, cracks, hairy beavers. I'm not into dicks, tools, weapons, cocks, shafts and bell ends.'

But it was, inevitably, the racist material that attracted the greatest condemnation. Some of the gags were constructed in conventional fashion. 'They're fucking taking over,' he'd say (assuming we knew who 'they' were); 'before long, that fish shop'll be called fucking Harry Ramadan's.' Other bits, though, didn't quite work as comedy. 'I'm not saying that all Muslims are terrorists,' ran one line. 'But isn't it funny how all terrorists are fucking Muslims?' The rhythm is right, but the structure promises wordplay that doesn't come. That was unusual. Brown wrote his own material and was a good technician – he had to be to achieve and sustain his level of success – yet when it came to immigration, he abandoned his craft. And there were occasions when there was simply no joke at all, just frustration: 'I don't mind asylum seekers driving taxis, but I wish they'd learn to speak fucking English.'

That line got a massive roar from his audience. It wasn't, however, a howl of hatred. Rather it resembled the dark delight of a football crowd cheering a particularly heavy tackle by a defender who was one of their own. Written down, stripped of the live interaction, his gags come across harsher than when delivered in an exasperated Teeside accent by a man who looks deliberately ridiculous. Brown was the village idiot, licensed to say the unsay-able on behalf of the serfs, to mock the morals that govern society, and ridicule the po-faced puritans who would police speech and culture. This stuff didn't have to be crafted; simply the fact that it was uttered was sufficient. The audience reaction was the punchline.

Brown was, in effect, creating a bubble in which normal rules didn't apply, a place where impure thoughts could be spoken aloud. But it was very definitely a comedy gig, not a political rally. The audience was not being incited by the clown onstage, not being wound up and charged to go out into the world. On the contrary, the roar sounded like a release of tension, so that the punters might return to normal life, having been purged. It was a comic catharsis.

It did, though, have a political element. There was a recognition of the sentiments expressed. Brown said in a 2007 interview that he'd noticed a change in how this material was being received. 'When asylum seekers first started coming here I was talking about it on stage, but now that it's in the news, when I talk about it people are on their feet applauding.' And he was clear that he meant what he said in his act: 'behind every joke a comedian makes there's a serious point'.[10] The roar of approval was also the sound of the audience registering their acknowledgement of that serious point. There's no joke without fire.

The mounting number of council bans became a serious problem. It enhanced Brown's outlaw status, of course, but hit revenues and, in the absence of media exposure, he needed the live work. He couldn't understand why he was being singled out. 'Compared to Jimmy Carr's act, I'm like the archbishop of Canterbury,' he protested.[11] That wasn't really true, and anyway it entirely missed the point. Jimmy Carr was a horse of a very different off-colour.

Born in 1972, Carr was a grammar-school boy from Buckinghamshire who went to Cambridge University and then got a marketing job at Shell, before leaving to train as a psychotherapist. Where Roy Chubby Brown had resolved to become an entertainer while in a jail cell, Carr did so on a spiritual retreat in Greece. Within a couple of years, he was on television, initially hosting *Your Face or Mine?* on E4, then becoming ubiquitous on the panel-show circuit, specialising in amoral, one-liner wit.

His stage presence was very different too. With his smart suit and haircut, like a model in a 1961 Burton's menswear catalogue, he was an anachronistic throwback to the likes of Bob Monkhouse. He talked about having 'a head shaped like a potato'[12] but was good-looking enough to attract teen fans. 'He's frickin' gorgeous,' wrote one on an internet message board. 'I wish I was eighteen, so then I could go see him and stalk him all the time. That would be sweet.'[13] People didn't tend to say that about Roy Chubby Brown.

Even so, there were points of comparison. Both men had a Stakhanovite work ethic and both had a reputation for taboo-breaking assaults on political correctness, usually accompanied by a little chuckle of pleasure at their own daring. But Carr was careful not to overstep the line too far when broadcasting, and it helped that he looked and sounded middle class, so that it was assumed he was simply playing the naughty schoolboy. 'As many have discovered before him,' noted the *Observer*, 'a posh voice gives you licence to express outrageously tasteless and illiberal sentiments.'[14]

Certainly, there was a distance from the material, so that although many objected to, say, Carr's rape jokes – 'What do nine out of ten people enjoy? Gang rape.' – no one believed that he was actually a rapist. When Brown told jokes about hitting his wife, it was hard to ignore the fact that in 1996 he pleaded guilty to assaulting the mother of his two children. He was fined and ordered to pay £250 compensation, which she considered lenient: 'It cost me £700 in dental fees to have four teeth and damaged nerves repaired after he hit me.' During the attack, she said, he shouted that she was an 'ugly cunt'. Just like he did onstage.[15]

The other difference between them was that Brown tended to give the knife an extra twist. When Carr did jokes about disability, they'd be sly, slick gags: 'They say laughter is the best medicine, so maybe, just maybe, if we all keep laughing at people in wheel-chairs ...' And he held up his crossed fingers. This, on the other hand, is Brown: 'I was bullied at school. I'll never forget this lad saying to me, "Hey, fat fucker! Porky! Lard arse!" One day I just lost my temper with the fucker and tipped him out of his wheel-chair.' It's a joke that – with minor adjustment – could have come from Carr. But then Brown adds an extra line, tossed casually into the shocked laughter at the wheelchair reveal: 'Down's syndrome or not, I kicked the cunt.' The additional comment casts a shadow back over the gag, taking it from distasteful to disturbing.

In the mid-1990s, as the alternative comics broke into and then transformed mainstream entertainment, the limits of what was acceptable had been fairly well drawn. Observational humour about the differences between men and women was okay, so long as it was relatively benign; gags about homosexuality less so, unless delivered by a homosexual, in which case they were almost mandatory. Ethnic minorities were very definitely not acceptable as subjects, and neither were most nationalities, save for the Germans, French and Italians. (Americans would have been fine, but they were considered more suited to anger than humour.) Serious physical disability was out of bounds, body size was not, mental health was borderline. All social classes were considered fair game.

But increasingly these conventions were being breached. At one end of the spectrum, there was the jovial figure of Al Murray, whose character the Pub Landlord was jingoistic and xenophobic (but not racist) in a way that managed to have its beer and drink it. He was 'the provisional wing of UKIP', according to Garry Bushell in the *People*.* 'Being in character lets Murray get all the laughs and none of the disapproval.'[16] And at the other extreme there was the most successful comedy sketch show of the era, *Little Britain*, which transferred from Radio 4 to BBC Three in 2003, and thence to BBC One. Drawing on the children's comic tradition of the *Beano* (filtered through *Viz*), Matt Lucas and David Walliams revived gags long since believed to have been buried – blackface, cross-dressing, obesity – and added a new cruelty and crudity with vomiting, incontinence and gerontophilia.

The *Observer* columnist Nick Cohen saw Lucas and Walliams, along with the more aggressive Frankie Boyle, as 'cowardly comedians who pick on the poor rather than the powerful'.[17] Jeremy Hardy, the most politically committed survivor of the 1980s generation, judged his own work by similar standards. 'I think my role is to afflict the comfortable and comfort the afflicted,' he explained. 'As Chris Rock said, we should be punching up not punching down.'[18]

Hardy himself, however, could also cause upset. A 2004 routine

---

* Murray didn't see it like this. At the 2015 general election, he stood against Nigel Farage in South Thanet, representing the Free United Kingdom Party (FUKP). He came sixth, some 15,708 votes behind second-placed Farage.

on his Radio 4 show, *Jeremy Hardy Speaks to the Nation*, hadn't translated well into print: 'If you just took everyone in the BNP and everyone who votes for them and shot them in the back of the head, there would be a brighter future for us all.'[19] Coming from a former *Guardian* columnist with a near-residency on national radio, it didn't quite sound like 'punching up'. The BBC explained that this was actually a satire on anti-fascists: 'He wasn't inciting anyone to violence, he was lampooning the attitudes of the left and its attempts to rationalise all types of behaviour and views.' But Burnley Council, which then had six BNP councillors, was unimpressed and scrapped a scheduled performance by Hardy at one of its venues. 'I wouldn't say he was banned,' observed a council spokesperson.[20] 'More cancelled.'

It was hard to see who was going to be offended, since members of the BNP were unlikely to be fans of Hardy's work, but then the same principle held true for Roy Chubby Brown. Audiences knew what to expect with Brown, as they did with Jimmy Carr. Each was creating a comfortably unsafe space where people could come together and listen to wicked thoughts that were forbidden in the real world. They were doing what comedians have always done: cheeking their betters, poking fun at public morality, pointing up the fallen nature of humanity and the frailties of the human body. And a huge part of the appeal was saying naughty things that jarred with the state-endorsed, non-judgemental celebration of diversity and inclusion.

There remained, though, a stubborn disparity between these comedians. However much outrage Carr was said to provoke,* it didn't stop him appearing on television; he still had his job as presenter of the panel game *8 out of 10 Cats* (2005). Brown, by contrast, was a broadcaster *non grata* throughout his career.

---

* As with his much-condemned 2009 gag: 'Say what you like about the servicemen amputees from Iraq and Afghanistan, we are going to have a fucking good Paralympics team in 2012.'

There was little doubt who was the truly transgressive artist. But what precisely was his offence?

In Brown's early days, the language he used was sufficient to keep him off the screen, but the standards of what was permissible had changed since then. In 2005 the BBC broadcast *Jerry Springer: The Opera*, a satirical work that, said the *Sunday Times*, 'portrayed Jesus as a homosexual and contained some 400 swear words, including c*** and f***'.[21] Even Brown struggled to match that output. In any event, he was intelligent enough to know that, like Carr, he'd have to tone it down should he ever get the chance to appear on television. That wasn't really why he didn't get invited onto *Room 101* or *Have I Got News for You?* or even *8 out of 10 Cats*.

Nor was ribald material quite as frowned upon as once it had been. Brown started in an era when special permission had to be sought from the IBA to allow a sitcom, *Robin's Nest* (1977), to show an unmarried couple living together. Thirty years on, Donald Stewart in *Benidorm* (2007)* shared Brown's grubby gluttony for sex, as in his description of the night before he and his 'very accommodating' wife came on holiday, when he had 'six of the lads' round to his house. 'The thing is, if you've got a beautiful wife, to me it would seem churlish to keep her to yourself,' he says. 'Mind you, at the end of the night her vagina looked like a pair of padded coat-hangers. I had to pay for extra leg-room for her on the plane.' As a former theatrical agent who 'used to handle Frankie Howerd in the 70s', the one thing Donald didn't have in common with Brown was his homophobia. 'In the late 60s, I had an old drinking partner, Martin "Lucky" James,' he reminisces. 'We used to go out on the lash, come back to his mum's in Gallowhill, and Lucky would bugger me senseless. Great times.' Such material was now acceptable in a mainstream sitcom.

---

* When Kenny Ireland, the actor who played Donald, died in 2014, tributes included one from Alex Salmond, the first minister of Scotland.

In truth, it wasn't vocabulary or subject matter that kept Brown off television, it was fear that he meant what he said. As Ricky Gervais, another often controversial comic, explained, 'You tell a sick joke with the express understanding that neither party is really like that.' It was doubted that Brown and his audience had that understanding, and the reason for the doubt was class. 'Roy Chubby Brown is the most significant English male comedian of the past quarter-century,'[22] wrote the academic Andy Medhurst in his study of comedy and English identity, *A National Joke* (2007); 'he is a living, breathing, swearing, shocking (to some) reminder that class matters.'[23] More specifically, Brown's problem was one of education. He hadn't been to university, and neither had his audience, so it was suspected that he and they were not properly schooled in modern manners.

Here was the great division in British comedy and, perhaps, in society more generally, a line drawn in the sand by tertiary education. From John Major onward, governments pursued a policy of increasing the number of students, and the gulf in society between those who had been to university and those who had not was becoming ever more apparent.

That gulf was cultural more than economic or even academic. In addition to their educational role, universities passed on orthodox values of liberal decency. In the context of comedy, a degree certificate was a licence to laugh at taboos, because it proved you knew why those taboos were important and could be trusted to place an ironic fig leaf over the offending areas. The subject of the degree mattered less than the fact it existed. Derren Litten, who created and wrote *Benidorm*, had studied acting for three years at the Central School of Speech and Drama, while stand-up Johnny Vegas – who starred in the show, and who looked and sounded as if he came from the old tradition of working-men's clubs – had taken ceramics at Middlesex University. As the *Sunday Times* put it, Frankie Boyle was 'a kind of Roy Chubby Brown for people who've been through further education'.[24]

There was a potential danger here, of course. If taboo-breaking comedians did have a cathartic role, acting as a pressure valve to release feelings we knew we shouldn't have and wanted to vent safely, what were the consequences of denying this to half the country? Brown's absence from television, combined with the council bans, made it look to his fans rather as though they themselves had been deemed unacceptable, too ill educated to be allowed access to their own culture. The fact that it was the same councils that had been responsible for their education merely added injury to insult.

II

'If you were planning a country from scratch,' observed the *Rough Guide to Britain* in 2006, 'you would never force England, Scotland and Wales together into a single United Kingdom.'[25] And the splits were not simply at the historical borders; there was also a growing separation, said the *Guide*, between, on the one hand, 'overweight, football-mad, beer-swilling, sex- and celebrity-obsessed TV addicts', and on the other, 'animal-loving, tea-drinking charity donors thriving on irony and Radio 4'.[26]

The divisions were more numerous than that, of course, and growing. Britain was rediscovering its multicultural nature. Historically, the country had long accepted the reality of cultural diversity, most obviously on geographical and class lines; you could see it in the social weight accorded to accents and vocabulary, or in the way that bear-baiting and cockfighting had been suppressed in 1835, but fox hunting and hare coursing were legal until 2004. But over the second half of the twentieth century, this plurality had been in decline, cultural differences flattening out. The post-war generation that came out of the grammar schools and art schools had changed the feel of the country; upward social mobility was met with a fashionable embrace of what was seen as working-class authenticity, and there had emerged, from the 1960s through to the 90s, a largely shared culture across classes in a way that not been the case since the Industrial Revolution.

It was a popular, middlebrow kind of culture, looking more to America than Europe, and it centred on television. The duopoly of BBC and ITV – with the minor additions of BBC Two in 1964 and Channel 4 in 1982 – ensured that the vast majority of the population, for whom television had become part of their everyday routine, consumed much the same programming. As the century closed, however, the market was becoming far more competitive, with all the big players in decline. In 1990, BBC One and ITV had 82 per cent of the audience share between them;[27] by 1999[28] that had fallen to 59 per cent.* The British were taking to the new digital, multi-channel world with more enthusiasm than the industry had expected.

Soon after, there came further technology that changed viewing habits. The digital recording innovations of TiVo arrived in Britain in 2000, the same year that the internet service provider Freeserve ran trials of high-speed broadband, promising to replace the dial-up modem and to allow video content to be streamed satisfactorily. Internet television duly materialised, with 4 On Demand launched in 2006, followed by BBC iPlayer and ITV Catch Up. In the past, the audience had been united in time, if not space; now even that was disappearing as people began to shake free of the schedules.

The fragmentation of the television audience suggested that perhaps the country wasn't as culturally cohesive as it had appeared, that although there had been what one might call a pooling of cultural sovereignty, divisions remained. The new

---

* In 1999 ITV was the most watched channel with 31 per cent of the audience, followed by BBC One (28 per cent), BBC Two (10), Channel 4 (10) and Channel 5 (5), the balance made up by the new satellite and cable broadcasters.

diversity in broadcasting was partly a consequence of a people asserting separate identities, but partly too it helped shape that development, with the material that it produced, the stories it chose to tell.

One of the ways that existing broadcasters dealt with the desire for new channels was to create their own niche stations. The most striking in those early days was E4, a subsidiary of Channel 4 aimed at the youth market, which launched in 2001. It began with American imports, but became better known for commissioning its own teen series, the likes of *Skins* (2007), *The Inbetweeners* (2008) and *Misfits* (2009).

These shows broke new ground in their casual depiction of sex, drugs and alcohol in a generation seeking short-term fixes. 'We're playing it right on the edge,' said Bryan Elsley, co-creator of *Skins*. 'It's funny, moving and offers no solution. It doesn't attempt to deal with issues.'[29] There were issues, though, plenty of them, in this drama about Bristolian sixth-formers, written by 'the youngest team in British drama history'.[30] There's Anwar, struggling to deal with the conflicts between his Islamic heritage and secular society; he's happy to break the prohibition on drinking, but homosexuality is a step too far. 'I'm just a Muslim,' he says. 'Gay's just wrong.' Happily, his best friend, Maxxie, is gay, and an acceptance of difference is reached. There's Cassie, who speaks about anorexia in a way seldom seen in the media: 'I stopped eating and then everyone had to do what I said. That was powerful. I think it was the happiest time of my life. But I had to stop before I died, because otherwise it wasn't fun.' And there's Sid, a bespectacled virgin who masturbates to *Asian Fanny Fun* magazine.

Pornography also loomed large in *The Inbetweeners*, a sitcom about four schoolboys at a suburban comprehensive. 'I don't think I've ever been on the internet and not ended up having a wank,' reflects Neil, while Jay, the immature braggart of the group, is sufficiently well versed in porn terminology to give Roy Chubby

Brown a run for his money, talking about girls in terms of crack, snatch and gash, fanny, pussy, clunge, minge and axe-wound. It's not just the children; their parents are seen as equally sex-obsessed. When Simon's father moves into a hotel during a marital separation, he asks Simon for the loan of his laptop: 'The movie channels in here are a bit soft, if you get what I mean?' There's a running gag that Neil's father is gay; you can tell because 'he wears tight denim shorts to do the gardening'. When Neil says his dad's a bit short of money, Jay's reflex response is: 'Spent it all on butt plugs, did he?' Elsewhere, Will is horrified to discover that his mother's been trying internet dating: 'Finding out your mum is on Facebook is bad enough, but finding out she's using it to look for cock is beyond the pale.'

Nor do the teachers inspire any respect. 'It's not so much a calling these days as a graveyard for the unlucky and unambitious,' explains Mr Gilbert, whose dislike of his pupils doesn't conceal a kind heart. 'Between you and me, the only reason anyone teaches these days is because they've taken a more relaxed view on police checks in recent years.' This perhaps explains 'Paedo' Kennedy, 'a sexual predator in a waistcoat', according to Will, 'a man who it seemed incredible the school continued to employ'. He has a strange attraction to Neil, because 'Neil is catnip for paedos.'

There's more of the same in *Misfits*, a fantasy show which centred on a group of young offenders caught in an electrical storm that gives them each a superpower, some more conventional than others. Simon can become invisible, but Alisha's 'gift' is that anyone who touches her is overcome by lust; when Simon touches her, he blurts out that he wants to urinate on her breasts, and it seems reasonable to assume that his fantasy life is also porn-driven. But again it's the parents who go the furthest. Nathan's mother explains that she's come to terms with her new partner's wish to identify as a dog: 'If that's who he is, I've got to accept it. Some men dress up in women's clothing.' And Nathan replies, 'Yeah, they're just sick perverts.'

Bryan Elsley was clear that there was a moral core to *Skins*, because teenagers are 'highly moral individuals. They have a very strong sense of what is wrong and what is right.'[31] But there was also a bleak, brittle hedonism to much of this work. 'We are designed to party,' declares Nathan in *Misfits*. 'Yeah, so a few of us will overdose or go mental. But Charles Darwin said you can't make an omelette without breaking a few eggs. And by eggs, I do mean getting twatted on a cocktail of Class As.' He's responding to a quasi-religious cult called Virtue, founded by Rachel, who has acquired powers of irresistible suggestion. 'We're trying to encourage self-respect, responsible behaviour, respect for the law,' she says. 'All this drinking and the drugs and the anti-social behaviour – you don't need to behave like this. You can be so much better.' But Nathan remains unconvinced: 'I'm a screw-up, and I plan to be a screw-up until my late twenties, maybe even my early thirties.' There was not an overabundance of hope on display.

Nor was there in Channel 4's most acclaimed drama of the decade. Writer Paul Abbott was born in Burnley in 1960, the second-youngest of eight children. His mother left home when he was nine, his father when he was eleven. 'I was twelve and a half when I had my first fuck,' he said. 'I didn't know anyone who hadn't by the time they were twelve. We were all shagging like rabbits.'[32] Dissatisfied with the way 'TV usually only engages with sub-working-class culture in cartoons, sketches* or documentaries,'[33] he created *Shameless* (2004), a long-running series set on a desperately grim estate in Manchester.

The sprawling cast of characters drink, take illegal drugs and enjoy promiscuous, and sometimes violent, sex: 'I want you to bite me! Treat me rough! I want you to spit on me!' They steal from shops, businesses and each other, they cheat the benefits

---

* These sketches included most famously the characters Vicky Pollard on *Little Britain* (2000) and Lauren Cooper in *The Catherine Tate Show* (2004), with their respective catchphrases 'Yeah, but no, but' and 'Am I bovvered?'

system, and they expect to be provided for by the state; the card game pontoon is known locally as maisonette 'cos when you turn twenty-one, that's what you get off the council'. A soldier who's served in Iraq comments that Basra 'is a right dump. Mind you, it's not as bad as round here.' There is poverty and, more than that, poverty of spirit. The *Independent on Sunday* called it an 'unflinching depiction of a family of the Tories' worst nightmares: northern benefit scroungers, thieves and pissheads'.[34]

At the centre of it all is the compelling figure of Frank Gallagher. Father of at least nine children (the mother of the first six left him for another woman), he seldom drives the action but serves as a chorus figure, commenting from inside the chaos. He's a self-obsessed, self-pitying, alcoholic bully, who's acquired a handful of random, isolated bits of knowledge on his stumble through life, and sees himself as a working-class sage. There is racism on the estate, but he'll have no part of immigrant-blaming. 'If they all went on strike, we'd be legless,' he says. 'Shops, hospitals, the entire fucking transport system. If every immigrant on this sceptred isle downed tools for one day – one day – we'd come to a total fucking standstill.' And he remains committed to democratic socialism: 'People forget that it took centuries, but the working man's vote is the most powerful weapon you'll ever possess. Lest we forget.' The irony, of course, is that he almost certainly would forget, or else be too drunk to get to the polling station. And anyway he is very definitely not a working man; he's unemployed, unemployable, surplus to society's requirements.*

'It's not blue collar,' said Abbott in 2011, as an American adaptation got under way; 'it's no collar.'[35] And it brought to the screen a part of British life many preferred to ignore. Early

---

* In a BBC documentary *The Class System and Me* (2008), John Prescott encountered a young woman on a London council estate who described herself as: 'Middle class. I ain't got loads of money, I'm not poor.' When he suggested she was actually working class, she retorted, 'But I don't work.'

series were filmed in West Gorton, Manchester, one of the most deprived areas in the country; it had more anti-social behaviour orders issued than anywhere else, and houses were said in 2005 to be on sale for as little as £8,000.* Viraj Patel, a local shopkeeper, testified to the show's accuracy: '*Shameless* shows real life here and in other parts of Britain. It isn't far-fetched at all.'[36]

The real-life equivalents of the characters in *Shameless* were seldom seen on mainstream television, save in the daytime forum of ITV's *The Jeremy Kyle Show* (2005), a *Kilroy* for the underclass. Here melodramas of sex, crime and addiction were played out, parading people's misery before a censorious host who was armed with the results of DNA tests and lie detectors. Topics discussed might include 'I'm sleeping with my stepdaughter but is her baby mine?' or 'Where was my boyfriend when he said he was behind the chicken shop?' or 'I'm a binge drinker and a drug dealer ... but I'll be a great dad.'

It was a 'human form of bear-baiting', said a judge in Manchester hearing a case that arose from the show,[37] or, according to television critic Victor Lewis-Smith, 'the latter-day equivalent of those seventeenth-century people who used to visit Bedlam to be entertained by the mad antics of the inmates'.[38] But the participants were neither animals nor lunatics; they were consenting adults, probably with enough experience of television formats to understand what they were doing. And was the ritual humiliation here any worse than the way members of the public were treated by Anne Robinson on *The Weakest Link*, or by Simon Cowell on *The X Factor*? Or even how the public themselves, egged on by the media, collectively bullied participants in reality TV shows? The fact that people chose to go on *The Jeremy Kyle Show* might have been regrettable, but there was no shortage of guests over its

---

* House prices in the north-west were lower than they were nationally, but still averaged £168,000 at the time. (*Guardian* 4 December 2005)

fourteen-year run; it was the one place they could tell their own stories.*

More to the taste of prime-time schedulers was the bling-glam world of *The Only Way Is Essex* (2010), a structured-reality show featuring young people obsessed with manicures, pedicures and cosmetics, designer clothes, big hair, fake tans and – for the women – fake breasts. It made stars of the likes of Joey Essex ('I still don't really know what GCSE stands for'[39]) and Amy Childs, a beautician who popularised the vajazzle and rejected the diction-ary definition of an Essex girl. ('Who done the dictionary though? Is he from Essex?'[40]) Appearances could be deceptive, however: Childs had been privately educated, as had other *TOWIE* cast members including Gemma Collins and Megan McKenna.†

Television in the new century was attracted to the extremes and, at the other end of the spectrum from *The Jeremy Kyle Show*, that meant that people deemed a bit too posh in recent years now found a warmer welcome. One of those who marked the changing of the times was Hugh Fearnley-Whittingstall, a journalist edu-cated at Eton and Oxford, who became an unlikely TV chef. His first series was *A Cook on the Wild Side* (1995), but he really made his name with a succession of shows set in a gamekeeper's lodge in Dorset, from where – starting with *Escape to River Cottage* (1999) – he regularly served what one reviewer called 'a cocktail of bucolic idyll shaken up with a splash of cold realism, managing to have a quiet giggle at the expense of escapist urges at the same time as pandering to them'.[41]

Unlike previous cookery shows, this was pure spectator sport. There was no pretence that the viewers would ever test his

---

* A 2008 survey of viewers saw Kyle's show voted the worst daytime programme ever. In second place was the BBC's *The Daily Politics* with Andrew Neil. (*Daily Star* 9 January 2008)
† This was even more apparent in a rival structured-reality series *Made in Chelsea* (2011), with the likes of Ollie Locke and Georgia 'Toff' Toffolo.

assertion that 'squirrel's back legs are delicious roasted'[42] or follow his recipes for crispy pigs' ears, calf's testicles or fried rook-breast. It was presented as entertainment, and the appeal was that of an unkempt free spirit romping through the countryside. Above all, he insisted, he wasn't a professional: 'I'm just having a laugh and making a living.'[43]

A variation on the same theme came with Nigella Lawson, daughter of Margaret Thatcher's chancellor, Nigel. After private school and Oxford, she had initially been employed by the *Spectator*, a magazine edited at varying points by her father and her brother, before going on to write columns in various other organs. She became sufficiently known that in 1995 she joined the newly launched Talk Radio as a presenter. It didn't work out. Those were still the days of new lads, mockneys and Pulp's 'Common People'; Tony Blair was affecting an Estuary accent, and poshness was out of fashion. So when, just a couple of weeks into her career, Lawson mentioned on air that she had her baby's nappies delivered (the internet had yet to make the idea of home deliveries commonplace), she was deemed to be 'out of touch with ordinary people', and was sacked by the shock-jock station. 'Wow!' exclaimed columnist Lowri Turner in the *Sunday Mirror*. 'Does Nigella also employ a cook, a chauffeur and someone to test for any stray peas lurking under her mattress?'[44]

The answer to the first of those questions was soon to be answered. Lawson clearly had no need to employ a cook, for in 1999 she published *How to Eat*, and the following year was launched as a TV chef. Filmed in her own far-from-modest marble-clad kitchen and gracious dining room, and promising 'minimum effort for maximum pleasure', *Nigella Bites* (2000) made her a star. Despite the title, she didn't actually bite. Instead, she oozed and schmoozed and enthused. Reviewers strove to capture the appeal. 'Voluptuous Nigella' was 'a little bit shy, a little bit breathless'; she was 'a very mucky pup' who was to be found 'pouting – oh cruel and terrible beauty – into the camera'.[45] She was also seen as something of a throwback to more glamorous times. 'With her pale skin, extravagant pre-Raphaelite hairdo and finishing-school accent,' wrote Roland White in the *Sunday Times*, 'she looks like she should be stepping out of a Sunbeam Alpine somewhere on the French Riviera while Roger Moore holds the door open.'[46] In the *Observer*, Martin Bright talked of her 'giggling like a naughty schoolgirl' and offered a different cultural reference from the 1960s: 'she throws in little flirty glances and double-entendres like an extra from *Carry On Up the Aga*'.[47]

It seemed as though the class trappings that had been a handicap on Talk Radio were now an asset. And in the same year that *Nigella Bites* debuted, a BBC reality TV show, *Castaway 2000*, brought Ben Fogle to public attention. He had earlier been turned down as a children's television presenter, supposedly because 'his accent was too posh',[48] but he was now acceptable. A corner had been turned.

There was, it seemed, a place for the posh presenter on television in the new century, as long as they conformed to off-the-peg fantasy-figure stereotypes: Fearnley-Whittingstall as the eager eccentric; Fogle as the action adventurer; Lawson as 'the popular, all grown-up head girl who everyone had a crush on'.[49] There was also the boisterous prankster, Jeremy Clarkson, who fronted the relaunch of motoring show *Top Gear* (2002); the hockey captain, Clare Balding, who left the racetrack to host *Olympic Grandstand* (2000); the swot, Stephen Fry, now best known for his 'brainy banter'[50] as presenter of *QI* (2003); and the class clown, journalist Boris Johnson, who was elected Tory MP for Henley in 2001 and hosted the panel show *Have I Got News for You* for the first time the following year.* Later there would be cheeky schoolgirls Mel

---

* 'It galls me,' regretted John O'Farrell, former writer on *HIGNFY*, 'that a satire show on which I worked for five years could have played a crucial part in launching the career of such a deeply destructive politician.' (*Things Can Only Get Worse?* p. 77) Team captain Ian Hislop was also apologetic: 'There

Giedroyc and Sue Perkins being indulged by housemistress Mary Berry on *The Great British Bake Off*, the biggest television show of 2014–16.

All were unmistakably upper-middle class, all were privately educated, and all shared a certain lightness of being, giving the impression that they rather enjoyed life. In the age-old English division of cavalier and puritan, they were cavaliers. They were amateurs – gifted amateurs, but amateurs nonetheless – enthusiasts rather than experts, and they proved enormously appealing to a large slice of the public. Middle England – the realm of Classic FM, the National Trust and the *Mail on Sunday* – was alive and well, and it liked its fantasies of peculiar toffs and posh totty. It especially liked those who, rather than nag their audience, gave permission for fun and frivolity.

If there was a class counterpoint to Fearnley-Whittinstall and Lawson, the upper-crust cooks of Channel 4, it could be found in the form of Essex-born Jamie Oliver, whose BBC series *The Naked Chef* (1999) established his chirpy, laddish persona. In 2005 he launched a crusade with *Jamie's School Dinners*, trying to improve the meals cooked in a school kitchen, as he introduced broccoli and fish onto menus previously dominated by fried, processed foods; these latter were symbolised by the Turkey Twizzler, a meat product manufactured by Bernard Matthews.

Accompanied by a wider campaign, Oliver did succeed in securing new government guidelines for school dinners, and his initiative found justification in an Essex University study that showed his healthier diet improved academic performance and

---

is a sense of guilt that part of his success is built on his performances on our show.' (*Daily Star* 25 March 2013) This seems unnecessarily self-flagellating. Other print journalists, who would not have been immediately familiar to a mass audience, appeared on the show before Johnson did: Robert Harris, Michael White, John Diamond. It was just that he was better on TV than they were.

reduced truancy. A further victory came with the withdrawal from sale of the now disgraced Twizzler. But the series was most notable for the protests it generated. The image that lasted was of parents pushing fast-food takeaways through playground railings, providing sustenance for children deprived of their traditional fare. Here was working-class resentment at the do-gooding endeavours of the governing elite. Because, despite all his blokey mannerisms, Oliver was now perceived to be a member of that elite, one of those busybodies who nagged about diet and smoking. Co-opted by the puritans, he wasn't fun any more.*

In 1937, the future Labour minister Douglas Jay had written that 'in the case of nutrition and health, just as in the case of education, the gentleman in Whitehall really does know better what is good for people than the people know themselves'. For some, Oliver was seen as the modern embodiment of that sentiment. He was mocked by comedians Harry Enfield and Paul Whitehouse, whose characters Jamie and Oliver were two oversized teenagers, unable to pass a fast food outlet without filling their faces, staggering from Fatso Burger to Shitty Fried Chicken, and sustaining themselves in between with sacks of potato crisps and two-litre bottles of fizzy drink.†

The rise of the posh presenter exemplified one of the more remarkable phenomena of the time: the growing cultural power of independent schools. In *The Old Boys* (2015), David Turner's history of the more venerable institutions, he concluded that 'academically, scientifically, economically and pastorally' the sector had never been healthier: 'if there is a golden age of the public

---

* 'I say let people eat what they like,' Boris Johnson told the Tory conference. 'Why shouldn't they push pies through the railings?' (*Financial Times* 4 October 2006)

† In *Shameless*, on the other hand, Frank Gallagher's twins were called Nigel and Delia, after the TV chefs Slater and Smith.

schools, it is now.'[51] The growth in the numbers of pupils from overseas meant that the international reach of British schooling was as wide as it had been in the days of empire, but it was at home that the influence was greatest.

Only around 7 per cent of the population went to fee-paying schools, but a series of studies by educational charity the Sutton Trust showed how strong their presence still was in the establishment, disproportionately represented at the top of the civil service, the army, the legal, journalistic, scientific and medical professions. There was no great surprise here, but perhaps there was in the way that popular culture was similarly dominated: it was variously reported, for example, that 42 per cent of British BAFTA winners and 19 per cent of Brit Award winners had been to fee-paying schools.[52] Among the latter were Lily Allen (Bedales), James Blunt (Harrow), Dido (Westminster), Laura Marling (Leighton Park), Chris Martin (Sherborne), Marcus Mumford (KCS Wimbledon), Florence Welch (Alleyn's) and Will Young (Wellington).*

Some of the leading crime and thriller writers dominating the bestseller lists were likewise privately educated: Lee Child (King Edward's), Nicci Gerrard, half of Nicci French (Alice Otley), Paula Hawkins (Collingham), Peter James (Charterhouse). So too were several of the comedians we've already encountered: Harry Enfield (Richard Collyer), Matt Lucas (Haberdashers'), Michael McIntyre (Merchant Taylors'), Al Murray (Bedford), David Walliams (Reigate Grammar).† When Eddie Redmayne and Benedict Cumberbatch were in competition for the Best Actor Oscar in 2014, it was billed as a battle between Eton and Harrow, and it

---

* Radiohead, whose members met at Abingdon School, were nominated fourteen times for a Brit Award between 1994 and 2004 without ever winning.
† 'My accent may sound rather unfamiliar, possibly even rather exotic, to some of your ears,' teased Simon Evans, the best stand-up of the time. 'If you are struggling to place it, it is in fact: educated.' His clipped delivery sounded posh enough, but he'd come out of state schools.

felt like a return to the days when Old Harrovian actor Simon Williams could jokingly comment, 'Character acting for me is playing an Old Etonian.'[53]

Over a third of British medallists at the 2012 Olympics had been to independent schools, and, as ex-cricketer Ed Smith pointed out, the England XI in the summer of 2011 featured eight public schoolboys, compared with just one back in the winter of 1987.[54] (This was probably a symptom of the decline of sporting opportunity within the state system, rather than a tribute to the independent sector.) Of the major sports, only boxing and football remained almost exclusively working-class – world super-middleweight champion Chris Eubank Jr (Shoreham) and footballer Frank Lampard (Brentwood), captain of Chelsea and England, were rare exceptions.

The version of private education depicted in fiction, however, gave little indication of engaging with the modern world. 'Peregrine Manor School is very old, very expensive and only accepts very high-profile offspring,' explains DS Sandra Pullman at the start of a 2012 episode of *New Tricks*, and we suspect immediately that there are skeletons as well as corpses to be found in these closets. 'This school was founded to provide an education for English boys and girls,' declares the head, Elizabeth Clayton, and retired detective Brian Lane clarifies her point: 'You mean *white* English boys and girls? Your ancestor, Edwin Clayton, he was against the abolition of slavery, wasn't he? And your grandfather, Arthur Clayton, was one of Oswald Moseley's most fervent supporters.' He concludes: 'I haven't seen a single Asian or black pupil in this place. Not one.' As it turns out, she's not just racist, but also a blackmailer, bleeding an MP to supplement the declining income from school fees.

It was relevant perhaps that the episode in question, 'Old School Ties', was written and directed by Julian Simpson, who had been educated at Felsted School. Most such critiques of public schools were by those who'd been there. In literature, the most extreme account of bullying was in *Engleby* (2007) by Sebastian Faulks (Wellington). The play *South Downs* (2011) by David Hare (Lancing) depicted, in the words of critic Michael Billington, 'the pain, loneliness and insecurity that seem inseparable from an English public-school education'.[55] And *Gentlemen & Players* (2005) and *Different Class* (2016), two thrillers by Joanne Harris (Wakefield Girls), were savage in their depiction of class prejudice and stunted emotions at the fictional St Oswald's Grammar. Similarly, Andrew Marr (Loretto) reflected in his novel *Children of the Master* (2015) on the school attended by one future Labour MP, as compared with the world of another: 'Emotional survival in this pleasant – so, so pleasant – place, with its choir which did Purcell, and its glossy, neatly lettered rolls of honour, was harder than in the drab council estates of Ayrshire.'[56]

Against the negative visions of these old boys and girls, the one outstanding addition to the canon of public-school literature came from the state-educated J. K. Rowling, creator of the Hogwarts School of Witchcraft and Wizardry. Not everyone was impressed with the institution. In a much-reported assault on the Harry Potter saga in 2000, writer Anthony Holden (Oundle) lamented that Hogwarts was not a comprehensive, 'a school of the kind with which most of those millions of young readers can identify'.[57] Clearly he was wrong, since the success of the books showed that readers *did* identify. But then the popularity of the genre had never been about class, but about escape from parental control. The securely structured but child-dominated world of the boarding school still had the same fantasy allure as had Tom Brown's Rugby and Billy Bunter's Greyfriars in earlier generations. Perhaps more so in a world of family break-up and domestic instability. The Harry Potter books and films – with all their time-hallowed paraphernalia of dormitories, boarding houses and games fields, and their depiction of what one real-life headmaster called a 'sense of community, activity and excitement'[58] – helped make independent schools acceptable again.

More broadly, there was a shift happening, driven largely by the rise of the internet. Cultural expression was growing at an extraordinary rate because the means of production and distribution were becoming so available, and in the process it was splintering into a myriad of directions. There was not the cohesion of old. Popular culture had been the glue that bound the country together as it navigated its post-imperial decline. Now it was losing its stickiness. So in pop music, for example, the Spice Girls, who disbanded in 2001, might have been the last group that really mattered, that meant something beyond record sales and outside their own constituency. And because there were now so many alternatives, so much material available online for free, the financial rewards were not what they were. It helped if one had the security of family support, hence all those privately educated pop stars and comedians. The return of poshness, of the old order, was a function of cultural fragmentation.

Politics was slower to change than culture. In Westminster, being openly posh was at odds with the principle of meritocracy to which lip service had long been paid, and there was a reluctance to flaunt one's privileged background. Tony Blair (Fettes), the first public-school prime minister in over three decades, tended not to refer to his education, knowing it was a potentially sensitive point. Certainly it provided Michael Howard with his best line in the House of Commons. In 2003, as the two party leaders argued over the tripling of university tuition fees, Howard declared, 'This grammar school boy will take no lessons from that public school boy on access to higher education.'[59] It was a jibe that hit home and disarmed the prime minister. Come the general election, however, the public-school boy still won. And the Tories responded by choosing as Howard's successor an unashamedly posh leader.

5

Cameron and Blair

I

On 2 August 2003 Tony Blair broke Clement Attlee's record to become the longest continuously serving Labour prime minister. Now, two further milestones were visible on the horizon: his tenth anniversary in Downing Street would fall in May 2007, and beyond that lay Margaret Thatcher's modern-day record for longevity, which he would reach in November 2008. The only serious obstacle in his way was the increasingly restless ambition of Gordon Brown.

There was, admittedly, also the question of a general election, but that was not expected to be a major impediment. The

Conservative MPs had replaced Iain Duncan Smith with Michael Howard not in the hope of winning, but simply to avoid annihilation. Nonetheless, Howard himself was optimistic, pinning his hopes on a new campaign director, Lynton Crosby, a much vaunted political strategist from Australia.* Crosby introduced the phrase 'dog-whistle politics' to Britain: messages that wouldn't provoke undue alarm, but whose underlying meaning would be heard by the lost voters at whom they were aimed. 'Are you thinking what we're thinking?' was the main slogan for the 2005 campaign, suggesting that the Tories understood what people wanted to say if only they were permitted. 'It's not racist to impose limits on immigration,' ran one poster, sending a signal that was, wrote Jonathan Freedland in the *Guardian*, aimed at 'all those people who have opinions that begin "I'm not racist, but ..."'[1] It was 'the most shameful, racist campaign I can remember by a major party', fumed John O'Farrell, 'designed primarily to whip up fear and divide communities'.[2]

On the other hand, the Labour Party was also accused of dog-whistling. Earlier in 2005 there had been a poster with the faces of Howard and his shadow chancellor Oliver Letwin – both of whom were Jews – superimposed on flying pigs, and another with Howard looming out of a dark background, swinging a pocket watch to hypnotise the public; 'a Shylock-style pose', according to the *Daily Mirror*, though some saw it as more akin to Fagin.[3] 'The last British politician to exploit anti-Semitism was Oswald Mosley,' thundered former *The Times* editor William Rees-Mogg; 'is it now Tony Blair?'[4] Even Lynton Crosby professed himself shocked: 'That Fagin poster was racist. I hadn't encountered that

---

* In Duncan Smith's last weeks as leader, Crosby had given a briefing session to the shadow cabinet, trying to persuade them that if John Howard could become prime minister in Australia, then Duncan Smith could be here: 'Howard is dull as batshit so your man can do it too.' (*Australian* 16 February 2004)

kind of anti-Semitism before.'[5] These things did have an impact, as a Tory canvasser in Richmond, Surrey, discovered that year. 'I don't like Blair,' a Labour voter declared. 'But if you think I am going to vote for a fucking Welsh Jew-boy like Michael Howard, you must be fucking joking.'[6]

There were other slogans in the 'Are you thinking' vein: 'What's wrong with a little discipline in schools?' 'I mean, how hard is it to keep a hospital clean?' 'How would you feel if a bloke on early release attacked your daughter?' 'Put more police on the streets and they'll catch more criminals. It's not rocket science, is it?' All were intended to convey a tough, common-sense approach to politics, even at the risk of reviving the 'nasty party' tag.

It shored up the core support, but seemingly failed to win new converts.* At the election the Tories increased their vote share by less than one point and, although they gained 32 seats, still had fewer than 200 MPs, compared with 355 on the Labour benches. Tony Blair had won a third successive general election, the only Labour leader ever to do so, and if his majority of 66 was lower than the previous two victories (179 and 167), it was still impressive; only Clement Attlee in 1945 and Harold Wilson in 1966 had done better in Labour's history.

Beneath the headlines, though, the signs were not good. The Don't Knows won again; Labour shed another million votes from its already poor performance in 2001, and barely one in five of the registered electorate voted for the government. Meanwhile, the party was looking like a husk of its former self: membership had halved since 1997 and was now not much more than 200,000. The invasion of Iraq had damaged Blair, probably irreparably. 'If you believe that I stood up there and told a whole lot of lies then that is the reason for not voting for me,' said Blair,[7] and many followed his advice; there was a peeling off to the Liberal Democrats, who had the best post-war result for a third party. 'There is a very

---

* 'Are you sinking like we're sinking?' offered comedian Linda Smith.

real danger,' said the former cabinet minister Mo Mowlam,* 'that Tony Blair could do to Labour what Margaret Thatcher did to the Tories: split the party for a generation.'[8]

The most striking feature of the 2005 election was that the Conservatives outpolled Labour in England. Labour's success, let alone its big majority, was dependent on an electoral map that gave it a slight advantage, and on its support in Scotland, where it took 41 of the 59 seats. In the event that the SNP made progress, Labour would struggle to win a national election.

There was, therefore, something positive for the Tories to take from the Howard interregnum: they had a solid, if narrow, base upon which to build. As to who would supervise construction, there seemed little doubt. Four weeks on from the election, the psephologist Anthony King announced, 'The contest for the Tory Party leadership is now all but over.' He was reacting to a YouGov poll of Conservative members that showed overwhelming support for David Davis.[9]

Davis was then 56 years old and, for a Conservative MP, had an unusual backstory that he was not shy of sharing. Born to an unmarried mother – who was herself the daughter of a communist hunger marcher – he grew up on a council estate in south London and went on to get a science degree while also serving with the SAS in the Territorial Army. In Parliament since 1987, he had managed to alienate many on his own side. Some of his colleagues complained that he was 'lazy, divisive and arrogant'.[10] One said he was 'a tough guy who hasn't achieved anything and doesn't even read books';[11] another that he was 'a thug, a bully and a careerist'; while yet another explained that he was disliked 'because he's such a rude fucker'.[12] When the recently promoted shadow home

---

* The most popular minister of the first New Labour term, Mowlam had left the Commons in 2001 and opposed the Iraq war. She died in August 2005, just two weeks after Robin Cook suffered a fatal heart attack.

secretary David Cameron emerged as the stop-Davis candidate, he won the backing of four successive Tory leaders – John Major, William Hague, Iain Duncan Smith and Michael Howard* – who were all said to think Davis was 'devious' and 'untrustworthy'.[13]

At the 2005 conference, the would-be candidates were invited to make a speech, and Cameron launched himself with an outburst of optimism. 'Our best days lie ahead,' he urged. 'There is a new generation of businessmen and -women. We can lead that new generation. We can *be* that new generation.' He called for a caring internationalism ('for the people of Darfur and sub-Saharan Africa who are getting poorer while we are getting richer'), and he ended in a way that the younger Tony Blair would have recognised: 'I want to inspire a new generation with Conservative dreams.'

The content was limited but the style was impeccable: he looked assured and agreeable as he roamed the stage, speaking without a script. His best moment came at Labour's expense. At their conference the previous week, an 82-year-old peace campaigner had been ejected from the hall after he called out 'Nonsense!' during Jack Straw's speech, and had then been detained by the police under the Prevention of Terrorism Act.† 'If at any stage you want to shout "Nonsense!" then go ahead, because we believe in free speech,' joked Cameron. 'But I'd be grateful if you wouldn't shout "Nonsense!" all the way through.'[14] He exuded self-confidence.

The audience in the hall loved it, political commentators were impressed. With Davis delivering 'the worst speech of his

---

* Of the other previous leaders, both Margaret Thatcher and Edward Heath had withdrawn from public life. Heath died in July 2005, and that December Carol Thatcher revealed that her mother had dementia.

† Tony Benn reported a story of a delegate to the 2004 Labour Party conference being refused admission because he was wearing a T-shirt with the slogan 'I believe in peace'. He was apparently told that 'there were no political statements allowed in the conference'. (Benn, *More Time for Politics* p. 204)

life' (in the words of Ken Clarke),[15] Cameron's odds halved over-
night, making him the new favourite; a new YouGov poll of
party members, a fortnight later, showed him on 59 per cent. The
other candidates – Clarke (again) and Liam Fox – were knocked
out of the contest by the MPs, leaving the membership with a
choice between the veteran bruiser Davis and the young charmer
Cameron. And on 6 December 2005 the result was announced,
with Cameron winning by a margin of two to one. Unlike the previous occasion, the system had this time produced a leader who
played to the electorate, not merely to the activists. The removal
of Iain Duncan Smith had signalled a new seriousness among
MPs, and now, after three defeats in a row, it seemed as though
the members too had decided that enough was enough.

Asked to define his vision of conservatism, Cameron offered
'the idea that we are all in it together, that we are one country,
one nation'.[16] Inclusivity was his pitch, along with a bright-eyed
optimism: 'Let sunshine win the day!' he exclaimed in his first
conference speech as leader.[17] He was in favour of the environment, and to prove it he had a windmill fitted to the roof of his
house (it didn't work) and cycled to work (followed by an official
car, carrying his papers). A climate-change photo opportunity
was staged in the Arctic; he said we should listen to the concerns
of anti-social youth ('Hug a hoodie,' as the *News of the World*
paraphrased it[18]); and he talked about our responsibilities to each
other: we needed a big society, not a big state.

He was a new kind of post-Thatcher Conservative: modern,
metropolitan, pragmatic. 'I'm not a deeply ideological person,' he
said; 'I'm a practical one.'[19] In so far as he had a political philosophy, it was much the same as that of Tony Blair: the ideological
battles of the twentieth century were over ('We had won') and the
task now was to use 'Conservative means to achieve progressive
ends'.[20] Above all, he was relaxed, perhaps because, having been
Norman Lamont's special adviser on Black Wednesday in 1992,

he felt he'd already been through the worst of storms. 'He seems unflappable and comfortable in his own skin,' admired Michael Portillo,[21] now cast as the John the Baptist of Tory modernisation. In short, Cameron was – and was intended to be – the Conservative Party's answer to Tony Blair, a newer, less tainted version.* And in his first outing at prime minister's questions, he taunted Blair as last year's model: 'He was the future once.'[22]

Cameron was also in touch with the cultural times. His wife, Samantha – photogenically pregnant with their third child at the time of the leadership contest – may have been a direct descendant of Nell Gwynn and the daughter of an eighth baronet, but she'd been a 'hippie-like art student' in Bristol,[23] where she'd hung out with the cool crowd and been taught how to play pool by trip-hop star Tricky, while jewellery designer Jade Jagger was a guest at their wedding. Dave (as he liked to be known) wore chinos and Converse sneakers, and proclaimed his love of the music of the Smiths and the Boomtown Rats, the comedy of Billy Connolly and the recipes of Hugh Fearnley-Whittingstall. (Though he also endorsed Jamie Oliver: 'A great man. I have all his cook books.'[24])

Pursuing cultural credibility, he became the first politician to appear on the BBC One chat show *Friday Night with Jonathan Ross*, though the encounter was perhaps a little more laddish than he might have wished. 'Did you, or did you not, ever have a wank thinking of Thatcher?' asked Ross; while Cameron floundered, the host added his own personal testimony: 'I tried, but it was a challenge even for me.' It was tacky and distasteful, but not much more so than the BBC's more heavyweight interviewers. 'David Cameron, do you know what a pink pussy is?' was Jeremy Paxman's opening question on BBC Two's *Newsnight*. 'Do you know what a slippery nipple is?'[25] (They were cocktails, and the tenuous justification for mentioning them was that they were available

---

* Impressionist Rory Bremner said of Cameron, 'The man does a better Blair than me.' (*Daily Telegraph* 8 December 2005)

cheaply in a bar owned by a company of which Cameron was formerly a non-executive director.)*

Cameron's campaign to win hearts and minds was never going to be enough in itself to reverse the anti-Tory sentiments that dominated the fashionable end of culture, and there was still plenty of sniping. 'He's like a songwriter who's eternally ripping off someone else's song and just changing the odd line a little,' said Oasis songwriter Noel Gallagher, seemingly without irony,[26] while Alan Bennett thought he 'could have been a child actor', a profession which he observed was 'ideally suited to tyrants in the making'.[27] *Coronation Street* star William Roache, a long-standing Conservative supporter, felt it was a little early – 'I think David Cameron's one for the future'[28] – but model Paula Hamilton was won over: 'I think he speaks sense.'[29] Others saw a personal appeal. 'He is fanciable and he is the sort of man you want your daughter to marry,' enthused Anne Robinson,[30] and even ex-Labour MP Oona King, who'd just lost her seat to George Galloway, agreed: 'Let's face it, Cameron is good eye candy.'[31] *GQ* magazine named him the ninety-second-sexiest man in Britain.[32] Again there were echoes of the young Blair, confounding the old joke that politics is show business for ugly people.†

The most common line of attack was on Cameron's privileged background, as summed up by himself: 'I have the most corny CV possible. It goes: Eton, Oxford, Conservative Research Department, Treasury, Home Office, Carlton TV and then Conservative

---

* Paxman was beginning to look as bored with his job as Robert Kilroy-Silk had been. Earlier he'd asked Tony Blair about publisher Richard Desmond becoming a Labour donor, given the material that had made Desmond his fortune: '*Horny Housewives, Mega Boobs, Posh Wives, Skinny and Wriggly* – do you know what these magazines are like?' Blair, his face frozen in a grin that shaded into a grimace, managed to blurt out, 'No.' (*Newsnight* 16 May 2002)

† 'Isn't it fantastic to have a leader of our party we can sleep with, with the lights on?' comedian Jo Brand had exclaimed in 1994. 'Tony Blair – isn't he gorgeous?'

MP.'[33] He was the first Tory leader in forty years to have been privately educated and, although this too was merely following Blair's example, it was seen in some quarters as a weak point. 'If Tories think an Old Etonian toff's the answer to their problem, they must be asking the wrong question,' scoffed the *Daily Mirror*'s Kevin Maguire.[34]

But Maguire hadn't noticed the change in cultural attitudes over the last few years. Cameron was undeniably posh, but he never pretended otherwise, any more than did Stephen Fry, Jeremy Clarkson or Boris Johnson. Like them, Cameron didn't adapt his accent. He did present himself as a normal family man – most notably in a video blog called WebCameron – but the shots of him at home showed a kitchen that was nearly as desirable as Nigella Lawson's. He was casual, charming and concerned, flattering us, as a nation, that we had moved so far beyond our old obsessions with class that now even an Old Etonian could dream of one day becoming prime minister.

It was easy to mock, of course. The television satire *Party Animals* (2007) caricatured the new Tories as 'Listening to Kanye West on their iPods, wearing flip-flops, hugging hoodies.' The first fictional portrayal of Cameron himself came the same year in the TV drama *The Trial of Tony Blair*, where he was played by Alexander Armstrong,* cycling to his office with some edgy hip hop on the soundtrack. 'I'm sorry, but the bike has to go,' he tells his staff as soon as the door is closed on the press pack. 'I'm absolutely knackered. Bloody green politics!' Desperate to change out of his Lycra, he has to wait for his jeans and T-shirt (this being the designated outfit for the day) to arrive in the Lexus that's just pulling in round the back.

Even so, the repositioning strategy did work. The aim was, in the terminology of the time, 'to detoxify the Conservative brand'.[35] The 2005 campaign – 'Are you thinking what we're thinking?' – had been

---

* An Old Dunelmian rather than an Old Etonian.

'too right wing and rather mean-spirited', Cameron concluded.[36] That had been the nasty party. So he tried to neutralise Labour's most effective line of attack, that the Tories couldn't be trusted with the health service. 'Tony Blair once explained his priority in three words: education, education, education,' he said in his first conference speech as leader. 'I can do it in three letters: NHS.'[37] He was a genuine advocate for the service, praising in particular its care for his oldest child, Ivan, and he acknowledged progress in a way no Tory had yet done. 'In some ways political correctness is a good thing,' he said. 'I don't want my disabled son to be called a spastic.'[38]

The Tories had changed, and the easiest way to demonstrate that was to talk about inclusivity and diversity. The fact that Cameron was an Old Etonian was no handicap; as the Queen had shown at the Golden Jubilee, these were ideals that even the poshest could endorse. More than that, they were causes that the posh were eager to get behind. Had the Tories chosen a leader from a working-class background in David Davis, there would have been a different emphasis. During the leadership campaign, Davis had written of the need to end multiculturalism, defining it as 'allowing people of different cultures to settle without expecting them to integrate into society'.[39]

That was what Cameron wanted to distance himself from, and to make the point crystal clear, he visited South Africa, where he met Nelson Mandela, now 88 and widely acclaimed as a secular saint. He had led the African National Congress, described by Margaret Thatcher as 'terrorists', and Cameron took the opportunity to renounce that view, apologising for 'the mistakes my party made in the past with respect to relations with the ANC and sanctions on South Africa'. Far from being a terrorist, Mandela was 'one of the greatest men alive'.[40] This was the kind of thing guaranteed to infuriate the keepers of the Thatcherite flame, the likes of Bernard Ingham and Norman Tebbit,* and it duly did just

---

* Lord Tebbit also objected when the party logo was changed from a flaming

that. So too did Cameron's apology for Section 28. As the Blair blueprint showed, there was no harm in being attacked by those in one's own party who the public thought were extreme.

'I've never felt that the left and the right were closer together,' Jonathan Ross said to David Cameron. 'It's kind of hard to tell you guys apart at the moment.' He added, 'I don't think that's necessarily a bad thing'. There was undoubtedly a standardisation of style, attitude and policy in British politics. There was also a downward shift in age. A generation or two back, it had taken someone until their fifties to get to the top of a party, but Cameron was just 39 when he became leader of the opposition. He was two years older than William Hague had been on taking the job, two years younger than Tony Blair in 1994, and the same age as Charles Kennedy on becoming Liberal Democrat leader in 1999. This was very much the modern trend: educated, metropolitan, middle-class young men with a plausible, unstuffy manner and a promise of managerial competence.

The only slight hiccup came with the Lib Dems. Kennedy was one of the few politicians who was actually liked by the public, a friendly, cheerful figure with an easy TV manner and a nickname, Chat Show Charlie, that was meant derisively but actually reflected his popularity. In early 2006, however, it emerged that beneath his image as a convivial tippler with a fondness for Scotch, there lay a far more serious drinking problem. A large section of the parliamentary party effectively staged a coup and removed him from his job, replacing him, in contravention of the prevailing fashion, with Menzies Campbell, who was 65 and could pass for 70. The satirists and cartoonists had a field day; the new leader was regularly depicted on a Zimmer frame or stairlift, or just shuffling along in carpet slippers, often assisted by nurses. Within months,

---

torch to an oak tree, which he said more closely resembled a 'bunch of broccoli'. (Hernon, *The Blair Decade* p. 182)

there was unrest among the MPs and threats of another coup. 'It's very unfair,' complained Campbell. 'It's convenient for commentators who want to drive me out to hit me with the age thing. But that ain't going to happen – I'm going nowhere.'[41]

He was right about it being unfair, but wrong on his prognosis. Nineteen months after becoming leader, he too was forced out. He hadn't even lasted as long as Iain Duncan Smith. 'To watch a decent man being kicked to death is not an edifying spectacle,'[42] reflected Lib Dem MP Vince Cable; 'shafted by a shower of shits', added his colleague Mike Hancock.[43] There was some talk of Kennedy making a comeback, but that didn't happen, and instead the party opted for Nick Clegg. He was a 40-year-old ex-public schoolboy (Westminster), a former bureaucrat with the European Commission and, according to reports, 'seen by many in his party as its answer to David Cameron'.[44] Normal service had been restored, and the Lib Dems had their very own plausible young man again.*

If Tony Blair had had his way, Labour would have followed suit. As the end of his premiership came into sight, he worried that a Gordon Brown succession would betray his vision: 'I just totally disagreed with what I knew he was going to do.'[45] Instead he looked for an alternative in David Miliband, who'd been his chief policy adviser in the days of opposition and through the first term, before being elected as an MP in 2001. Miliband[†] got his first ministerial appointment within sixteen months, and entered the cabinet at the age of 40 as environment secretary in 2006. It was a rapid rise – reflecting the dearth of talent coming through – but could have been even more spectacular; Blair had been tempted

---

* Rory Bremner said Clegg was even more difficult to impersonate than Cameron. 'I imagined meeting him and him asking "Can you do me?" I was going to say "No, can you?"' (*Birmingham Mail* 20 March 2010)
† 'I can't get used to these new metric politicians,' complained comedy writer Andy Hamilton.

to give him the Foreign Office, only deciding against it because, according to Peter Mandelson, 'Gordon would have seen it as a boost for the credentials of a potential leadership challenger.'[46]

Around the same time, Blair appeared on Radio 5 Live's football phone-in 6-0-6 (there was a World Cup to discuss). Tailoring his message to his audience, the prime minister said that Miliband was his very own Wayne Rooney, by which he presumably meant that here was his young superstar, though it wasn't the best comparison: the Manchester United and England striker was then inhabiting an oxygen tent, trying to hurry back from an injury so he could participate in a tournament where he was destined to score no goals and to be sent off in yet another quarter-final defeat.[*]

The problem was that, while no one doubted Miliband's intelligence or ability, there was little evidence of the killer ambition needed to make it to the very top of politics. 'I still can't believe it when I look around the cabinet table that I am there,' he marvelled, even as Westminster buzzed with talk of a possible leadership bid.[47] Indeed, it wasn't entirely clear that he wanted to be in front-line politics at all. He'd earlier confessed that he hadn't intended to become an MP; his eyes were rather set on 'running some big charity'.[48] So he politely rejected Blair's suggestion that he stand against Brown. Various other names were touted as possible challengers to Brown – Charles Clarke, Alan Milburn, John Reid – but none was truly plausible as the heir to Blair. In the absence of Miliband, it was almost inevitable that Brown would succeed, via coronation rather than election.[†]

---

[*] Blair said on 6–0–6 that England had a 'very, very good chance' of winning the World Cup. Instead it was won by Italy, ending 24 years of hurt.
[†] In the event, there was a half-hearted challenge from the left by John McDonnell, but it didn't get far. In order to be on the ballot paper, a candidate required nominations from 44 Labour MPs (12.5 per cent of the PLP) and McDonnell got only 29 of them, including the left contenders in the next two leadership contests, Diane Abbott and Jeremy Corbyn.

By now, knowing he was on his way out, Blair had become much more bullish. As he approached a decade in office, he was, he said, 'at the height of my powers', and was determined to get as much done as possible in the time remaining to him. Where once he sought the approval of the people, he was now dismissive of 'party or even public opinion, provided I thought what I was doing was right and would work for the long-term interest of both party and public'. Most controversially within Labour ranks, he got an education bill through the Commons only with the votes of David Cameron's Tories. He didn't seem to care. His stubborn solidarity with America over Iraq at whatever political cost (it was hard to imagine any other Labour prime minister pursuing the same path) was turning out to be the rule, not the exception. 'Being in touch,' he later wrote, 'was no longer the lodestar. "Doing what was right" had replaced it.'

For many in the party, the last straw came in the summer of 2006, when Israel responded to a Hezbollah attack with a massive assault on Lebanon, and Blair refused to condemn the Israelis. He justified himself by saying he was staying true to his 'world view',[49] but Jack Straw, now leader of the House, was unimpressed: 'The gap between Tony's "world view" and that of most other people was now beyond conciliation.' And anyway, the terminology made him worry: 'In my book, a "world view" is a dangerous and mis-guided notion, its proselytisation inevitably leading to the most simplistic categorisations.' The word increasingly used of Blair in these last months was 'messianic'. It was almost, reflected Straw, 'as if he was willing his own martyrdom'.[50] When Roy Hattersley suggested to a cabinet minister that Blair 'would be crucified' over his education reforms, the reply was: 'He thinks that there are historical precedents for it happening to people like him.'[51]

That September, a number of junior ministers led by arch-Brownite Tom Watson* staged a coordinated resignation, trying

---

* He 'wouldn't have blown his nose without Gordon's say-so', in the words of Peter Mandelson. (*The Third Man* p. 424)

to force Blair's hand. John Prescott dismissed it as 'the Corporals' Revolt',[52] but it proved sufficient, and Blair was bounced into announcing that he would indeed resign the following year. He stayed long enough to achieve his decade as prime minister – marked by an opinion poll showing that 69 per cent of the public thought he would 'be remembered most for the Iraq war'[53] – but he fell some way short of Margaret Thatcher's record.

II

Just before lunchtime on Wednesday 27 June 2007, Tony Blair rose for his last ever session of prime minister's questions. He began, as he had done for years now, by reading out the names of those who had died in Iraq and Afghanistan since his last appearance: Major Paul Harding, Corporal John Rigby, Drummer Thomas Wright. Much of the following half-hour was occupied with tributes from rival party leaders and good wishes from backbenchers, but there were still some members with political opinions to express. 'Does he not think,' asked Jeremy Corbyn, 'that it is time to give a timetable to bring the troops out of Iraq?' Blair did not think that. Fighting al-Qaeda in Iraq, he insisted, was still necessary: 'We will not beat them by giving in to them. We will only beat them by standing up to them.' Others were more concerned with continuing problems in the National Health Service.

Blair, however, wanted to end not with issues but with a defence of his profession. 'Some may belittle politics, but we who are engaged in it know that it is where people stand tall,' he said in his closing remarks. 'If it is, on occasions, the place of low skulduggery, it is more often the place for the pursuit of noble causes. I wish everyone, friend or foe, well. And that is that. The end.'[54]

He left the chamber to a standing ovation from all sides – after David Cameron had urged the Tories to join in. 'Margaret Beckett was in tears,' it was reported, and had to be comforted by the home secretary John Reid, 'while others looking moist-eyed included Tessa Jowell and Hazel Blears.'[55] And so, amid tears and cheers, Tony Blair left Westminster, stepping down not only as prime minister but as an MP.

This wasn't normal. He was only the second incumbent since the war to leave Downing Street and Parliament simultaneously.* The standard practice was to remain in the Commons until at least the next general election, which gave the outgoing premier a transition period between high political office and post-parliamentary life. There was the inevitable reduction in stature, of course, but at least the psychological adjustment could be made in a familiar and mostly friendly world, for Parliament is at times a sentimental institution and tends to be indulgent of the semi-retired. But despite being a superlative performer in the chamber, Blair had no fondness for the place – 'I've never pretended to be a great House of Commons man,' as he said in his final words – and he simply walked away.

By the standards of other prime ministers, he left office at pretty much his own speed and on his own terms. He would have preferred to stay an extra year, but he'd been able to announce his departure many months in advance. Which meant he'd had time to plan for his future. There was, after all, his age to consider. He was very young to be in such a position. His ten predecessors in office had an average age of 71 when they left the Commons; he was just 54, and consequently there was some speculation concerning his post-Downing Street career. The only comparable figure was John Major, who had been 58 when he retired as an MP, but there hadn't been any such questions about his future; it was just assumed that he'd slip quietly into the role of greybeard

---

* The first had been Anthony Eden, who resigned in 1957 after the Suez Crisis, amid allegations that he had lied to the House when sending British troops into action, and whose premiership is remembered solely for a foreign policy disaster.

elder of the establishment. As he did. No one, on the other hand, believed that Blair was ready to quit the world stage just yet.

What the immediate future might hold was explored in fiction. Robert Harris's novel *The Ghost* was published in the late summer of 2007, just before the Labour Party conference that would see Gordon Brown's first speech as leader. Here, an ex-prime minister is holed up in a private mansion on Martha's Vineyard, Massachusetts, out of season, and cuts a forlorn figure, 'stripped of his power, abused by his enemies, hunted, homesick'. He's meant to be writing his memoirs, but he's not a man temperamentally suited to looking back. 'It's losing power – that's the real trouble,' explains his wife. 'Losing power, and now having to sit down and relive everything, year by year.'

His life is one of high security, travelling in private jets and in cars with inch-thick windows that can't be opened because the vehicle has to be kept 'air-tight against chemical and biological attack'.[56] Yet this is a man who has increased the dangers for everyone else. 'There was a time when princes leading their people into battle were on the front line,' Harris told the press. Now, 'our leaders are swaddled in security, with bomb-proof cars and pampered and ferried around like dictators until the day they die, while the rest of us, on the tube or whatever, are liable to be blown up in their wretched War on Terror. It seems to me to be morally wrong.'[57]

Harris was at pains to stress that his character – named Adam Lang – was not to be taken as a portrait of Blair. 'It's a fictional prime minister,' he said when appearing on *Have I Got News for You*. 'It's entirely drawn from my imagination.' And the audience laughed, for they understood the game, just as they knew there could be only one model for a fictional premier who was subservient to American interests, whose military involvement in Iraq was messy and controversial, who had a media-unfriendly wife more intelligent than he, whose reputation was that of a liar and so on and on.* In a fine piece of left-liberal wish-fulfilment, evidence emerges that Lang is complicit in a war crime, and seems destined for the International Criminal Court on the Hague.

The same premise was the basis of the first screen portrayal of Blair in retirement, Alistair Beaton's *The Trial of Tony Blair*, which aired in January 2007, some months before his departure. It was set in 2010, as Gordon Brown wins Labour a fourth consecutive term, but this time with a majority of just two, after Blair – desperate not to be eclipsed by his successor – leaks embarrassing emails to sabotage the campaign. Still continuing their feud, Brown takes his revenge by waving through a UN resolution to pursue a war crimes prosecution, ensuring that Blair is arrested and committed for trial in the Hague.

So cocooned has (the fictional) Blair become that he struggles to believe what's happening. 'I took this country to war because it was the right thing to do,' he rants to his publisher. 'It was the right thing for Britain, and one day history will judge me. And it'll be the liberal journalists, the sneering intellectuals, the appeasers, the bloodless, spineless chattering classes of which you are obviously a member, those will be the ones found wanting, those'll be the ones in the dock of history, not me.' Despite the public bravado, he worries in private: 'It won't be Iraq they'll remember me for, will it?' and his wife is stumbling in her reassurance. 'No,' she falters. 'No, I'm sure it won't be.' Ultimately, though, he can't silence his doubts. 'What have I achieved?' he despairs. 'In my time in government? What I have achieved?'

---

* Pierce Brosnan played Lang in the film adaptation, *The Ghost Writer* (2010), and said of his preparation for the role: 'I looked at Tony Blair, his performance of Tony Blair being prime minister and his persona.' (*World Entertainment News Network* 17 February 2010) Alec Beasley, the prime minister in David Hare's BBC series *The Worricker Trilogy* (2011–14) was similarly seen as a Blair figure, which was also denied. 'Oh no,' said Hare. 'We based him on Putin.' (*Guardian* 22 February 2014)

A bleakly comic variation on the theme was seen the following year in a Harry Enfield and Paul Whitehouse sketch. Back when Blair had been prime minister and therefore important, mega-bank HSCB Lorgan Stanley had offered him a position at £1 million a year for one day a week. But now he's left office, they've forgotten all about his existence, until he turns up, ready to start work. There's nothing for him to do, so they send him out to Starbucks for coffee and treat him as an unwanted, irritating office boy, passed from office to office, looking ever more lost and pathetic.

The sheer quantity of fiction inspired by Tony Blair, particularly on-screen, was remarkable. In *The Trial of Tony Blair*, he was played by Robert Lindsay (reprising his role from 2005's *A Very Social Secretary*), while others who portrayed him included Jon Culshaw in *Churchill: The Hollywood Years* (2004); James Larkin in *The Government Inspector* (2005); Damian Lewis in *Confessions of a Diary Secretary* (2007); and Stephen Mangan in *The Hunt for Tony Blair* (2011). Most celebrated was Michael Sheen's depiction in Peter Morgan's trilogy: *The Deal* (2003), *The Queen* (2006) and *The Special Relationship* (2010). And then there was Christian Brassington in the dramatised sections of the docudrama *Tony Blair: Rock Star* (2006), a youthful long-haired incarnation, playing strip spin-the-bottle with other ex-public-school friends in 1970s London, complete with full-frontal nudity. (Anonymous female nudity, of course, not that of Blair himself, though we do see him in nylon underpants.)

There was also a procession of fictional prime ministers who evoked the spirit of Blair. The best known was in the film *Love Actually* (2003), written and directed by Richard Curtis, where Hugh Grant played a premier known only as David, who strongly resembled, well, Hugh Grant really, casually charismatic as ever. But there was definitely a touch of Blair as well, the early-years Blair, the one who offered hope and decency and general niceness, a Blair still riding high on the optimism of the 1997 election.

David's big moment comes at a joint press conference with the US president, when he goes off-script to stand up for Britain. 'We may be a small country, but we're a great one too,' he says. 'And a friend who bullies us is no longer a friend. And since bullies only respond to strength, from now onward, I will be prepared to be much stronger. And the president should be prepared for that.' The scene entered the political language. 'Although he has acknowledged that many people want him to have a *Love Actually* moment and stand up to the president,' reported *The Times* in 2006, 'Mr Blair has said it just is not going to happen.'[58]

Growing disillusion with Blair was the starting-point of Sally Wainwright's *The Amazing Mrs Pritchard* (2006), in which a supermarket manager from Yorkshire launches a new party and unexpectedly defeats the unnamed but easily identified prime minister. ('He did lie about Iraq,' says a checkout worker; 'he didn't tell the truth, anyroad.') The references were there even in historical drama. In the BBC One Saturday teatime show *Robin Hood* (2006), Dominic Minghella continued the time-honoured tradition of reinventing England's greatest myth for contemporary times. We first see this Robin of Locksley as he returns from the Middle East, a veteran of the Crusades, questioning England's involvement in the campaign. 'Is it *our* Holy War?' he asks. 'Or is it Pope Gregory's?' And in reply, the evil Sheriff of Nottingham echoes Blair's words: 'We stand shoulder to shoulder with Rome.'

Even more pronounced was Blair's treatment in *Doctor Who*. In 'Aliens of London/World War Three' (2005), written by Russell T. Davies, it transpires that Downing Street has been infiltrated by an alien race, the Slitheen, disguised as humans. In the panic that follows the crash of a spacecraft in London, one of their number is appointed acting prime minister and makes a familiar-sounding announcement: 'Our inspectors have searched the sky above our heads, and they have found massive weapons of destruction, capable of being deployed within forty-five seconds.' Consequently, he declares war on behalf of humanity. 'He's making it up,' says the Doctor. 'There's no weapon up there, no threat.' An obscure – but definitely human – backbench MP, Harriet Jones, wonders, 'Do you think they'll believe him?' and the Doctor's companion Rose snaps, 'Well, you did last time.'

It takes a missile strike on 10 Downing Street to foil their dastardly plan, and for the Doctor to remember that he knows the name of Harriet Jones from forthcoming history: 'Future prime minister, elected for three successive terms. The architect of Britain's golden age.'

Sadly, the hope and promise of the decent premier prove illusory. Harriet Jones returned in another Davies story, 'The Christmas Invasion' (2005). Now prime minister, she stands up to the Americans in her own *Love Actually* moment: 'You can tell the president, and please use these exact words: he's not my boss and he's certainly not turning this into a war.' But as yet another group of hostile aliens (the Sycorax this time) are defeated and sent on their way by the Doctor, Jones orders a strike on their spaceship, which is destroyed as it retreats. The Doctor is disgusted by what is essentially a war crime and, his trust in her destroyed, he decides to undermine her premiership by starting a rumour about her health: 'Don't you think she looks tired?' The jibe came at the end of a year in which it was repeatedly said of Blair[59] that he'd been 'looking tired in recent months and showing visible signs of ageing'.*

There was a darker tone in Davies's other prime minister for *Doctor Who*. In 'The Sound of Drums' (2007), Harold Saxon proclaims his allegiance to truth ('The government told you nothing. Well, not me!'), stands up to the Americans, and we learn that 'The president is said to be furious that Great Britain has taken unilateral action.' Everyone, it seems, has fallen for Saxon's hypnotic charm, though the appeal is elusive. 'What was his policy?

---

* Not everyone shared this opinion. 'You look good,' the 62-year-old Colonel Gaddafi told him. 'You are still young.' (*Observer* 28 March 2004)

What did he stand for?' challenges the Doctor, and his companion Martha can't quite put her finger on it: 'I dunno. He always sounded – good. Like you could trust him. Just nice. He spoke about – I can't really remember, but it was good.'

This aura of benevolence is, of course, just a cover. Harold Saxon, it transpires, is none other than the Doctor's arch-enemy, the Master. A tabloid journalist discovers that his persona is a fabrication: 'It's a lie. Everything's a lie.' And as Martha's father, a black man, is bundled into the back of a van by armed police, he screams at the neighbours, 'It's your fault! All of you! You voted Saxon – you did this!'

In these fictional portrayals of prime ministers, there were common ingredients: the tensions between truth and lies, between principle and compromise, between Britain and America – and behind everything, the fact of war. This had become the dominant narrative of Tony Blair's premiership even before he left office: that the honeyed words of hope had been drowned in a flood of falsehood, that he had sold out the interests of his own people, that behind his populism lurked an anti-democratic authoritarianism.

None of this was particularly new. 'Politicians have always been despised for hypocrisy and dishonesty,' observed prime minister Stanley Baldwin in 1925.[60] Nonetheless, the sheer quantity of fiction during and immediately after Blair's premiership suggested that there was something more here than simply the traditional British cynicism about politicians. There was no comparable treatment of, say, James Callaghan or John Major, while Gordon Brown got portrayed solely because he was standing next to Blair. Of post-war prime ministers, only Margaret Thatcher inspired so much work, and most of the dramatic depictions of her came after she left Downing Street. The story of Blair, however, exerted a deep pull on the national imagination from Iraq onwards.

There was a difference. Thatcher was a divisive figure because her policies had such an impact on the lives of so many Britons;

the same was not true of Blair, whose domestic policies were far less radical and far-reaching. In his case, it was the man, not the politics, that determined the perception.

In the early months of his premiership, when there were allegations that Bernie Ecclestone's donation to Labour had influenced government policy on cigarette sponsorship of Formula One, Blair had gone on television and asked to be judged on his character: 'I think most people who have dealt with me think I'm a pretty straight guy, and I am.'[61] His pitch had worked. Then, he was taken as a man of his word. After years of a Tory government enmired in scandals and sleaze, the electorate had put its faith in this fresh-faced, clean-handed young leader, convinced that he was not like other politicians. And then he took the country to war.

As the former home secretary Charles Clarke wrote at the time, 'The Blair premiership is a classic illustration of the potential for good intentions to turn to dust.'[62] The fall from grace had a tragic, almost mythic, element to it, because so many had made an emotional investment in him. It was personal, so that Iraq felt like bad faith, a breach of promise, and people wanted to understand what had gone wrong. Consequently, the publication of his memoirs, A Journey, in 2010 attracted a great deal of attention; there was a wish to understand what had happened.

Not all the interest was positive. He was obliged to cancel a scheduled book-signing at Waterstone's flagship store in Piccadilly for fear that demonstrations would get out of hand ('Blair suffers rioters block,' was the Sun's headline[63]), and a proposed launch party at Tate Modern was similarly abandoned. He did manage a signing in Dublin, but 'eggs and shoes were hurled by protestors' and there was an attempt at a citizen's arrest.[64] These disturbances occasioned some concern. 'Blair-hate is no conventional political criticism,' deplored an editorial in The Times. 'It is an ugly, visceral reflex that is anti-American, anti-British and anti-democratic.'[65]

The controversy helped ensure that the sales expected of the book were realised. In Britain it shifted a third of a million copies, the second-largest figure for a political biography in recent times.* 'Dan Brown and J. K. Rowling are the competition here,' exaggerated a spokesperson for Waterstone's.[66] American sales were even higher. In anticipation of the memoirs' success, publisher Random House had paid Blair a reported advance of £4.8 million. And that fed into the next chapter of the tale, because in his first years out of Downing Street, there was a great deal of media discussion of Blair's earnings in his reincarnation as global statesman.

He was appointed representative of the Quartet on the Middle East – the UN, EU, USA and Russia – and although the post was expenses only, he supplemented his prime-ministerial pension with advisory work for JPMorgan Chase and Zurich Financial Services. And then there was income from the lecture circuit: in 2008 he was reported by *The Times* to be 'probably the highest-paid public speaker in the world'. The paper estimated his earnings in the year since leaving Downing Street as being in excess of £12 million.[67] The *Daily Telegraph*, meanwhile, came up with the figure of £15.89 million for the first two years, with Cherie Blair adding a further £1.64 million.[68] This kind of wealth might be expected of retired American presidents, but it was unknown for prime ministers,† and it made Blair look grubby. It brought to

---

* Authenticated sales figures for the British book trade date back only to the launch of BookScan in 1998, thereby missing Thatcher's *The Downing Street Years* (1993), which was said to have sold 300,000 copies in hardback alone. In the wake of Barack Obama's election as US president in 2008, a British edition of his memoir, *Dreams from My Father* (1995), sold over 700,000 copies.

† Thatcher had also made money on the lecture circuit, but not to this extent. She earned around $1.5 million a year after leaving office, as well as $500,000 a year as an adviser to the tobacco company Philip Morris. She did, however, get a bigger advance than Blair for her memoirs: around £6 million for two volumes. (Moore, *Margaret Thatcher* pp. 750 and 752)

mind Peter Mandelson's old comment, 'We are intensely relaxed about people getting filthy rich'.[69] It also shredded the last scraps of Blair's original appeal. He had been seen as not only 'a pretty straight guy' but also a regular guy, someone who inhabited the same world as us. Now he very clearly didn't; the gap between politicians and public was greater than ever.

Perhaps more concerning for Blair himself was that the really high-profile job was to remain tantalisingly out of reach. In late 2007 and again in 2014 there was talk of him being appointed president of the European Council, but the job went instead to Herman Van Rompuy, ex-prime minister of Belgium,* and then Donald Tusk, ex-prime minister of Poland. And so passed Blair's chance of real standing in international politics. He still had a role advising the government of Kazakhstan, but it wasn't quite the same thing, and, despite the financial reward, there was the irritation of critics carping about his support for a regime whose human rights record was – according to Amnesty International – 'disgraceful'.[70]

For his detractors, Blair's post-premiership career compounded his crimes. The trajectory seen in the fictional dramas was from decent man to great deceiver, from Bambi to Bliar. Now, more charges were laid against him in the court of public opinion. The reports of filthy riches were read as him having cut and run. The refusal to apologise for Iraq meant that the rhetoric of his detractors rose; the warmonger became war criminal. And then there was the gift to satirists: he was an envoy to the Middle East, despite his responsibility for two unresolved conflicts in which

---

* Van Rompuy became best known in Britain for Nigel Farage's verbal assault in the European Parliament: 'You have the charisma of a damp rag and the appearance of a low-grade bank clerk … I can speak on behalf of the majority of the British people in saying: we do not know you, we do not want you, and the sooner you are put out to grass, the better.' (*Daily Telegraph* 26 February 2010)

British soldiers were still being killed and wounded. These things besmirched his reputation further. They also harmed the image of politics.

When Blair reflected on his time in office, he concluded, 'the decade had been reasonably successful'.[71] It was a fair assessment. Judged by the normal criteria applied to prime ministers – that is, on domestic rather than foreign policy – there had undoubtedly been achievements. In later years, as the mood in his own party turned decisively against him (at the 2011 Labour conference, the mere mention of his name provoked loud booing), it was these successes that his supporters tried to trumpet.

There had been a substantial reduction in child and pensioner poverty, increased spending on public services, the construction of new schools and hospitals (even if they hadn't all been paid for yet), and the refurbishment of much social housing, although not enough new build. These things could be eroded, of course, through spending cuts and lack of maintenance, while some other achievements – a rise in educational attainment, a decline in crime – relied upon statistics that not everyone trusted. But there had been structural changes too, with the minimum wage, the devolution of power to Scotland and Wales, peace in Northern Ireland, and some significant, transformative legislation: the Human Rights Act 1998, Freedom of Information Act 2000, Disability Discrimination Act 2005, Equality Act 2006.

Further, when Blair left office, the economy was still in good shape, as it had been throughout his decade, with low inflation, high employment and steady growth; even when France, Germany and America went into recession at the beginning of the century, the UK had continued to thrive. Economic growth had been around for so long that it was almost possible to believe those boasts of having put an end to boom-and-bust. Few paid heed to the first tremors of the coming earthquake, already being felt in early 2007, and the public mood remained relatively buoyant.*

There had also been advances for gay rights, seen as emblematic of the country's acceptance of diversity. This was very much in line with New Labour's view of itself, but it was too nervous of appearing 'loony left' to put the reforms to the electorate; they weren't mentioned in a manifesto until 2005, when they were presented as fait accomplis. The legislation on civil partnerships and the like was primarily the result of cultural, rather than political, pressure: it was television and film that had changed attitudes and Blair was riding a national mood, not setting the agenda. Nonetheless, the electoral success of New Labour did mean that the Conservatives also had to change to adapt to this new reality. Perhaps this fact represented the biggest impact of Blair's premiership. His three consecutive election victories dragged the centre of British politics towards the left on social issues. Most significantly, the Sure Start programme and greater funding of childcare and nursery places increased the state's involvement in the rearing of children.

These were all things that Blair and his supporters could chalk up to his credit, successes to set against the failure to put Britain at the heart of Europe and the catastrophe of Iraq. Given the extraordinarily favourable circumstances of 1997, however, and given ten years in power, the pickings were a little thin. 'The tragedy of this prime minister is that he promised so much but delivered so little,' said David Cameron,[72] and one didn't have to share Cameron's faux sorrow to believe that he had a point. It

---

* Ipsos-Mori regularly conducted a survey asking whether people thought the economy would improve, stay the same or worsen over the next year; from the results was generated the Economic Optimism Index. In the first six months of 2007, up to Blair's departure, the EOI was running at an average of minus 27, roughly the same level it had been all century. The following year, it plummeted to an average of minus 54.

seemed a poor return for a man who had so often felt the hand of history on his shoulder.

'Journalists are calling it the Blair Decade,' wrote novelist Sebastian Faulks in 2007, 'but it wasn't really. It was the decade of Islam and IT. Mr Blair has left hardly a fingerprint on the years and, in a liberal democracy, that is perhaps how it should be.'[73] That wasn't how Blair saw his political mission. His task had been to change the nation, to usher in a new world. It wasn't just policy; it was about politics itself, the third way. 'I could see the twentieth century left/right debate of Western politics dying on its feet,' he wrote, 'just getting in the way of what needed to be done.'[74] Subsequent events proved him wrong, at least for the immediate future. The economic crisis that hit the world shortly after he left office gave renewed impetus to the right and – to a lesser extent – the left, while in Britain and its fellow travellers in Europe the third way floundered.

The impact of that crisis suggested that Blair was not quite as aligned with cultural and political evolution as he thought. He saw the state, he said, as a structure that 'actively empowers people to make their own choices and does not try to do it for them'.[75] But that implied a democratic spirit not always evident in a leader whose thinking depended on the practice of authority right through society: 'My theory of leadership is that it's the same whatever you're doing, whether you're running a corporation, a football team or a country.'[76] He was prepared to pursue his own beliefs, regardless of party or public support, and he wanted others to share his sense of determination. So his public-sector reforms focused on giving greater powers to school heads and to the chairs of NHS foundation trusts. The model was the public schools: 'They have strong leadership, and are allowed to lead. They are more flexible. They innovate because no one tells them they can't.'[77] Similarly, he was attracted to the idea of the powerful city mayor, though he rowed back when he realised that Ken Livingstone was going to get the plum job in London.

Despite his claims to meritocratic modernity, Blair's approach often looked rather old-fashioned, still 'the gentleman in White-hall', even if he was now wearing an open-necked shirt. In his memoirs, he wrote that the Conservative Party had clambered onto a populist bandwagon in its opposition to student fees, 'But such bandwagons are dangerous if they are heading in a direction with which serious, elite cross-party opinion disagrees.'[78] He was, of course, part of that serious and elite opinion, so although he regarded himself as a radical reformer ('I'm naturally attracted by iconoclasm')[79] the country saw him as part of the establishment. And by the end of his premiership, the establishment was starting to lose its moral authority, not least because of him.

Leadership, for Blair, required self-belief and absolute assurance. In 2005 journalist Paul Scott published *Tony and Cherie: A Special Relationship*, which told sensational tales of the prime minister's wife engaging in 'white witchcraft' and a 'New Age sexual technique'. It also included the story of her first encounter with Princess Anne, when she introduced herself with the line 'Do call me Cherie,' only to be rebuffed with a frosty 'Actually, let's not go that way. Let's stick to Mrs Blair.'[80] Downing Street was outraged, denying the truth of Scott's claims, but the Princess Anne incident, at least, was genuine, for it turned up in Cherie Blair's autobiography and again in her husband's. His response was characteristic. Anne's behaviour was 'discordant in our democratic age', he conceded, but it displayed 'an admirable determination not to be concordant'.[81] The disapproval feels perfunctory, the admiration genuine.

Blair himself was temperamentally averse to confrontation. 'It was always amicable,' wrote John Prescott of their disputes. 'No screaming and shouting.'[82] David Blunkett went further: 'Tony has never been rude in his life.'[83] Or, as Jack Straw put it, 'Tony does not do rude.'[84] And maybe therein was the contradiction for the man who wanted to be seen as a strong leader. He was an emollient politician who prided himself on his ability to listen, but still he envied and respected those more definite and unyielding than he, whether they were the Princess Royal, the US president or Rupert Murdoch, and he aspired to walk their walk. He had great visions for the world; what he perhaps lacked was the weight to sell these visions to a nation that was not seeking greatness.

He was, though, for a brief while, a major figure on the international stage – 'We were big players,' he would say in later years[85] – and he attracted compliments and criticism accordingly. 'A piddling, posturing pygmy,' said Robert Mugabe,[86] while Bob Geldof sniffed, 'He's all right,'[87] and George W. Bush struggled to find the words to express his admiration: 'He's much more kind of lofty and eloquent than I am.'[88] Labour MP Frank Field took a dim view: 'Tony Blair reminds me of a water spider. It skims across the water, but once it has gone, you can't tell that it was ever there.'[89] His greatest achievement of all was undoubtedly the peace process in Northern Ireland, and the taoiseach Bertie Ahern duly paid tribute: 'Tony Blair leaves a priceless legacy of peace and agreement.' The most enthusiastic verdict was that of Cherie: 'I'm sure history will judge him very well,' she said. 'I think he will be up there with Churchill.'[90]

6

Bust and Broken

I

Despite the decline of religion in public life, politicians were still asked from time to time to name their favourite hymn. The results were mildly interesting, if seldom revealing: Ann Widdecombe and David Blunkett went for established classics – 'How Great Thou Art' and 'Dear Lord and Father of Mankind' respectively – while Michael Howard took the diplomatic option of 'I Vow to Thee, My Country', more a patriotic song than a hymn (and the favourite of the late Princess Diana).[1]

Less obviously, when Gordon Brown was asked by the BBC's *Songs of Praise* in January 2005 for his favourite hymn, he nominated 'Jerusalem'. No doubt he was telling the truth, but it seemed odd that the son of a Church of Scotland minister, whose knowledge of hymns was presumably extensive, would opt for the song – sensual rather than sacred – that had become England's unofficial anthem. Dorothy-Grace Elder, a former MSP for the Scottish National Party, was suspicious: 'More politics than piety, Brown's careful selection was a wannabe PM's early bid for acceptance by Middle England.'[2]

If so, there was just cause for New Labour to be nervous, for it had been a long time since a non-English leader had been successful at the polls. Neil Kinnock had certainly suffered in England from anti-Welsh prejudice, and Brown's Scottishness might similarly have counted against him, particularly at a time when devolution had given nationalism a boost. As he moved ever nearer the premiership, Brown was increasingly to be found making speeches about the 'common qualities and common values that have made Britain the country it is. Our belief in tolerance and liberty which shines through British history. Our commitment to fairness, fair play and civic duty.'[3]

It was the kind of thing that Tony Blair used to do effortlessly, but it felt like hard work with Brown, as if he were lacking in sincerity. He wasn't. But an integral part of Brown's Britishness was a stiffness of manner, a social shyness that made it difficult for him to play the role of political salesman.

Previously, he had taken refuge in his mastery of detail, particularly of the complexities of a tax system that he was making ever more intricate. As the *Observer* put it, he was 'seen as high-handed, intellectually precious and out of touch with "real people"'.[4] He constructed a shell that journalists found impenetrable and infuriating. 'I'm convinced Gordon Brown bores 99 per cent of any audience,' said BBC journalist John Humphrys. 'I once interviewed him for 38 minutes and he gave the same answer to every question. And he doesn't care that everyone finds him so boring.'[5] The Tory view was much the same. 'He has the charisma of a coffin lid,' was Michael Portillo's rather harsh evaluation,[6] and Dominic Cummings dismissed him as 'Scottish, grim, unsmiling, and not fully human'.[7] That last charge was often heard. 'He makes efforts to be "human",' observed Hugo Young of the *Guardian*, but 'it is rather hollow, even though well meant.' And, he added, 'He has a sense of humour. He can see the point of jokes. He can laugh, though seldom at himself.'[8]

He was a serious politician and an awkward human being. Perhaps Robert Harris came closest: he 'suffers from a kind of political Asperger's syndrome. Intellectually brilliant, he sometimes seems socially barely functional: a little bit odd.'[9]

As chancellor, none of this was a great impediment; it might even have helped mark him out as more weighty and considered than Blair. Brown's spin doctor, Damian McBride, believed the serious but scruffy image – 'his dandruff, his unkempt hair and his skew-whiff ties' – was part of the appeal: 'Boris Johnson without the jokes.'[10] McBride believed he should be allowed to be his 'laddish' self in his media appearances, doing 'things he was very good and natural at – like talking about sport'.[11] Polling evidence, however, suggested that there was a gender issue, that Brown trailed David Cameron among women voters, and laddishness wasn't going to help. So began a media campaign to establish that – despite all appearances to the contrary – he was just a normal kind of guy. It wasn't entirely successful, and he faced some mockery for an interview with *New Woman* magazine in which he revealed that he had no preference between briefs or boxer shorts (so long as they came from Marks & Spencer), that he was aware of the rabbit design of vibrator, and that he could drop an indie-rock name: 'Arctic Monkeys on the iPod really wake you up in the morning.'[12]

Accompanying the charm offensive was the repeated assertion of Britishness. In the weeks leading up to his coronation as Labour leader, he promised the creation of 200,000 jobs, telling employers – particularly in construction, retail and hospitality

– that they should not be recruiting abroad. 'It is time to train British workers for the British jobs that will be available over the coming few years.'[13] At the TUC conference in September 2007, his first as prime minister, he promised 'British jobs for British workers',[14] and later that month, at the Labour conference, he returned to the theme, squeezing in eighty mentions of 'Britain' or 'British', compared with just eight references to 'Labour'.[15]

The bit that stuck was that phrase 'British jobs for British workers', and it did him little good. From the left came the reminder that this was an old BNP slogan, while the right pointed to government figures released that summer showing that, although 2.1 million jobs were created in the first decade of New Labour, more than half of them had been taken by foreign workers.[16] In any event, it was difficult to see how any such policy could be realised within the rules of the European Union.

Nonetheless, Brown's speech got a broadly warm welcome because he was still in his honeymoon as prime minister. The media consensus was that he had a successful first summer, confidently handling a succession of crises, although in truth most were small-scale replays of previous issues: a minor foot-and-mouth outbreak, thwarted terrorist attacks in London and Glasgow.* There were also extreme weather conditions – it was the wettest May–July since records began – leading to extensive flooding; Brown visited the affected areas and was appropriately concerned and resolute.† In September 2007 a new poster was

---

* The latter incident saw members of the public assist the police in apprehending two terrorists who'd rammed a burning car at the door of Glasgow Airport. This prompted one of the *Daily Record*'s most celebrated headlines: 'Hero Cabbie: I kicked burning terrorist so hard in balls that I tore a tendon in my foot.' (4 July 2007)
† The bishop of Carlisle saw the floods in terms of climate change and the introduction of civil partnerships: 'We are reaping the consequences of our moral degradation, as well as environmental damage.' (*Sunday Telegraph* 1 July 2007)

unveiled, portraying him as a man of substance not spin. 'Not flash, just Gordon' was the slogan, created by Saatchi & Saatchi.

There were also a few policy announcements, the most eye-catching being the abandonment of plans announced by the Blair government to license the 'first Las Vegas-style supercasino' in Manchester.[17] This was billed as evidence of Brown's much vaunted 'moral compass',[18] legacy of the low-church heritage he shared with Margaret Thatcher and Tony Benn,* though the fact that ten smaller casinos were allowed to go ahead somewhat betrayed his principled objection to gambling.

None of it amounted to much more than looking serious and prime ministerial in front of television cameras. Still, he'd had such a problem with his media image previously that his assured performance gave him a boost. The transition from the decade of Blair was proceeding more smoothly than had been expected. Just a few months earlier opinion polls had suggested that, if Brown became prime minister, the Tories would have an eleven-point advantage, enough to secure a majority government. It hadn't worked out like that. Labour were seven to ten points ahead, and registering a substantial lead on the key issues of leadership and the economy.

It was not until early 2007 that the world outside the financial services industry became aware of what the *Financial Times* referred to as 'the craze of lending to borrowers with weak credit histories'.[19] It appeared that in recent years, while the sun had been shining and there was hay to be made, a new form of banking had been pioneered in America. Lenders had been offering what were called lower-quality loans – or, even more euphemistically, sub-prime mortgages – and then spreading the risks attached to such debts in complex bonds that mixed the secure with the suspect.

---

* At the funerals of both Thatcher in 2013 and Benn in 2014, the old John Bunyan hymn 'He who would valiant be' was sung.

These were then packaged and repackaged, sold and sold again, spinning around the globe in ever more intricate webs. Structured finance, they called it, and it was the future, an exciting new world born of the computing power that now dominated the markets.

The rationale was that there was security in having risk spread so widely; this was, like the internet, a decentralised network that could not easily be brought down. But still it rested on subprime borrowers, and, by definition, they could not be relied upon; in the event of an economic downturn, they would be the first to be hit. And so it happened. Towards the end of 2006, the American property market suffered a slump. Defaults and late payments went up, and the vulnerability of the global network of risk was exposed. The contagion spread like an internet virus. In February 2007 London-based bank HSBC issued a profit warning related to its American mortgage book, and saw its share price fall.

The bankers held their nerve. There was no need to change direction. 'This genie simply will not go back into the bottle,' said the head of structured finance at the New York investment bank Lehman Brothers. Indeed, so optimistic were Lehman that they were busily helping the 'trailblazing Northern Rock' – formerly a humdrum Tyneside building society, now a thrusting young bank – to develop 'new and yet more sophisticated types of financial instrument'.[20] And why not? The rapid expansion of Northern Rock was reaping fine rewards, and in early 2007 the bank reported figures* that showed annual profits up by 16.5 per cent.[21] Reports in April that it 'was to start offering subprime mortgages underwritten by Lehman Brothers'[22] were seen by the markets as a positive move, and its valuation rose still further.

But over that summer, doubts about the stability of the subprime market became ever more insistent. What had been an

---

* It later transpired that Northern Rock was not averse to falsifying figures. This, wrote Gordon Brown, 'should have led to prison sentences'. (*My Life, Our Times* p. 299)

obscure business story buried away in the back of the broadsheets was now breaking into the news pages. Non-specialist readers struggled to make sense of the jargon of collaterised debt obligations, asset-backed commercial paper, structured investment vehicles, securitisation vehicles – let alone why anyone thought it was a good idea to lend 110 per cent of the value of a property on an interest-only mortgage to someone classified as subprime.

It transpired that they weren't the only ones failing to grasp the fine detail. Within the industry everyone now knew there was a problem with bad debt, but the system was so labyrinthine that no one knew how serious the problem was or where it might manifest itself. Financial institutions, unsure who or what could be trusted, became nervous of lending to each other. There was growing talk of a 'global liquidity crisis'[23] and the phrase 'credit crunch' entered general speech.

In Britain, Northern Rock in particular was heavily exposed, with hundreds of millions invested in American mortgage-backed securities. Its aggressive model of long-term fixed-rate mortgage deals also left it vulnerable when British interest rates were put up – as they were – in an attempt to dampen an over-inflating economy. In the summer of 2007, unable to repay its own loans and unable to raise funds elsewhere, Northern Rock was forced to approach the Bank of England for an emergency bail-out.

News of negotiations over this application was broken by the BBC on a Thursday evening in mid-September. It sent the Northern Rock share price into free fall – ending the next day down nearly 60 per cent since May, with no end in sight – and sparked a rush of depositors to high-street branches, thousands queuing up to withdraw their money before the bank went under. For a couple of days there was panic. Northern Rock's website collapsed, and telephone switchboards were unable to cope with the deluge of calls. Some branches closed, having run out of money; others stayed open late to serve the never-ending queues; police were deployed to keep order in the streets and, in Cheltenham, to deal with an angry couple who barricaded the manager in her office, demanding that they be given their savings. An estimated billion pounds was withdrawn on the first day. The newly appointed chancellor of the exchequer, Alistair Darling, tried to reassure the public that action was being taken, but many weren't listening. 'I never believe anything this government tells me,' said one of those queuing up at a local branch. 'They said there were weapons of mass destruction in Iraq and how many of our lads have died?'[24]

Three months into his premiership, Gordon Brown had a genuine crisis on his hands, unprecedented in modern Britain; in the 150 years since the last run on a high-street bank, 25 prime ministers had been and gone. And it looked perilously close to home. Northern Rock had demutualised to become a bank in the early months of the Labour government, and was the biggest private employer in Newcastle upon Tyne, one of the party's strongholds. Its risk committee was headed by Derek Wanless, the man entrusted by Brown in 2005 with leading an inquiry into the future of the NHS. It was even the shirt-sponsor of Newcastle United football club, of which Tony Blair was a fan.

Opposition parties tried to fix the blame on Brown – 'It's his credit boom and it looks as if he has failed to regulate it properly,' said Tory MP Michael Fallon[25] – but in the early days the government largely got the benefit of the doubt and won broad public support for its response. Because, after the initial stumble, the combination of Brown's authority and Darling's dull calmness brought some stability at the start of the following week. The Bank of England loan was approved and guarantees were given for savers' deposits. Further, Darling said, the government would take the same action for any other bank that encountered similar problems.

It was only a temporary respite, and there was no indication that any lessons had been learned in the banks; when the Liberal Democrats, in a spirit of inquiry, sent someone to Northern Rock asking for a 125 per cent mortgage, he was offered one unconditionally.[26] Over the next months, the company required further injections of capital, until in February 2008 the government finally grasped the nettle and took Northern Rock into public ownership, with taxpayers now liable for £55 billion of loans and underwritten guarantees. Nationalising a bank was a spectacular U-turn for a prime minister who had ridden the wave of lightly regulated finance.*

With the crisis apparently over, there was much talk in autumn 2007 of a snap election to confirm Gordon Brown's premiership, talk that originated in off-the-record briefings from within Brown's circle. The government was in the ascendancy and the Tories – as they made their way to Blackpool for their conference – were widely considered to be on the ropes, battered into near-submission by what Tony Blair called 'the big clunking fist'[27] of the new prime minister. Where Brown ruled a united party, there were whispering campaigns against David Cameron, suggestions that he was viewed with contempt by senior colleagues. He had only days to 'save the Conservatives from self-destruction', warned the *Sun*, branding his task 'Mission Impossible'.[28]

Seven days later, the outlook had been completely transformed. The Labour lead in the polls had been heavily cut – even eliminated in some surveys – and the news from the marginal seats was even worse, with Labour behind by six points. 'A week ago Cameron and Osborne looked like men facing certain and crushing defeat, falling back in some disorder under the weight of Labour's attacks,' wrote the *Guardian*'s Larry Elliott; now they'd had 'a Dunkirk moment'.[29]

The crucial factor was George Osborne's conference speech, promising that a Tory government would abolish stamp duty on properties under £250,000 – benefiting some 90 per cent of

---

* Bradford & Bingley – another building society that had demutualised to become a bank – was similarly nationalised later in 2008.

all first-time house-buyers – and raise the threshold for inheritance tax from £300,000 to £1 million. These were big, popular
moves, particularly for property owners in south-east England.
Even more inspired was the pledge to subsidise the tax cuts by
imposing a levy of £25,000 a year on those 'fat cats' living in the
UK while registered as non-domiciled and therefore not liable
for British tax. The Tories were wooing the middle classes, from
Chingford to Cheltenham, who felt they'd been taken for granted,
even fleeced, in recent years. In particular, the inheritance tax proposal (never implemented) proved very popular.

'I have never rated George's understanding of financial and
economic matters,' wrote Vince Cable, 'but he is a political opera-
tor of some substance and this was a brilliant move.'[30] Brilliant
enough to panic Brown into abandoning plans for an early vote,
while foolishly refusing to admit that he'd been influenced by the
polls.

The dithering over whether to call an election diminished
Brown. He later talked of Tory inheritance tax plans 'dreamed
up on the playing fields of Eton',[31] which merely emphasised his
failure: a Labour leader shouldn't have been so easily thrown by
a policy that touched so few. It was 'the greatest misjudgement
of Gordon's long career, utterly changing the way he was perceived and defined', said Damian McBride,[32] and Jack Straw's
verdict was damning: 'The cabinet and the PLP's confidence in
him was severely damaged – and never recovered.'[33] Even Brown
himself eventually admitted he 'mishandled' the situation,[34] and
he seemed somehow a less substantial figure. 'He looks like he's
been inflated – but not enough,' concluded comedian Ross Noble.

Thereafter nothing really went right again. There was an
endless series of minor missteps, most of them inconsequential
but together giving the impression of a leadership and a party that
had – as commentators now said – lost control of the narrative.
Obviously, it didn't really matter that when Brown did a web chat
with the social networking site Mumsnet, he refused twelve times

to answer a question about what was his favourite biscuit. But this sort of thing was part of the game of modern politics,* and his failure to respond meant that nothing else he said was heard. The users of the site were quick to pour scorn on his inept performance. 'Maybe he needs to consult with his advisers on what would be the most vote-winning biscuit to admit to liking?' was one much-quoted comment.[35] More than ten days later, he sent some packets of chocolate-chip biscuits round to the Mumsnet offices, saying they were his favourite. Which merely gave the story another run out in the press.

Nor did it matter much when the Labour Party, in a desperate attempt to paint the Tories as unreconstructed Thatcherites, produced a poster based on *Ashes to Ashes*, with David Cameron wearing Gene Hunt's snakeskin boots and sitting on the bonnet of his Audi Quattro. 'Don't let him take Britain back to the 1980s,' read the slogan,[36] and David Miliband explained that it was 'a powerful reminder of the damage which the Tories did to Britain'.[37] He clearly hadn't spotted that Hunt was actually a roguish hunk, and that the poster gifted a tough-guy image to a young, inexperienced leader previously considered a bit of a softie. 'We wish we'd thought of it,' said a Tory source admiringly, and they did the next best thing; they appropriated the image and added their own slogan: 'Fire up the Quattro – it's time for change.'[38]

A similar miscalculation was seen in the Crewe and Nantwich by-election in May 2008. Labour's campaign played heavily on the class of Tory candidate Edward Timpson, a privately educated toff who came from the family that owned the Timpson shoe-repairing firm (founded 1865). 'Mr Timpson has been ambushed by Labour activists in top hats and tails,' it was reported.[39] The result was an 18 per cent swing against Labour, and the Tories'

---

* When they were asked (and of course they *were* asked), David Cameron went for oatcakes, and Nick Clegg hedged his bets: Rich Tea for dunking, or Hobnobs without the dunking.

first by-election gain in over a quarter-century. This was three weeks after Boris Johnson* had beaten Ken Livingstone to win the London mayoralty. Having started as an 8–1 outsider, Johnson recorded the largest vote any individual candidate had managed in British electoral history, over a million first-preference votes, with a campaign that was personality based and barely mentioned the Conservative Party.† Being a toff was not the electoral disadvantage Labour believed.

Labour's presentational mistakes attracted attention partly because there was so little policy to talk about. After that first flurry of excitement, Brown's premiership simply didn't live up to its promise; the hopes of Labour activists that, in John O'Farrell's words, 'we would see far more radical changes once Gordon was no longer held back by the man next door',[40] were not to be realised. Brown had opposed things that Blair did or wanted to do, but he didn't come up with alternatives. If not academy schools, foundation hospitals and tuition fees, then what? Other policies that he had disapproved of under Blair – identity cards, 90 days' detention without charge for terrorist suspects – were now revived as he sought to look tough. None of it seemed coherent, none of it set the agenda. He had a 'tendency to react to events as he had in opposition', concluded Peter Mandelson,[41] who'd been given a peerage and brought back into the cabinet, another sign that things hadn't really changed.‡ He 'tried his best,' said cabinet

---

* On the all-important biscuit question, Johnson nominated chocolate digestives.

† This was despite the *Guardian* wheeling out a long list of celebrity Londoners to say how appalling the prospect of Johnson as mayor was, from rapper Ty ('I'd be petrified') to writer Blake Morrison threatening to emigrate, to designer Vivienne Westwood: 'It just exposes democracy as a sham, especially if people don't vote for Ken.' (1 May 2008)

‡ 'It's so heart-warming to see him slithering through the TV studios again,' said Diane Abbott. 'I think he has added to the gaiety of the nation.' (*Sun* 6 October 2008)

minister Peter Hain, 'but somehow we never really escaped the gloom and drift which steadily engulfed us under his premiership'.[42] The new prime minister seemed to be struggling with his responsibilities. 'Gordon is finding it much harder than he thought it would be,' admitted his wife, Sarah.[43]

There was perhaps a sporting parallel. Blair liked to associate himself with Alex Ferguson, the all-conquering manager of Manchester United, to whom he gave a knighthood in 1999 after a treble-winning season that saw victories in the Premier League, FA Cup and Champions' League. Ferguson's assistant then had been Steve McClaren, who went on to become a manager in his own right and was later appointed England coach. It wasn't a successful tenure. In a lacklustre series of performances, England failed to qualify for the European Championship for the first time in 24 years, their hopes finally trampled into the mud of Wembley Stadium in a 3–2 defeat by Croatia in November 2007. The press were merciless. 'What a bunch of losers,' howled the front page of the *Daily Star*. 'Hopeless, hapless, helpless,' agreed the *Guardian*. The match was played in heavy rain, and the sight of McClaren sheltering under an umbrella aroused particular scorn. 'Great leaders inspire their men to glory,' said the *Daily Mail*. 'Steve McClaren will be remembered as a wally with a brolly.'[44]

The comparison with the beleaguered prime minister was the subject of one of George Osborne's better jokes, delivered the next day: 'Gordon Brown is fast becoming the Steve McClaren of British politics. The number two who couldn't hack it at number one.'[45]

II

In late August 2008, Alistair Darling gave an interview to the *Guardian* that painted a bleak picture. Economic conditions were 'arguably the worst they've been in sixty years', he said. 'I think it's going to be more profound and long-lasting than people thought.' The next twelve months would be critical, especially since the government had lost public support. 'People are pissed off with us,' he admitted.[46] His gloomy comments were not appreciated by his colleagues, but they were justified. It turned out that Northern Rock in the autumn of 2007 hadn't been the crisis itself, merely the harbinger of the crisis.

Through 2008 the scale of the financial problem was gradually uncovered. Banks and their affiliates had been behaving in the most extravagant and hazardous manner, without regulation or even recognition; in the words of Gordon Brown, a 'shadow banking system had proliferated without politicians being aware of it'.[47] And in September 2008 the concerns became acute. The US government stepped in to take over the Federal National Mortgage Association and the Federal Home Loan Mortgage Company (commonly known as Fannie Mae and Freddie Mac), which between them underpinned much of the American mortgage market, and which had been hit hard by the housing slump. A week later, the high-risk practices of the big investment banks finally came home to roost when Lehman Brothers posted the biggest bankruptcy filing in history. By the end of the month Washington had had to persuade the Bank of America to buy up another failing investment bank, Merrill Lynch, while two others – Goldman Sachs and Morgan Stanley – had hastily restructured themselves in order to come under federal protection. The credit crunch was rebranded as a financial crisis.

The impact was global, and was felt severely in Britain, where financial services were a large part of the economy.* Over the

---

* When Labour took office in 1997, the financial and insurance industries accounted for 5.9 per cent of GDP; ten years later, this had risen to 8.6 per cent, and the economic output of the sector had very nearly doubled in real terms. (House of Commons briefing paper, *Financial Services: Contribution to the UK Economy*, 31 July 2019)

summer of 2008, as the credit squeeze intensified, inflation rose and house prices began to slide. In early October, the London stock market suffered its worst one-day fall for over twenty years, and the stability of the entire banking system came into ever sharper question. In a swift and decisive response, the government announced a rescue package with a mixture of loans and guarantees and an offer to buy bank shares, all worth a total of £500 billion. The scale of the undertaking was huge, mind-boggling, very nearly matching the whole of government expenditure for the previous year. It was a vast investment in protecting the system, a desperate emergency measure deemed necessary because the banks were – in the phrase of the day – 'too big to fail'. The most affected institution, for example, and therefore the one in which the state acquired the largest stake, was the Royal Bank of Scotland; as Vince Cable pointed out, 'the RBS balance sheet was fifteen times the size of the Scottish economy'.[48]

'This is not a time for conventional thinking or outdated dogma but for the fresh and innovative intervention that gets to the heart of the problem,' announced Brown,[49] and for once he was on the front foot. The British response set a pattern repeated elsewhere, most importantly in America. And it succeeded in its short-term aims. The immediate crisis, the fear of complete collapse, passed. The political impact on the public, however, on those being asked to foot the bill for bailing out the banks – that was yet to be felt.

In January 2009, the International Monetary Fund warned that the coming year would see the world's worst economic performance for more than six decades, adding that, of the major industrialised nations, the UK would face the deepest problems in what came to be called the Great Recession.[50] Indeed, the economy was already contracting when Darling spoke to the *Guardian* back in August. By the time that growth returned, in the third quarter of 2009, GDP had fallen by more than 7 per cent, allowing for inflation, a bigger fall than that experienced in either of the recessions during the long Tory government of 1979–97. And unemployment was nudging 2.5 million, a million higher than the relatively stable levels so far in the century. Some of the most familiar retailers – Borders, MFI, Threshers, Woolworths, Zavvi – went out of business.

Desperate measures were taken in mostly vain attempts to boost industry and consumer confidence. Money was injected into the economy through what was called quantitative easing (printing money, as it used to be known), and the rate of VAT was temporarily cut. So too were bank lending rates, though that change wasn't so temporary: in December 2007, the Bank of England interest rate stood at 5.75 per cent; fifteen months later, it was 0.5 per cent, the lowest in the Bank's 300-year history, and was to remain at that level right through to 2016, when it was cut still further.

It was the end of the long boom. And it was effectively the end of Gordon Brown's premiership. The fact that he won international plaudits for handling the crisis simply didn't cut much ice at home. He was the man who'd repeatedly promised an end to boom and bust, and here was the biggest bust in living memory. Global factors were far beyond his control, of course, but he'd been happy enough to take the credit in the good times, and there was little inclination to cut him any slack now. Why had he not known what was happening? Why was there no proper regulation?

Above all, there was a bitter, lingering taste of injustice. Bankers had engaged in wildly speculative and dangerous practices, and when it had all gone wrong, the taxpayer was left to foot the bill. 'Never has so much money been owed by so few to so many,' as Mervyn King, governor of the Bank of England, put it.[51] And there was a recession. No one was held accountable before the law, and the wrong people were paying the price.* As on 9/11, the kaleidoscope had been shaken, but this time the pieces had

---

* Some looked in admiration to countries such as Iceland, where several bankers were jailed and the former prime minister was prosecuted.

been carefully reassembled in exactly the same pattern. In short, it didn't seem fair, and fairness was as integral to Brown's political pitch as was his reputation for economic stability.

Even at the outset, there were indications that his reputation wouldn't survive. In October 2008, the street artist Banksy left a message tied to a lamp post behind the Royal Exchange in the City of London: bunches of flowers attached to wads of fake £20 notes, and a card addressed to the prime minister that quoted the words of the Libertines' debut single from 2002: 'What a waster! What a fucking waster, you pissed it all up the wall.'[52]

At a more elevated level, there were those who felt that while the government might have shored up the crumbling superstructure, it had done nothing about the rotting foundations. The most powerful voices came from those with a moral rather than a political position. 'It seems like the addict returning to the drug' was the verdict of archbishop Rowan Williams on Gordon Brown's economic rescue package,[53] and the Pope made much the same point in his blessing on New Year's Day 2009: 'It's not enough, as Jesus said, to put patches on an old suit.'[54]

Meanwhile, the Queen took advantage of a visit to the London School of Economics to ask another, related question: 'If these things were so large, how come everyone missed them?'[55] It was a fair point; the crash of 2008 did little for the reputation of economists, the high priests of finance. And the idols of Wall Street and the City of London were now seen, in the title of a book by Larry Elliott and Dan Atkinson, published that summer, as the Gods that Failed. Elsewhere, the Ipsos-Mori poll that had been tracking the public's trust in various professions since 1983 saw a sharp fall in the standing of government ministers, and of politicians generally, all the way back to levels seen in the dying days of John Major's premiership.

Gordon Brown took most of the political blame for the crash, but if there was a single hate figure, it was Sir Fred Goodwin, the chief executive officer of RBS, who resigned in late 2008 just before the bank posted an annual loss of £24 billion, the largest ever recorded in Britain. He was known as Fred the Shred, a reference to his practice of cutting costs and staff – although he enjoyed a suite at the Savoy and a dozen chauffeur-driven Mercedes – and was condemned as epitomising the reckless gambling and bland incompetence of the banking industry; the feeling only intensified when it was discovered that, although he could be – and was – stripped of his knighthood, he still had the compensation of a £700,000 annual pension.*

Even before the crash 'ruptured our confidence in the rationality of the market economy' (in Tony Blair's words),[56] there had been the sense that a super-rich elite was splintering off from the rest of society. The first ten years of the New Labour government, wrote the BBC's business editor Robert Peston in 2008, had seen 'an extraordinary increase in the income of the top 1 per cent of earners, an even bigger increase for the top 0.5 per cent, and a still bigger rise for the top 0.1 per cent'.[57]

There had been for some time a steady trickle of stories about the vast sums of money being paid to senior executives, and about the little or no tax paid on that income. Stories about, for example, Philip Green. He might have been the CEO of the Arcadia Group – which included Burton, Dorothy Perkins and Topshop – but the shares were actually owned by his wife, Tina, via a Jersey-based firm, while she herself was resident in Monaco. Happily for the Greens, this arrangement meant she didn't come under the regime of HM Revenue & Customs, so that when she received a £1.2 billion dividend in 2005, it attracted no tax in Britain.

There was further disquiet in 2007 when Nick Ferguson,

---

* 'People feel anger and contempt over this,' said Norman Tebbit, arguing that Goodwin and others should have been put 'in the dock at the Old Bailey because it would have done more good than any amount of regulation'. (*Daily Telegraph* 10 May 2013)

chairman of the private equity fund SVG Capital, pointed out that he paid a lower tax rate than normal people because of rules introduced by Gordon Brown nearly a decade earlier. Under a scheme intended to promote enterprise, selling a business asset held for a minimum of two years attracted just 10 per cent capital gains tax. Meanwhile, someone on minimum wage – someone employed, say, as a cleaner by a private equity firm – would, from 2008 on, be able to work just nineteen hours a week before becoming liable for 31 per cent tax and National Insurance. The injustice was spelled out by Ferguson himself: 'Any common-sense person would say that a highly paid private equity executive paying less tax than a cleaning lady or other low-paid workers can't be right.'[58] But there seemed to be a lack of common-sense people setting the rules.

Much anger centred on the end-of-year bonuses paid to bankers, which had spiralled into fantasy in the last days before the crash. It was reported that the financial year 2006–07 saw some 4,200 people working in the City of London receive bonuses of a million pounds or more, a rise of 40 per cent on the previous year.[59] These were curbed a little in the immediate aftermath of the crisis – hitting firms that dealt in luxury goods* – but to the fury of the public normal service was soon restored.

Culturally, the rapacious capitalist was becoming ever more entrenched as a type in popular drama on television, often with extreme right-wing politics thrown into the mix. 'We are on the edge of an abyss,' says Robert Osbourne, a wealthy businessman in the spy series *Spooks* (2002). 'I'm going to take this country back one street at a time.' He's busily sponsoring race riots, while also smuggling illegal immigrants into the country. 'Little by little

---

* A collapse in sales was reported, for example, by staff at Fettered Pleasures, a north London retail outlet that specialised in upmarket sadomasochistic and bondage equipment – padded leather cages and the like. The shop closed in 2011, though the name survived as a mail-order business.

this country will change. We bring the foreigners in, we choke the asylum system and shove immigration in people's faces.'

The BBC series *Hustle* centred on a gang of confidence tricksters whose motto is 'You can't con an honest man,' ensuring that our sympathies lie with the crooks, not their victims. In a 2004 episode they target Sir Anthony Reeves, CEO of a utilities company who's overseen a huge fall in profits and big rises in bills, an 'inept piece of mismanagement' that earns him a £500,000 payoff. One of the gang fills in the background: 'Sir Anthony verges on the xenophobic, staunch defender of the pound, hates anything European. He refers to anyone who earns less than a hundred thousand a year as a member of the Great Unwashed.' Another murmurs sarcastically, 'Nice man!'

The same year, the TV movie *Fallen* centred on a businessman who was once a candidate for the BNP but has more recently turned to direct action. He's been smuggling missiles into the country from the Middle East, planning to commit a false-flag terrorist outrage that'll be blamed on Islamic extremists. 'We Brits have become a little too hospitable for our own good,' he explains. 'All these immigrants flooding into the country, and nobody does anything about it. Watch how fast that changes if a civilian aircraft gets shot out of the sky.'

And again in 2004, a senior police officer in *Murder City* has to decide which of two inquiries deserves the lion's share of his limited resources. There's a missing sixteen-year-old girl from a nice suburban family, or there's 'a parasitical, money-grubbing quantities trader', who's been found dead: 'no friends, no family, a loner, no one even liked him'. In this modern take on Bernard Shaw's *The Doctor's Dilemma*, there's not a moment of hesitation: the case of the trader is immediately downgraded.

Aside from the corporate crooks, the London seen in *Spooks*, *Hustle* and *Murder City* – and in *Demons*, *Luther*, *Sherlock* and a host of others – was a glossy hi-tech city of corporate buildings and waterfront views, shot in stylish, rapid-cut photography and populated by good-looking multicultural young people. It was a long way removed from the down-at-heel sleaze of a generation back; all that survived from the past were picturesque alleys and railway arches, deserted and darkly tense. And for many Britons, this alien, futuristic London was the problem. It was seen to be drifting away on its own, becoming a cosmopolitan city of the world, run by faceless financiers and owned by foreigners with dubious funding. It didn't even look like the rest of the country: the 2011 census showed that over a third of London's residents had been born abroad (a quarter born outside Europe), with white British people now a minority. And it was the home of exotic insular tribes of the kind satirised in smart sitcoms – the political advisers of *The Thick of It* (2005), or the 'self-facilitating media node' that is *Nathan Barley* (2005) – insecure, boastful young men and women, full of sound and futility, for whom there is nothing beyond their own in-crowd of superannuated adolescents.

Most Londoners, of course, were neither Russian oligarchs nor Hoxton hipsters. But all could see that the city was changing rapidly, and many were feeling excluded. 'This London was not the capital her parents had known,' reflects a character in P. D. James's *The Murder Room* (2003). 'Theirs had been a more peaceable city and a gentler England.'[60] In particular, the cost of housing, whether owned or rented, was becoming prohibitive to all but the very wealthy (or those on benefits), hollowing out the middle classes. For years, trade unions had been warning that essential public-sector workers – teachers, nurses, firefighters, police officers – were being priced out of the capital, with a knock-on effect in other desirable locations: not just the Thames Valley and Surrey, but Bath, Brighton, Cambridge, Oxford, York. In the film *Wimbledon* (2004), a couple are seen riding the London Eye and gazing out across the city. 'One day,' he says, 'none of this will be ours.'

*

'As communism died in 1989, capitalism died in 2008,' observed Cardinal Cormac Murphy-O'Connor, the archbishop of Westminster.[61] If that overstated the case, there was certainly a perception that economic inequality was becoming unsupportable and perhaps unsustainable. And the danger for politicians was that they were too easily seen as being on the wrong side.

There was, for example, a gossipy story in 2008 about what Peter Mandelson did or did not say to George Osborne when the two men met socially in Corfu. They were on a superyacht owned by the Russian oligarch Oleg Deripaska, 'often described as Russia's richest man,'[62] along with financier Nathaniel Rothschild and media executive Elizabeth Murdoch.* The story didn't really linger, but the image did, the idea that senior members of the two rival parties moved in such very elevated circles. It looked decadent. Or there was the culture secretary Tessa Jowell, whose husband David Mills was a corporate lawyer acting for Silvio Berlusconi. Mills was alleged in 2006 to have taken a £340,000 bribe from the Italian prime minister, and although he insisted that Jowell was 'entirely blameless',[63] it wasn't the kind of association that reflected well on Labour.

Or there was the biggest sex scandal of the Blair years, when home secretary David Blunkett resigned from the cabinet in 2004, caught up in stories of his affair with a woman who was not only married to a 'multi-millionaire husband',[64] but also the publisher of conservative magazine the *Spectator*. And this was Blunkett, the Sheffield boy who'd fought poverty and blindness to reach the political heights, and who was meant to be a tribune of the working class, the scourge of the metropolitan élite.†

---

* Osborne 'has two kinds of friends – the Haves and the Have Yachts', joked Frank Skinner.

† When John Prescott was revealed to have had a two-year affair, on the other hand, it was more predictably with his diary secretary, and the story was treated humorously in the press, particularly the detail that, although he

Above all, there was the long-running saga of the loans-for-peerages scandal. The allegation was that supporters of Labour had lent the party large sums (which, being loans not gifts, did not have to be declared) and had subsequently had their names put forward for honours. It was an old accusation. The difference this time was that the stories resulted in an eighteen-month police investigation. The Labour Party's fundraiser Lord Michael Levy was arrested, among others, and Tony Blair himself questioned on three occasions as a witness, the last time in the month he left office. Such a thing had never happened before, and although no charges were brought against anyone, it looked shabby. In a 2008 episode of the sitcom *Outnumbered*, a boy standing for election to his school council is found to have given his classmates twenty pence each, and his parents remonstrate with him. 'You see, Ben, that isn't how democracy works,' says his father, and then catches himself. 'What am I saying?'

These things tarnished Labour. And while the party pointlessly pursued its anti-toff campaign in, say, Crewe and Nantwich, the public had concluded that in this new world of them and us what counted was not inherited class, but a sense of values, a need for empathy, however nebulous this might be. It was the lesson that should have been learned from the veneration of Nigella Lawson as domestic goddess and the denigration of Jamie Oliver as a meddler. A public-school education was no longer the issue; people wanted politicians who understood them and shared their interests, rather than hobnobbing with the super-elite in finance and the media, let alone oligarchs from eastern Europe and beyond. This was why Blair's post-premiership wealth attracted such hostility.

'gave a four-times-a-night performance', he was physically under-endowed. He 'might have the body of a saveloy but in the department where it matters he is a chipolata', chortled the *Sun*, helpfully printing a life-size picture of a two-inch cocktail sausage for those who hadn't experienced the joys of a 1970s-themed finger-buffet. (4 May 2006)

Dissatisfaction with politicians came to a head in 2009 when the *Daily Telegraph*, having acquired full, unredacted records of the expense claims of MPs, began publishing the information.

This was a scandal that had been years in the making. In the 1980s, as salaries in the City of London began their sharp rise, MPs were looking down the river from Westminster, envious of the earning power of old university chums. There was a limit to how far they could push their own pay, though, so other benefits were found instead. In 2001, for example, MPs had voted themselves an above-inflation pay rise of £4,000 a year, and at the same time increased their additional costs allowance by a further £4,000 and improved the return on their pensions. By 2007, when Sir Philip Mawer, the parliamentary commissioner for standards, warned that there was abuse of the system, an MP's basic salary stood at around £60,000 a year, with an additional £104,000 for office and administration costs, plus expenses. It was material related to this latter category that the press had been after for some time. Occasionally a story would emerge – as when home secretary Jacqui Smith was found to have claimed for a Virgin Media bill that included two pay-per-view porn movies – but the Commons fought hard to keep its privacy.

And then a cache of over a million documents was leaked to the *Telegraph*, which put a team of 25 people on the story and ran it for all it was worth. For weeks there was a daily diet of injury and insult, as revelation after revelation crawled into the public glare. The details made MPs appear both venal and ridiculous. There was Tony Blair's £6,990 bill for roof repairs, claimed two days before he left office; there were the mock-Tudor beams fitted to John Prescott's house and the love seat in Douglas Carswell's garden; there was the servicing of the boiler for Michael Ancram's swimming pool, the cleaning of Douglas Hogg's moat, the clearing of wisteria from David Cameron's chimney. And, at the pinnacle, there was Sir Peter Viggers's duck house, costing £1,645, the object that came to symbolise the whole affair. Individual claims were disputed and sometimes refuted, but the sheer weight of detail made its own impact.

Given how often people had voiced their cynicism about politicians, it might have been expected that this would simply be taken as evidence of what was already known. But it hit harder than that. There was real anger and contempt. The recession was starting to bite, and the bank bail-out was still fresh in the mind. But the numbers involved in the economic crisis were so vast as to be meaningless; not so with the parliamentary expenses. Even more acute was 'the insight into MPs' lives', as David Cameron put it, the scrutiny of 'a class that seemed completely out of touch with normal people'.[65]

'We know no spectacle so ridiculous as the British public in one of its periodical fits of morality,' wrote Thomas Macaulay in 1831, and here was a fine fit of morality.[66] Public fury was turned on MPs to a degree that shook Westminster. Radio phone-in shows had a field day, and the studio audience on *Question Time* was overtly, jeeringly hostile to any politician – of whatever party – who had the courage to appear on the panel. All were assumed to be feathering their own duck houses. 'The whole thing is a catastrophe of massive proportions,' wrote Michael Spicer,[67] who'd unsuccessfully tried to claim £23.95 for a Christmas tree, but did get over £100,000-worth of work done on his Worcestershire manor house.[68] He said of his Tory colleagues, 'They are traumatised, hurt and damaged.'[69] It was, said Vince Cable, 'the biggest political crisis in my lifetime'.[70]

Even in clear cases of wrongdoing, the majority were abuses of a system that was almost designed to be abused. Most notably, the second-house-allowance rules gave MPs a good deal of leeway over what constituted a secondary residence, and permitted them to flip between primary and secondary whenever it proved advantageous. Or, in the case of married Tory MPs Andrew MacKay and Julie Kirkbride, it permitted her to claim mortgage payments for the family home in her constituency, and him to do the same for their Westminster flat. 'They effectively had no main home but two second homes,' observed the *Telegraph*, 'and were using public funds to pay for both of them.'[71]

However lax the regulations, though, some had overstepped a legal as well as moral line. Labour MPs David Chaytor, Jim Devine, Eric Illsley, Denis MacShane, Elliot Morley and Margaret Moran were prosecuted and found guilty on various charges of fraud and false accountancy, and given prison sentences – with the exception, following psychiatric evidence, of Moran. Also jailed were two Conservative peers. The damage to Parliament's reputation went further still. In an attempt to seize the initiative, MPs decided that Michael Martin, the Speaker of the House of Commons, had mishandled the crisis and had lost the confidence of the public; he became the first Speaker to be forced out of office for over 300 years.*

As the scandal grew, Gordon Brown posted a video on YouTube, a garbled torrent, telling the electorate that he understood their concerns and promising that change was coming. 'MPs need to have the humility to recognise that the country has lost confidence,' he said.[72] It amounted to very little, and his appeal failed to pacify a deeply disgruntled public. He didn't help his cause by breaking into an awkward, inappropriate grin at random moments. This tic had been noted before – Chris Mullin referred to it as his 'mirthless smile, switching on and off like a neon sign'[73] – but was now becoming a standard feature of his appearances, presumably to address the perception that he was lacking in warmth. It was an invitation to mockery. Simon Hoggart wrote in the *Guardian*, 'It's the smile a 50-year-old man might use on the parents of the

---

* Some in the House had never taken to Martin, a former sheet-metal worker from Glasgow, and he faced what Peter Hain called 'snotty class prejudice'. (*Outside In* p. 361) In his nine years in office, he never made the same public impact as his predecessor, Betty Boothroyd, or successor, John Bercow.

23-year-old woman he is dating, in a doomed attempt to reassure them.'[74] Jon Gaunt in the *Sun* settled for calling the prime minister a 'grinning, gurning gargoyle'.[75]

The YouTube video merely deepened the depression among Labour MPs. 'Why on earth did they let it go out?' wailed an ex-minister, and a backbencher observed sadly, 'I've never known morale so low.'[76] A few months later, in June 2009, the scale of Labour's crisis became clear when the party came third in the European elections, securing just 15 per cent, its lowest share of a national vote in 99 years. Council elections, held on the same day, were just as bad.

As the government limped towards the end of its term, it was looking as weak and doomed as had that of John Major in the mid-1990s. And just as divided. It was now assumed that Brown was not able to win the next election, and a succession of would-be coups were mounted in an attempt to dislodge him. There were round-robin letters and resignations, and open attacks from the ex-ministerial ranks. Brown's biographer Steve Richards recorded an encounter between David Cameron and former Labour minister Charles Clarke in the summer of 2009. 'Don't worry, we'll get rid of Gordon before the election,' promised Clarke, and Cameron retorted, 'That's exactly what I'm worried about.'[77] Each incident inflicted further damage, whether it were Clarke saying he was 'ashamed to be a Labour Member of Parliament'[78] or Europe minister Caroline Flint accusing Brown of treating women in cabinet as 'little more than female window dressing'.[79]* Perhaps if it had

---

* This was not new to Brown. For all the talk of Blair's Babes, New Labour had always been a very male enterprise. Margaret Beckett was the most senior woman in the party, the elected deputy leader who had stood in as leader on John Smith's death and served in cabinet right through the Blair years; yet she rates just eight mentions in his memoirs, the last of them in a 'worst of all worlds' reshuffle, when she was promoted to foreign secretary. She is never heard from again.

all been coordinated, it might have worked, but Labour lacked the ruthlessness displayed by the Tories when dispatching Margaret Thatcher or Iain Duncan Smith. Or even that of the Liberal Democrats when discarding Menzies Campbell.

In January 2010, there was one last attempt to change leader, when two ex-cabinet ministers, Patricia Hewitt and Geoff Hoon,* called for a secret ballot of MPs. It was too late. 'The election was imminent,' concluded Jack Straw. 'We were now, to coin a phrase, all in it together.'[80] Nor was there any support for a change in the wider party: a poll that month showed 71 per cent of Labour voters thought Brown was the best leader currently available.[81]

So he stayed in office, eking out the last days of a deeply disappointing premiership, looking, said Ken Clarke, 'so pale-faced that he was almost dysfunctional, and I really did fear for his well-being'.[82] He'd been touted as the anti-Blair, the man who would restore self-respect and core principles to a hurting party, and none of it had come to pass. There was even a return to the sleaziest side of spin, when Brown's press secretary, Damian McBride, was obliged to resign in 2009 after emails were leaked revealing plans to spread untrue and offensive rumours about Tory MPs and their spouses.

There had been a lack of policy initiatives, and perhaps that was understandable because, despite the endless Westminster gossip about Blairites and Brownites, the dispute had always been essentially personal, not political. After all, Brown had built much of New Labour himself. The PFI projects, the sprawling tax regime, the light-touch financial regulation, the tax credits – it was all his, all the economic contortions that attempted to weld

---

* Two months later, both Hewitt and Hoon were among MPs suspended from the Parliamentary Labour Party after being covertly filmed by Channel 4's *Dispatches* apparently offering their services to a fictitious lobbying company. Hoon explained that he was looking for 'something that bluntly makes money'.

social justice onto a low-pay, low-tax system without strong trade unions. None of this was going to change under his premiership.

Even if he had wished to make a significant shift in direction, his hands were tied by the enormous drain on the public purse of the financial crash. His intervention on that occasion was the most significant moment of his time as prime minister, and, in a famous stumble in the Commons, he talked of having 'saved the world, er, saved the banks'.[83] In his memoirs, he amended this a little – 'The leaders of the world agreed on concerted action that may have saved the world from a second great depression'[84] – but he was still clear that he'd played a pivotal role. But even if one accepted that his actions had been necessary and timely, this wasn't really what his supporters had hoped for. He was supposed to change society, not reconstruct a banking system that had failed so spectacularly.

For a man who appeared to be such a heavyweight politician, Brown's career seemed strangely insubstantial. He had many of the attributes one would want – an agile intelligence, a seriousness of manner, an ability to command a platform, a moral commitment to combating poverty – but somehow he was less than the sum of his parts. Perhaps it was because of the painful political lessons he'd learned. He was 32 when elected to Parliament, 46 by the time he entered government, and those 14 years of powerless opposition shaped him; his espousal of New Labour came from the same bitter experience as that of Tony Blair.

As with Blair, there was a lingering sense of disappointment. Brown was the longest-serving chancellor since William Pitt the Younger,* having already spent five years in preparation as shadow chancellor, yet he changed the country less than had Geoffrey Howe or Nigel Lawson. His most substantial legacy was the minimum wage, a policy that had been in Labour manifestos since 1987, when Roy Hattersley was shadowing Lawson. Some of the underachievement was the product of the caution learned in the

---

* Pitt doubled up as prime minister.

lean years, but some of it was down to his self-indulgent insubordination, his running battles with the man elected leader by the Labour Party and prime minister by the country. Brown helped create New Labour and guide it into office, and then played a huge role in squandering the best opportunity the party had ever had.

His premiership resembled that of another ex-chancellor, James Callaghan, who'd become prime minister in 1976, two years into a government, taking over from the multi-election-winning Harold Wilson. Neither won a general election, and both were sunk by a crisis that undermined their proudest boast: the ability to work with the unions in Callaghan's case, economic stability in Brown's. There was also a parallel failure to catch the electoral tide, delaying until it was too late. When Callaghan faced speculation about calling an early election in 1978, he teased the media with a rendition of Vesta Victoria's music-hall classic 'Waiting at the Church'. Brown could have matched him with Marie Lloyd's 'My Old Man': 'I dillied and I dallied, I dallied and I dillied ...'*

In an earlier generation, he would still have been a major figure in the Labour Party, and he would have been better suited to times when politics was taken more seriously.† But in the twenty-first century, when dealing with the media was a primary requirement, he floundered. John Prescott once said of him, 'He could be a miserable bugger, Gordon.'[85] And in those last months in Downing Street, sinking ever further into gloom and despondency, the prime minister's public appearances exuded a sense of wretchedness that made the occasional flash of that unconvincing smile still more incongruous.

---

* By contrast, when chancellor John Major took over from Margaret Thatcher in 1990, he went on to win a general election.
† 'The paradox is that as politics has become less ideological, its coverage has become more sensationalist,' reflected Robin Cook. (*The Point of Departure* p. 262)

7

Grooming and Abusing

I

The death of Labour MP Bob Cryer in a motorway crash in April 1994 was felt deeply on the left. His obituary in the *Independent* was written by Tam Dalyell, and at his funeral Dennis Skinner was in the chair, with speakers including Tony Benn, Arthur Scargill, Bernie Grant and Jeremy Corbyn. Cryer had never had the highest public profile, but he was respected in the right circles: Skinner called him 'a full-time committed socialist',[1] and his widow, Ann, said he was a 'lifetime rebel'.[2]

There was an attempt to get her to stand in the ensuing by-election, but she declined. 'It was too soon,' she explained later.

'I wasn't up to it.'[3] The idea was a good one, though. Born in Lytham St Annes in 1939, Ann Cryer (née Place) had always been political – she came from a family of suffragettes and socialists – and in 1961 she'd been elected onto Darwen Council in Lancashire: 22 years old, working at the Blackburn telephone exchange, and the youngest councillor in the country. Later that year she met her future husband Bob Cryer at the Labour Party conference in Blackpool. In 1964, in Harold Wilson's first general election victory, he stood as a candidate in Darwen, but failed to unseat the long-serving Tory MP Charles Fletcher-Cooke.

A decade later, though, Cryer succeeded, elected in 1974 for Keighley, a town to the north-west of Bradford, West Yorkshire, which he represented until it fell to the Tories in 1983. He then spent a term in the European Parliament, before returning to Westminster at the next election as MP for Bradford South.* He was a member of the Bennite left, and for two years back in the 70s had served as an industry minister in James Callaghan's government, before a principled resignation over policy. Beyond politics, the Cryers shared a love of railways, and appeared, together with their children John and Jane, as extras in the film *The Railway Children* (1970), Bob having advised on the earlier BBC adaptation of the story.†

Although she turned down the idea of contesting Bradford South in 1994, Ann Cryer remained an important figure in Yorkshire politics, and was subsequently persuaded to go for Bob's original constituency in Keighley. 'You can't remain a widow all your life,' Tony Benn told her.[4] She was a popular candidate and

---

* Bob Cryer's claim to political trivia fame was that in 1989 he became the first MP, apart from the Speaker, to be heard in a televised debate in the Commons, interrupting scheduled proceedings with a point of order.
† In 2013 the British Board of Film Classification received its first ever complaint about *The Railway Children*; 43 years after its release, someone suggested it might encourage children to play on rail tracks.

won the seat in 1997 on a 10 per cent swing, defeating the man who had deposed her husband thirteen years earlier. In the same election her son John Cryer became MP for Hornchurch.

Like Bob before them, Ann and John Cryer were clearly on the left of Tony Blair's Labour, and were marked down early on by Peter Mandelson as 'potential rebels'.[5] They lived up to their reputation, joining the Campaign group of MPs and voting against the government on the controversial issues of the day: welfare, war, student fees. In September 1998, when a list was compiled of the most rebellious of the new Labour intake, John was ranked fourth out of 184 MPs, while Ann was at number five. 'I must stand by what I believe. There are situations where I feel at odds with the government.'[6]

If that was all very much in the family tradition, she was nonetheless adamant that she was not going to be 'Bob Cryer mark two'.[7] And in due course, she began to upset not just the leadership but those on her side of Labour as well.

Somewhere around one in six of the population of Keighley was British Asian, the large majority of them Muslims of Pakistani or Bangladeshi heritage. Soon after her election, Ann Cryer began to hear stories of girls being sent to the Indian subcontinent to be married against their will, even, on some occasions, being 'forced to marry at gunpoint'.[8] These were arranged marriages that had turned to coercion. As journalist Satinder Chohan wrote in the *Guardian*, 'Forced marriages can entail abduction, violence, sexual abuse, rape and even murder.'[9] Cryer spoke out on the issue repeatedly from 1998, becoming the first to raise it in Parliament, and her pressure helped lead to the 2007 Forced Marriages Act.

More controversially, she also criticised the practice of bringing spouses over from Pakistan or Bangladesh for arranged marriages, however consensual, arguing that it was holding back social progress. 'I want the Muslim community to be as prosperous as the Sikh and Hindu communities have become,' she said, 'but I believe it is being held back by marriages to men who know nothing of the culture over here, who often don't speak the language.'[10]

In 2001 she went a little further still and, speaking this time about brides coming from the subcontinent, suggested that 'we must think about requiring would-be spouses to have a language qualification'. That brought her into conflict with the ruling Labour group on Bradford Council, but she was unrepentant. Nor did it escape her notice that the loudest voices against her were those of men. 'They want me to shut up and stop questioning the right of Asian males to dictate to Asian females,' she said. 'As long as Asian women don't have English they are without rights.'[11]

Her comments also attracted national criticism. Shahid Malik, a member of Labour's National Executive Committee, said she was 'doing the BNP's work' and called for the parliamentary whip to be withdrawn. 'Without doubt there are racist undertones in what she is saying and it will be viewed as Islamophobic,' he said. Iqbal Sacranie of the Muslim Council of Britain joined the condemnation: 'She's trying to find fault with the victims, the very people being marginalised.'[12] And in his *Independent* column, comedian Mark Steel denounced the idea of immigrants having to speak English: 'It's not that all those who support it are racist, but they surrender to the racists.'[13]

Meanwhile, back in Bradford, a Liberal Democrat councillor, Mozaquir Ali, had waded in, calling for Cryer to be 'prosecuted for inciting racism'. And shortly afterwards, the Labour Party offices in Keighley were vandalised by a gang of youths: the windows were smashed, and the back door decorated with a graffitied image 'of Osama Bin Laden in front of New York's doomed twin towers and various obscenities'.[14]

'What I am trying to do,' Cryer explained, 'is to speak over the heads of the self-styled Asian leadership and also the white politically correct. They're almost thought police, because they are telling me what I should be thinking and what I should be saying.'

But she also acknowledged that these were difficult waters. 'The reason I had never mentioned this before was because I had a fear of being called a racist and of course I am not. If I'm a racist, I am also a Dutchman.'[15]

The attacks, noticeably, were still all coming from men. The young women who Cryer was seeking to protect were not much heard from. Two years later, though, Monica Ali's acclaimed first novel *Brick Lane* (2003) did give them a voice. The story was of Nazneen, an eighteen-year-old woman from a Bangladeshi village who comes to the East End of London for an arranged marriage to a man more than twice her age. She 'could say two things in English: sorry and thank you', and although her husband is a comically absurd figure, not a monster – he doesn't beat her, for example – he discourages her from leaving the high-rise council flat they occupy. 'Why should you go out?' he asks rhetorically.[16] Nazneen does eventually go out, and finds a life of her own, but the social isolation of the early pages lingers on as an alternative outcome. Her position was one that Ann Cryer would have recognised from her caseload.

It was in early 2002 that Cryer first heard stories about gangs of men in her constituency exploiting young girls for sex and prostitution. Information was hard to come by, but gradually a picture began to emerge. It appeared to be not just a couple of isolated individuals, but a network, a loose association of night workers, men employed by minicab firms, takeaway restaurants and the like. They were targeting the girls they met, enticing them with alcohol, presents and drugs, and ultimately having sex with them. There were stories of girls being shared with other men, and of them being prostituted. Some were underage, and crimes were certainly being committed, but it was difficult to get the victims to talk; some were emotionally reliant upon the men, others too drunk or damaged to remember what had happened to them.

A 2003 report from Bradford Youth Services confirmed that

there was a serious problem. Of the 45 teenage girls interviewed for the survey, around 80 per cent said they had had sex before they were sixteen, sometimes because they were forced, sometimes for money or to get a bed for the night. A spokesperson for Barnardo's, who'd been working with victims of child prostitution for some time, welcomed the study: 'Young women across Bradford and Keighley are systematically trapped and exploited in sometimes extremely dangerous sexual relationships when they are still children in the eyes of the law.'[17]

After eighteen months of investigation, Cryer announced that her office now had 'a list of more than sixty names of men who are alleged to have lured girls, some as young as eleven, to have sex with them'.[18] And in the most explosive revelation, she added that there was a racial dimension to the story: 'I am merely pointing out fact in saying that all the victims of these terrible crimes are white girls and all the alleged perpetrators are Asian men.'[19]

The men on Cryer's list came from the Pakistani and Bangladeshi communities, and the allegations of gang rape and prostitution suggested that the abuse might have become culturally entrenched. The local police, however, were unconvinced. 'Superintendent Whyman said he did not think there had been any systematic exploitation of young girls,' reported the local newspaper. 'He stressed he did not see the problem confined to the Asian community and that grooming girls for sex was endemic.'[20]

The first conviction came in November 2003 – twenty-four-year-old Delwar Hussain found guilty of having sex with a thirteen-year-old – and in 2004 others were arrested and charged. The official account remained that there was no racial or cultural element to the offences. 'The investigation we have done has arrested both Asian and white men,' said Colin Cramphorn, the chief constable of West Yorkshire Police, pointing to Britain's high rate of teenage pregnancies, 'with the fathers being of all races'.[21]

Cramphorn's comments came in response to a Channel 4 documentary, *Edge of the City*, that featured some of the victims. Anna

Hall, the producer and director of the programme, explained that she'd stumbled into the subject, her original intention having been to document the daily lives of social workers. 'We weren't looking for this issue,' she said. 'It just kept surfacing. Social workers said, "You can't do that story because it's too difficult." What did they mean by "too difficult"? Too racially sensitive?'[22]

The stories in the documentary were jaw-dropping, including a thirteen-year-old said to have more than a hundred sexual partners, and the programme's conclusion was firmly in agreement with Cryer's findings: 'What's devastating for such a multiracial area is that in Bradford the girls are white and the men overwhelmingly are Asian.'[23] Hall's overriding sense was one of horror that 'blatant abuse was going on under people's noses, and no one seemed able to prevent it'.[24]

Edge of the City was scheduled for transmission in May 2004, but was postponed at Cramphorn's request.* 'The broadcast will increase community tension across Bradford with the consequent risk that it will provoke public disorder,' he said.[25] Furthermore, it was an insensitive time to be screening such a programme since there were local elections that month, and then, in June, elections to the European Parliament. Anything that reflected badly on a particular racial group might help the far right in those polls. In short, warned Lee Jasper† of the National Assembly Against Racism, the documentary 'could inadvertently act as a recruiting sergeant for the BNP'.[26]

The fear was that there might be a rerun of 2001, when riots had broken out in several northern cities: Bradford, Burnley, Leeds, Oldham. Disturbances in Bradford, in particular, where over 300

---

* It was eventually screened in August 2004.

† Jasper had been a key figure in Ken Livingstone's mayoral team in London since 2000, and would later stand in the 2012 Croydon North by-election for Respect before rejoining Labour in 2016.

police officers were injured, were said to be 'the worst race riots in more than twenty years'.[27] They had been sparked by tensions between white and Asian populations, with additional fuel provided by the presence of the far-right British National Party and – according to the home secretary David Blunkett – of 'the Socialist Workers Party and hangers-on who made matters worse and played directly into the hands of the far right'.[28] Since then, the BNP had grown substantially.

The party was undoubtedly capable of provoking conflict on the streets, but there remained the question of whether it might also pose an electoral challenge. Under the leadership of Nick Griffin, it made its first impact in 2002, when three BNP councillors were elected in Burnley. That was a small enough victory to be dismissed in most quarters. The salient point about the local government elections that year, said the *Independent on Sunday*, was how little support the fringes enjoyed: 'the three main parties secured around 95 per cent of the votes cast'.[29] In *The Times* Michael Gove pointed to the victory of several Asian Tories: 'The bigger but less dramatic story about these elections may not be the rise of racism as an electoral factor but its ebbing as a consideration in many voters' minds.'[30]

Reports from Burnley suggested that this might be too optimistic. The BNP success was sufficient to bring the town, briefly, to national attention. What emerged was a tale of two ghettos. First, there was the 'poor white country' of Burnley Wood, a dense network of terraced streets, 'as grim and violent a place as you can see in Britain', where 'men wander in vests and women in slippers';[31] parts of it were said to 'resemble a war zone, with burned-out housing, abandoned cars and rubble in the streets'.[32] It was here, 'on a piece of land strewn with broken glass, dog dirt, litter, remnants of fires and surrounded by boarded-up houses', that the three BNP councillors held their first press conference.[33]

And then, a mile or so to the north, there was the Asian equivalent in Daneshouse, the eighth-poorest ward in the country. The

2001 census showed that over 90 per cent of those in the Borough of Burnley were white, with just 7 per cent of Asian origin, mostly from Bangladesh. The complaint from Burnley Wood was that the larger families in Daneshouse consumed a disproportionate share of what little public spending the council had at its disposal. 'I only voted for the BNP because Labour isn't doing anything around here for whites,' said one resident. 'Someone has to step in and make sure the whites get their fair share,' agreed another. 'I'm disgusted with my Labour candidate. Where the hell was he when we needed him?'[34]

In the 2003 round of local elections, the BNP contingent on Burnley Council rose to eight. There were further victories in Stoke, Broxbourne and Calderdale, though Nick Griffin failed to get elected in Oldham. It still wasn't clear if this was a significant electoral threat. Certainly, Shahid Malik, the Labour politician who'd accused Ann Cryer of 'doing the BNP's work', was keen to downplay the successes. 'We've got to get this into perspective,' he said. 'There are some 22,000 councillors in this country, the BNP will have got fifteen or so.'[35]

Malik himself had been born in Burnley – his father, Rafique, had served as mayor of the town in 2000–01 – and he would go on to become the first Muslim minister in a British government. In the 2005 general election, he was returned for Dewsbury, the West Yorkshire constituency that gave the BNP their best showing that year, with over 5,000 votes. They still came fourth, though, and the Conservative candidate in second place was Sayeeda Warsi – like Malik, a Muslim child of immigrants from Pakistan – so perhaps Michael Gove's point about the decline of racially motivated voting had merit.

Nationally, the BNP fielded 119 candidates in 2005, up from 33 in the previous general election. As leader, Nick Griffin had the pick of the constituencies and chose to stand against Ann Cryer in Keighley. He came fourth, with 9 per cent of the vote, while Cryer was re-elected with 45 per cent and an increased majority.

'Over the last seven years I have raised issues that some people have found unpalatable – for example: forced marriages; honour killings; the need to learn and speak English; managed migration,' she said. 'Now is the time to send a clear message to the outside extremists that they are not welcome and that we will not allow them to destroy our towns.'[36]

Those, of course, were not the issues that the BNP focused on. Instead it made great play of the sexual exploitation cases that she'd also highlighted. And it did so in the crudest terms it felt it could get away with. 'There is something about these Asian blokes that they like these young girls,' said Phil Edwards, the party's official spokesperson; 'something to do with their religion, they cannot get it in their own communities.'[37]

In July 2004, the BBC screened *The Secret Agent*, a documentary containing undercover footage of BNP members. One boasted of having committed a violent assault during the Bradford riots, another fantasised about machine-gunning Muslims. Nick Griffin also featured, calling Islam a 'vicious, wicked faith' and talking about the arrests of Muslim men for grooming under-age girls for sex: 'The bastards that are in that gang, they are in prison so the public think it's all over. Well, it's not. Because there's more of them.'[38] He was subsequently charged with incitement to racial hatred, though acquitted.

Those who believed Ann Cryer was aiding and abetting racists by speaking out about the ethnicity of sex offenders saw the steady rise of the far right as proof of their argument. From another perspective, however, this was merely shooting the messenger, and it was the child abusers themselves who were acting as 'a recruiting sergeant for the BNP'. If appalling crimes were being committed, and if there was indeed a racial or cultural dimension, a pattern of offending, then the greater offence for an MP would be to remain silent. That really would be aiding and abetting.

That there was such a dimension became ever harder to ignore.

Nick Griffin's claim that 'there's more of them' proved to be accurate. A decade on, in 2015, a further fifteen men were convicted of rape and other offences against underage girls in Keighley. By that stage, the scale of the problem was being revealed in a string of court cases. This was no isolated local phenomenon; there were convictions for street grooming gangs – as they became known – operating in the same manner in Aylesbury, Banbury, Bristol, Derby, Halifax, Huddersfield, Newcastle, Oxford, Peterborough, Rochdale, Rotherham and Telford. An official inquiry found that in Rotherham alone there had been an estimated 1,400 victims over a sixteen-year period: 'most of the victims in the cases we sampled were white British children, and the majority of the perpetrators were from minority ethnic communities'.[39] Complaints had been made in 2001, yet the first convictions secured only in 2010.

The reluctance of the authorities to get involved was a particularly shocking element in the cases. One of the girls from Rotherham told *The Times* of an incident in 2008 when the police raided the house she was in, responding to a report of a girl's screams. She herself was then arrested, charged and convicted of being drunk and disorderly, while the three British Pakistani men found in the house were released without charge. She was thirteen years old at the time. Shortly afterwards she became pregnant, though she didn't know by whom: her thirty-year-old abuser had lent and rented her out too many times for her to keep track; some who assaulted her wore balaclavas to conceal their identity, some were 'old men with grey beards'.[40] The abuse she suffered was key to the conviction in autumn 2010 of five men for rape and sexual activity with a child.

'We had social workers telling us they'd been trying to get the police to take this problem seriously for years,' said Maggie Oliver, a Manchester detective who worked on an investigation in Hulme and Rusholme. That operation 'identified dozens of young victims and dozens of suspects' but was closed down in

2005 with no arrests made 'due to concerns over costs among senior command'. The pattern was the same, said Oliver: 'men of largely Pakistani heritage were abusing vulnerable white girls'.[41]

There were those who continued to insist that this was not a cultural issue, that to say otherwise was merely to perpetuate – as a 2011 *Guardian* headline put it – 'Our ignoble tradition of racialising crime'.[42] The following year, Sue Berelowitz, the deputy children's commissioner for England, said on Radio 4 that the grooming gangs were not just Asian Muslims. 'It's not a problem confined to one community,' she insisted. 'It is absolutely happening across all ethnic and religious groups.' In response, the *The Times* columnist David Aaronovitch summed up the situation as it then stood: 'of sixty-eight recent convictions involving street grooming, fifty-nine were of British Pakistani men'.[43]

The particular case that sparked this exchange was the conviction of nine British Pakistani men in Rochdale for rape, the trafficking of girls and other offences. And with those guilty verdicts, a corner seemed to have been turned. Mohammed Shafiq, of the Rochdale-based Ramadhan Foundation, was unequivocal: 'to say that ethnicity is not a factor in these crimes is a lie'.[44] Alyas Karmani, an imam and a Respect councillor in Bradford, spoke of the dual worlds inhabited by young men of Pakistani and Bangladeshi descent. There was the traditional realm of family, business and mosque, and then there was the modern consumerist world of the West. The fault line, as so often when cultures clash, lay with sex. 'Oral sex and anal sex are taboo in the British Pakistani community,' Karmani explained. 'Sex is seen as only for procreation and only in the missionary position.' In complete contrast, there were the temptations of 'the over-sexualised, material and lust-driven English lifestyle, where women are scantily clad, binge-drinking is a mainstream form of entertainment and porn is a massive factor'.[45]

Mohammed Shafiq was equally clear why the police and social services had been so tardy in responding to the stories. 'They fear being called racist,' he told *Panorama* in 2008.[46] He later argued that if there were racist behaviour, it was working in the other direction; the crimes of the grooming gangs constituted 'a form of racism that is abhorrent and totally unacceptable in a society that prides itself on equality and justice'.[47] He added, 'The reality is that there is a small minority of Pakistani men who think white teenage girls are worthless and can be abused with impunity.'[48]

The silence of most mainstream politicians stemmed from the same concerns. 'There must have been councillors and MPs all over the country who knew what was going on but were terrified,' said Ann Cryer; 'terrified of being labelled a racist.' Denis MacShane, who'd been Labour MP for Rotherham, regretted he had not done more, but as a '*Guardian*-reading liberal leftie', he was just following the prevailing orthodoxy: 'I think there was a culture of not wanting to rock the multicultural community boat.'[49] Similarly, when the abuse of arranged marriages was raised in government circles in 2004, Paul Boateng, Britain's first mixed-race cabinet minister, had slapped down discussion: 'Political dynamite. Don't touch it with a barge pole.'[50] This was the real reason that the street grooming gangs had been such a gift to the BNP: the fact that – with rare exceptions such as Cryer – politicians were so reluctant to raise their voices. In their absence, Nick Griffin had rushed to fill the vacuum.

The other side to this tale of abuse and neglect was the lack of concern in some official quarters for working-class children, many of whom had been in care homes and young offenders' institutions. There was an argument, too, that they weren't listened to because they were seen as damaged, unreliable witnesses. 'There's clearly an issue of ethnicity,' conceded Keir Starmer, the director of public prosecutions, in 2012. 'But if we're honest it's the approach to the victims, the credibility issue, that caused these cases not to be prosecuted in the past.'[51] He introduced new guidelines to ensure that complaints were taken seriously regardless of who was making them.

The consequences of the slow official response were twofold. Hundreds of young girls suffered horrendous abuse that could have been prevented had action been taken sooner. And beyond the immediate victims, many more people felt betrayed. As Mohammed Shafiq put it, an official attitude seemed to have emerged in which 'anxieties about racism trump common sense and compassion'.[52] The scandal was not that there was a conspiracy or cover-up, but that those whose job it was to protect the vulnerable had turned away their faces. They thought they were doing so for the right reasons, but they were wrong. They were wrong philosophically, showing an obsession with skin colour that rivalled that of the BNP, and they were wrong politically: the 'multicultural community boat' did not require its crew to turn a blind eye to vicious crime. Those in authority – police officers, politicians, council officials – were seen to have failed, and trust in institutions was damaged.

Rotherham Council, meanwhile, seemed to have its own priorities. In November 2012 it took three east European children away from their foster parents, saying that since the couple were members of UKIP, they were therefore likely to be racist. The council later insisted that there was no blanket ban on membership of the party, and that this particular case was very complex for reasons that couldn't be revealed because of confidentiality. The first official to be interviewed, however, had been more forthcoming: she said the stumbling block was UKIP's wish to end the 'active promotion of multiculturalism'.[53]

That story broke during a by-election campaign in Rotherham. Labour held on to the seat with a reduced margin, but the Conservatives, runners-up last time, now trailed in behind UKIP, the BNP and Respect, while the Liberal Democrats had slipped from third to eighth place. The extremes were closing in.

II

Sir Jimmy Savile OBE KCSG died on 29 October 2011, just two days shy of what would have been his eighty-fifth birthday. It had been an extraordinary life. Born into poverty in Leeds, a Bevin Boy working in the mines during the Second World War, he'd risen to an exalted, if ill-defined, position in the establishment: trusted by Margaret Thatcher, befriended by the Prince and Princess of Wales, knighted by Pope John Paul II. He was a regular presence on radio, television and advertising for four decades, and was probably the biggest charity fundraiser Britain has ever known. He was also a completely ridiculous figure, with his dyed hair and gold jewellery, his tracksuits and cigars, his inane patter that degenerated over the years till there remained little beyond cobwebbed catchphrases and random yodels.

He was a mess of contradictions: a disc jockey who claimed never to have owned a record; a children's television presenter who said he didn't like kids; a member of Mensa who fought a hundred bouts as a professional wrestler. He was a man who professed no interest in politics, yet appeared in election broadcasts for both the Conservatives and Liberals in 1974; who had no medical qualifications, but had a room set aside for him at Stoke Mandeville and Broadmoor Hospitals. 'To most people I am a question mark,' he said in 1968.[54]

And somehow, in between the absurdities and the achievements, his life changed the texture of the country. He was one of the first to run dance halls where the music came from records not live acts; he introduced the notion of pop celebrity to the BBC, most notably on *Top of the Pops* and *Jim'll Fix It*; and he pioneered the sponsored endurance event – in 1971 he walked from John O'Groats to Land's End, and a decade later competed in the first London Marathon, one of over 200 marathons he ran for charity. His *Daily Telegraph* obituary concluded, 'he was simply an odd chap'.[55]

His death also changed the texture of the country. Initially, there was a sort of amused reverence. The flags flew at half-mast over the Queen's Hotel in Leeds, where his gold-painted coffin lay in state next to a table bearing sacred relics: a half-smoked cigar in an ashtray, the books from his two appearances on *This Is Your Life*. Thousands came to pay their respects, and if the mood was less than sombre – one mourner came dressed as Santa Claus, because 'I thought Jimmy would appreciate it'[56] – the affection was genuine. For many, he was seen as one of the good guys, one of their own, the working-class kid who'd made it big and not forgotten them.

The lying-in-state was followed by a procession through the streets of Leeds – spectators chanted 'Jimmy, Jimmy' as the cortège passed[57] – and then, on the third day, a requiem mass, before the burial outside Scarborough. Savile went to his grave in a tracksuit and in the honorary green beret awarded to him by the Royal Marines. At his request, his coffin was set at a 45-degree angle, so that he would be looking out to sea, and was encased in concrete to deter any would-be grave robbers. In due course, a headstone was erected reading, 'It was good while it lasted.'[58]

It didn't last much longer.

Savile received his knighthood 'for charitable services' in 1990, but it was a long time coming. Margaret Thatcher had begun lobbying for him in 1983 and been repeatedly refused by the honours committee, with Robert Armstrong, head of the home civil service, expressing 'continuing misgivings' and saying 'we remain worried'.[59]

They weren't the only ones. Dark stories about Savile had been in wide circulation for years. He'd never made any secret of his voracious and promiscuous sexual appetite; indeed he had frequently bragged of it, telling tales of how he and his entourage enjoyed the attentions of eager young women, how they got into scrapes trying to evade the parents. 'I train my men well,' ran the last words of his autobiography. 'To date, we have not been found out. Which, after all, is the eleventh commandment.'[60] Within the music industry, he was regarded as a sexual predator with a taste for teenage girls and a casual disregard for the age of consent. Everyone knew stories of him picking out girls from the audience on *Top of the Pops*, and technicians on the show said they didn't let their daughters come in for the filming if he was the presenter.

'We all blocked our ears to the gossip,' broadcaster Esther Rantzen said later; 'there was gossip, and there were rumours.'[61] According to BBC producer Wilfred De'Ath, who worked with Savile in the 1960s, it was more even than that: 'He never attempted to hide this predilection, so it was generally known that he was into young girls.'[62] Nor was his behaviour any secret on Fleet Street. 'I have known he abused underage girls for more than forty-five years,' said Brian Hitchen, former editor of the *Daily Star* and *Sunday Express*. He hadn't published anything during Savile's lifetime, though, because 'Britain's libel laws too often help make those like Savile untouchable.'[63] BBC broadcaster Paul Gambaccini, who said he'd been 'waiting thirty years' for the truth to emerge, offered another reason why the press backed off, suggesting that Savile used his charitable activities as moral leverage: 'He was called and he said, "Well, you could run that story, but if you do there goes the funds that come in to Stoke Mandeville – do you want to be responsible for the drying up of the charity donations?" And they backed down.'[64]*

It took a year after his death for the stories to break. The first sign came, oddly, at the Edinburgh Fringe in August 2012,

---

* One of the few to speak publicly about Savile was comedian Jerry Sadowitz. 'He's a child-bender,' he said in a 1987 routine. 'That's why he does all the fucking charity work: it's to gain public sympathy for when his fucking case comes up.' Another view saw the charity fundraising as a kind of penance. The serial killer Culverton Smith in the *Sherlock* episode 'The Lying Detective' (2017) was loosely based on Savile; he's a wealthy well-connected entrepreneur who believes his philanthropy makes up for his crimes: 'If life is a balance sheet, and I think it is, why, I believe I'm in credit!'

when Bernie Byrnes's play *How's About That Then?* addressed the rumours head on. 'A paedophile is a person who has an erotic interest in prepubescent children,' said the fictional Savile. 'I ain't got that. Ephebophilia, as it happens, means adults with an erotic interest in individuals in their mid- to late adolescence. Guilty as charged.'[65] The following month, ITV broadcast *The Other Side of Jimmy Savile*, a documentary based on interviews with several women who claimed to have been abused by Savile. All were under the age of consent at the time of the abuse, and one was under fourteen.

And with that programme, the dam burst. Hundreds of alleged victims came forward right across the country, and the Metropolitan Police established Operation Yewtree to investigate the claims against Savile. Its report, published in January 2013, found that he had committed sexual offences, including rape, against at least 450 people. Most of the victims had been girls aged thirteen to sixteen, though some were adults, some were boys, and some were under the age of ten. Perhaps most shocking of all was the revelation that his crimes were committed not just within his showbusiness world, but in schools, hospitals and prisons: he had exploited his access to the nation's institutions to abuse with impunity. And other institutions – the BBC, the press, various police forces, the Crown Prosecution Service – had failed to take action. Clearly, most had simply averted their gaze, but the suspicion remained that some had gone further, had protected, perhaps even colluded with, Savile.

The fall from grace was as spectacular as the career that preceded it. His *sui generis* status remained, but now distorted and inverted, so that the media that had once lauded him now denounced him as 'the most evil and the most prolific paedophile of all time'.[66]

And when that was not enough to satisfy the appetite for monsters, the press ran stories claiming that 'Twisted Jimmy Savile may have sexually abused corpses as well as kids.'[67] Or there were suggestions that Savile might have known mass murderer Peter Sutcliffe, the Yorkshire Ripper, whose third victim was killed near one of Savile's homes. 'At first sight the suggestion that Savile might be connected with the crimes committed by Sutcliffe will seem far-fetched,' admitted criminologist Professor David Wilson. 'Yet predatory paedophiles and serial killers are the awful products of common forces which, in their case, were allowed to develop unchecked.' And forensic psychologist Dr Ian Stephen advised the police to 'keep an open mind' on whether Savile himself was a killer: 'It is possible that he upped the game. There is always that risk with people who are sensation seekers.'[68] There was no evidence of any such thing, and the absurd extravagance of the reports served only to belittle the real horror in a way that did no justice either to Savile's victims or to the cause of truth.

Meanwhile Operation Yewtree had been extended beyond Savile to take in allegations against other figures from the entertainment industries, with sensational results. Nineteen men were arrested as part of Yewtree, of whom seven were found guilty on various charges between 2012 and 2015. The worst offender was a doctor at Stoke Mandeville (though there was no connection with Savile) who received a 22-year sentence. Inevitably, though, it was those whose names were already known to the public who attracted the most attention: entertainer Rolf Harris and broadcaster Stuart Hall, media publicist Max Clifford (who died in jail), already disgraced pop star Gary Glitter (who received sixteen years).

Of the other celebrities who got dragged into the investigation, Dave Lee Travis was acquitted of all but one charge – groping the breasts of a 22-year-old woman – for which he was given a suspended three-month sentence. Nine of those arrested were never even charged, though the damage to their lives was considerable in financial and personal terms: Paul Gambaccini spent a year on police bail, comedian Freddie Starr said he'd contemplated suicide during the investigation, and fellow comic Jim Davidson

– whose lost bookings cost him a claimed £500,000[69] – described the experience as 'pretty traumatic'.[70]

There was also Jonathan King, pop impresario and broadcaster, who had earlier been given a seven-year sentence for having sex with underage boys. He emerged from jail in 2005, still protesting his innocence and entirely unrepentant; he wrote and filmed a musical of his trial, *Vile Pervert* (2008), which showed he hadn't lost his knack of writing catchy pop songs, even if they now had titles such as 'The True Story of Harold Shipman' and '(There's Nothing Wrong with) Buggering Boys'. In the wake of Yewtree, as other police forces mounted their own inquiries, King was arrested again and charged with 23 sex offences. This time, however, the case was thrown out by the judge, who had stern words for the behaviour of the police in bringing the charges. 'The integrity of the criminal justice system and processes have been undermined publicly,' she said, adding that the case seemed to have been brought solely because of 'concerns about reputational damage to Surrey Police'.[71] The force had received an allegation about Savile in 2003 but had taken no action and, in going after King now, seemed to be trying to compensate for past failures.

The sudden prominence of stories about child abuse in the past stirred a memory of earlier allegations. Back in 1981 the Tory backbench MP Geoffrey Dickens had stood up in the Commons and, against the advice of the attorney general, had revealed that Sir Peter Hayman, a former high commissioner to Canada and deputy director of MI6, was a paedophile. A couple of years earlier, it transpired, Hayman had been investigated by police, who found 'a mass of pornographic material' in his flat, but he was not prosecuted.[72] There was outrage following Dickens's speech, directed not at Hayman but at Dickens himself. David Steel, Liberal Party leader, suggested his action might have been an abuse of parliamentary privilege; *Observer* columnist Alan

Watkins argued that MPs should curb that right, and the police questioned Dickens, demanding he reveal his source.

The failure to prosecute Hayman, said Dickens, showed that there was an 'establishment cover-up',[73] and he went on to claim that he'd discovered a paedophile network that included 'big, big names – people in positions of power, influence and responsibility'.[74] It all sounded a little conspiracist, especially coming from Dickens. Nicknamed Bunter for his huge size, he was almost a caricature of the hanging-and-flogging Tory; Matthew Parris said he had 'the bearing of a master butcher, the opinions of a taxi driver, the voice of a foghorn'.[75] He thundered against homosexuality as much as paedophilia, and was even prepared to toss satanism, witchcraft and necrophilia into the mix. 'Children are sacrificed sexually to the lust and gratification of the coven,' he told the press. 'And that's not all. Bodies have been taken from the grave and their heads cut off. People have cut the heads off and then sexually assaulted the skeleton.'[76] Consequently, few serious people paid Geoffrey Dickens any attention.

Dickens died in 1995, but the story that there was a paedophile ring at the top of the establishment never quite disappeared. And in the wake of the revelations about Jimmy Savile, it resurfaced.

This time it was promoted by Tom Watson, a Labour MP who shared Dickens's propensity to bulk ('an overfed Che Guevara' was one colleague's assessment[77]) and his willingness to engage the press with newsworthy statements; shortly after his election in 2001, he was to be found calling on the home secretary to ban a new album by Gary Glitter.[78] A week after the launch of Operation Yewtree, in October 2012, he demanded in the Commons that the police 'investigate clear intelligence suggesting a powerful paedophile network linked to Parliament and Number Ten'.[79]

The ensuing investigation centred on the Elm Guest House in Barnes, south London, which had operated as a gay brothel until it was raided by police in 1982. Now, stories emerged that boys from a nearby children's home had been taken to the place for the pleasure of powerful men. 'Paedo VIPs are feared to have abused vulnerable underage boys for years' was the summary of the *People*, which made much of the running on the story.[80] Among the politicians, judges and police officers alleged to have frequented Elm Guest House was Leon Brittan, home secretary 1983–85. And those dates were significant, for it was said that in 1984 Geoffrey Dickens had handed him a dossier on establishment paedophiles, and no action had been taken. No wonder there was a cover-up, mused conspiracy theorists, if the home secretary himself were part of a child-abuse ring.

Watson pursued the story in the Commons and, immediately after Brittan's death in January 2015, wrote a piece for the *Sunday Mirror* accusing the late politician of 'multiple child rape'. He quoted 'one survivor' who said Brittan was 'as close to evil as a human being could get'.[81]

That survivor was known only by the pseudonym Nick, and his story was being promoted by a website for investigative journalism called Exaro ('Holding power to account' was its slogan). Nick confirmed that he was one of those abused at the Elm Guest House, and added various other locations, including the Carlton Club. And he said that the abuse was not just sexual: two children had been tortured to death, and a third murdered to silence him. The identities of those alleged to have been involved in these atrocities were withheld by police, but in August 2015 one of the accused, former Tory MP Harvey Proctor, went public and named others who were being investigated. They included Edward Heath, Lord Bramall, Michael Hanley and Maurice Oldfield, men who had served respectively as prime minister, chief of the general staff, and heads of MI5 and MI6.[82]

This was beyond sensational. Indeed, it was beyond credence. Homosexual paedophiles with a taste for murder are extremely rare, and those who exist tend to operate on their own. The idea that four of them should simultaneously occupy such a powerful quartet of establishment posts – let alone that they would risk sharing their practices with a despised backbencher like Proctor – was almost impossible to credit, even before one came to the absence of any evidence at all for the supposed murders. Who on earth would believe such an absurdity?

To their credit, most of the media trod very warily, while still reporting the allegations, which were just too irresistible to ignore. However, Exaro had support not only from Tom Watson but also from George Galloway, on the television stations Press TV and RT (owned by Iran and Russia respectively), and from James O'Brien, host of a phone-in show on LBC radio. 'I don't know whether Ted Heath abused children,' wrote the latter. 'But I am certain that the allegations against him have to be examined publicly.'[83] Even as Watson was belatedly apologising for that 'as close to evil' comment – there was no evidence against Brittan – O'Brien was still pursuing his theme, while protesting, 'I hate this story. It frightens the life out of me.'[84]

Much more importantly, the Metropolitan Police – wary of past failings, conscious of the new guidelines introduced by Keir Starmer – believed the story, as detective superintendent Kenny McDonald made clear in December 2014: 'Nick has been spoken to by experienced officers from the child abuse team and from the murder investigation team, and they and I believe what Nick is saying is credible and true.'[85] It was neither credible nor true, and after the tottering tower of lies finally collapsed the only prosecution that emerged from the multi-million-pound inquiry was that of Nick himself. In 2019 he appeared in court under his real name of Carl Beech on charges of perverting the cause of justice and of child sex offences – for it turned out that, unlike his alleged abusers, he actually was a paedophile. He was sentenced to eighteen years in jail.

Many of the claims investigated by Yewtree and others dated to the 1960s and 70s, when attitudes, at least in official quarters, had been different. The sexual abuse of children was certainly not acceptable – hence Jimmy Savile covering his tracks – but as long as it remained at a relatively low level, it could be dismissed in official quarters as an unfortunate fact of life. Many of those in positions of power had attended all-male boarding schools in the pre-war years, and even if they hadn't experienced abuse themselves, they knew that it happened; along with flogging, fagging and the Officers' Training Corps, it was something to be endured.

And that extended to institutions over which they had oversight. The occasional teacher with roving hands was to be expected; like the heavy drinker, he was to be regretted and managed, without making too much of a fuss. Abuse wasn't really covered up, it just didn't seem important enough to be worth causing trouble over.

When Norman Tebbit was asked about the allegations of the early 1980s, he didn't rule out the idea that the establishment had closed ranks: 'If there was a cover-up, it was almost unconscious. It was the thing that people did at that time.'[86] That certainly was true. Stories about Liberal MP Cyril Smith had appeared in *Private Eye* in 1979 – rumours about him spanking and sexually abusing boys – and he'd been interviewed by his party leader, David Steel. Forty years later, Steel acknowledged that he'd 'assumed' Smith's guilt but had taken no action;[87] indeed, he had subsequently allowed Smith to be awarded a knighthood.* It all reinforced the underlying assumption of those period detective shows: despite whatever happy childhood memories we had, the recent past of our country was a place of moral corruption and misery.

In all classes, the shame that was attached to having been abused meant that it was not something to be spoken of in personal terms. Culturally, it was addressed mostly through black humour, as in Uncle Ernie's song 'Fiddle About' from the Who's opera *Tommy* (1969), alongside which ran a vein of nudging, knowing

---

* Smith died in 2010. Two years later, the Crown Prosecution Service admitted that he should have been prosecuted following an investigation in 1970.

jokes about sexy schoolgirls. Now, there was a whiff of nostalgia for such jokes; in a 2008 episode of the sitcom *Peep Show*, Mark remembers a scoutmaster from his childhood: 'Leyton was a bit of a paedo, but not in a bad way. Just boosting you over the climbing wall, making you run round the camp in your pants. It was old-style paedo-ing, before it got such a bad name.'

In the Swinging Sixties, some had also explored the far frontiers of the permissive society. The song 'Sodomy' from the American musical *Hair* (1967) listed various – apparently approved – sexual practices: oral sex, anal sex, masturbation and also pederasty. Few actually advocated paedophilia, of course, but there were those arguing that the age of heterosexual consent, set way back in 1885, was outmoded, a Victorian value that could and should be swept away. By the mid-1970s even figures of great liberal respectability such as John Robinson, former bishop of Woolwich, and Patricia Hewitt, general secretary of the National Council for Civil Liberties (later Liberty), were calling for the age of consent to be lowered to fourteen, and home secretary Roy Jenkins set up a committee to look at the proposal.*

The Paedophile Information Exchange, a campaigning organisation launched in 1974, found some allies in the gay rights movement, affiliated to the NCCL, and was listed by the National Association for Mental Health (later Mind) 'as one of the "organisations to write to" for sexual minorities'.[88] PIE's chairman, Tom O'Carroll, who argued for an age of consent of four, was taken seriously enough for his book *Paedophilia: The Radical Case* (1980) to be reviewed in *Gay News*, *New Society*, the *New Statesman*, the *Times Educational Supplement* and the *Times Literary Supplement*. On the other hand, PIE was attacked in the media

---

* In France, a 1977 petition calling for the abolition of age-of-consent laws attracted the signatures of virtually every intellectual of any standing, from Jean-Paul Sartre and Simone de Beauvoir to Roland Barthes, Jacques Derrida and Michel Foucault.

by moral reformer Mary Whitehouse, in Parliament by Geoffrey Dickens, and on the streets by the National Front. There was a cultural and class divide here, and the public was on the side of the moral conservatives rather than the social liberals.

What had happened in the years since then was the rise on the left of feminism, with its insistence that the personal was political. That which had previously been endured in private was now part of public debate, and the voices of victims began to be heard. Male violence against women and children, particularly sexual violence, was higher on the agenda than it had ever been, as politics began to catch up with public opinion; for nothing aroused greater fury and disgust than child abusers. Which is why there was such anger when it appeared that officialdom had comprehensively and repeatedly failed the people. Street grooming gangs were permitted to operate; Jimmy Savile was questioned by police but not prosecuted; stories of institutionalised abuse in children's homes were hushed up. Police, prosecutors, politicians – far too many had turned a blind eye.

And then, with Savile's death, came the over-reaction. This was a 'watershed moment', said Keir Starmer. 'The approach of the police and prosecutors to credibility in sexual assault cases has to change.'[89] Exposed as having been incompetent at best – probably complacent, possibly even complicit – police and others now allocated enormous resources to pursuing the innocent. Twenty officers had spent ten hours searching the house of 92-year-old Lord Bramall, a man who'd served in the Normandy landings and been awarded a Military Cross in 1945. Whatever it was that they expected to find more than 30 years after the alleged offence, it was not discovered. And all this was on the uncorroborated say-so of a single witness, whose story was no more plausible than those told by people claiming to be alien abductees. ('They too must be believed,' mocked Jonathan King.[90]) Cliff Richard's home was similarly searched, this time with live coverage on the BBC after a police tip-off; it was the start of a 22-month investigation that resulted in no charges being brought, and large sums of money being paid in compensation by the South Yorkshire Police and the BBC.

The inquiry into the Rotherham abuse concluded that early warnings were ignored as 'a politically inconvenient truth'.[91] The same could be said elsewhere: it was simply easier to let things lie. For too long, the vulnerable were abandoned, the innocent were persecuted, the guilty went unpunished. And faith in the social infrastructure was damaged, because no institution came out of these incidents with any credit at all. The police had failed to act (but then over-reacted), the media had failed to ask questions, the NHS had facilitated Savile's abuse. A 2013 episode of the police thriller *Luther* centred on a vigilante killer who explains why he has resorted to direct action: 'The criminal justice system was created to protect us from people who would do us harm. But time and again, it fails in that purpose.' When he later hangs a paedophile, he does so in front of a cheering mob.

8

Coalition and Cohesion

I

Gillian Duffy was a widow and a grandmother, 66 years old, retired, having previously worked for the council, caring for vulnerable children. She was a lifelong Labour supporter, so when, during the election campaign of 2010, she popped out to buy a loaf of bread and caught sight of Gordon Brown, she seized the opportunity to try to speak with him. Meeting the public wasn't on his agenda – he was supposed to be visiting offenders on a community-service programme – but she persisted and was eventually brought over to have a word. Like most of the population, she was a little disgruntled with things, but she was perfectly courteous and, over the course of a five-minute conversation, raised a wide range of issues, including the national debt, education, tuition fees and taxes on pensioners. In the middle of her scattergun remarks, she also mentioned immigration. 'You can't say anything about the immigrants,' she said. 'All these eastern Europeans what're coming in – where are they flocking from?' They moved on to other subjects, she had her say, Brown responded well, and they parted with a handshake and a shared laugh. There was no story here, nothing for the evening news bulletins. This was no Sharron Storer moment.

Except that Brown was capable of turning a non-event into a crisis. Failing to notice that he was still wearing a Sky News radio microphone, his comments as he was driven away were recorded for public consumption. 'Should never have put me with that woman,' he grumbled. 'Whose idea was that?' What did she say, he was asked, and his reply was devastating: 'Oh, everything. She's just a sort of bigoted woman that said she used to be Labour. I mean, it's just ridiculous.'

Brown's next engagement was a Radio 2 interview with Jeremy Vine, during which a tape of his remarks was played to him for the first time. A studio camera showed him as he listened back to what he'd said; head hung low, his face covered by his hand, as though the implications were hitting him in real time, he looked deeply dejected. It was, said those who knew him, a characteristic pose when he was concentrating. But for everyone else, it gave the appearance of a beaten man, and it became one of the defining images of Brown.

In desperation, the campaign schedule was abandoned and the prime minister whisked off to Gillian Duffy's house, where he spent an hour talking with her. 'I'm mortified by what's happened,' he said as he emerged. 'I've given her my sincere apologies. I misunderstood what she said.' Unfortunately, he was wearing that silly smile again.

The incident was widely described as a gaffe. At best, it

made Brown look rude and arrogant. 'What does he mean, "that woman"?' asked Duffy. 'It's not nice, it's not nice at all.'[1] For some – the leader writers at the *Daily Express* and the *Daily Star*, for example – it showed that he held much of the electorate in contempt. But perhaps there was something deeper here, something far more fundamental. His 'bigoted' was clearly a response to her comment on eastern Europeans. For him, that was what the whole encounter had been about: she complained about immigration, and she must therefore be racist. Duffy's perspective was very different. 'What was bigoted in what I said?' she asked, genuinely baffled. 'I just asked about the national debt.'[2]

It wasn't his condemnation of her opinion that was so revealing; it was his failure even to hear what she was saying. The other issues she raised – tuition fees, taxation, the economy – simply hadn't registered with him. It turned out that he was much more obsessed with race than she was.

The meeting of Gordon Brown and Gillian Duffy was the one moment on the campaign trail that really registered in the 2010 general election. Apart from that, everything was dominated by the television debates between the three leaders. Indeed, politicians felt the debates were too dominant, sucking the energy out of the campaign. But the 2001 and 2005 campaigns, when there were no such events, hadn't exactly been noted for their vibrancy either. Perhaps it was just that conventional campaigning was looking tired.

And anyway, the debates were a significant development. Britain had never experienced such a thing before because, ever since they were first mooted in 1964, one side had wanted them and the other had not; there had never been a common interest in participation. But now Brown had nothing to lose, so low was Labour's standing in the polls, while Cameron, far from certain of victory, fancied his chances in a TV studio. And so a series of three encounters was arranged, on ITV, Sky and BBC successively. Nick Clegg, with 62 Liberal Democrat MPs behind him and 22 per cent of the vote last time, was also invited to participate, but the Scottish National Party leader Alex Salmond was – to his fury – excluded, despite having 6 MPs and a 1.5 per cent share.

Most attention, of course, focused on the first debate, since it had the advantage of novelty. It was 'an historic moment in television and political history', said host Alastair Stewart. There was a studio audience, but they didn't applaud or interrupt, and the three men were on polite first-name terms with each other. Though there were no killer blows – or even decent one-liners – the winner was undoubtedly Clegg. He was relaxed, concerned and plausible, successfully portraying the others as old politics while he was the alternative.

Mostly, though, he won because hardly anyone knew who he was; up until this point in the campaign, he'd been escorted in public by his popular Lib Dem colleague Vince Cable, serving to identify him. Now the public got a good look at Clegg, and they liked what they saw. He had a freshness that appealed to the disillusioned. 'It's a bit like a newcomer promoted to the Premiership beating Chelsea and Manchester United on the first two Saturdays of the season,' said psephologist John Curtice.[3] The phrase that stuck was 'I agree with Nick,' as both Brown and Cameron tried to associate themselves with the Young Pretender. There was a surge of support, and in some polls the Lib Dems briefly overtook Labour. The papers dubbed it Cleggmania, though they couldn't decide whether the term was serious or ironical.

The remaining two debates also lacked any memorable moments, but the experiment was deemed by most of the media to have been a success. It didn't, though, do much to reinvigorate the political process. The low numbers of voters in 2001 and 2005 had been put down to the inevitability of the outcome or possibly to the fact that, with sustained economic growth, everything seemed to be okay. Neither of those factors was present this time, but although turnout was up a little, it was still historically low at 65 per cent.*

The boost that the Lib Dems had got from their new media profile was so great that there was genuine surprise when it didn't translate into actual votes at the election; the party increased its share by a single point and dropped five seats, though presumably things would have been worse without Cleggmania. The Tories did well, gaining 96 seats, but not well enough, falling short of the number needed to form a majority government. With a hung Parliament for the first time since February 1974, only one thing was sure: Gordon Brown had lost. It was a catastrophic result for his party, which shed 97 seats, its worst collapse since the great split of 1931. Labour attracted the votes of just 8.6 million people, only a handful more than Michael Foot had managed in 1983, and its share was down to 29 per cent, lower than that recorded by John Major's Conservatives in 1997. The only consolation was that it could have been worse: at the start of the year, some polls had shown the Tories with a twenty-point lead, and in the end it was just seven.

Brown remained in place over the weekend, trying to stitch together a deal that would keep him in office, if only for a few months, but it was a doomed endeavour. He lacked the political authority to lead a minority government, and even if he got the Lib Dems on board, he'd still be short of a majority; support from nationalist MPs from Scotland and Wales would also be required, which seemed unlikely. Five days after the election, he announced his resignation as prime minister.

In the meantime, the Conservatives and Liberal Democrats had found that they got on rather well with each other. Which was, ironically, a tribute to the success of New Labour; Cameron had moved so far towards the centre that he could now announce

---

* Excluding 2001 and 2005, one had to go back (again) to that atypical election of 1918 to find a lower turnout.

the formation of a coalition government, with Clegg as deputy prime minister and four other Lib Dems in cabinet.* On a lovely spring afternoon, with blossom in the air and birds in song, Cameron and Clegg gave a joint press conference in the Downing Street Rose Garden. Briefly, the shadow of the financial crisis was banished, and the mood was one of optimism and hope. The two men looked so comfortable with each other that the *Daily Mail* compared them to television presenters Ant and Dec, while Polly Toynbee in the *Guardian* suggested it looked like a civil partnership.

Television satire show *The Revolution Will Be Televised* (2012) summed up the historic development: 'In 2010 the British public was treated to its first coalition government since the end of the Second World War, an unequal coming-together of David Cameron's Conservative Party, who have pretty much most of the power, and that other party with Nick Clegg.'

Liam Byrne, the outgoing chief secretary to the Treasury, had never enjoyed much of a public profile, but he achieved unwanted notoriety with the note he left behind for his successor, the Lib Dem David Laws: 'Dear chief secretary, I'm afraid there is no money. Kind regards and good luck!' It was meant to be a joke, an echo of when chancellor Reginald Maudling had left a similar message in 1964: 'Sorry, old cock, to leave it in this state.'[4] But Laws decided not to take it lightly and made the document public, presenting it as a signed confession of Labour sins.

That note became a vital piece of evidence in the narrative that the Coalition wanted to push. A combination of the recession and the bank bail-out meant that the country was engaged in vast levels of borrowing, and this was now painted as typical of Labour's inability to run the economy. 'Last year our budget

---

* Vince Cable was business secretary, working alongside Osborne, of whose 'understanding of financial and economic matters' he'd been so disparaging.

deficit was the largest it has ever been in our peacetime history,'
said the new chancellor, George Osborne. 'This is the legacy of
thirteen years of fiscal irresponsibility.'[5]

If that was economically simplistic, it was nevertheless effective
politicking. The one person who could perhaps have combatted
it by mounting a robust defence of Labour's record was Gordon
Brown, but he'd resigned as party leader. He didn't stay around to
argue his case and, though still an MP, was seldom seen in Westminster.* Instead he disappeared in a puff of sulk, leaving deputy
leader Harriet Harman to mind the shop for the next four and a
half months while a new leader was elected.

Four candidates swiftly emerged: David Miliband, his
younger brother Ed, Andy Burnham and Ed Balls. Four white
men, all aged between 40 and 44, who had been political advisers
before they entered Parliament and had then been fast-tracked
into cabinet.† For a party which proclaimed its faith in diversity
and inclusion, it wasn't ideal. There was an alternative over on
the left, where Diane Abbott had put her name forward, but she
stood no chance of getting the support of 33 MPs, the requirement to be on the ballot paper. So David Miliband, his own
position secured, decided he'd nominate her and encouraged
others to do the same.

Now there really was diversity. Abbott was a woman, the first
black candidate ever to stand for the leadership and considerably
older than her rivals; Burnham hadn't even taken his A levels when
she was first elected to Parliament. There was also a diversity in
politics – she was anti-Iraq, pro-spending, pro-immigration – but

---

* He did get take up some highly paid speaking engagements, if not as highly
paid as his great rival; a speech in Delhi in 2010 earned him a reported £741 a
minute, compared to the £6,667 a minute picked up by Tony Blair in Manila
the previous year. (*Sunday Times* 30 January 2011)
† In a radical break with convention, however, Burnham had been to
Cambridge University rather than Oxford.

that was a side issue; she was included primarily for cosmetic reasons, and stood no chance of winning.*

Media attention centred on the Milibands, because they emerged as the front-runners and because fraternal conflict was such a good storyline. It was not hard to believe that the two men were brothers. They were both bred-in-the-bone politicians – their father, Ralph, had been one of Britain's leading academic Marxists – and both had been intelligent, competent ministers. They were clean-cut, decent and urban; smart-casual, with Fuzzy-Felt hairlines. Of the two, David was the more conventionally good-looking; at Oxford he'd been nicknamed Donny after 1970s teen star Donny Osmond – 'because of his haircut and Colgate smile', said a contemporary[6]. But Ed was endearingly lopsided, the gawky but cute one in a boy band. In 2001 the *Guardian* had reported that 'sexy Eddie's been getting love letters from admirers of his Woody Allen geek-chic look',[7] and that imagery was still around. The contest was 'The meek vs the geek' said the *Independent on Sunday*, without specifying which was which.[8] Columnist Matthew d'Ancona said that whenever he saw them, he found himself 'humming Rolf Harris's "Two Little Boys"'.[9]

'Not since Cain and Abel ...' wrote George Galloway,[10] and others went for the same image, though Nick Cohen had the better biblical parallel with the story of Jacob tricking his older brother Esau into selling his birthright for a mess of potage.[11] For many people, those of a traditional cast of mind, this was precisely what was happening. David had first rights, just by virtue of being older; consequently, he'd been 'stabbed in the back' by Ed.[12]

Because it was Ed who won. In what was billed as Blair vs Brown: the Next Generation, it was the Brownite who emerged

---

* Jack Straw, who managed Brown's leadership campaign in 2007, was happy there was only one name on the ballot paper: 'There's enough risk in politics without manufacturing it.' (*Last Man Standing* p. 493) MPs might have been wise to heed his words, even if they got away with it in 2010.

victorious, having secured the backing of some big names, including the 1980s leadership double-act Neil Kinnock and Roy Hattersley, and, more importantly, the three largest unions: Unison, Unite and the GMB, led by Dave Prentis, Len McCluskey and Paul Kenny respectively. But what was most striking about the campaign was his young, enthusiastic, passionate fans. 'Ed speaks human,' they insisted, explaining that David was just a nerd, a dry theoretician, whereas their candidate was a man who connected with the people. 'He has got the X Factor,' as Kinnock put it.[13] The clincher was that Ed had only been elected to Parliament in 2005, so he hadn't been there for the Iraq debate and had clean hands; he said he would have voted against the invasion.

Though David put a brave face on his defeat, he looked hurt and wounded by the experience. He declined to serve in Ed's shadow cabinet and in 2013 quietly made his excuses and left Parliament, moving to New York City to head the International Rescue Committee, finally realising that dream of 'running some big charity'.[14] Instead, shadow chancellor Ed Balls emerged as the other big figure on the opposition front bench.*

And so the two Eds faced up to Cameron and Osborne, with Clegg somewhere in there as well. All displayed the same lack of diversity as the pre-Abbott Labour leadership candidates: born within a five-year period, all but one with PPE degrees from Oxford (philosophy, politics and economics),† they represented the final triumph of the professional politico-media class that had been taking over Westminster for two decades. Journalist Martin Bright called them the Adrian Mole generation,[15] after Sue Townsend's fictional diarist, born in 1967. (Mole's journal had come to an end by the Coalition years, but neither Townsend

---

* Miliband's first choice as shadow chancellor was Alan Johnson, but he resigned after three months when he discovered his wife was having an affair with his police protection officer.
† Osborne had been to Oxford, but had studied modern history.

herself[16] nor Adrian's fans had any doubt that he would have voted for Nick Clegg and then been 'incredibly disappointed'.[17]) In 2009 Vince Cable wrote, 'We face the prospect of rule by charming but utterly inexperienced young men armed with only a sense of entitlement to run the family estate.'[18] He'd been talking about Cameron and Osborne, but as far as much of the public were concerned, they all looked the same.

The convergence of politicians of all the major parties meant that the election was, as Mark Haddon wrote in his novel *The Red House* (2012), 'a national soap opera in which the closeness of the result was more exciting than the identity of the winner'.[19] Whichever government emerged, it would have looked much the same and would have followed broadly the same economic path, since so few options were available. The country, and the world, had begun to recover from the after-effects of the banking crisis, but the future was uncertain; the Eurozone looked as though it might fall apart at the seams, and there were dire warnings of a double-dip recession, of deflation, of mass unemployment. The Keynesian solution – injections of capital by government – had already happened, with the bail-out of the banks and an economic stimulus package, and Liam Byrne was right: there was no more money. Tax receipts were down and, given the scale of the national debt and the huge deficit feeding that debt (£167 billion a year at the election), cuts in public spending were politically inevitable; all major parties were in agreement on that.*

A year before the election, George Osborne warned that Britain had 'moved from an age of prosperity to an age of austerity',[20]

---

* Mervyn King, governor of the Bank of England, was reported to have predicted that 'whoever wins this election will be out of power for a whole generation because of how tough the fiscal austerity will have to be'. (*Scotsman* 30 April 2010) The Labour manifesto could only promise no cuts until 2011, at which point 'spending will be tighter'.

and as chancellor he continued to talk a tough game. In June 2010 he announced a first package of tax rises and spending cuts in what was billed as 'the harshest budget for thirty years'.[21] That took us back to the first of Margaret Thatcher's recessions, and there were many commentators agreeing with the predictions of the new Labour leadership that the result would be the same as in the 1980s. But despite the rhetoric, Osborne imposed a slow squeeze rather than shock treatment. Public employees faced wage freezes rather than redundancies; interest rates were kept low (helping public debt move to private pocket), and the cuts were focused primarily on local authorities, most of whom had sufficient reserves and fat for the effects not to be felt immediately. It was called austerity – 'we were never afraid of using the word', said David Cameron[22] – though it was less dramatic than that sounded; Cameron added that public spending was being reduced by just one pound in every hundred. There would be an impact down the line, but by then, it was hoped, the economy would have recovered.

The mantra throughout was that definition of Conservatism suggested by Cameron shortly after he became leader: we were all in this together. The first budget, for example, saw cuts to housing benefit, but also a levy on banks and a freezing of the Queen's income from the Civil List. Nonetheless, reduced spending was obviously disproportionate in its impact, hitting those individuals who relied most on the state and those areas where weak business infrastructure was combined with high levels of public-sector employment; a 2010 report by the credit information company Experian suggested that Middlesbrough, Plymouth and the Wirral were particularly vulnerable.[23]

Even so, the Coalition years did not see a repeat of the early 1980s: in fact, employment rose and unemployment fell. Growth did remain sluggish for three years, but there was a gradual recovery. The problem came elsewhere with a crisis in productivity. Even in the strike-hit 1970s and through the recessions of the

1980s and 90s, productivity had continued its upward path, with just the occasional brief blip. But now, and for a full decade after the crash, the graph flatlined. Consequently, wages stagnated and few felt the benefit of economic growth.

The most significant development of the Coalition years was welfare reform, a programme entrusted to a figure the public had forgotten. After being ousted from the Tory leadership, Iain Duncan Smith had pursued his vision of compassionate Conservatism, co-founding a think tank, the Centre for Social Justice, to develop policies that would combat deprivation and poverty. Much of its work addressed cultural as much as economic factors – addiction, family stability, gangs – and sought solutions in grass-roots projects rather than central government. The welfare state, it was argued, had become a trap, fostering dependency; what was needed was a complete overhaul of philosophy as well as practice in order to restore personal responsibility. It was a project that attracted Cameron, and after the 2010 election he plucked Duncan Smith from the backbenches, appointing him work and pensions secretary. The task was to undertake a revolution – these were '"once-in-many-generations" changes', according to welfare reform minister Lord Freud[24] – and it fell foul of both the Treasury and public opinion.

The big idea was universal credit, a single benefit to take the place of six existing payments, which was intended to taper off as a recipient found employment, ensuring that, as the sound bite went, 'nobody is better off on benefits than in work'.[25] It was intended to simplify and improve the system, but the transition ran massively over-budget and was still nowhere near its implementation targets when Duncan Smith left office in 2016. Nonetheless, it looked likely to be the lasting legacy of the Coalition government.

Meantime, there was also the more prosaic aim of saving money. 'Cuts, innit?' as a character in J. K. Rowling's *The Casual Vacancy* (2012) says.[26] The major target was disability benefit, where the numbers had grown rapidly over the last two decades because, said Osborne, successive governments had used disability as a way of massaging the unemployment statistics.[27] The answer was a fitness-for-work assessment, a test administered not by the claimant's own GP, but by employees of ATOS Healthcare, a private company awarded the contract by the DWP. Unsurprisingly, only a minority were deemed unfit for work, and stories emerged of appalling errors; figures showed that over a 26-month period, 2,380 claimants died after being taken off employment support allowance.[28]

There was also what the government called the spare room subsidy and what everyone else called the bedroom tax. Those claiming housing benefit who were in social accommodation would henceforth see a reduction in their payments if they were deemed to be under-occupying their property – if they had a spare bedroom. Most eye-catching was the introduction of a cap on benefits, set at £26,000, the average rate of pay. It was, Osborne told the Conservative conference in 2010, a simple principle: 'Unless they have disabilities to cope with, no family should get more from living on benefits than the average family gets from going out to work.'[29] It was believed that this would affect around 50,000 households, most of them in London, since housing benefit was what pushed the total up.

Beyond those hit directly by the changes, there were more widespread complaints of delays in the payment of benefits, and the application – sometimes harsh, sometimes unjust – of sanctions against claimants deemed to have broken regulations. Short-term relief for these problems was addressed by a referral to a food bank, such as those run by the Trussell Trust, the country's largest, but by no means only, provider; they supplied three days' worth of essentials, and there was a maximum of three applications per person. By 2015, the Trust had 445 operations nationally, with over a million referrals a year, a growing proportion being those who were in poverty despite being in employment, many from among the 700,000 people now on zero-hours contracts.

Food banks were not unique to Britain – there were said to be twice as many in France – but that mattered little; there was still a sense of shame that working people were queuing for charity because of hunger.

Many of the reforms built on initiatives of the previous government. It was Labour who had appointed ATOS to conduct the work-capability assessments, while the bedroom tax merely extended into social housing earlier restrictions for those in the privately rented sector. Other policies – the cap, the withdrawal of child benefits from high-earning households – were not unthinkable had Labour won the election; the party's manifesto had some tough talk about there being 'no option of life on benefits'.* There were plenty of denunciations of Coalition callousness in the liberal media, but they never really cut through to the mass of the public, perhaps because most people were unaffected. 'Is the "bedroom tax" the new Poll Tax?' asked the BBC and the *Guardian* and the *Huffington Post*.[30] It wasn't. Instead there was a lot of support for the reforms, led by right-wing newspapers with an inexhaustible supply of stories about people abusing the system.

There was, to take just one example, the 24-year-old Sunderland man reported by the *Sunday Times* to have had eight children with eight different women, though it might have been as many as twelve with eleven; no one was sure, not even him: 'I've never even seen some of the kids I'm supposed to have fathered.' He was on incapacity benefit for a bad back.[31] There were even jokey celebrity stories that fed into the same narrative. One of the audience favourites in the 2010 series of *The X Factor* was a large, hairy medallion-man named Wagner – 'the Beast of Brazil', as the papers dubbed him[32] – who sang, danced and played the bongos with an enthusiasm that his ability couldn't match. The *Sun* took

---

* There was also a continuity in personnel: Lord Freud had produced a report on welfare reform for Tony Blair in 2007 and had been an adviser to Gordon Brown's government.

pleasure in revealing that, even as he was cavorting across the nation's screens, he was claiming incapacity benefit after injuring his shoulder.*

The rhetoric was of shirkers and workers, skivers and strivers, the undeserving poor versus 'people who have worked hard all their lives, who have done the right thing' (Ed Miliband's words, though all leading politicians used much the same formulation).[33] This went back a long way – in 1968 Labour minister Judith Hart had said the welfare system could not afford even 'one person scrounging his living from the state'[34] – but it had a greater airing during austerity.

Beyond the individual stories, there were parts of the country that – as *Shameless* illustrated – had been neglected for years before the 2008 crash and showed no sign of recovery. The Office for National Statistics identified an area centred on the Lower Falinge Estate in Rochdale as the most benefit-dependent neighbourhood in the country: 84 per cent of the 1,030 adults were unemployed.[35] Or there was James Turner Street in Birmingham, which grabbed the nation's attention in 2014 when it was the subject of the documentary series *Benefits Street*. Nine out of ten residents were said to be on benefits, and the show provided four hours of sensational storylines culled from a year's filming, complete with the usual fiddling, shoplifting, alcohol and drug abuse. This was all a gross distortion of reality, complained everyone who knew the subject or the neighbourhood, but it was Channel 4's most watched show that year.

Broadly, then, the public was in support of reforms to the benefits regime. Opinion polls showed approval of the benefits cap, though half wanted the limit to be lower.[36] As Osborne said, the

---

* He wasn't the first. In 2009 a 73-year-old man from Sutton Bonington, Nottinghamshire had a moment of fame in 2009 after his display of breakdancing on *Britain's Got Talent*; the experience turned sour when it was discovered he was in receipt of £70 a week for a bad leg.

cap was 'what the British people mean by fair'.[37] However, what the British also meant by 'fair' was that the rich shouldn't exploit the system either. There was much criticism of comedian Jimmy Carr and singer Gary Barlow when they were revealed in 2012 to have used clever schemes to reduce their tax bills. More troubling were the parallel stories about big business. Only its shareholders were happy that American coffeeshop chain Starbucks had a turnover of £398 million in Britain in 2011, and yet had made a loss of £33 million, so didn't pay any corporation tax at all.[38] Other companies – Google, Amazon, Facebook, Vodafone – were also busily engaged in finding loopholes in the regulations. Their tactics were perfectly legal, and serious commentators were at pains to note that there was a difference between avoiding and evading taxation. Most people, though, made no such distinction and preferred 'dodging'. Whatever it was called, many had the feeling that we weren't really all in it together at all.

And then there was the most contentious issue of all for the Coalition: the decision in December 2010 to increase university tuition fees from £3,000 to £9,000 a year. Other changes were also made – including an increase in the income threshold at which the loans would be repaid and a time limit, so that it was estimated that only a quarter of students would ever repay the full debt – but it was that headline figure that seized the public imagination. Ed Miliband's Labour opposed the policy, while accepting the principle; they said they would cap fees at £6,000, merely doubling the previous limit. The real problem, though, came for the Liberal Democrats, who had pledged during the election to abolish tuition fees altogether. Twenty-one Lib Dem MPs, including Charles Kennedy and Menzies Campbell, voted against the increase, but the leadership reluctantly agreed to back it, and the decision did the party great harm. Opinion polls tracked a rapid decline in support; from a 23 per cent share at the general election, they were, within a year, down to single figures.

If it hadn't been tuition fees, it would have been something else. This was always going to be a bumpy road for the Lib Dems because so many of the 2 million voters gained since 2001 were defectors from Labour, driven away by Iraq, who saw themselves as being on the left. Hostile to the Tories, they viewed coalition as akin to collaboration. And because the party disproportionately attracted graduates and undergraduates, tuition fees became the symbol of betrayal.

In the country more widely, the policy reversal was seen as evidence that no politician, not even nice Nick Clegg, could be trusted to keep their promises. Which was perhaps a reflection of Britain's inexperience when it came to coalition government; it seemed a little unreasonable to expect the junior party to get its own way on every issue without any compromise at all. In fact, the Lib Dems achieved a great deal of their agenda – on environmental policies, the pupils' premium, a big rise in the income-tax threshold – but all was obscured by tuition fees, a policy that had been buried away on page 33 of their manifesto.

Clegg was accused in some quarters of being prepared to sell his own grandmother in pursuit of power – which didn't really ring true; he'd joined the Liberal Democrats after all – and the party became the butt of endless jokes. Either Lib Dem politicians had become Cameron's stooges ('I was only following orders,' says Mark in *Peep Show*, 'like Vince Cable') or they were simply duplicitous, as in Alexander Armstrong's introduction to a TV game show: 'My clever guests will be showing more mental leaps than Nick Clegg looking at his manifesto promises.'

The country house is one of the most familiar symbols in British fiction, the organic solidity of its class structure – standing in for the nation at large – regularly threatened by interlopers, criminals and meddling officialdom. 'There is no narrative base that can provide members of every level of society, sleeping under a single roof, more believably than a great house before the First War,' as Julian Fellowes said in 2009.[39] He'd been commissioned to write a drama series for ITV, and the press was suitably excited; in these dark recessionary times, Britain was ready for what the *Sun* hoped would be 'a bodice-ripping period drama'.[40]

Downton Abbey (2010) didn't disappoint. The plotlines were simple, the dialogue unchallenging, the characterisation painted in broad strokes. The familiar social hierarchies were firmly in place. 'We all have different parts to play,' says the Earl of Grantham, 'and we must all be allowed to play them.' The same message is heard below stairs, mostly from the butler, Carson: 'A good servant at all times retains a sense of pride and dignity that reflects the pride and dignity of the family he serves.' Above all, it looked beautiful, generously stocked with the pleasures that viewers of Edwardian dramas had come to expect: repressed passion and stern duty; snobbery, steam trains and side saddles, all dressed up in corsets and starched uniforms. It was easy to watch, and even easier to overlook what a high level of craft it took to appear this effortless.

The show was a huge hit, and exported well, particularly to America, where it was showered with awards, from a Golden Globe for best supporting actress to an Emmy for outstanding hairstyling. Guinness World Records said it was 'the most positively reviewed television programme in history'.[41] So when, in his 2012 budget, George Osborne cut the top rate of income tax to 45 per cent,* the opposition's cultural reference was obvious. This budget, said Ed Miliband, was all too reminiscent of *Downton Abbey*: 'A tale of a group of out-of-touch millionaires who act like they're born to rule but it turns out they are not very good at it.' He added, '*We* all know it's a costume drama. *They* think it's a fly-on-the-wall documentary.'[42]

It was a good joke, and played to the image of the government being out-of-touch toffs, but for much of the public, particularly

---

* It had been 40 per cent under Labour, but Alistair Darling had left behind a postdated increase to 50 per cent, to take effect in April 2011.

outside London, it didn't establish a clear dividing line. Because Miliband himself, despite the fact he'd gone to a comprehensive school, was perceived to be as remote as the Old Etonian prime minister and the Old Pauline chancellor. When the *Independent* ran focus groups to explore the state of class in modern Britain, 'we found that people regarded Cameron and Miliband as equally "posh"'.[43] Similarly, when Alex Salmond denounced 'the Westminster elite', he pointedly added, 'and that includes Ed Miliband'.[44] And when Ed Balls regularly taunted David Cameron in the Commons with the cry of 'Flashman!' the reference to the bully in *Tom Brown's School Days* seemed a little odd coming from Balls, privately educated and – like Miliband – the son of a university professor. (Michael Balls had also taught at Eton, though not during Cameron's time there.)

There were, of course, policy differences between the parties, even between the two parts of the Coalition, but the impression created by the Adrian Mole generation was that the political class all came from the same world, and that it was very different to the one inhabited by ordinary people. The clearest example came as that 2012 budget began to unravel.*

Hot food sold in takeaway restaurants had long been subject to VAT. This didn't, however, apply to shops, even though many supermarkets had introduced a hot-food counter, so that Tesco or Sainsbury's could now sell a hot sausage roll baked on the premises without charging the VAT that a fast-food outlet would have to add. Broadly speaking, large retailers benefited at the expense of small businesses. Osborne announced that he was closing this loophole. And then wished he hadn't.

The supermarkets barely featured in the coverage, and attention focused instead on Greggs, the Newcastle-based bakery chain

---

* The 2012 budget came under such severe criticism that it was branded an 'omnishambles', a term borrowed from *The Thick of It*. In private, the favoured expression was 'clusterfuck', from the same source.

which had more than 1,500 outlets nationwide and which – alongside its budget-price sandwiches and jam doughnuts – also sold hot food in the form of steak bakes, cheese-and-onion pasties and sausage rolls. They were, wrote Deborah Ross in the *Independent*, 'the world's least artisan bakers',[45] but they had loyal customers, often on low incomes. In 2010 workers at Glasgow Airport protested at the threatened closure of a branch of Greggs, arguing that this was an attempt to gentrify the airport: 'Greggs, it seems, are too working class.'[46]

It was also a company that had an eye for publicity, and it found support in the tabloids, whose readers were the chain's principal customers. Osborne's budget was a tax on Greggs pasties, went up the cry, and Pastygate was born. 'Let them eat cold pasty,' mocked the front page of the *Sun*,[47] following this with 'Who VAT all the pies?' and a pledge to fight 'the hated pasty tax'.[48] A model dressed as Marie Antoinette followed Osborne around, brandishing a tray full of pasties; a trio of page 3 girls was sent out into the streets to distribute sausage rolls to the public; and, in shocked tones, it was revealed that caviar remained exempt from VAT.

This last point didn't seem entirely relevant, since it was hard to know where one might find caviar served hot, let alone sold as a takeaway, but it did indicate that this was seen as a class issue. When Osborne was asked at a press conference when he had last bought a pasty, he admitted that he couldn't remember and was ridiculed for being out of touch. Forewarned, Cameron had an answer ready when he was similarly challenged: he'd had a pasty from the Cornwall Pasty Company at Leeds railway station. This, however, was interpreted by some as evidence of his posh lifestyle (it wasn't Greggs) and then as dissembling when it emerged the Leeds outlet had actually closed in March 2007 – and anyway it was a takeaway restaurant so it already paid VAT. Meanwhile Miliband and Balls hurried along to the nearest Greggs and, in the presence of reporters and news crews, self-consciously ordered sausage rolls as though they did this sort of thing all the time.

Right-wing Tory MP Nadine Dorries took the opportunity to lay into the leadership: 'Unfortunately, I think that not only are Cameron and Osborne two posh boys who don't know the price of milk, but they are two arrogant posh boys who show no remorse, no contrition, and no passion to want to understand the lives of others – and that is their real crime.'[49] Again, though, the public wasn't convinced that the opposition was much different. Throughout this period, as earnings fell behind inflation, Miliband spoke of a 'cost of living crisis' for 'the squeezed middle', a loose demographic that swept up most of the population, but when asked about the size of his family's weekly shopping bill, he gave a figure below the national average and was greeted with derision.*

In this instance, the Pastygate campaign achieved its objective and forced a government U-turn. Recognizing when he was beaten, Osborne simply abandoned the policy. If the whole strange episode illustrated anything, it was that, in an era when so many institutions were losing the confidence of the people, Greggs the Bakers had quietly become integral to the life of the nation. It was the working-class Marks & Spencer, to be messed with at your peril. 'Beware symbolism' was Cameron's conclusion.[50]

II

In April 2011, 30 years on from the fairy-tale wedding of Prince Charles and Lady Diana Spencer that had so enchanted the

---

* On another occasion, Cameron demonstrated how to deal with such trick questions. Asked the price of a loaf of bread, he explained that he didn't really buy bread, he baked his own, and in a fine political twist, added that he used a flour called Cotswolds Crunch, made by millers based in his own constituency.

nation,* the couple's first-born son, William, married Kate Middleton, and the nation was enthralled again. The narrative was irresistible: here was the second in line to the throne marrying a commoner, a woman whose mother had been an air hostess; the *Daily Express* was not alone in seeing the story of 'an ordinary girl marrying a prince as the ultimate victory of the classless, mobile society'.[51] Kate wasn't actually common in the sense that common people understood the term – her father's family had known royalty for generations, and she had been privately educated at Marlborough – but still it was a lovely fantasy.

As was to be expected, the occasion was a triumph. On a special bank holiday Friday, a million people turned out to line the London streets, another 26 million watched on television (2 billion worldwide), and there were street parties across the land. All the ceremonial trappings of state and church – carriages, uniforms, bishops, RAF flypast – were tastefully displayed against the familiar backdrops of Westminster Abbey, the Mall and Buckingham Palace, and the causes of both glamour and grandeur were honoured. Everyone agreed that this time the couple genuinely were happy, that Diana would have been proud, and that the monarchy was safe in the hands of this new generation of royals.

It was a big event on social media – during the ceremony, there were 74 mentions every second on Facebook – and the public's running commentary added a new dimension to such events, shaping the media coverage in real time. It was evident, for example, in the huge attention given to the supporting cast, for which there had been no equivalent at Charles and Diana's wedding. The online consensus was that the younger siblings of the couple delivered the sex appeal to complement the stateliness: Harry was the dashing young prince, and a Facebook group dedicated to the bride's sister (the Pippa Middleton's Ass Appreciation

---

* Charles had remarried in 2005, this time to Camilla Parker-Bowles, and was looking much happier than he had ever done.

Society) instantly attracted 100,000 fans. Meanwhile, Prince Andrew's daughters, Beatrice and Eugenie, were scorned for their clothes sense; 'like the Ugly Sisters from Cinderella', shuddered style expert Nick Ede of Sky's reality TV show *Project Catwalk*.[52]

Even in these new-media times, the venerable tradition of people writing to the tabloids to express their patriotic pride was still observed. 'Britain has its failings but no other country can put on a show like Kate and Wills' wedding.' 'There is no doubt at all that pomp and pageantry is what we do best.' 'The royal wedding, with all its pomp and pageantry, showed the world why this country is still great.' 'The royal wedding has put the feel-good factor back into this country and for the first time in years I feel proud to say I'm English.' When the couple kissed on the Buckingham Palace balcony, 'for us commoners that was the icing on the cake'.[53]

There was one jarring political note. Tony Blair and Gordon Brown were not among the guests. There was no obligation to invite them since, despite appearances, this wasn't a full state ceremony, but David Cameron and John Major were there, and Margaret Thatcher had been asked (she declined on grounds of ill health).* A correspondent to the Scottish edition of the *Sun* was pleased the Labour pair were excluded: 'They are champagne socialists who clearly do not give a monkey's about the hard-working people of this country. William and Kate clearly do care.'[54]

The royal wedding was a rare moment of national unity in the Coalition years. There was, for the first time since the war, a government that commanded majority support – between them, the Conservatives and Liberal Democrats had taken nearly 60 per cent of the vote – but this engendered no sense of cohesion and provoked no move towards consensus: opinion polls showed the

---

* Thatcher had already made her last public appearance, and died on 8 April 2013.

numbers approving of coalitions did not increase.[55] The country was still divided, still uncertain and unhappy. If the enthusiasm for William and Kate showed that people wished this were not the case, any optimism was soon snuffed out. For that summer of 2011 saw two hugely destabilising episodes.

The first came with the shaming of the press. The print media was already in decline, under serious and sustained pressure from the internet. Between the election years of 1997 and 2010, the ten national dailies* saw a combined fall in circulation of over 25 per cent. Worst hit were the *Daily Mirror*, which lost over half its sales, and the *Daily Express*, with only the *Financial Times* and *Daily Star* bucking the trend. The situation was even worse for the Sunday papers,† which saw a fall of nearly 40 per cent, despite the addition of a new title in the *Daily Star Sunday*.

The decline was inevitable, but the crisis of 2011 was self-inflicted. It was a story long in the breaking and it started with royalty. Some years earlier, the practice had grown up at some newspapers of employing private investigators, sometimes to acquire personal details of celebrities, sometimes just to keep an unfriendly eye on them. Methods were straying into criminality, and the Metropolitan Police and the Information Commissioner's Office began pursuing inquiries. Things took a decisive turn with a 2005 story about Prince William in the *News of the World* which could only have come from messages purloined from the mobile phones of William's closest aides. The story had been written by the paper's royal editor, Clive Goodman, and in January 2007 he appeared in court to plead guilty to charges of conspiracy

---

* Ranked by 2010 sales, these were: *Sun, Daily Mail, Daily Mirror, Daily Star, Daily Telegraph, Daily Express, The Times, Financial Times, Guardian, Independent.*
† Similarly ranked: *News of the World, Mail on Sunday, Sunday Times, Sunday Mirror, Sunday Telegraph, Sunday Express, People, Daily Star Sunday, Observer, Independent on Sunday.*

to intercept communications. Also pleading guilty was Glenn Mulcaire, a private investigator retained by the newspaper on a six-figure contract, who specialised in these practices; the subjects of his operations included figures from showbusiness, sport and politics, as well as the royals.

'This case is not about press freedom,' the judge told the accused. 'It is about grave, inexcusable and illegal invasion of privacy.'[56] And he sentenced Goodman and Mulcaire to four and six months respectively. The *News of the World* insisted that their behaviour was exceptional, unacceptable and entirely unknown to Goodman's superiors, but the editor of the paper, Andy Coulson, resigned as a matter of principle, since it had happened on his watch. That wasn't the end of the matter, though. The *Guardian* kept the story alive, convinced that Goodman was not an isolated case and that the police themselves were involved, selling information to journalists. Meanwhile some of those whose phones had been hacked began proceedings against News International, owner of the *News of the World*.

The fact this couldn't be put to bed was difficult for the incoming government. Four months after leaving the *News of the World*, Andy Coulson had taken up a new job as the Conservative Party's director of communications, brought on board to lend his tabloid sensibilities to David Cameron, then in opposition, just as the *Daily Mirror* journalist Alastair Campbell had done for Tony Blair. It was a risky appointment. Coulson continued to deny any knowledge of phone hacking under his editorship, but that left hanging, as the *Guardian* pointed out, a dangerous question: 'If he didn't know, why didn't he know?'[57]

In 2011, a new police inquiry was opened and arrests started to be made. And in July that year, the story finally grabbed centre stage when it was revealed that among those whose phones had been hacked were the murdered schoolgirl Milly Dowler, and relatives of dead British soldiers and of 7/7 victims. This went far beyond celebrity; it wasn't just the usual targets, those who had chosen to be in the media – Wayne Rooney, Abi Titmuss, George Galloway. This could be any one of us, caught up in a personal tragedy and then exploited by the media.

The disclosures triggered a major crisis. Within days, News International announced the closure of the *News of the World*, founded in 1843 and Britain's biggest-selling Sunday title. In other developments, Rebekah Brooks, the former *Sun* editor, resigned as chief executive of News International, and Sir Paul Stephenson resigned as commissioner of the Metropolitan Police. Also, Andy Coulson was arrested: he had known after all, and though by this stage he'd left his Downing Street job, it did not reflect well on the government. The man the prime minister had chosen as his chief spin doctor was, in 2014, convicted of conspiracy to intercept messages and sentenced to eighteen months in jail.

Other individuals were also convicted, and more newspapers implicated, but it was the *News of the World* that really mattered. More than a newspaper, it was a national treasure; it was to Fleet Street what the Carry On movies were to the British film industry, or Beryl Cook to the art establishment. In its modern tabloid form, it wasn't quite the same as it had been in its postwar class-defying pomp when its circulation could hit 9 million, but it still had a whiff of those times, of a world without Sunday trading, when the sabbath was a day of tedium broken only by the shenanigans nudgingly chronicled in what was fondly known as the *Screws*. 'I suppose one ought to be grateful,' wrote Alan Bennett in his diary, 'for phrases like "intimacy took place".'[58] And, one might add, for 'I made my excuses and left,' and 'improper suggestion', and 'an act too disgusting to describe in a family newspaper'. In due course, the *Sun on Sunday* rose to take its place on newsagents' shelves, but never in the affections of the nation.

This was a paper that had always portrayed itself as being on the side of decent, ordinary folk, and many readers were genuinely horrified at the betrayal of trust shown by the hacking of

Milly Dowler's phone. Of all newspapers, the *News of the World* should have known the public's attitude to child victims.

The banking crash, the expenses scandal, now phone hacking – it seemed as though a wildfire was tearing through the institutions of the establishment, destroying public confidence. Yet however disruptive all this had been, the second crisis of summer 2011 revealed new layers of discord.

On Thursday 4 August an unarmed 29-year-old man named Mark Duggan was shot dead by police in Tottenham, north London. Such fatalities were becoming rare, for the number of deaths in police custody or following contact with the police was in sharp decline. Even on the broadest measure (including pursuits and road traffic incidents) the annual average in 2001–05 was 91 such deaths in England and Wales, falling to 48 in the following 5-year period, and then to 32 in 2011–15.[59] But still there were controversial cases,* and a shockingly low level of prosecutions for unlawful killing. In this instance there was a great deal of local anger, a belief that Duggan's killing was unjustified and that the police response was woefully inadequate.

The following Saturday evening, fights between youths and police in the streets of Tottenham turned into a riot, accompanied by outbreaks of arson and looting. The next day there were further, worse disturbances elsewhere in London, and the disorder then spread to much of the rest of England, not just to the obvious big cities – Birmingham, Bristol, Leeds, Liverpool, Manchester – but also to Basildon, Birkenhead, Cambridge, Chatham, Croydon, Derby, Gillingham, Guildford, Gloucester, Luton, Northampton,

---

* Among them: the shooting of Jean Charles de Menezes on a Tube train after the failed terrorist attacks in July 2005; the death of Ian Tomlinson after being assaulted by a police officer while walking past a demonstration in 2009; the supposed suicide of David Emmanuel (better known as reggae star Smiley Culture) during a police raid on his house in 2011.

Nottingham, Oxford, St Albans, Salford, Slough, West Bromwich and Worcester, with minor incidents elsewhere.

There had been other street riots in recent months. In November 2010 a student demonstration against tuition fees had seen trouble flare outside the Millbank office block that housed, among other tenants, the Conservative Party. To chants of 'Tory scum', windows were smashed, a huge pile of placards was set alight outside, and some protestors managed to break in, setting off the fire alarm and gaining access to the roof. Banners were displayed reading 'This is what democracy looks like' and 'Clegg, you sell-out'.[60] The protests, said Labour backbencher John McDonnell, 'showed the best of our movement'.[61]

And in March 2011, 500,000 people had attended the largest-ever TUC rally to protest against austerity and to hear Ed Miliband tell them that they were walking in the footsteps of the suffragettes and civil rights campaigners and all those 'that have marched in peaceful but powerful protest for justice, fairness and political change'.[62] Some factions on the march opted for power rather than peace. UK Uncut, a group that campaigned for a crackdown on tax avoiders, used the demonstration as an opportunity to occupy Fortnum & Mason, and there were attacks on other shops and clashes with the police. Dozens were injured and there were a couple of hundred arrests.

On both those occasions, things had got out of hand for a brief period in a small part of central London. But August 2011 was a different order of magnitude altogether. For five nights, it seemed as though social order had simply broken down in large areas of England. London saw the worst of it, with disorder right across the city. The prevalence of mobile phones – these were the first major riots of the social media age – meant that the disturbances were swift-moving, short-lived, seemingly random, with the police desperately trying to keep up with developments, as though playing whack-a-mole across the capital. By the third night, an extra 10,000 officers had been deployed in London (leaving some other forces short), and there was talk of using plastic bullets and water cannon, of calling in the army.*

There were battles with the police, but there was also a level of criminality that went beyond anything seen in recent memory. Cars, lorries, buses and ambulances were burned out. Houses were robbed, passers-by mugged, people driven from their homes by fire. And there was looting on an industrial scale. Virtually every big-brand store had one or more branches ransacked, from Bang & Olufsen to JD Sports and Primark. Local independent shops were also targeted, some because there were electrical goods, jewellery or alcohol to be stolen, others just for the fun of it: there was no logic to arson attacks on a bakery, a restaurant, a newsagent, even a Greggs. The incident that received the most coverage was the torching of the House of Reeves, a family-run furniture store in Croydon founded in 1867, where firefighters couldn't reach the blazing building because of the mobs on the streets. 'I have never seen such a disregard for human life,' said a local man. 'I hope they rot in hell.'[63] This had become destruction for its own sake. Internet retailer Amazon reported that sales of baseball bats rose by 5,000 per cent.

Five people were killed in the riots, hundreds were injured, thousands arrested. Magistrates' courts sat through the night to deal with the surge of cases, and when that proved insufficient, video links were set up with police stations to run virtual courts. The headlines tried to catch the wanton violence: 'Yob rule', 'Carry on looting', 'National Lootery', 'Anarchy in the UK', 'Rabble without a cause'.[64]

---

* This was the favoured option of the many celebrities who used Twitter to keep the nation informed of their views. From sports stars Kelly Holmes and Rio Ferdinand to film director Michael Winner and columnist India Knight, all agreed that the army was the answer. As Piers Morgan tweeted, 'it's time for the Army to defend the pro-British public against these anti-British thugs'. (8–9 August 2011)

There was, as ever, much earnest analysis of why this had happened, since it all seemed a little removed from the death of Mark Duggan. The truth was probably that, seen from inside a mob, a temporary breakdown of social order can be exciting, thrilling. Having the police on the defensive was simply fun, though lip service had to paid to loftier causes. 'Everyone was on a riot, just chucking things, chucking bottles, breaking into stuff,' enthused a girl in Croydon, although her friend hastily added, 'It's the government's fault.'[65] It was an explanation that fell some way short of satisfactory. The austerity programme of the Coalition might have affected the response to the riots ('The scale of government cuts is making it harder for the police to do their jobs,' said shadow home secretary Yvette Cooper),[66] but surely was not the cause. It did not explain, for example, the mob that gathered outside Birmingham Children's Hospital, intent, it appeared, on arson, until seen off by staff. And anyone inclined to see this as a rebellion of the dispossessed might pause at the reports that on Marchmont Street in central London, the only shop to have its windows smashed was Gay's the Word, the country's leading lesbian and gay bookshop; there was no looting there, just criminal damage. Nor was there to be a repeat of the rioting, even though government cuts bit harder in later years.

Inevitably, thoughts turned to the riots of the 1980s. The most serious of those had also been in Tottenham, where PC Keith Blakelock was murdered on the Broadwater Farm estate in 1985, but a local shopkeeper insisted there was no comparison: 'That was contained on a housing estate, this is a hundred times worse.'[67] More apposite, perhaps was the spate of unrest in 1981, starting in Brixton, south London, and spreading across the country. That too had been at a time of economic difficulty, in the early days of a cuts-driven government (and in the year of a royal wedding), yet this felt different, and not just in scale. 'Then, a sense of social injustice burned as fiercely as the buildings and the cars,' wrote the *Liverpool Echo* in an angry leader column. 'This time there is no oppressed, indignant and voiceless population. Social campaigners have been replaced with hooded thugs united not by injustice but by malicious intent, by boredom and by communication networks that are named "social" but sometimes can be anything but.' The editorial was headlined: 'Morons, criminals and feral copycats'.[68]

Perhaps that slid too easily over the fact that the initial spark was the killing of an unarmed black man by the police. Yet there were many who agreed with a Brixton café owner: 'It's just an excuse to go shopping.'[69] The 1981 riots had famously coincided with the Specials' 'Ghost Town', a bleakly beautiful protest song, reaching number one in the charts. This time, the top single was Cher Lloyd's 'Jagger Swagger', a song of celebrity, status and success. 'You should get some of your own,' advised the lyrics. 'Count that money, get your game on.'[70]

And as the images of social collapse were beamed around the world, some worried about the impact on the economy and on London's big moment, now less than a year away. Matt's cartoon in the *Daily Telegraph* showed a Londoner giving directions: 'The Olympic stadium? Turn left at the second burned-out bus and right at the looted electrical store.'[71]

The opening ceremony for the 2008 Olympic Games in Beijing was on a scale never seen before in the event's history. It started with 2,008 drummers playing bronze instruments in regimented choreography, and got bigger from there. A cast of many thousands, drilled and disciplined, worked in perfect harmony to produce spectacular effects and moments of great beauty. This was what a totalitarian regime could do to show off to the world, given a budget reported to be in excess of $100 million. It was a triumph of the collective over the individual, and set a standard that may never be matched again.

Certainly it was never going to be matched by London, where the next Games were held in 2012, and where the ceremony budget was just £27 million. That was still an extraordinary sum to spend on a single performance, however, and the show's director, Danny Boyle, was used to making a little go a long way: his films *Train-spotting* (1996), *28 Days Later* (2002) and *Slumdog Millionaire* (2008) – for which he got an Oscar – were made for less than that between them. 'We took advantage of the financial limitations and tried to produce something with twice as much heart,' he said.[72]

The event he staged was a funny, irreverent, emotional love letter to Britain. It opened with a green and pleasant landscape being transformed by the Industrial Revolution, and ended with Tim Berners-Lee, inventor of the World Wide Web, tweeting a message of democratic revolution: 'This is for everyone.' In between there was a riot of pop culture, the focus falling on the second half of the twentieth century. It was a more polished performance than the Golden Jubilee pageant a decade earlier, but the tone of gleeful eccentricity was not dissimilar. The stadium was visited at various points by village cricketers, Jarrow marchers, dancing suffragettes, Sgt Peppers, Chelsea Pensioners, Windrush immigrants, pearly kings and queens, and spring-heeled punks with oversized heads, while a swarm of Mary Poppinses flew in to defeat monstrous puppets of villains from children's literature, from Captain Hook to Lord Voldemort. It was entirely without cynicism, without irony even, and silly enough for Rowan Atkinson in Mr Bean mode to do a fart joke. When grime star Dizzee Rascal appeared, it was inevitable that he'd perform his number-one hit 'Bonkers' (2009).*

The only thing missing was a fleet of London cabs, but they were there for the closing ceremony, five of them, each carrying a Spice Girl. This performance was even more implausible than the

---

* There were limits, though; David Cameron said he'd 'vetoed one of the more bonkers ideas – a section featuring Gerry Adams and Martin McGuinness'. (*For the Record* p. 377)

opening ceremony: the massed bands of the Foot Guards played Blur's 'Parklife'; Timothy Spall as Winston Churchill recited Caliban's 'Be not afeared' speech from *The Tempest*; Eric Idle led the crowd in 'Always Look on the Bright Side of Life', accompanied by morris dancers, roller-skating nuns and Welsh women; DJ Fatboy Slim spun some discs while a hippy bus in psychedelic livery turned itself into a giant octopus. It was that kind of show.

In between the two ceremonies, the Games were – said all the British commentators – a magnificent spectacle of sport, and the public agreed. There had been real fears that the whole thing would be a disaster, but it turned out to be a feel-good event. It helped, of course that the home team did extremely well, winning 65 medals and coming third in the overall table, behind the USA and China. (In Sydney in 2000, that had been 28 medals and a tenth-place finish.) And some of the British successes were in big events as well, not just the sports that involved boats and horses: Mo Farah won gold in the 5,000 and 10,000 metres, as did Jessica Ennis in the heptathlon, Andy Murray in the tennis, and Nicola Adams in boxing, the first woman ever to do so. It was exciting stuff for British viewers, though for the international audience there was nothing to rival the highs of Beijing, when Jamaican sprinter Usain Bolt set world record times in both the 100 and 200 metres, and American swimmer Michael Phelps won an unparalleled eight golds.

The celebratory mood extended to the Paralympics, which enjoyed their best staging. The opening ceremony featured Stephen Hawking and a depiction of the Large Hadron Collider, as well as a performance of Ian Dury's anthem of disabled defiance 'Spasticus Autisticus' (1981), originally banned by the BBC to the dismay of its writer, and now joyously broadcast around the world. In the medal table, Britain again came third, this time behind China and Russia.*

---

* The London Games were also notable for the crowd's pleasure in passing

The most impressive performance of all was that Olympic opening ceremony, with its attempt to define Britain's image. There was, though, some confusion overseas, particularly concerning the long section in praise of the National Health Service, with hundreds of children in illuminated hospital beds that danced around the stadium, and the inexplicable unveiling of a weird giant baby's head.* 'It is a strange sort of nation that can turn a hospital bed into a symbol of national pride,' snorted Peter Hitchens in his *Mail on Sunday* column.[73] But that was the point. This was indeed a strange sort of nation, a mixed-up, muddled-up, shook-up nation that embraced eccentricity, creativity and tradition. There was amazing innovation but also a love of national myths. And one of the myths held most dear was the NHS.

Britain had long ago decided that this was a modern marvel. 'It is the envy of the world,' explained the *Daily Herald* in 1958, on the tenth anniversary of the founding. 'Whenever a foreigner meets one of our fellow-countrymen, ten to one the first subject he will bring up is our Health Service. There isn't another like it.'[74] Half a century later, on its sixtieth anniversary, the same line was still commonplace. 'The NHS is the envy of the world,' said Labour health minister Ann Keen, 'and this diamond jubilee year offers us an exceptional opportunity to celebrate a unique British institution.'[75]

Universally admired, yet not imitated – it seemed contradictory somehow. And there had always been awkward types pointing to other systems that offered better results. A 1964 editorial in the *British Medical Journal* was already warning that the service was slipping behind its rivals: 'We doubt, indeed, whether any medical

---

its verdict on visiting politicians: David Cameron and George Osborne got heavily booed, while Gordon Brown and Boris Johnson got cheered.
* It was supposed to represent ultrasound imaging, but the television commentary omitted to mention that.

organisation on the continent of Europe looks upon Britain's NHS as other than inferior to its own system.'[76]

But such heretical views were seldom heard nowadays. This was, in the phrase used by politicians of all stripes, 'our NHS'. Every comparable European country shared the same medical advances, offered the same treatments; only the British made a fetish of the delivery mechanism for those treatments. In a fragmented country, this was one of the things – perhaps *the* thing – that held us together. It wasn't only about medicine, but also identity, a wish to express a common endeavour, a need to share and to belong; it was the Labour Party's great contribution to the nation's mythology. The fact that no one else was sufficiently impressed to adopt the same system simply made it more completely British. When David Cameron summed up his priorities in three letters, it was an acknowledgement that the NHS was now an article of faith.

'The National Health Service is the closest thing the English have to a religion,' Nigel Lawson had observed in 1992,[77] and the comparison became familiar; Peter Hitchens wrote of 'the bizarre worship of the NHS as a state religion',[78] and Matthew D'Ancona of 'our national secular religion'.[79] When Justin Welby* was enthroned as archbishop of Canterbury in 2013, his sermon referred to the creation of the NHS, like the abolition of slavery, as an example of 'Christ-liberated courage'.[80] The Reverend Stephen Greasley, chairman of the Derby Forum of Faiths, was prepared to go further; when a man asked him why we don't see miracles these days, he answered, 'But we do. Every day. The blind see and the lame walk. The National Health Service is God's greatest instrument for healing.'[81]

Nobody went that far about the BBC, but it too was a nationalised treasure that came out of the Olympics very well. The

---

* After the state-educated George Carey and Rowan Williams, Old Etonian Welby was a return to the tradition of public-school primates.

corporation ran a full 27-channel internet service, so that not a single shot in the double-trap shooting was missed, nor a single tack in the Men's Finn class.* Also having a good Olympics was the army; the task of ensuring security had originally been contracted out to private firm G4S, but a fortnight before the start it admitted it couldn't get the staff, so soldiers had to be sent in. Together with the vast body of enthusiastic volunteers known as Games Makers, the cheerfulness of the squaddies ensured a mood of goodwill.

But the institution that emerged as the ultimate victor was, perhaps inevitably, the monarchy. The single most inspired and memorable image of the Games came in the opening ceremony, when a filmed insert saw James Bond, played by his current inhabitant Daniel Craig, arrive in a black cab at Buckingham Palace to be shown into the royal presence. 'Good evening, Mr Bond,' she said, and allowed herself to be escorted out to a waiting helicopter. As it flew across London, with 'The Dam Busters March' on the soundtrack, it was waved at by well-wishers and by the statue of Winston Churchill in Parliament Square (animated for the occasion). Cut to the stadium in real time, as the helicopter hovered, and both Bond and Her Majesty parachuted out. A few moments later, the Queen, wearing the same frock as in the film, made her entrance into the royal box. Even more than the Golden Jubilee, this was the defining moment of the Queen's late years, the longest-lived – and soon to be longest-reigning – British monarch sharing a joke with a fictional character, tradition and popular culture paying tribute to each other.

In the troubled years ahead, many would look back on the 2012 Olympics as the nation at its best: the grubby worlds of banking, politics and press temporarily eclipsed by the great institutions that could still bring people together – the NHS, the BBC, monarchy, the creative industries. The tone was set by that opening

---

* Gold medals for Britons Peter Wilson and Ben Ainslie respectively.

ceremony, proclaiming the continued cultural power of the UK, presenting a celebratory, self-confident multi-ethnic image. It was the biggest shared moment of its time,* and one with a deep emotional charge. 'Danny Boyle's ceremony was the most spectacular thing I've seen in my life,' said Delia Smith, the country's best-loved cook. 'It made me feel proud to be British, which I don't think I was before.'[82]

---

* UK viewing figures for the opening ceremony peaked at 27 million, the biggest TV audience since Hilda Ogden left *Coronation Street* on Christmas Day 1987. As comedian Katy Brand said, 'So if the UK viewing audience was 27 million, and it cost £27 million, then it's the best bloody pound I have ever spent.' (*Independent* 29 July 2012)

9

Europeans and Europe

I

For centuries, cockle picking in Britain was little more than a cottage industry, a laborious task – harvesting the shellfish by hand, raking through the sand at low tide. The product was part of staple seaside fare, as seen in comedian Ken Dodd's 1968 description of the Golden Mile in Blackpool: 'Cockles, oysters, winkles and candyfloss, brandysnaps, fish and chips or scampi and, for the upper classes, chips eaten from the *Guardian*.'[1] By the turn of the century, however, cockles had become fashionable in upmarket restaurants, a substantial export trade was developing, and the industry was becoming more intensive. Concerns began to be raised over unscrupulous employers, said to be both exploiting their workers and depleting the beds by taking small cockles as well as the fully grown. It was still mostly done by hand, though.

In 2003 several productive areas in Scotland and Wales were closed because of contamination – a recurrent problem, due to pollution – and large numbers of cocklers turned instead to Morecambe Bay in Lancashire, with its expanse of sands and mudflats. Increased competition meant that corners were cut and risks taken. Technically, a permit was required to fish in Morecambe Bay, but no one had the resources to enforce this, as local Labour MP Geraldine Smith pointed out: 'You can't stop people turning up and going on the beach at eight o'clock on a dark winter's night, especially as there's about £6 million worth of cockles just lying on the beaches.'[2] She was speaking after a night in February 2004, when 21 people lost their lives, dragged underwater by a rapidly turning tide and drowned.*

Most of the dead were young men, all were Chinese, all had been brought into the country illegally and were working for gangmasters who paid them a pittance and provided slum accommodation. 'We're talking about up to forty people living in these houses,' said a police officer. 'There are mattresses on the floor, hardly any food, and poor heating.'[3] These workers had no experience or training, and knew nothing of the tidal patterns.

This was increasingly the nature of the industry. A police raid the previous season had seen 37 Chinese cocklers arrested in Morecambe Bay on suspicion of immigration offences. And what was true of shellfish gathering was also the case in other areas of low-skill casual labour, especially agriculture and horticulture. Around the same time, immigration officers 'estimated that about 2,000 Chinese migrants had appeared in the King's Lynn area of Norfolk'.[4]

---

* Twenty-one bodies were recovered. It is possible that the death toll was higher.

Complaints about unscrupulous gangmasters employing and exploiting foreign labour – often illegal immigrants – had been around since the 1980s, and in 1998 the Labour government had issued a code of practice, agreed with the National Farmers' Union. The problems continued, however, largely driven, it was argued, by large retailers relentlessly squeezing suppliers on price. Some Whitehall departments had been reluctant to press for registration and regulation, but in the aftermath of Morecambe Bay, action became unavoidable. The Gangmasters (Licensing) Act 2004 began the long process of trying to regulate employment practices in industries that had become reliant on a lack of oversight.

This was the reality behind the cheap food that found its way onto British tables, a reality that few cared to look at too closely. A notable exception came in *Two Caravans* (2007), Marina Lewycka's novel of migrant workers, with its description of 'Sunnydell Chicken Farm and Hatchery'. A Pole named Tomasz finds employment here, loading a 'crop' of 40,000 chickens from a windowless hangar onto lorries bound for the abattoir. He's paid six pounds an hour, from which is deducted tax, insurance, travel and accommodation (a room shared with five others). Even then, six pounds is not the real rate, because 'for every hour you work you do another voluntary'.[5] The account is Dickensian in its disgust at the treatment of humans and animals alike, both abused in pursuit of profits. 'I'm sure that there isn't one chicken farm where all these awful things happen,' said Lewycka. 'I'm also sure that they all do happen: just not on the same day and in the same place.'[6]

And as the gentle, melancholic Tomasz finds himself being brutalised by the experience, he becomes reflective. 'Is he freer here in the West today than he was in Poland in the years of communism?' he wonders. 'Is he really any freer than those chickens in the barn, packed here in this small stinking room with five strangers, submitting meekly to a daily horror that has already become routine?'[7]

*

'Walk down some streets in west London these days and you could be in downtown Warsaw,' observed a French news agency in 2008: 'from thriving Polish supermarkets and cafés to the hum of Slavic chatter and rich smell of Polish dumplings.'[8] But it wasn't just London. The wave of migrants from eastern Europe was one of the biggest developments of the new century, touching almost every part of England, including many which had previously seen very little immigration at all.

In May 2004 the European Union, then fifteen nations strong, expanded south and east, taking in Cyprus, the Czech Republic, Estonia, Hungary, Latvia, Lithuania, Malta, Poland, Slovakia and Slovenia. Two other countries – Bulgaria and Romania – applied but were deemed not yet ready: they joined three years later.* It was the EU's biggest ever enlargement, increasing the population of the Union by around a quarter, and while Cyprus and Malta were considered straightforward, the absorption of the former communist states raised fears that large numbers of people might leave low-wage, low-employment economies in search of better-paid work. The prospect of mass migration meant that the cherished principle of free movement within the Union was temporarily suspended; a seven-year transition period was implemented, during which each of the existing members was permitted to put its own restrictions on immigration from the east. Most did so, but not Ireland, Sweden or the UK, which set no limits on workers entering the country.

The British government was reassuring: it wouldn't be much of an issue. 'The number coming here for employment will be minimal,' said immigration minister Beverley Hughes.[9] She was speaking as the Home Office published a report estimating that there'd be between 5,000 and 13,000 arrivals a year. This estimate was based on the assumption that other countries – France,

---

* Croatia subsequently joined in 2013.

Germany, Italy, Spain – would also have an open-door policy. When it turned out that wasn't the case, no adjustment was made, and the number 13,000 remained; it was still being quoted in the press right up to the date of accession. 'No minister ever used such a figure,' protested home secretary David Blunkett,[10] but equally no minister corrected it either. As with the 45-minute claim in Iraq, the government let the error stand, and thereby supplied its opponents with ammunition.

Some disputed the official figures from the outset. The pressure group MigrationWatch estimated around 40,000 would come from east Europe each year.[11] But MigrationWatch was, according to Blunkett, just 'a tinpot one-man organisation'[12] and easily lumped in with what Andy McSmith in the *Independent* described as 'an ominous coalition of Conservatives, bigots, tabloid newspapers, and anxious intellectuals'.[13] Among those tabloids, the most vociferous was the *Daily Express*. 'Millions of poverty-stricken workers plan to invade prosperous western Europe in search of a better life,' it warned in a typical piece. 'Tens of thousands will head for Britain alone.'[14]

And herein lay the problem. Even before the accession countries joined the EU, political positions had been taken and battle lines drawn. As the date drew nearer, Tony Blair spoke of 'a potential risk' of there being larger numbers than had been anticipated, and was immediately criticised. 'This is a knee-jerk reaction,' said Keith Best of the Immigration Advisory Service. 'It's pandering to the *Daily Mail* and *Daily Express*.'[15] Free movement had become an article of faith in polite society, and any opposition to it carried the whiff of racism. 'We live in an increasingly globalised world,' said Brendan Barber, general secretary of the TUC. 'Our best response is not to yield to little England, but recognise that the best way of avoiding a rush to the bottom is to fully embrace Europe; and that means accepting the free movement of labour as well as capital and goods.'[16] The logic was not obvious.

Exact figures were impossible to determine,* but in the first five months of the enlargement, the government estimated that 75,000 immigrants made their way to Britain from eastern Europe, prompting a rapid change in government messaging: 'It was decided to present the figures as good news, evidence of a thriving economy etc.'[17] The good news got better and better; two years on from the accession, there were an estimated 350,000 Polish people living in Britain. Other nationalities were also represented,† but it was the Poles that made the most impact, because there'd been nothing on this scale before. 'From one country, in a very short space of time, it must be the largest influx we have ever seen,' observed David Coleman, professor of demography at Oxford.[18] ('Coming over here, doing the jobs we're not prepared to do because we've all got worthless degrees in media studies,' grumbled comic Al Murray in his persona of the Pub Landlord.)

It was an extraordinary development in British history, and it wasn't entirely clear why it had come about, why Britain hadn't imposed any restrictions on free movement like comparable countries. One explanation was that the British government had simply been wrongfooted, hadn't realised until too late that other members of the EU would abandon such a key principle. There was also, though, the timing. When the decision was made in 2003, the government's preoccupation had been the invasion of Iraq. Divisions within the EU on the subject meant that Britain was in danger of losing influence, and the accession states looked like allies. Speaking in the Iraq debate in March that year, Tony

---

* This was even more so with illegal immigration. In May 2006 home secretary John Reid announced there were around 400,000 illegal immigrants in Britain, while admitting that the true figure would never be known. The same month it transpired that some of those worked as cleaners in the Home Office.

† To take just one example, in 2001 there were 8,600 UK residents who'd been born in Latvia and Lithuania; that rose to 170,000 ten years later.

Blair drew attention to the fact that all ten countries were 'in strong support of the position of this government'.[19] Free movement would bring them into Britain's sphere of influence and, in the words of Jack Straw, 'rebalance the EU away from Paris and Berlin, particularly after Iraq'.[20]

The other explanation that was offered came from a former Labour speechwriter, Andrew Neather, in an article addressing the unprecedented rise in immigration more generally. And it was unprecedented. In the 1960s and 70s, more people left Britain than arrived, so that in 1968, for example, the year of Enoch Powell's Rivers of Blood speech, net migration stood at minus 56,000. That began to turn in the 80s, and by 1997, when Labour came to office, annual net migration stood at plus 48,000. And then there was a surge. In the re-election year of 2001, it soared to 179,000, the highest level yet recorded, and went on to rise still further, boosted by the accession countries, so that it reached 267,000 by the next election. These were the net figures; looked at another way, annual immigration topped 500,000 a year in 2002 and stayed there for the rest of the decade.[21]

Neather claimed this was a 'deliberate policy' designed 'to open up the UK to mass migration'. There was an economic advantage, but that wasn't the sole motivation: 'mass immigration was the way that the government was going to make the UK truly multicultural'. An added benefit was 'to rub the Right's nose in diversity and render their arguments out of date'. The government had no wish, however, 'to discuss what increased immigration would mean, above all for Labour's core white working-class vote'. It was 'too metropolitan an argument', so that 'while ministers might have been passionately in favour of a more diverse society, it wasn't necessarily a debate they wanted to have in working men's clubs in Sheffield or Sunderland'.[22]

Between the census of 2001 and that of 2011, the number of British residents who had been born in a foreign country increased by more than 3 million, so that they now accounted for more than one in eight of the population. As Neather said, 'Part by accident, part by design, the government had created its longed-for immigration boom.'

'One of the first things that strikes people who come to the UK from Poland is how chubby everyone is,' wrote a 24-year-old Polish student at Birmingham University. She'd grown up without crisps, chocolate, fizzy drinks and other capitalist indulgences, and as she looked around Britain, she concluded, 'I have definitely not missed out on much.'[23] An alternative take on British culture came from the Imbeciles, a Bulgarian punk trio unimpressed on their arrival in London in 2003 to see T-shirts being sold that displayed Soviet iconography. Their debut single spelled out their reaction: 'From those of us who lived through it, you can keep your T-shirts, they don't mean shit.'[24]

Much of the migration from eastern Europe followed traditional paths into the cities, to London and Liverpool, Birmingham and Hull – where it was said that 'most of the spare shops on Spring Bank have been taken up with Polish supermarkets and Kurdish hairdressers'.[25] Some nationalities congregated in particular areas: Bulgarians in Herefordshire, Slovaks in Warrington, Lithuanians and Latvians in Peterborough.* And there were less obvious destinations too, such as Carlisle, twinned with the Polish city of Słupsk. 'In Scarborough, North Yorkshire, Polish grocery shops have sprung up,' noted the *Sunday Telegraph*. 'In Great Yarmouth, Norfolk, a policeman has taught himself to speak Lithuanian so he can chat to locals on his beat.'[26] By 2013 Polish had become the third most commonly spoken language in the country, behind English and Welsh, but ahead of Punjabi and Urdu.

Connections were made with other communities: there was

---

* By 2009 over 9 per cent of the population of Peterborough had come to the city from overseas, most of them from eastern Europe.

a report from Bradford of 'an Asian family running a chain of thriving Polish supermarkets',[27] while the owner of the Biedronki supermarket in Gloucester said that his customers were 'not just from Poland, Romania or Slovakia but many people from Asian countries'.[28] There were other crossovers too. In Lancashire, the managing director of a property management company began erecting to-let boards written entirely in Polish. 'I think the niche is there,' he told the press, 'and people from Poland are respectful people. They look after the properties.'[29] In December 2006 the *Reading Chronicle* became the first British newspaper to publish a Polish-language edition.

It was estimated in 2007 that Polish expats, 80 per cent of whom were aged between 18 and 34, spent £4 billion annually. Their purchasing power was such that in 2006 Tesco, Britain's biggest retailer, began stocking Polish food, and two years later launched a Polish-language version of its home-delivery website. Some products had a wider impact. In particular, Polish beer – brands such as Tyskie, Zywiec and Lech – became a familiar sight in supermarkets, corner shops and pubs, increasingly consumed by British drinkers. 'We started stocking it a couple of years ago in Wakefield, Yorkshire,' said a spokesperson for the pub chain J. D. Wetherspoon. 'We now sell it all over the place.'[30]

This wasn't like previous large-scale immigration. It was predominantly white and Christian, factors that might have facilitated integration. It was also, however, more rapid, more widespread and, because many were merely making a temporary move to places of higher employment, more transient. As academic Ann White noted, 'Eastern Europeans see themselves as citizens of the EU rather than migrants.'[31] Consequently, despite the food shops, there remained a cultural segregation. There was no presence, for example, in the 2012 Olympic Opening Ceremony.

Even in popular culture, eastern Europeans were scarcely visible. There were some footballers (Petr Čech of the Czech Republic and Bulgarian Dimitar Berbatov won the Premier

League with Chelsea and Manchester United respectively), but they weren't household names in the way the first French stars – Eric Cantona, David Ginola, Thierry Henry – had been; they weren't asked to front major advertising campaigns. There was music being made but much of it remained separate: rapper Noizy, 'arguably the king of Albanian hip-hop',[32] grew up in Woolwich, south London, but while his records reached number one in his homeland, they did not feature in the British charts. The one major exception was pop singer Rita Ora, a Kosovar who grew up in Notting Hill, west London and was big enough to become a judge on *The X Factor*. And then there were the scantily clad and briefly successful Cheeky Girls, identical twins from Romania who made their name with the million-selling single 'Cheeky Song (Touch My Bum)' in 2002.*

The old British vision of eastern Europe had been a place of feudalism, superstition and adventure – the Ruritania of Anthony Hope's *The Prisoner of Zenda* (1894), the Transylvania of Bram Stoker's *Dracula* (1897) – subsequently overlaid with the sinister imagery of the cold war. Nowadays, the cities of the region were becoming more familiar with the growth of tourism, particularly with stag and hen parties, but there remained a belief that beyond the bars and the busy streets lay an almost medieval world. In the British mind, there was also a north–south divide; Poland and the Czech Republic were one thing, Romania and Bulgaria another. In his film *Borat* (2006), Sacha Baron Cohen's title character is from Kazakhstan, but the scenes depicting his home village – complete with town rapist, prematurely aged peasant population and guns in the kindergarten – were actually filmed in Glod in Romania. When Jeremy Clarkson visited Romania in a 2009 edition of *Top Gear*, he described it as 'Borat country, with Gypsies and Russian playboys'.[33]

---

* In 2008 Gabriela Irimia of the Cheeky Girls announced her engagement to Lib Dem MP Lembit Öpik (he was of Estonian extraction, though born in Bangor, Northern Ireland). Sadly, the relationship was not long lived.

The sense remained that this was a strangely alien culture; it looked mostly familiar but was separate. One of Harry Enfield's regular characters was a diffident middle-class man who buys his coffee from Café Polski every day because he's besotted with Magda, one of the two Polish women who work there. There's a melancholic tone to the sketches, stemming from the Englishman's inability to communicate. The women are by turns rude, aloof, friendly, flirty, with no apparent rhyme or reason, and the fact that he can't understand what they say to each other makes his confusion more acute. The familiar sight of a balding, middle-aged man mooning over someone young enough (as she points out) to be his daughter becomes a metaphor for two cultures that can't quite seem to meet.

In middle-class reality, there was much praise for the Polish builder, who did the kitchen extension, and the Czech nanny, who was so good with the children. This was not shared by the Essex plumber, who believed his wages were being undercut. As Norman Tebbit said, 'For some people, immigrants are an endless supply of au pairs, for others they're competition for jobs.' He himself, as it happened, fell into the first camp; he employed incomers to help care for his wife, who'd been paralysed by an IRA bomb in 1984. 'They work hard, they save hard,' he explained. 'There doesn't seem to be the same motivation amongst young British people. I think the schools are at fault, the welfare system.'[34]

Nowhere in Britain was more affected by the enlargement of the EU than Boston, Lincolnshire. According to the 2001 census, 98.5 per cent of the town's population were white British, and the only substantial foreign community comprised just 249 Germans.[35] Ten years later, it had the largest proportion of eastern European residents in the country, with 10.6 per cent of the population having been born in one of the accession countries, around 6,800 people. Those were the official statistics; most believed that they greatly understated the reality.

The economy in this part of Lincolnshire relied heavily on agriculture and food processing – a quarter of the fruit and vegetables in British supermarkets came from round here – and there was seasonal employment to be found, picking and packing in the fields and factories. In the 1980s and 90s, this casual work had attracted the unemployed from South Yorkshire and the east Midlands, where heavy industries were in decline. Then at the turn of the century, there was the start of an influx of foreign workers, primarily Portuguese, but also Kurds and the first few eastern Europeans.

This aroused some suspicion from locals. Rumours began to circulate of businesses displaying 'No English' signs, and of migrant workers being given grants to buy cars. The stories weren't true but they found a ready audience. 'Foreigners have been a rarity until now, so visitors from overseas are an exotic species,' explained a local resident. 'Anything that is said about them could be believed to be true.'[36]

In the 2004 European elections, the British National Party outpolled the Liberal Democrats in Boston, and temperatures rose later that year during the Euro 2004 football tournament, when the BNP circulated a leaflet falsely alleging that the council and the police had banned the St George flag. On the night of France's stoppage-time victory over England, there was a riot involving some two hundred people, of whom sixteen were later charged. Police cars were overturned and set on fire, an off-licence was looted and torched, and even a charity shop was smashed up; according to the *Sun*, there was a million pounds' worth of damage.[37]

It was not an isolated incident. The drama of England's defeat sparked disturbances across the country, in places as diverse as Birmingham, Bletchley, Cambridge, Cheshunt, Colchester, Croydon, Liverpool and Wakefield. Nonetheless, there was something different about Boston, a distinct racial undertone. The rioters were said to have been chanting 'I'd rather be a Paki than a Kurd' as police stopped them from reaching their primary target, a Kurdish café in the town. 'In the past, there has been a failed attempt at petrol-bombing us,' said a worker at the café; 'we have been warned on numerous occasions to get out of Boston.'[38]

By 2007, it was being reported that 90 per cent of businesses in Lincolnshire were reliant on foreign labour, increasingly now from east Europe, recruited there by gangmasters. 'Eastern Europeans came because they were desperate,' explained the Reverend David de Verny, an Anglican priest who worked with migrants. 'They undercut the Portuguese.' Some were reported to be working twelve-hour shifts, seven days a week, and receiving a pittance in pay. As the manager of the Citizens Advice Bureau in Boston explained, 'They come over, and the gangmaster leases a house, packs it full with, say, twelve people, and takes the money directly from their wages to cover rent at extortionate rates.'[39]

The arrival of large numbers of mostly young people brought new pressures on housing and on education. At the start of 2006, there were 85 children in Boston primary schools who didn't speak English; a further 96 arrived that year, and signs in school playgrounds were now written in 5 languages.[40] Government spending had not allowed for such rapid population growth, and the infrastructure was creaking. 'We are not crying wolf,' said Lincolnshire's chief constable, Tony Lake, in 2007. 'The situation is very fragile. Without extra funding we will not be able to provide the service that people rightly expect.'[41]

Even so, many felt the economic impact on the town was positive. 'Migrant workers have brought Boston back to life,' said a local businessman.[42] The journalist Mary Riddell grew up in Boston in the 1960s, and forty years on, described its rebirth under the impact of immigration: 'The place is richer and more cosmopolitan than it has been for decades, if not centuries.' She argued that, although there were difficulties, 'native Bostonians are winners'.[43]

Wages were low, but so too was unemployment. And the

economy seemed sustainable, so that when the recession came in 2008, Boston wasn't as badly hit as other places; retail sales nationally fell by 8 per cent, but by just over 2 per cent in the town, and unemployment was not the same issue it was elsewhere.[44] There were social problems, though, outlined in 2012 when the local council commissioned a report into 'issues such as drinking on our streets, licensing of HMOs,* employment protection issues, zero-hour contracts, and a review of our licensing regulations for off-licences'.[45] Twenty-eight recommendations to guide the council and the police were made, and crime, violent crime and complaints of anti-social behaviour were said to have fallen as a result.

The report was praised by Cambridge academic Mary Beard, appearing on a 2013 edition of *Question Time*, broadcast from Lincoln. It was 'the most impressive single document I have read on this issue', she said.[46] An audience member, Rachel Bull, a 35-year-old office manager from Boston, angrily disagreed. 'The facilities are at breaking point because of these people coming into the country,' she said. 'There are hardly any locals here any more because they're all moving away. You go down to Boston High Street and it's just like you're in a foreign country. It's got to stop.'[47] There was sustained applause as she continued: 'I may not be as clever as her or have been to university, but this is my family's home town and I wanted to say how it really is for the real people that live here.' She herself was half-Polish, descended from refugees who fought in the war, and she was keen to stress that this wasn't racism. 'I don't blame the migrants,' she insisted. 'I blame the government for not realising the impact it's having on ordinary people – or managing it.'[48] It was essentially the point that Gillian Duffy had been trying to make.

A decade on from the 2004 riot, Stephen Stray, editor of the *Boston Standard*, reflected on how things had changed. 'Seeing

---

* Houses in multiple occupation.

the damage done by that day ten years ago was one of the saddest episodes I have encountered in my time in journalism,' he wrote. 'It's been heart-warming to see that we have not had any repeats of such incidents.'[49]

Indeed, there were no outbreaks of mob violence now, and although there remained ghettos of exploitation in and around Boston, there was also some integration in many workplaces. That didn't extend, however, much beyond the working day. Separate pubs, clubs and churches, together with social media and satellite television, meant that different cultures could co-exist without a great deal of interaction. 'These are two worlds running parallel,' warned the Reverend de Verny in 2007. 'They ignore each other. But I'm not sure how long that can go on.'[50] Somehow, it did go on. When journalist Emily Dugan visited Boston for her book *Finding Home: Real Stories of Migrant Britain* (2015), she described a town that was stable but segregated, with 'an atmosphere of division that puts up unseen walls between "eastern European" and "British" areas, souring the community and prompting mistrust on both sides'.[51]

The arrival of east Europeans brought change to the country as a whole, but the change was mostly intangible. There were plenty of academic studies (not all of them funded by EU money) that showed immigrants were making a net contribution to the economy and weren't holding down wages, but it was harder to measure the sense of cultural unease. And there was a much bigger issue beyond the economy. It was perhaps the temporary nature of this immigration that was a little disturbing; in places more accustomed to social stability than transience, the sense of people just passing through was a psychological, almost a philosophical challenge. And it raised an awkward question that hadn't really turned up before. What did it say about the country if people *didn't* want to put down roots here?

What was most striking was that public disquiet at what was happening tended to be directed at those in power. A poll in the

Sun in 2007 showed that over 50 per cent of people thought the government had been dishonest about the level of immigration. But while four in five worried about the strain on public services, half the population agreed that immigration was good for the country.[52] As a 2007 leader column in the *Coventry Telegraph* put it, 'Who could argue against the diversity that's enriching our city – the Polish shops alongside the Irish, the Lebanese restaurants alongside the Italian and the Asian, the Lithuanian workers bringing their skills here.'[53]

II

In October 2001, Tony Benn visited the London School of Economics to give a lecture on the democratic case against the European Union. It was an old favourite of his – he'd been speaking on the subject for nearly thirty years – but he was struck this time by the lack of interest that he met. 'You must realise the whole academic establishment takes Europe now for granted,' explained his host, Dr Richard Heffernan; 'there's no question of whether you should or shouldn't be in. It's studied, but not criticised, rather like communism in Russia.'[54]

Heffernan was right. Despite the irritating buzz of UKIP gadflies, British membership of the EU was a settled affair, and in all the best circles – academic, political, business – it was assumed that continuing convergence of the member states was both inevitable and desirable. Talk of Britain joining the euro faded away in public, but, according to José Manuel Barroso, president of the European Commission, private discussion continued. 'I know the majority in Britain are still opposed,' he said in 2008, 'but the people who matter are thinking about it.'[55]

The public were indeed opposed to the single currency. And to further integration generally. And, for a very substantial minority, opposed even to membership itself. Shortly after Blair was elected in 1997, with his promise to put Britain at 'the heart of Europe', the pollsters Ipsos-Mori asked how people would vote if there was an in/out referendum: 44 per cent said in, 37 per cent out. The same question a decade on showed a slight hardening of views on both sides: 51 to 39 per cent.[56] It was cultural as much as political. Most of England did not feel part of the European family, instead looking beyond to the English-speaking world. 'The good Lord knew what he was doing when he put water between us and the rest of Europe,' said Margaret Thatcher in 2002,[57] and many felt the same in their gut. Certainly, many Conservative Party members did.

For David Cameron as leader, however, Thatcher herself was part of the problem, and in his first conference speech as leader, he deliberately distanced himself from her positions. The Tories had been pursuing their own, dated agenda, he said, fixating on grammar schools, private healthcare and tax cuts; above all, it was time to stop 'banging on about Europe'.[58] Some assumed that he was therefore pro-EU, but that wasn't the case. 'I am much more Eurosceptic than you imagine,' he told Labour Europhile Denis MacShane in 2005.[59]

In pursuit of decontaminating the Conservative brand, Cameron did his best to sideline the issue, but it didn't go away. Just as Blair never got rid of the hard left in Westminster, so the old Eurosceptic Thatcherites loitered still on Cameron's backbenches. One of them, Nicholas Winterton,* spoke at Tony Blair's last appearance in the Commons, asking why the government had not fulfilled its promise to hold a referendum on the EU's Lisbon Treaty. He got a loud cheer from his colleagues, but

---

* His wife Ann Winterton, also an MP, had earlier had the whip withdrawn for a month after a speech, made shortly after the cockle-picking disaster, included a joke on the subject: 'Two sharks were circling round the Atlantic and one says, "I'm sick of eating tuna." The other replies, "Fancy going to Morecambe for a Chinese?"' (*Daily Mirror* 26 February 2004)

the prime minister was unimpressed. Noting the 'guttural roar', Blair remarked, 'If I were the leader of the Conservative Party I would be worried about that.'[60]

The issue Nicholas Winterton raised – the Lisbon Treaty – was contentious and, as it turned out, momentous. It hadn't started as a treaty. Originally, there was to be a constitution for the EU, a declaration of what the Union stood for and how it would operate in its new expanded form. A specially formed body called the European Convention deliberated for fifteen months in 2002–03 and produced a draft constitution for presentation to the European Council. It was, said Peter Hain, Britain's representative at the convention, little more than 'a tidying-up exercise',[61] though Joschka Fischer, the German foreign minister, had bigger aspirations than that: 'Creating a single European state bound by one European constitution is the decisive task of our time.'[62]

The constitution was signed in 2004 by representatives of all 25 member states, but had still to be ratified by each of those countries. Several decided that they would hold a referendum on the question, and there was pressure on Tony Blair to do the same. He was opposed to any such thing, though it was hard to construct a coherent argument for refusing; he'd promised he'd have a referendum before joining the single currency, he'd held referendums in Northern Ireland, Scotland, Wales and London on devolving powers – why not this? There was one obvious reason, as Peter Mandelson acknowledged: 'we might lose it'.[63] Early indications were that more than half the electorate were prepared to reject the constitution, with only 16 per cent in favour.[64]

But there were big figures in the cabinet who disagreed with Blair. None wished to leave the EU, of course, but they saw the constitution as too politically sensitive to be pushed through Parliament against the public will. Better to fight and lose than face the wrath of the electorate. Some shared the public impatience with Europe. 'One of the many reasons for the fading popular support for the EU is its wilful wasting of money,' wrote Jack Straw,[65] who also complained of 'irritations, frustration, pomposities, and the ever-present efforts of a self-serving administration in Brussels to extend its powers'.[66] David Blunkett was no fan of that administration either: 'They don't seem to get how people feel; they don't understand the instinct, the almost automatic suspicion of bureaucracy, of the dead hand and, above all, of things that are so far distant that they can't be influenced.'[67]

In April 2004, with European elections looming, Blair unexpectedly announced that there would after all be a referendum on the constitution. It would be, he insisted, a one-off binding poll: 'If the British people vote no, they vote no. You can't then start bringing it back until they vote yes.'[68] One reason offered for his change of heart was that it was a trade-off to ensure the support at the next election of Rupert Murdoch's newspapers (a *Sun* headline had earlier declared that not having a referendum would be 'The biggest betrayal in our history').[69] 'A deal was done,' a Downing Street source was reported to have said,[70] causing Ken Clarke to comment that it was 'a terrible blow to parliamentary sovereignty. I foresee that in ten years' time we can expect to have referendums on every subject where some of the newspapers don't agree with Parliament.'[71]

Opposition leaders, however, welcomed the announcement for their own reasons. Michael Howard set out his stall against the constitution, saying it would be 'bad for our democracy, bad for jobs and bad for Britain', while Charles Kennedy worried that there was a rise in anti-EU sentiment, which was why it was 'so essential' to have the referendum.[72]

Having committed to the idea, Blair saw the possibility of making it a much more fundamental argument than simply the narrow question of the constitution. 'I thought we might just turn it into a referendum that was effectively: in or out,' he wrote in his memoirs. 'I rather fancied mounting a really big public argument on an issue I felt strongly about and on which I was right.'[73] The problem, though, was that a referendum campaign would dominate his third term, and losing that vote – a very real possibility – would bring his premiership to an unsatisfactory close. In the event, it didn't matter. In June 2005, referendums in France and the Netherlands rejected the constitution, and that was that. 'What a sigh of relief I breathed,' admitted Blunkett,[74] and Straw felt the same: 'I could not contain my delight.'[75]

It was not, however, the EU's way to accept meekly such a setback. 'It was dead,' wrote Peter Hain of the constitution. 'But my work was not.'[76] In 2007 began the process of drafting what would become the Lisbon Treaty. This included the great majority of the aborted constitution, including the most controversial measures: steps towards common foreign, security and defence policy, and the extension of qualified majority voting into new areas of policymaking, so that the wishes of national governments could be overruled by a majority of their peers.

The Lisbon negotiations started early in Gordon Brown's premiership, when things were still going well, and he felt strong enough simply to rule out a referendum this time. David Cameron, on the other hand, was at his lowest ebb and – despite not wishing to bang on about Europe – was prepared to offer a hostage to fortune. 'I will give you this cast-iron guarantee,' he wrote in the *Sun*. 'If I become PM, a Conservative government will hold a referendum on any EU treaty that emerges from these negotiations.'[77] By the time he became prime minister, however, the Lisbon Treaty was a fait accompli, all signed and ratified, and he'd already ruled out a retrospective referendum. The guarantee wasn't worth the scrap iron it was cast in. He returned to the *Sun* with another pledge, that he would legislate to ensure any further concession of national sovereignty would require a referendum: 'Never again should it be possible for a British government to transfer power to the EU without the say of the British people.'[78] Nevertheless, this wasn't enough to silence the cries of 'Betrayal' from his right wing.*

Perhaps the least likely response to the Lisbon Treaty came from the Liberal Democrats, whose leader Menzies Campbell launched a bold new policy in 2007: 'It is time to end the shadow-boxing over Europe. A referendum, "in or out", would clear the air.'[79] Nick Clegg continued the demand when he became leader, and the party's 2010 manifesto promised both a referendum on the euro and an in/out referendum the next time that a treaty proposed 'fundamental change in the relationship between the UK and the EU'. It was an idea that was also gaining some support in the Conservative Party. In 2009, Eurosceptic MP Michael Spicer suggested the same in/out vote to his leader. 'What happens if the "outers" win?' asked Cameron doubtfully, and Spicer replied, 'Then either come out or threaten to do so as a strong bargaining counter.'[80]

The concern for the Conservatives was that the subterranean rumbling and grumbling of Euroscepticism in the country was becoming hard to ignore, and a real challenge was emerging outside the party. Having survived the fiasco of Robert Kilroy-Silk's attempted coup, UKIP had become a more serious proposition. In 2006 Roger Knapman stood down at the end of his four-year term as leader, allowing 42-year-old Nigel Farage to take over.[†] He was already – for what it was worth – the party's

---

* It did, however, get passed into law as the European Union Act 2011, subsequently repealed by the European Union (Withdrawal) Act 2018.

† Farage won the leadership election comfortably. Coming fourth in a field of four was businessman David Noakes, who left the party the following year, with a UKIP official calling him 'a swivel-eyed loon whose insane conspiracy theories make the rest of us look as mad as a box of frogs'. (*Sunday Telegraph* 25 February 2007) A decade or so later, Noakes pleaded guilty to money laundering and other charges. 'We've had more than our fair share of wrong 'uns,' shrugged Farage at his party conference in 2012. (*Irish Times* 5 March 2012)

biggest figure, commanding far more airtime and column inches than any of the others, and wielding backstage power for some years. Implausibly, he would turn out to be the most influential British politician of the era.

Farage was born in Kent in 1964,* and joined the Conservative Party in 1978, inspired by Sir Keith Joseph, Margaret Thatcher's mentor, who'd come to give a talk at his school. But he began to lose faith with the party after Thatcher's Bruges speech in 1988. It wasn't that he disagreed with her assault on the European dream of ever-closer union; precisely the opposite – it was the failure of the Tories to follow her lead that alienated him. He became increasingly convinced that the political establishment had betrayed the country, and in 1993 he volunteered to help Alan Sked, who was standing as an anti-federalist candidate in the Newbury by-election. One of his tasks in the campaign was to drive Enoch Powell down from London for what was to be the penultimate public appearance by the grand old man of Euroscepticism; the encounter, he later wrote, 'awoke all sorts of aspirations in me which I had not even acknowledged before. It inspired me.'[81]

Shortly thereafter he became a founder member of UKIP, and joined the national executive committee. In 1994 he had his first experience as a parliamentary candidate, finishing fourth in the Eastleigh by-election, just 169 votes clear of Screaming Lord Sutch and the Monster Raving Loony Party.

In later years, some would accuse him of vanity and ruthless ambition, but these were not the acts of a power-hungry man. To create a new national party from scratch, without benefit of experience, big names or financial backing, was a ludicrous proposition for anyone with aspirations to a career in politics. At this stage, Britain still had first-past-the-post elections for Europe as well as Westminster, and there was no chance whatsoever of

---

* He was therefore just on the cusp of the Adrian Mole generation, though the fictional comparison most often cited was Toad of Toad Hall.

winning anything. Nonetheless, Farage dedicated himself to the hopeless project. He turned out to be a good speaker, both in dusty village halls and, eventually, in television studios.

He was also accused of wanting to take Britain back to the 1950s. Actually, Farage's image was more that of a late-1970s chancer: pinstripe suit, cigar in one hand, glass of malt in the other, the kind of man who'd bunk off work to go to the races, roar with laughter at off-colour jokes, leave no corner uncut when dealing with taxes and expenses. He gave the impression that, along with Arthur Daley in *Minder*, he might have an unpaid tab at the Winchester Club. Or that he might run into Gene Hunt at the Lodge. And many of those who enjoyed *Minder* in its original run, or who revelled in the politically incorrect world of *Life on Mars*, found that they rather liked Farage. If you thought that the smoking ban and lectures about five a day and binge drinking were evidence of the nanny state, then this was your man. Likewise if you hankered after old-school history that comforted rather than confronted and didn't seem to be telling you off, or if you thought Roy Chubby Brown was funnier than Jimmy Carr, or if the phrases 'political correctness' and 'health and safety' made you snort. He was spoken of almost as one of the family – the roguish uncle of childhood, perhaps – and he became the latest of those mono-named right-wing figures who turn up occasionally in British politics, the plain-speaking patriot: Winston, Enoch, Maggie, and now Nigel.

He wasn't really a man of the people at all, he was a privately educated stockbroker, protested his critics (of whom there were many). This was true, but he was yet another who, in the early twenty-first century, didn't try to disguise his poshness and discovered it merely enhanced his popular appeal. The key to his success was his authenticity. He didn't pretend to be anything other than what he was; he didn't prevaricate or dissemble, he was absolutely sincere. And he was passionately devoted to his cause. Above all, he gave the impression that he was having fun, enjoying himself.

'You see, you try to turn everything into a joke,' Nick Robinson of the BBC said to him as though it were an accusation, failing to understand that – unless times are really desperate (as in 1979) – the English will always favour the cavalier over the puritan.

The first fruits of his leadership came in the 2009 European elections. Gordon Brown was past his honeymoon at this point, and the Conservatives scored their third consecutive victory in the poll, though their share of the vote was hardly commanding, little better than in 2004 when triumph had been followed by disaster at a general election. The real story was the second-place performance of UKIP. This was the first national election since 1918 in which a party other than Tory or Labour had finished in the top two, a remarkable result.

Just as the Conservatives had UKIP to worry about on their right flank, however, UKIP had a similar problem with the British National Party to *its* right. In 2009 the BNP came sixth, behind the Greens, but they still got nearly a million votes and emerged with two MEPs, their first elected members and the best performance by a far-right party in British history. Later that year, the party's leader Nick Griffin was invited onto *Question Time*, a controversial decision that many feared would legitimise the party, though the electorate seemed to have done that already. Certainly the public interest was there: the episode gave the show its highest ever audience figure of 7.9 million viewers.

It proved, though, to be the BNP's high-water mark. Griffin's attempts at respectability provoked splits in the ranks, while anti-fascist groups raised the level of their campaigning, and the public exposure tended to repel rather than attract new support. In the 2010 local elections, the party lost most of the council seats it was defending, and in the general election held the same day, it failed to make the breakthrough for which it had hoped. It did, though, get more votes than the Scottish National Party managed, and although it was outpolled by UKIP, its average per candidate was better.

In fact, 2010 was an even bigger disappointment for UKIP than it was for the BNP. Farage had stood down as leader, so he could concentrate on his attempt to win the Buckingham seat of John Bercow, the new Speaker of the House of Commons. This was considered very poor form, since the Speaker was traditionally unopposed by major parties,* but it seemed to give the party a fighting chance of registering an upset. It was a mistake. Nobody paid any attention to the BNP's new leader, the Tory defector Lord Pearson, and the party got far less media coverage than it had in the 2009 campaign. The manifesto didn't help, drowning its core message in a tidal wave of policies, from a flat-rate income tax to the restoration of caning in schools, from limiting the number of foreign players in football teams to banning offshore windfarms.† Farage later described it as '486 pages of drivel'.[82] Nor did he fare well in Buckingham, coming in third behind not just Bercow but also an ex-Tory MEP running as a pro-European independent. The most notable moment came on the day of the election; a two-seater plane that was supposed to be towing a UKIP banner failed to get properly airborne, and both the pilot and Farage were injured when it crashed. It was hard not to see the accident as symbolic of party fortunes, a return to the chaotic early days.

But then, perhaps re-energised by his brush with death, Farage got a grip. 'I think the accident made him more ruthless and more single-minded,' said a UKIP colleague.[83] By the end of the year, he was back as leader and the party entered its purple patch. With the Liberal Democrats in coalition and Ed Miliband's Labour failing to convince, there was room for a new recipient of the protest vote. UKIP stepped into the breach. It was in the Coalition

---

* Though the previous Speaker, Michael Martin, had been opposed in Glasgow Springburn by the SNP in 2001 and 2005.
† There was also heady talk of returning to traditional livery for trains and the reintroduction of Pullman carriages.

years that Farage became one of the most famous politicians in the country, a familiar sight not only on news bulletins and *Question Time* (he made fourteen appearances in 2010–14), but also on the likes of *Have I Got News for You*, where he displayed good humour even when being teased about extremism; invited to participate in a game where he had to identify party supporters as being either Fruitcake or Loony, he happily played along.

That reference was to David Cameron's description of UKIP members as 'fruitcakes, loonies and closet racists'.[84] But that had been back in 2006, when the new Tory leader was not banging on about Europe. These days, he was taking Farage's ragtag army far more seriously.

To start with, the Conservatives were not a united party, even leaving aside the question of Europe. Two other issues in particular angered the traditional right. The first was foreign aid. This had been the fashionable issue of 2005. The group Make Poverty History was campaigning for the cancellation of the debts of developing countries and for better aid programmes, demands that inspired a day of multi-star concerts called Live 8, broadcast on BBC television.* The same year the BBC also screened Richard Curtis's film *The Girl in the Café*, which talked of a 'casual holocaust' of 30,000 children dying of extreme poverty every day. 'I think we're fighting today for something as big as the abolition of slavery,' says the fictional chancellor of the exchequer, a heavyset Scot. That was also the year Cameron became Tory leader, and he embraced the cause, pledging to maintain levels of spending on international development; once in government, it was one of only two departments, along with health, to have its funding ringfenced. For him it was a totem of decency, though for some

---

* Named after the 1985 Live Aid concerts, and staged to coincide with a G8 meeting in Scotland, where the British government was seeking international action on global poverty.

Tory voters it was seen as a mistaken priority. In the wake of the recession, they argued, the government should be looking after its own people.

And then there was the introduction of gay marriage in the Marriage (Same Sex Couples) Act 2013. Cameron had apologised for Section 28 already, but this was something else again, removing the last great legal discrimination between heterosexual and homosexual. How could anyone say the Tories were the nasty party when he was taking the initiative on such a liberal issue? Gay marriage wasn't very controversial in the country – an opinion poll in 2009 had found 61 per cent in favour[85] – but many Tories saw it as being either morally wrong, or unchristian, or a distraction from the economic agenda, or personally distasteful, or a mix of these factors. And so, although the bill passed easily through the Commons, that was thanks to Labour support; more Tory MPs voted against it than for it, and many constituency branches saw a significant loss of members.* Cameron was 'out of touch with his party', said backbencher Stewart Jackson. 'Both gay marriage and EU migration feed into a narrative that too much emphasis is going to the liberal metropolitan elite and not enough to the blue-collar working vote that Margaret Thatcher had the support of.'[86]

The departure of some of the party's more right-wing membership wasn't in itself a worry; frankly, they were seen as part of the contamination that the brand could do without. The trouble was that they now had somewhere to go, and it was voters as well as activists who were being lured away. Presenting itself as the very antithesis of that liberal metropolitan elite, UKIP saw a steady rise in support, and half of those switching from Tory said they did so because of gay marriage.[87]

---

* The Conservative Party has never published official membership figures, but it's estimated that they 'fell by more than half from 273,000 to 134,000 between 2002 and 2013'. Most of that was on Cameron's watch. (Audickas and Keen, 'Membership of UK Political Parties', p. 10)

There was a new momentum now. Implausible though it seemed – impossible almost – UKIP was starting to look like a player in domestic elections, not just the Europeans. There were seven parliamentary by-elections in Britain between November 2012 (Rotherham, a Labour seat) and June 2014 (Newark, Conservative), and although UKIP didn't win any, it came second in six of them.*

These were difficult times for the prime minister. The Coalition government was at its lowest ebb, nursing its wounds after the 2012 omnishambles budget, and there were concerns that the drift from Conservative to UKIP might yet become a serious split. The EU itself was looking shaky, scarred by mass unemployment and a sovereign debt crisis that revealed just how precarious the economic position of the so-called PIGS (Portugal, Italy, Greece, Spain) was, trapped in the Eurozone with Germany effectively holding the purse strings. Pressure grew on the Tory leadership to take the initiative. 'Europe is now in play in a way it hasn't been for a long, long time,' a cabinet minister told the press. 'All options are on the table and clearly withdrawal is one of the options.'[88]

The rise of Euroscepticism in Britain had not gone unnoticed. As Michael White reported in the *Guardian* in 2012, 'Brussels has a new word: "Brexit".'[89] But Brussels didn't appear to be overly worried. In 2014 a recalibration of financial contributions to the EU was announced: France and Germany would have to pay less, while the UK was handed a bill for an additional £1.7 billion. Partly this was because illegal activities were now calculated as part of GDP; prostitution was estimated to generate £5.3 billion a year in Britain, and the drug trade another £4.4 billion. This wasn't helpful to the European cause. As comedian Roisin Conaty observed, 'It feels like the EU are doing that thing where you're

---

* There was also a by-election in the Sinn Fein-held seat of Mid Ulster, which UKIP did not contest.

going out with someone and they want you to dump them, so they just start behaving really badly.'

Finally, David Cameron took the decisive step. 'The next Conservative manifesto in 2015 will ask for a mandate from the British people for a Conservative government to negotiate a new settlement with our European partners,' he announced in a speech in January 2013. 'And when we have negotiated that new settlement, we will give the British people a referendum with a very simple in or out choice. To stay in the EU on these new terms; or come out altogether. It will be an in/out referendum.'[90]

After the Lisbon Treaty referendum guarantee, there was no question of Cameron backing down. If, that is, he came out of the next election with a majority government. And the consensus in political circles was that this wasn't going to happen. The received wisdom was that incumbent governments didn't increase their share of the vote, and the best that Cameron could hope for, it was argued, was another coalition. In which case, some argued, he might be able to wriggle out of his commitment, blaming his partners, though he insisted he would not. But all this was for the future, and the offer of a referendum was much more about surviving the present. Because there was general agreement about the motivation here. 'Mr Cameron's announcement is not driven by principle but political expediency,' opined the *Daily Mirror*. 'This is about placating the right in his party and saving Tory seats at the next election by quashing the threat posed from UKIP.'[91] What remained uncertain was whether it would work.

Two moments from the 2014 European election campaign encapsulated Nigel Farage's appeal. First there was a debate with Nick Clegg on television. When Clegg came to write his account of the Coalition, he began with this encounter, clearly still trying to make sense of it. Because there was no doubt that Farage emerged the winner, acclaimed as such by 69 per cent of viewers, according to the polls.[92]

How could this be? wondered Clegg. Farage had expressed his admiration for Vladimir Putin at a time when the Russian leader's involvement in Ukraine was being denounced by all right-thinking commentators. Surely any British politician who supported such a leader would 'put himself firmly on the wrong side of public opinion'? Yet the public response had shown that Clegg's assumption was wrong. In retrospect, he wrote, he had underestimated the anti-elite message of the UKIP leader, and, by extension, failed to spot his own Achilles heel: 'I was the establishment figure, tarnished by several bruising years in office, defending a flawed status quo.'[93]

Perhaps though he still hadn't quite understood. The only issue from the debate he mentioned was the point about Putin, the subject which most viewers – though evidently not Clegg – probably regarded as being the least important of all. The studio audience did applaud Farage's comments on Ukraine, but it wasn't Putin they were approving; it was the UKIP leader's rejection of foreign adventures: 'I do not want to be part of an emerging, expansionist EU foreign policy.' Here was a politician who didn't want Britain to punch above its weight, and even a London audience in a BBC studio rather approved. *

The other moment came when phone-in host James O'Brien interviewed Farage on LBC Radio. This was a rare instance of Farage appearing uncomfortable and uncertain, rattled not so much by the content of O'Brien's questions, as by the sheer hostility with which they were delivered. The left-leaning O'Brien had made a successful career for himself by adopting the partisan

---

* The most revealing moment of the encounter came during the soundcheck. Asked what they'd done that day, Clegg looked smugly casual as he namedropped that 'actually' he'd met Bill Gates. Farage said he'd failed to live up to his attempt at self-discipline: he tried not to drink till 6 o'clock, but he'd yielded to temptation and gone to the pub at lunchtime. The audience knew which they preferred.

approach of right-wing shock jocks, and his open loathing of Farage allowed no room for the UKIP leader's usual saloon-bar affability.

The critical exchange came when Farage was challenged to defend his comment that he'd be concerned if a group of Romanian men moved in next door. What's the difference between that situation and a group of German children moving in next door? asked O'Brien.* 'You know what the difference is,' said Farage, but O'Brien denied any such thing: 'I honestly don't.' He returned to the theme at the end of the encounter: 'I do not understand why you use words like "Romanian" when describing who you would or would not like to live next door to.' By that stage, though, UKIP's press officer was bundling his man out of the studio, fearful that he was getting the worse of the encounter.

There was cautious condemnation in political circles. David Cameron accused Farage of saying 'some pretty unpleasant things'[94] but stopped short of characterising his comments as racist, and Ed Miliband followed suit: 'I think they were a racial slur but I don't think of Nigel Farage as a racist himself.'[95] The *Sun* pulled no such punches. Its leader column said of those remarks, 'This is racism, pure and simple: Romanians, he is suggesting, are criminals to be feared.'[96]

That was indeed the point that Farage had been dog-whistling: the belief that east European migration was adding greatly to crime in Britain. It was also one that he might have expected the *Sun* to share, given some of the paper's headlines in recent times: 'Our crime wave is good news for Romania', 'Beasts from the East', 'Capital hit by 28,000 Romanian criminals'.[97]

Whether it was true was another matter. Figures from the Office for National Statistics showed that there were more than 10,000 foreign nationals incarcerated in the jails of England and

---

* Farage was married to a German woman, with whom he had two children, hence the otherwise meaningless comparison between men and children.

Wales that year, just over one in eight of all prisoners. This was slightly disproportionate – 8.8 per cent of the general population were foreign, 12.7 per cent of those in prison – but understandably so: migrants were more likely to be young, as are those given custodial sentences, while foreigners tend not to receive lenient treatment in the legal system. The five foreign countries most represented in prisons were Poland, Ireland, Jamaica, Romania and Pakistan; and of those, four were also in the five most common nationalities in the UK. The exception was Jamaica, ranked twenty-eighth in the general population and third in prison.

So the stereotype at which Farage was hinting was misplaced: there was no great tendency towards criminality among Romanians living in Britain. But there were east European criminals. Not that it mattered. The interview hadn't really been intended to explore issues. It did its job: it got headlines, and both sides had their beliefs confirmed. Those who thought UKIP beyond the pale were jubilant that Farage had been 'hamstrung', 'skewered', 'humiliated',[98] while *Sunday Times* columnist Rod Liddle argued that the 'sanctimonious' O'Brien, 'swathed in self-righteousness', had added 'another 100,000 or so votes to UKIP'.[99]

If that were true, then it was only a minor contribution, because where 2009 was impressive, 2014 was spectacular. UKIP got 4.4 million votes, 26.6 per cent of the vote, and finished first; from 13 MEPs, it jumped to 24. It had representatives in all nine of the English voting areas, and in Scotland and Wales; only Northern Ireland remained immune. Some of its success was undoubtedly due to the collapse of the BNP, which shed 80 per cent of its vote from last time, but that still left over a million new UKIP supporters unaccounted for. Whichever way one cut it, this was an astonishing performance.

And then in August 2014 the party got its first MP, when Douglas Carswell, who represented Clacton, resigned the Conservative whip to join UKIP, followed the next month by Mark Reckless, Tory MP for Rochester and Strood. Both men stood again in by-elections and both were returned to the Commons. As incumbent MPs, they were special cases, but they did finally demonstrate that the UKIP label was not necessarily a barrier to electoral success in Westminster.

There was no doubt now, the party was a serious threat to the Conservatives.* 'UKIP was looking worryingly like part of the furniture,' reflected David Cameron.[100] The only way forward, argued some Tory Eurosceptics – Daniel Hannan, Jacob Rees-Mogg, Peter Bone – was for Cameron to come to an arrangement with Farage, some sort of electoral pact that would unite the right.[101] But what the story had shown thus far suggested precisely the opposite. Feeding UKIP only made it stronger. As Farage had noted when Cameron offered that in/out referendum, 'They're coming to play on our pitch now.'[102]

---

* Not just the Conservatives, though. As Tony Benn and Ken Coates had observed a decade earlier, UKIP had an attraction for disillusioned Labour supporters. Polling showed that a quarter of UKIP voters in 2014 would rather see Ed Miliband than David Cameron as prime minister. The story in local elections held the same day showed the damage being done to both parties: in Thurrock, Essex UKIP topped the poll, taking three seats from the Tories and two from Labour. Thurrock was an ultra-marginal Westminster seat, with a 92-vote Tory majority; if this result were replicated in a general election, Labour would lose votes but gain the seat.

Epilogue: Democracy

I

'It may be,' Peter Mandelson had reflected in 1998, 'that the era of pure representative democracy is coming slowly to an end.' Our political system had been created, he argued, in 'an age that has passed away', and in the future representative institutions would be 'complemented by more direct forms of popular involvement, from the internet to referenda'.[1] How this might work, what it actually meant in practice, was a bit vague, but his diagnosis had some merit: this was indeed a very different age.

The Reform Act of 1832, passed under the premiership of Lord Grey, laid the foundations for modern democracy in Britain.

At the general election that followed, there was an average of 1,787 electors for each member of the Commons. This meant that in the course of a five-year parliament, an MP of the 1830s could meet just one person a day and still get round the entire electorate, with over a month to spare. There would be class differences between those he met and, with Catholic and Jewish emancipation, religious differences too, but also a homogeneity: they would all be men, and they would all be men of property. He could reasonably aspire to represent them since he was cut from the same cloth.

By 2001, however, with the population having more than doubled in the intervening years, and with the franchise now extending to every resident over the age of eighteen (except prisoners, the insane and peers of the realm), the average electoral roll for a constituency was over 67,000; an MP would now need to meet 37 voters a day to see them all in five years. Those constituents were divided by sex, age, class, wealth, race, religion and creed in a way that would have been inconceivable to Lord Grey.

Equally startling would be the discovery of how far the state had extended into everyday life, particularly the number of voters with a direct pecuniary interest in the outcome of an election, whether as employee or as recipient of benefits. Alien too the professionalism of full-time politicians; the media training; the power of the leader's office; the number of ministers; the whips; the political advisers; the balance between Commons and Lords; and the fact that MPs were now expected to spend almost as much time in their constituencies, doling out advice and assistance, as they did addressing affairs of state in Westminster. Everything was different. Yet the structure was much as it had been in 1832, the democratic process still recognizable to a pre-Victorian time traveller. This was still a representative democracy – it's just that it didn't mean the same thing any more.

'The British media talked constantly of a political crisis, of a "fundamental malaise",' wrote Andrew Marr in *Children of the Master* (2015). 'What they really meant was that the people were in a right strop.'[2] It felt more than that. In the early years of the twenty-first century, as voter turnout declined and hostility towards politicians grew, there was much hand-wringing about apathy and a supposed mood of 'anti-politics'. But the multitudes who took to the streets for the Countryside Alliance in 2001 or Stop the War in 2003 (or both) were not apathetic and they weren't anti-politics. They were, though, unimpressed by the political process, particularly when the demands of both demonstrations were ignored.

The mainstream parties had essentially two responses to the sense of alienation. The first was to involve their members more, allowing them to make the biggest of all party decisions: the choice of leader. The Conservatives led the way with William Hague's reforms, which gave them Iain Duncan Smith, before MPs reasserted control. Then, under Ed Miliband – whose career closely paralleled that of Hague – the Labour Party adopted a similar though worse system, scrapping the electoral college that had weighted the various interests of the movement. To get on the ballot paper now required the support of 15 per cent of Labour MPs, and thereafter all members, affiliate members and registered supporters had an equal vote each. The result was the election of Jeremy Corbyn in 2015, who differed from Iain Duncan Smith in that he simply ignored Labour MPs when they passed a vote of no confidence in him; his power base was not in Parliament but among the activists, so he stayed in office to lose two general elections. Party members, it transpired, were still not representative of the wider public, still more preoccupied with their own concerns than with winning votes. For Labour, Iraq had become as destructive as Europe was for the Tories, and under Corbyn the Stop the War Coalition took over the party.

The second option was to offer devolution; if some power was passing up to the supranational state being built by the EU, then perhaps it could be balanced by a passing of power down.

Progress had been made in Scotland, Wales and Northern Ireland in the late 1990s, but not in England. The obvious answer was an English parliament – in effect a parliamentary committee comprising all MPs sitting for English seats – but politicians were nervous of the imbalance in size compared to the other nations.

Instead, many were attracted to the concept of 'the regions', a formulation much favoured by the EU and articulated by pro-European politicians. Unfortunately, the English have never thought of themselves as belonging to a region. Designating people as living in the South West, East of England or West Midlands won't stop them identifying with Cornwall, Norfolk or the Black Country, or from defining that identity in opposition to their neighbours: Devon, Suffolk, Birmingham. Only London had both a population large enough to be designated a region and a strong identity. The problem elsewhere was that there was too much history to be overcome; as Robert Tombs's magisterial work *The English and Their History* (2014) noted, 'not one European state is as old as Hampshire'.[3]

Nonetheless, in 2004 the government held a referendum in north-east England, asking whether people wanted a regional assembly. This was intended as the first in a series of such votes, rolling out around the country, with the north-east as the flagship. Few were convinced. 'What clearer evidence could there be of the growing gulf between leader and led?' fumed Sunderland MP Chris Mullin. 'I cannot recall a single letter from a citizen demanding a regional assembly, whereas the rulers of the north-east talked of little else.'[4] On a low turnout, the proposal was resoundingly defeating: barely one in ten of the electorate voted in favour.*

The regional assemblies were dead, but the mindset remained. In response to 'the charge from the rest of the country that no

---

* The No campaign was masterminded by Iain Duncan Smith's former director of communications, Dominic Cummings.

one in London listened', Gordon Brown held several cabinet meetings 'in the regions'.[5] It was an initiative that failed to change the weather.

So too the invitation to change the voting system, a cause long advocated by the third party and finally realised when the Liberal Democrats found themselves in government. In what was only the second ever UK-wide referendum, the people were asked in 2011 whether they wished to replace first past the post with the alternative vote, the system that had made Ed Miliband leader of the Labour Party. On an even lower turnout, the change was rejected by a two-to-one majority. It was simply not an issue that many cared about; of the 440 voting areas, only 10 supported the proposition, 6 of them London boroughs – Camden, Hackney, Haringey, Islington, Lambeth, Southwark – together with Cambridge, Edinburgh Central, Glasgow Kelvin and Oxford.

The following year, ten cities held referendums to see if they wanted elected mayors; just one – Bristol – voted in favour. Even less enthusiasm was generated by the Coalition's innovation intended 'to bring visibility and answerability to policing'.[6] The first police and crime commissioners were elected in 2012 on a pitifully low turnout, averaging 15 per cent. In the west Midlands, Labour's Bob Jones won, with the backing of just 5 per cent of the registered electorate.*

In fact, there was only one vote in the UK in this period that really inspired passion.

'This is the Scottish dilemma,' wrote the journalist and erstwhile Labour candidate Tim Luckhurst in 2002: 'Independence is rejected at the polls but cherished in the heart.'[7] At the time, the devolution of power to the Scottish Parliament seemed to be

---

* Four years later, the vote was held the same day as local elections and turnout increased to 26.6 per cent. Bob Jones's successor, David Jamieson, won nearly 14 per cent of the electorate this time.

working, both for the fledgling institution and for the Labour government in Westminster, which wanted an alternative to full independence.

Five years later, things looked very different. In the 2007 Holyrood elections, the Scottish National Party beat Labour for the first time, gaining another twenty MSPs in the 129-seat chamber and forming a minority administration. Taking office as first minister was Alex Salmond, who had spent ten years as SNP leader up to 2000, playing a key role in the devolution debate, and had returned to the job in 2004. A few months shy of his fiftieth birthday as he started his second leadership stint, Salmond was widely regarded as one of the shrewdest operators in British politics. Donald Dewar, Labour's great leader in Scotland, used to say he was 'sleekit',[8] and David Cameron observed, 'you had to count your fingers on the way out of a meeting with Salmond'.[9] He was, said Alastair Campbell, 'A man who fell in love with himself at an early age and has been faithful ever since,'[10] though others were more complimentary: 'he's an amazing man', enthused American businessman Donald Trump.[11]

Quite apart from his nationalist agenda, Salmond was adept at channelling dissatisfaction and casting himself as the outsider. 'Mr Salmond has made an art form of opposition,' wrote *The Times* columnist Michael Gove in 1998, in reluctant admiration; 'he is the Frank Sinatra of discontent, possessed of perfect political pitch and capable of making clichés bite as never before'.[12] He was a vociferous opponent of the invasion of Iraq – indeed, he had opposed Britain's involvement in the Kosovo War in 1999, which had been far less controversial – and he was scathing in his condemnation of Tony Blair's foreign policy: 'How can the prime minister pursue a shoulder-to-shoulder relationship with George Bush when he seems to spend most of his time on his knees?'[13] The Liberal Democrats benefited from anti-war sentiment in England, the SNP did so in Scotland.

Now Salmond had, as Blair said, 'got his feet under the table',[14] he had no intention of leaving, and he swiftly implemented some popular measures: the reduction and then abolition of NHS prescription charges, and the introduction of free university education – unless you came from another nation in the UK, in which case you had to pay tuition fees. In 2011 the SNP gained another 22 Holyrood seats to become Scotland's first-ever majority government, a spectacular result in a system designed to produce coalitions. Given how reliant Labour was on its Scottish seats in Westminster, it was a disturbing rejection of Ed Miliband's leadership, and coming so soon after UKIP's performance in the 2009 European elections suggested that the political map of the UK was being redrawn. Independence, it seemed, might be more than 'cherished in the heart'.

The real test would come, of course, in a referendum. And that was now inevitable; there was no point the SNP winning power unless they were prepared to push their one major demand. And so, in 2014, 700 years after the Battle of Bannockburn, came the most important referendum yet held. 'Should Scotland be an independent country?' was the question asked of Scottish residents, and the answer would determine whether the United Kingdom remained united. On the yes side, the SNP were joined by the Scottish Greens and the Scottish Socialist Party,* while the no camp contained the Tories, Labour and the Lib Dems. It wasn't an equal contest, but that rather suited the SNP; Salmond enjoyed being the underdog.

There was talk of skulduggery from both camps, but it didn't amount to very much: claims that the SNP government was leaning on and intimidating business leaders, and counter-claims that the Coalition government was threatening the Scottish people using what was dubbed Project Fear. The former allegations were mostly made by business leaders who'd declared themselves for no

---

* Not to be confused with the Socialist Party Scotland, the successor organisation to the Militant Tendency.

(so presumably hadn't been intimidated), while the latter seemed to be little more than difficult questions. What currency would an independent Scotland use, since sterling wouldn't be available? Would it join the euro, perhaps? What would happen to Scottish universities when they lost the fees of English students, now citizens of a fellow EU state? Could Scotland really stay in NATO while being anti-nuclear?

Among the rank and file, particularly on the yes side, there were insults and abusive language, but the ugliness was in bark not bite. In the latter stages of the campaign, Labour MP Jim Murphy was aggressively heckled by 'a noisy nationalist mob',[15] and had an egg thrown at him in Kirkcaldy. This was regrettable, but less violent than the 2001 egg-throwing incident with John Prescott in Rhyl; at least no one got punched this time.

What was striking about the campaign was the peripheral role of the English leaders. It was assumed that David Cameron, Nick Clegg and Ed Miliband weren't really much use to the no vote and so played little part. By the end Cameron was pleading with Scots not to make this about him: 'If you don't like me, I won't be here for ever,' he reassured them.[16] His main involvement was coming up with offers of ever greater powers for Holyrood if only Scots would agree to stay in the UK.

The real star of the no campaign was Gordon Brown, who peaked on the eve of polling with perhaps his best ever speech about why the Union mattered, not just economically but emotionally. Pacing the stage, he evoked shared sacrifice – 'there is not a cemetery in Europe that does not have Scots, English, Welsh and Irish lying side by side' – and shared endeavour: 'we built the health service together, we built the welfare state together, we will build the future together'. He praised with passion the great achievements of his nation, from the Scottish Enlightenment to the welfare state: 'They happen not in spite of the Union but because of the Union. And none of us is any less a Scot as a result of it.' And he called for solidarity and unity: 'if you're like me and a million more people who are convinced that the case for cooperation is greater than any case put for separation, then I say to you: hold your heads high. Show dignity and pride.'[17] It confirmed that all that talk about Britishness in the previous decade was absolutely genuine; he just hadn't managed to sell it to the English.

The other notable late contribution came on the Sunday before the vote. As the Queen left Crathie Kirk in Balmoral, a member of the public asked her about the referendum, and she stopped to reply, 'I hope that people will think very carefully about the future.'[18] This was generally interpreted to indicate her support for the Union. Indeed it would have been strange had she been in favour of having her kingdom divided beneath her, but the fact that she had commented at all was an indication of how narrow the polls were in those last days, some starting to show a yes lead. And the publicity her words received was an indication that, despite republican sentiment in the SNP, the monarchy still mattered.

It was a remarkably peaceful campaign, considering what was at stake. The last time a part of the UK had broken away, less than a century earlier, around 2,000 lives had been lost in the Irish War of Independence, with almost as many again in the civil war that followed, and a legacy of those conflicts had only just been resolved, leaving another 3,500 dead in the Troubles. There was nothing vaguely comparable in Scotland in 2014, nothing even on the same spectrum. Of course there wasn't. No one expected such a thing. But that was the point: for all the talk of a crisis in the political system, politics itself – the practice of resolving conflicts of interests in society without recourse to violence – was still functioning. It just needed people to feel that their say mattered.

The result refuted the charges of apathy and anti-politics, with turnout at nearly 85 per cent, the highest of any vote in the UK since universal suffrage and much higher than the most recent elections in Scotland to Westminster (63.8 per cent) or Holyrood

(50.5). Given a clear choice, a serious decision to be made, there was no shortage of engagement. People wanted to have their say on something that mattered. And the verdict was a convincing no, with a margin of victory of 10.6 per cent.

There was one nice irony among the results. The SNP had persuaded Westminster to allow a voting age of sixteen, assuming that young people were on their side; in fact, polling suggested that 16–24-year-olds were more likely to vote no. And there was one sour aftertaste. In his speech acknowledging the result, David Cameron, by his own later admission, struck entirely the wrong note by talking of introducing 'English votes for English laws'.[19] A moment for reconciliation was sullied by triumphalism and what was all too easily seen as typical English arrogance.

II

'There is,' wrote Nigel Farage in 2010, 'no reason – in theory – why we could not now be governed by *X Factor*-style voting on every motion currently before Parliament.' He added, 'we would make a better job of it than the political class'.[20] He was overstating the case – there was really no appetite for that much consultation* – but the analogy was appropriate.

Reality television, in the form of *Big Brother* (2000), *Pop Idol* (2001), *I'm a Celebrity … Get Me Out of Here* (2002), *The X Factor* (2004) and many, many more, was the broadcasting sensation of the time, ending the dominance of television by soap operas. Formats varied, but the essence was the same: a competition was run over several weeks, in which contestants were progressively eliminated until a single winner emerged; sometimes

---

* Even UKIP knew there was a limit. Its 2015 manifesto promised a referendum on EU membership, but then a maximum of a referendum every two years, on a subject to be chosen by public petition.

there was a panel of expert judges, but success and failure was ultimately determined by public vote. The word 'reality' referred to the (supposed) spontaneity and normality of proceedings, the suggestion that the genre could – like the docusoaps of the 1990s – make stars of everyday people, the likes of 'loud, drunk, coarse and ignorant' Jade Goody on *Big Brother*,[21] '48-year-old Scottish virgin' Susan Boyle on *Britain's Got Talent*[22] or self-described 'Muslim in a headscarf' Nadiya Hussain on *The Great British Bake Off*.[23] Much more significant, though, was the new element – audience participation and the sense of involvement that brought. To satisfy demand, the big shows had various spin-off series – the likes of *Big Brother's Little Brother* (2001) and *Big Brother's Big Mouth* (2004), which commented on the action and allowed viewers to have still more of a say.*

That didn't always suit the broadcasters. In 2008 the BBC's former political correspondent John Sergeant was a contestant on *Strictly Come Dancing*, despite his distinct lack of grace and agility. Columnist Rod Liddle dubbed him the Dancing Pig, and the tag passed into pub-quiz posterity.[24] Nonetheless, he was a hit. Week after week, he tripped over the light fantastic, delighting the audience with his plucky clumsiness and incensing the judges, who demanded he be voted off so we could get back to proper dancing. The conflict between panel and people grew so big, the media coverage overshadowing the entire show, that eventually Sergeant made his excuses and left of his own accord. 'There is now a real danger that I might win the competition,' he explained. 'Even for me that would be a joke too far.'[25]

'In life, the public don't always agree with the experts,' wrote Kelvin MacKenzie, and as the *Sun*'s former editor, he knew which side he was on: 'All retailers will tell you the public is always right

---

* Eventually, this trend would spawn *Gogglebox* (2013), in which we watched people watching television. The content they saw was unimportant; we were interested in their reactions to it.

– they pay the bills.'[26] His opinion was shared right across the tabloid media. In response to Sergeant's withdrawal, the *Daily Star* called for the removal of judge Arlene Phillips, identified as the one who 'drove him away with a blistering attack on everything from his personality to his posture', while the TV editor of the *Sunday Express* went further: 'this is meant to be the public's programme', he complained under a headline demanding 'Sack the judges'.[27] Much of the print media took the opportunity to give broadcasters a kicking. 'Why does the BBC have this desire to control?' asked a leader column in the *Scotsman*. 'Why does it feel the need to tell the nation what is good for it?'[28]

'The glorious British tradition of radical dissent now has a dancing footnote,' observed Tony Blair's former speechwriter Philip Collins, calling the public's stubborn support for Sergeant 'a two-fingered salute to authority'.[29] Even in the triviality of this skirmish, it was possible to see the battle lines being drawn. On the one side, those whose positions of power and influence required respect. On the other, a public that was beginning to find ways to flex its cultural muscles. And where culture went, politics was sure to follow.

The World Wide Web was released to the general public in 1991, provoking hopes and fears that this technology had the potential for changing society entirely. For the first decade or so, however, its impact was muted. Beyond the ability to communicate via email,* the rapid rise of the internet brought two central benefits. First, it expanded choice, so that one could access foreign newspapers and broadcasters, shop at remote outlets, consume uncensored pornography. Second, it made available such a body of information and knowledge that it constituted the greatest library in human history. The net's early successes reflected these roles: Amazon

---

* Not in itself a new technology; the Queen had sent her first email in 1976, while visiting an army base.

(1994) and eBay (1995); Google (1998) and Wikipedia (2001). This was not yet revolutionary; rather it offered bigger, better, faster versions of what already existed.

It was the arrival of social media that really changed the rules. Starting in 2003 with MySpace and LinkedIn, a new wave of platforms emerged: Facebook (2004), Twitter (2006), WhatsApp (2009), Instagram (2010), Snapchat (2011). Most significant of all was YouTube, launched in 2005, the biggest of the video-filesharing sites. This technology, combined with the advent of smartphones, allowed users easily to upload their own multimedia material. It covered virtually all the existing bases, save for pornography (other filesharing sites filled that gap),* but more importantly it added a new dimension: unfiltered access to other people's lives and thoughts. The format of the video diary had become familiar on television in the 1990s, but YouTube was a very different beast, for it exercised no editorial control.

By the second decade of the century, the likes of Alfie Deyes, Zoella and Tanya Burr were becoming internet celebrities by documenting their everyday lives, and were being followed by hundreds of thousands of other young people. They were superstars in their own world but almost entirely unknown outside, even when publishing houses, desperate for the youth market, began signing them up for ghostwritten novels, memoirs and self-help books. This was a generation that had still been in primary school when reality television promised the advent of a truly democratic culture; now, the YouTubers were the front line of the social media that began making that promise a reality.

They were also fulfilling the promise of modernism made a century earlier, the movement that had challenged the traditional emphasis on representation and narrative in art, literature and music. For those who grew up with the internet, it was not a library, as it had been seen by early adopters; that suggested the

---

* PornHub, XVideos and xHamster were all launched in 2007.

past, and there was no past here. Nor was there a future. This was a perpetual present, a literally endless procession of discrete, if not discreet, moments, inviting you to scroll and swipe for ever. Reality TV offered soap opera without plot lines, but it still had an end, a winner, in sight; social media went a step further and dispensed with both beginning and end. In these infant years, it was impossible to know the long-term impact of it all, but the internet carried a challenge to the concept of narrative itself; in a hyperlinked world, stories were outmoded.

There was excitement in some circles about the possibilities of the new technology reinvigorating politics. 'The beauty with the internet is that it allows politicians to have a two-way conversation where everyone is equal and every opinion is valid,' enthused John Prescott.[30] By the time of the 2010 election, around half the country was registered with at least one social network, 23 million of them with Facebook. Even if many of those accounts were opened in the haze of a drunken hour and forgotten the next morning,* there was still potential here. 'The next election will be the YouTube election,'[31] we were told, a 'new media election',[32] 'the first "internet election".[33] Alternatively, it was 'the Mumsnet election';[34] that site claimed 880,000 monthly users in 2010, and it was estimated that some 40 per cent were undecided voters. Politics in any formal sense, though, was less significant here than broad-brush perceptions of character; Gordon Brown stumbled on biscuits not budgets.†

---

* It was reported in 2006 that 200 million blogs worldwide were no longer being updated. (*Daily Record* 30 December 2006)
† Even before social media got big, Tony Blair had shown how to do this sort of thing in 2004 when he invited people to text questions to him. He gave just enough personal information to satisfy, revealing that he smoked his last cigarette fifteen minutes before getting married, and that his musical tastes were even more obvious than previously believed: his favourite guitar solos were those in the Beatles' 'While My Guitar Gently Weeps' and Lynyrd Skynyrd's 'Freebird', and his all-time supergroup would comprise John Lennon, Paul McCartney, Mick Jagger, Eric Clapton and Ginger Baker.

The platform with the most political content was Twitter, but its agenda could be deceptive. 'The vast majority of Twitter users are urbanites who work in new media, politics or journalism,' cautioned the *Guardian*. 'In its present form, Twitter is a tool for influencing influencers, not communicating with the electorate.'[35] In truth, the internet was still reliant on traditional media: the vast majority of video clips on social media were taken from television, while online commentators such as Paul Staines, who founded the Guido Fawkes blog (2004), were significant only insofar as their stories broke into the mainstream press.

There was also the question of demographics, because for the most part social media was the preserve of the young. And the young tended not to vote. According to Ipsos-Mori's analysis of the 2010 result, turnout among 16–24-year-olds was just 44 per cent, much lower than in any other age group.

Nonetheless, there was an implicitly political dimension to social media: the underlying assumption that 'ordinary' people should be heard. There were also those who believed they were anything but ordinary. 'Over the years, the media may have tried to shut out voices of dissent,' noted Farage, as he praised YouTube, 'but here is something that, despite their best efforts, they cannot stop.'[36] And the platform did attract those who felt excluded from, even censored by, the mainstream media, whether former Coventry City goalkeeper David Icke with his reptilian conspiracy theories, the far-right rabble-rouser Tommy Robinson, formerly of the BNP and co-founder in 2009 of the English Defence League, or comedian Russell Brand, who purveyed a vaguely spiritual anarchism.

Brand was briefly considered by some to be a serious political figure. In October 2013 – having already appeared on *Question Time** – he guest-edited an issue of the *New Statesman*, and to

---

* A second *Question Time* appearance in 2014 saw his most-quoted line, calling Nigel Farage 'a pound-shop Enoch Powell'.

mark the occasion was interviewed by Jeremy Paxman on *Newsnight*, an encounter that was viewed over 8 million times on YouTube in a fortnight, far beyond *Newsnight*'s normal audience figures. In print Brand's flowery style wore thin very quickly, but in person he was engagingly flirtatious, irreverent and passionate, talking of his 'absolute indifference and weariness and exhaustion from the lies, treachery, deceit of the political class that has been going on for generations now, and which has now reached fever pitch, where we have a disenfranchised, disillusioned, despondent underclass that are not being represented by that political system'. Although he had never voted, that was not him being apathetic: 'The apathy doesn't come from us, the people; the apathy comes from the politicians. They are apathetic to our needs, they're only interested in servicing the needs of corporations.' And in his most telling point, he linked the cynical detachment of the media, and of Paxman himself, to the new mood: 'You've spent your whole career berating and haranguing politicians, and then when someone like me, a comedian, goes, "Yeah, they're all worthless – what's the point of engaging with any of them?" you have a go at me.'

There was, he insisted, a revolution coming, and if he didn't know how or in what form, then why should he? He was an entertainer, not a political philosopher.* He didn't have any solutions, but that didn't mean he hadn't identified a problem. He was taken seriously enough during the 2015 election campaign for Ed Miliband to appear on his YouTube show *The Trews*, persuading him that voting wasn't actually such a daft idea. 'Russell Brand has endorsed Labour – and the Tories should be worried,' ran the headline above a *Guardian* column by Owen Jones.[37]

---

* Nonetheless, readers of *Prospect* magazine voted him the fourth most significant thinker in the world in 2015, following the publication of his book, *Revolution*. He was behind Thomas Piketty, Yanis Varoufakis and Naomi Klein. (*Guardian* 26 March 2015)

As it happened, the Tories didn't really need to worry. In the election, the Lib Dem vote collapsed, the post-referendum mood in Scotland saw very nearly a clean sweep for the SNP at Labour's expense,* and the Conservatives, despite only a small increase in its vote share, won a majority of seats in the House of Commons for the first time in 23 years. It's not that social media wasn't important, just that it didn't fit into what Brand liked to call 'the current paradigm'. To the YouTube generation, the leaders of the major parties – David Cameron, Ed Miliband, Nick Clegg – really did all look the same. The ones that stood out did exceptionally well: Alex Salmond in Scotland and Nigel Farage in England. UKIP got nearly 4 million votes (but only one MP) and, together with the Tories, the bloc committed to a referendum on Europe took 55 per cent of English votes.

The big test was yet to come. Tony Blair had lost his reputation when Iraq called into question his greatest asset: that he was a man of integrity. Gordon Brown foundered when the 2008 crash undermined his claims to financial stability and fairness. Now David Cameron, buoyed up by being on the winning side of the Scottish referendum in 2014 and the general election in 2015, was going to go for a third major vote the following year. It remained to be seen whether his most important quality – his breezy Old Etonian self-confidence – would be a help or a hindrance in the now inevitable EU referendum.

III

What had changed in those years? Primarily, it was that faith in authority had frayed badly. The monarchy† and the armed forces

---

* Of the 59 Scottish seats at Westminster, the SNP shot up from 6 in 2010 to 56 in 2015, while Labour slumped from 41 to 1.
† The popularity of the royal family was evidenced when Zara Phillips was

had come through unscathed, and the NHS – despite repeated scandals – had actually grown in stature, but most other institutions had fallen sharply in the esteem of the public. Newspapers had besmirched British soldiers and hacked the phone of a murdered child; banks had developed an addiction to gambling; the churches were preoccupied with sex and child abuse; local councils seemed more interested in snooping than providing services; similarly, the police, when not taking backhanders from the press, were more concerned with enforcing manners than catching burglars; while the criminal justice system, believed by many to be too lenient, saw an increase in the length of prison sentences but, thanks to the Criminal Justice Act 2003, a reduction in time served. Even the BBC had struggled, frittering away the licence fee on foul-mouthed presenters and navel-gazing executives. The impression, for many, was that you simply couldn't count on people in positions of power.

Above all, there were the politicians, whose reputation went from bad to much, much worse. Tony Blair had promised a new, more people-friendly politics, and so had Nick Clegg; after Iraq and tuition fees respectively, there was an anger that they had lied, that none could be trusted. In public, MPs uttered platitudes about 'understanding your concerns', and then badmouthed the electorate in private. They told people how to live their lives but were still regularly caught on hidden cameras touting their services to fake lobbying companies. Worse yet, the expenses scandal showed them playing the system more cynically – and certainly more profitably – than the feckless poor and the fraudulent disabled against whom they so often railed. Politicians took the brunt of public anger because, as Sharron Storer and Gillian Duffy made clear, they were held responsible for pretty much everything; they were the only ones we voted for, so they were the ones who were supposed to represent us.

---

voted BBC Sports Personality of the Year in 2006, 35 years after her mother, Princess Anne.

This was the visible side of the establishment, the side that the public saw running their lives, and the perception grew that none of them had fulfilled their duty of care to the nation. Institutions that were intended to serve the people seemed to be inward-looking, self-regarding, concerned with taking care of themselves. They had forfeited their right to authority because they had not lived up to their side of the implicit bargain: they had failed to provide the protection that was expected of the state.

At the most basic level, the War on Terror had only resulted in the country feeling less safe. There was fear of a shadowy, nightmarish enemy, one not only prepared to die, but intending to die, and with whom there could be no negotiation. Yet, despite much official handwringing about extremist clerics who 'radicalised' young British Muslims, action was painfully slow; it took eight years for the Egyptian preacher Abu Hamza to be extradited to America, eleven years to deport the Jordanian Abu Qatada to his homeland. The apparent inability of the country to rid itself of such unwelcome visitors angered many, as did the fact that British Islamist activist Anjem Choudary was not jailed until 2016, seventeen years on from the first reports that he was recruiting men for military training. The feeling grew that the people were being taken for mugs.*

The sense of insecurity was felt economically too. No one in this post-Thatcher era expected the government to adopt a hands-on approach to running the economy (though many dreamed), but it was surely still possible to regulate the more extreme aspects of banking. Or to ensure that some justice was meted out to the greatest transgressors. Or at the very least to have noticed what was going on – all those threats of dire consequences if we didn't join the euro, yet so few warnings of the sub-prime hurricane

---

* Conversely, there was no protection for those British citizens imprisoned in the US detention camp in Guantanamo Bay, Cuba – men who had been picked up in Afghanistan or Pakistan and held illegally for years without charge or court hearings.

heading over the Atlantic. In 2016, Michael Gove would observe of economists, 'I think the people of this country have had enough of experts,' and he was right; they had.[38]

Most powerfully, because most emotionally, those in power had failed to protect children. Street grooming gangs abused with impunity, and so had Jimmy Savile. In the new climate, many obscure, elderly men – retired teachers, sports coaches and others – were called to account for alleged crimes committed decades earlier; few of these prosecutions made the national media, but they were reported locally, and confirmed a feeling that there had been a conspiracy of silence.

The cumulative effect was a sense of frustration in the country, of being ignored, neglected. This was particularly true of the upper-working class and lower-middle class in white England. 'They had lived to see their simple patriotism derided, their morality despised, their savings devalued,' wrote P. D. James in *The Private Patient* (2008). 'If they protested that their cities had become alien, their children taught in overcrowded schools where ninety per cent of the children spoke no English, they were lectured about the cardinal sin of racism by those more expensively and comfortably circumstanced.'[39]

In a representative democracy, too many people felt unrepresented. It wasn't about policies, but about the political process itself. People wanted to be involved, to be consulted, as demonstrated by the high level of participation in the Scottish referendum. But on the biggest issues of the day – especially the war in Iraq and immigration – no one seemed interested in their opinion. This was despite the people having a decent track record: their scepticism on Iraq and their distrust of the single currency had surely been vindicated.*

---

* Possibly the single currency might have had more appeal if Ken Clarke's romantic suggestion of calling it the florin had been adopted. Instead, Germany went for the bureaucratically utilitarian euro.

They also wanted the community and cohesion of belonging; the enthusiasm for the Golden Jubilee, the NHS and the 2012 Olympics had shown that there was still such a thing as society. Further, this wasn't a static culture, resistant to change, and it wasn't in thrall to lunatic libertarians and rabid reactionaries; some truly profound changes, from same-sex marriage to the smoking ban, were accepted with barely a murmur because they were perceived to be just. Above all, disquiet at the extraordinary increase in immigration, which had transformed huge swathes of the country, was directed at politicians, not at foreign nationals. The racial violence seen in Boston in 2004 was a rare exception, not the rule.

The wish, as ever, was to live in a safe, stable society. And, perhaps, for the nation to have a quiet life. Way back in 1972, Alf Garnett, the London docker in Johnny Speight's sitcom *Till Death Us Do Part*, had spelled out his ideal future. 'What I reckon England ought to do, see, we ought to retire,' he explained. 'I think England ought to be able to sit back and put our feet up, and draw a pension from your upsurgent nations.' He exaggerated for comic effect, but the underlying attitude was much heard on radio phone-in shows in the twenty-first century. The idea of withdrawing a little from the world, of doing some basic housekeeping, was shared by those who opposed the invasion of Iraq and by those who opposed foreign aid.

And then there was the most significant trend of the time, the democratisation of culture. Social media often got a bad press, and not just during the 2011 riots. 'Twitter, the internet, generally, is tailor-made for the kind of mob-rule witch hunts which, in the Middle Ages, literally ended with people being burned,' pronounced Richard Dawkins.[40] Undoubtedly, there were some appalling instances of mass bullying, but they were rare and did not constitute most people's experience of social media; otherwise, the number of users would have fallen rapidly. What the internet offered was unmediated participation – there was no need of representatives here – and what most took from it was a social and cultural solidarity. One elitist's mob rule was another populist's democracy.

That a critical moment was approaching should have been apparent for years. The imbalance between culture and politics, between the democratic urge and the remoteness of the elite, was unsustainable. What was needed was a focus, a single issue that could stand proxy for all the concerns. It could have been an economic crisis or a paedophile scandal or, more likely, immigration. Instead it was Europe, and it was so because Nigel Farage – despite his multiple failed attempts to be elected to Westminster – was the most gifted campaigner of his generation.

In his second stint as UKIP leader, Farage channelled an amorphous mass of discontent into this one issue. Public anger, whether provoked by lying ministers, venal MPs, reckless bankers, cultural elites, sneering media, lenient judges, benefit scroungers, political correctness – all was wrapped up into Farage's crusade against the EU, together with concerns over immigration, crime, loss of identity, austerity, globalization. The rage of the overlooked was given a political focus: Brussels, with its unaccountable faceless bureaucrats who existed above national government and were known to no one. It was a fair target for an anti-elitist tendency to pick on, but it was ultimately a metaphor, a symbol for everything else that seemed to have gone wrong.

And mostly, again, it was about process. The referendum in 2016 on Britain's membership of the EU mattered because – finally, as it seemed to many – people were actually being consulted, and were being promised that this decision really was in their hands, that they could shape their nation's destiny. The UKIP slogan 'We want our country back', as articulated by Robert Kilroy-Silk in 2004, resonated even louder now. This had become an issue of democracy, the harbinger of a new era of participation.

The question that remained was the one posed in Russell T. Davies's *The Second Coming*: 'Do you think you're ready for that much power?' asked Steve Baxter. 'You lot? You cheeky bastards!'

References

Prologue: Faith

1. *The Times* 30 December 1999
2. Sampson, *Who Runs This Place?* p. 12
3. ipsos.com
4. *The Times* 2 April 2004
5. *Guardian* 8 March 2007
6. Ibid.
7. Hornby, *How to Be Good* pp. 36, 12, 204
8. Townsend, *The Woman Who Went to Bed for a Year* p. 73
9. *Daily Telegraph* 6 June 2003
10. *Independent* 21 June 2003
11. *The Times* 19 July 2003
12. *Daily Telegraph* 7 July 2003
13. *Daily Mirror* 7 July 2003
14. *Daily Express* 27 September 2002
15. *Sunday Times* 30 July 1995
16. *Daily Telegraph* 25 October 2008
17. *The Times* 24 December 2007
18. *Independent* 20 December 2007
19. *Sunday Telegraph* 5 August 2007
20. *Sunday Herald* (Glasgow) 10 June 2015
21. *Sunday Times* 5 April 2009
22. Russell, *Killer Plan* p. 250
23. *Sun* 8 September 2008
24. *Sunday Times* 18 October 2009
25. *Guardian* 16 March 2003
26. *Independent* 26 April 2003
27. *Daily Mirror* 18 March 2003

28. *Daily Express* 24 April 2003
29. Quoted *The Times* 8 April 2003
30. *Independent* 28 April 2003
31. *Sunday Telegraph* 21 August 2005
32. *Guardian* 16 July 2009
33. *Independent on Sunday* 6 January 2002
34. Public Health England, 'Measles notifications and deaths in England and Wales: 1940 to 2016' (July 2017)
35. *The Royal Liverpool Children's Inquiry* pp. 9–10
36. Billingham, *Scaredy Cat* p. 138
37. *Independent on Sunday* 2 December 2001
38. *Guardian* 14 March 1998
39. *Guardian* 20 November 2014
40. Dobbs, *The Lord's Day* pp. 126–7
41. Brown, *My Life, Our Times* p. 359
42. Blair, *A Journey* p. 513
43. *Guardian* 2 October 2001
44. Blair, *A Journey* p. 368

1: Peace and War

1. *Sunday Telegraph* 18 April 2010
2. *Herald* (Glasgow) 13 April 2010
3. *Birmingham Mail* 16 June 2010
4. *Daily Mirror* 13 April 2010
5. *Financial Times* 13 April 2010
6. *Birmingham Mail* 16 June 2010
7. *Birmingham Mail* 11 May 2001
8. *Coventry Telegraph* 17 May 2001
9. *Sunday Mirror* 20 May 2001
10. *Birmingham Post* 17 May 2001
11. *People* 20 May 2001
12. Blunkett, *The Blunkett Tapes* p. 261
13. *Sunday Mirror* 20 May 2001
14. Blair, *A Journey* p. 321
15. *Scotsman* 19 June 2001
16. Campbell, *The Blair Years* p. 530
17. Cook, *The Point of Departure* p. 121
18. Campbell, *The Blair Years* p. 717

19. *Daily Mirror* 1 January 2000
20. Prescott, *Docks to Downing Street* p. 305
21. *Sun* 19 July 2000
22. Mandelson, *The Third Man* p. 323
23. *Bremner, Bird and Fortune's Exit Poll*, 2001
24. Blair, *A Journey* p. 336
25. *Herald* (Glasgow) 11 January 2001
26. Spicer, *The Spicer Diaries* p. 451
27. *Guardian* 13 July 2001
28. Blunkett, *The Blunkett Tapes* p. 266
29. Mullin, *A View from the Foothills* p. 211
30. Blair, *A Journey* p. 340
31. Campbell, *The Blair Years* p. 554
32. Mandelson, *The Third Man* p. 329
33. Straw, *Last Man Standing* p. 491
34. Mandelson, *The Third Man* p. 329
35. Young, *The Hugo Young Papers* p. 739
36. *Daily Telegraph* 30 September 2003
37. O'Farrell, *Things Can Only Get Worse?* pp. 72–3
38. *Daily Telegraph* 26 March 2001
39. Prescott, *Docks to Downing Street* p. 315
40. *Sunday Telegraph* 9 January 2005
41. Blair, *A Journey* p. 483
42. *Evening Standard* 15 July 1999
43. *Independent on Sunday* 6 July 2003
44. Richards, *Whatever It Takes* p. 164
45. Mandelson, *The Third Man* p. 364
46. *The Times* 5 March 2005
47. Young, *The Hugo Young Papers* p. 782
48. Blair, *A Journey* p. 526
49. *Independent* 16 October 2004
50. *Guardian* 9 June 2001
51. *Evening Standard* 14 June 2001
52. *Daily Telegraph* 21 August 2001
53. *Sunday Times* 26 August 2001
54. Cook, *The Point of Departure* p. 39
55. Wheatcroft, *The Strange Death of Tory England* p. 253
56. *Independent on Sunday* 26 August 2001
57. Clarke, *Kind of Blue* p. 417

58. Young, *The Hugo Young Papers* p. 724
59. Ibid. p. 743
60. *News of the World* 25 November 2001
61. *Guardian* 5 October 2001
62. Ibid. 30 March 2002
63. *Daily Mail* 8 February 2002
64. *Guardian* 29 May 2019
65. *Daily Mirror* 21 October 2003
66. *Observer* 10 November 2002
67. *Independent on Sunday* 2 March 2003
68. *Independent* 5 June 2002
69. *Financial Times* 18 May 1998
70. Young, *The Hugo Young Papers* p. 723
71. Cook, *The Point of Departure* p. 259
72. *Independent* 31 May 1995
73. *Daily Telegraph* 8 October 2002
74. *The Times* 28 June 1995
75. *Sunday Times* 24 September 2000
76. *Guardian, Daily Telegraph* 8 October 2002
77. *Independent* 11 October 2002
78. *Daily Telegraph* 10 October 2003
79. *Independent* 1 November 2003
80. Cameron, *For the Record* p. 62
81. *Daily Mirror* 11 July 2001
82. *Daily Express* 12 September 2001
83. Straw, *Last Man Standing* p. 340
84. Mandelson, *The Third Man* p. 341
85. Speech to the Chicago Economic Club, 22 April 1999 (globalpolicy.org)
86. *Daily Mirror* 12 September 2001
87. *Guardian* 3 October 2001
88. *The Times* 20 July 1988
89. *Guardian* 25 October 2000
90. *Independent* 21 February 2000
91. Quoted Seldon, *Blair* p. 490
92. Quoted *The Times* 6 October 2001
93. *Sunday Mirror* 25 February 2001
94. Campbell, *The Blair Years* p. 566
95. Young, *The Hugo Young Papers* p. 790
96. Hansard 24 September 2002

97. Cook, *The Point of Departure* p. 216
98. *Sun* 25 September 2002
99. Blair, *A Journey* p. 453
100. Footnote in Campbell, *The Blair Years* p. 664
101. Associated Press News Service 5 February 2003
102. *The Times* 7 February 2003
103. *Guardian* 8 February 2003
104. *Independent on Sunday* 9 February 2003
105. Kampfner, *Blair's Wars* p. 265
106. Blair, *A Journey* p. 405
107. Cable, *Free Radical* p. 273
108. Prescott, *Docks to Downing Street* p. 215
109. Ashdown, *The Ashdown Diaries* p. 263
110. Hansard 17 March 2003
111. ICM, *Guardian* 21 January 2003; ICM, *Daily Mirror* 31 January 2003; YouGov, Channel 4/*Daily Mirror* 31 January 2003
112. *Observer* 11 November 2001
113. Rachel, *Don't Look Back in Anger* p. 442
114. *Independent on Sunday* 14 October 2001
115. *Birmingham Mail* 15 February 2003
116. *Daily Telegraph* 13 February 2003
117. *Sunday Herald* 16 February 2003
118. Bennett, *Untold Stories* pp. 323–24
119. McEwan, *Saturday* p. 32
120. Blunkett, *The Blunkett Tapes* p. 450
121. Cook, *The Point of Departure* p. 297
122. Campbell, *The Blair Years* p. 680
123. Blair, *A Journey* p. 372
124. Mullin, *A View from the Foothills* p. 462
125. Blair, *A Journey* pp. 467 and 478
126. Campbell, *The Blair Years* p. 700
127. *Independent* 17 May 2003
128. Blair, *A Journey* p. 452
129. YouGov, *Sunday Times* 1 June 2003
130. *Daily Mirror* 30 May 2003
131. *The Times* 26 June 2003
132. *Daily Mirror* 20 June 2003
133. *Independent on Sunday* 23 February 2003; *Independent* 4 June 2003
134. Campbell, *The Blair Years* p. 724

135. *Express on Sunday* 20 July 2003
136. Reported *Guardian* 20 July 2003
137. *Daily Mirror* 19 July 2003
138. Benn, *More Time for Politics* p. 131
139. Coe, *Number 11* p. 150
140. *Guardian* 1 March 2003
141. *Daily Mirror* 27 April 1999
142. NOP, *Independent* 7 February 2004
143. Mullin, *A View from the Foothills* p. 460
144. Blair, *A Journey* p. 392
145. *Financial Times* 24 January 2003
146. Blair, *A Journey* p. 410
147. *Sunday Telegraph* 6 January 2002
148. Jones, *Campaign 1997* p. 264
149. Blair, *A Journey* p. 509
150. Campbell, *The Blair Years* p. 719

2: Left and Right

1. *People* 5 May 2002
2. *Independent on Sunday* 31 March 2002
3. Cook, *The Point of Departure* p. 61
4. *Guardian* 1 October 1986
5. Ibid. 2 May 2000
6. Livingstone, *You Can't Say That* p. 451
7. *Daily Telegraph* 24 May 2001
8. Ibid. 24 May 2001
9. *The Times* 19 January 2002
10. O'Farrell, *Things Can Only Get Worse?* p. 26
11. *Independent* 14 September 2002
12. *Express on Sunday* 6 October 2002; *Financial Times* 12 May 2001; *Sunday Telegraph* 6 January 2002
13. *Birmingham Mail* 5 October 2001
14. *Independent on Sunday* 21 October 2001
15. *Guardian* 23 April 2010
16. *Scotsman* 24 March 2003
17. *Socialism Today* 74, April–May 2003
18. *The Times* 14 February 2003
19. *Guardian* 12 February 2003

20. *The Times* 19 January 2002
21. *Daily Telegraph* 22 March 2003
22. *Sunday Times* 19 April 1998
23. *Independent* 5 April 2004
24. *Guardian* 16 September 2002
25. Cable, *Free Radical* p. 304
26. *Guardian* 16 September 2002
27. Ibid. 16 March 2000
28. *Independent* 5 March 2003
29. *Sunday Times* 23 January 1994
30. *Guardian* 23 October 2003
31. *Daily Mirror* 24 October 2003
32. *Evening Standard* 25 January 2006
33. *Workers Power* June 2004
34. Benn, *More Time for Politics* p. 185
35. *Guardian* 23 October 2004
36. Cohen, *What's Left?* p. 310
37. *Red Pepper* April 2005
38. ICM, *Guardian* 16 March 2004
39. *1917* 28, 2006
40. *Independent* 5 April 2004
41. Benn, *More Time for Politics* pp. 288 and 290
42. *Evening Standard* 27 February 1974
43. Benn, *More Time for Politics* p. 129
44. *The Times* 29 August 2015
45. *Independent* 16 May 2013
46. *Observer* 26 July 2015
47. *Independent* 7 August 2015
48. Quoted Frankel, *Socialism: Vision and Reality* p. 48
49. *Liverpool Echo* 20 October 1983
50. *Independent on Sunday* 6 June 2004
51. *Sunday Mirror* 15 June 1997
52. *The Times* 24 June 2003
53. *Sun* 3 November 2001
54. *Independent on Sunday* 11 January 2004
55. *Evening Standard* 16 June 2004
56. *News of the World* 28 May 2000
57. *Evening Standard* 16 June 2004
58. Durham County Publications 3 December 2001

59. *Sunday Express* 4 January 2004
60. *Independent on Sunday* 11 January 2004
61. *Guardian* 10 January 2004
62. *Independent on Sunday* 5 June 1994
63. *The Times* 29 April 1994
64. *Independent* 12 October 1994
65. Farage, *Flying Free* p. 93
66. Ibid. p. 98
67. *People* 6 June 2004
68. *Financial Times* 21 March 2000
69. *Western Daily Press* 12 February 2001
70. *The Times* 29 April 2000
71. *Guardian* 26 February 2001
72. *Guardian* 9 February 2000
73. UK Independence Party election broadcast, 2001
74. *Western Daily Press* 15 June 1999
75. *Independent* 16 April 1997
76. *Daily Telegraph* 20 January 2004
77. *Guardian* 26 February 2001
78. Lancashire County Publications 24 August 2000
79. *The Times* 31 May 2004
80. *Daily Telegraph* 23 May 2014
81. *Independent on Sunday* 3 October 2004
82. *The Times* 22 January 2000
83. *Guardian* 9 February 2000
84. *Daily Express* 30 December 2003
85. *Evening Standard* 12 February 2002
86. *Evening Standard* 2 June 2004; *Daily Telegraph* 30 April 2004
87. *The Times* 30 November 2009
88. *Sunday Telegraph* 29 August 2004
89. Ibid.
90. *Sun* 17 November 2013
91. Ibid. 8 August 1998
92. Quoted *Observer* 21 May 2000
93. North Yorkshire County Publications 3 June 2004
94. *Guardian* 31 May 2004
95. Farage, *Flying Free* p. 155
96. *Daily Telegraph* 13 May 2004
97. Benn, *More Time for Politics* p. 189

98. Spicer, *The Spicer Diaries* p. 537
99. Clifford and Levin, *Max Clifford* p. 258
100. *Guardian* 19 June 2004
101. *Irish Times* 14 June 2004
102. *The Times* 29 April 1975
103. *Guardian* 4 October 2004
104. *Daily Mirror* 4 October 2004
105. *Sun* 4 October 2004
106. *Guardian* 5 October 2004
107. Farage, *Flying Free* p. 180
108. *The Times* 4 October 2004
109. *Independent on Sunday* 9 May 2004
110. Ibid. 23 January 2005
111. Ibid. 6 February 2005
112. *Financial Times* 16 April 2005
113. *Kilroy: Behind the Tan* BBC, 2005
114. *Independent on Sunday* 23 January 1994
115. *The Times* 18 November 1988

3: Past and Present

1. *Daily Telegraph* 14 May 2002
2. East Sussex County Publications 4 June 2002
3. *Birmingham Post* 3 June 2002
4. *Daily Mirror* 4 June 2002
5. *Birmingham Mail* 13 May 2002
6. *Daily Telegraph* 14 May 2002
7. *Independent* 17 May 2002
8. *Daily Telegraph* 5 June 2002
9. Kampfner, *Blair's Wars* p. 4
10. *The Times* 4 October 1995
11. *Express on Sunday* 12 November 2006
12. *Financial Times* 9 May 2006
13. *Guardian* 11 November 2004
14. Quoted *The Times* 27 November 2006
15. *Independent* 20 November 2006
16. Ibid. 27 November 2006
17. *Guardian* 24 August 2007
18. Ibid.

19. *The Times* 5 January 2002
20. *Herald* (Glasgow) 6 October 2000
21. *Daily Post* (Liverpool) 20 February 2009
22. *Guardian* 27 January 2005
23. Ibid. 10 September 2007
24. Quoted Lowe, *Mastering Modern British History* p. 575
25. *Sunday Times* 17 February 2019
26. *Sunday Telegraph* 28 March 2010
27. *Daily Mirror* 22 September 2007
28. *Sunday Times* 23 September 2007
29. *The Times* 26 March 2007
30. *Sun* 29 September 2007
31. *Guardian* 15 January 2004
32. *Daily Mirror* 5 February 2004
33. *Sun* 5 February 2004
34. Press Association 4 February 2004
35. *Daily Record* (Glasgow) 25 April 1997
36. *Herald Sun* (Melbourne) 20 October 2007
37. nhs.uk 23 February 2017
38. Robinson, *Friend of the Devil* pp. 63–4
39. *Financial Times* 8 June 2010
40. *Liverpool Echo* 12 March 2007
41. *Daily Telegraph* 9 June 2004
42. *Evening Standard* 18 April 2006
43. *Daily Express* 1 November 2008
44. Quoted *Observer* 18 September 2005
45. *Sunday Times* 9 October 2005
46. *Independent* 8 March 2001
47. *Bristol Evening Post* 16 April 2001
48. *The Times* 18 November 2003
49. *Sunday Express* 11 December 2005
50. *Daily Telegraph* 10 December 2005
51. *Guardian* 4 April 2013
52. *Gloucestershire Live* 14 October 2018
53. *Sun* 19 October 2018
54. bbc.co.uk 16 October 2018
55. *Daily Telegraph* 21 October 2005
56. *The Times* 7 February 2005
57. quoted *Daily Mirror* 10 January 2005

58. *Guardian* 31 January 2006
59. Ibid. 11 July 2008
60. Keys, *Thatcher's Britain* p. 3
61. *Daily Mail* 15 January 2005
62. *Independent* 15 January 2002
63. Lodge, *Deaf Sentence* p. 141
64. Livingstone, *You Can't Say That* p. 506

4: Class and Underclass

1. *Guardian* 19 June 2007
2. *Bristol Evening Post* 19 April 2013
3. Durham County Publications 31 December 2004
4. *Daily Post* (North Wales) 27 September 2017
5. *Bristol Evening Post* 19 April 2013
6. *Daily Post* (North Wales) 27 September 2017
7. *Evening Chronicle* (Newcastle) 25 January 2012
8. Ibid. 6 July 2018
9. *Sun* 24 April 1998
10. *South Wales Echo* 16 January 2007
11. *Hucknall Dispatch* 10 March 2010
12. *Yorkshire Post* 19 November 2004
13. *Sunday Times* 13 June 2004
14. *Observer* 7 December 2003
15. *Daily Mirror* 14 August 1996
16. *People* 20 March 2005
17. *Observer* 24 July 2011
18. *Bristol Evening Post* 28 November 2013
19. *Daily Telegraph* 16 September 2004
20. *Guardian* 3 November 2004
21. *Sunday Times* 2 November 2008
22. Medhurst, *A National Joke* p. 187
23. Ibid. p. 200
24. *Sunday Times* 28 December 2008
25. *The Times* 21 June 2006
26. *Financial Times* 21 June 2006
27. *The Times* 21 February 1990
28. *Independent* 6 January 2000
29. *Daily Record* 25 January 2007

30. *Sunday Times* 21 January 2007
31. *Daily Record* 25 January 2007
32. *Guardian* 7 February 2005
33. *Observer* 26 December 2004
34. *Independent on Sunday* 26 December 2004
35. *New York Times* 2 January 2011
36. *Daily Mirror* 17 February 2005
37. *The Times* 25 September 2007
38. *Evening Standard* 25 January 2013
39. *Daily Record* 26 August 2016
40. *Daily Mirror* 12 October 2010
41. *Independent* 15 February 1999
42. *Western Daily Press* 8 February 2001
43. *The Times* 20 February 1999
44. *Sunday Mirror* 16 April 1995
45. *Birmingham Mail* 13 September 2000; *Independent* 31 August 2000; *Daily Record* 30 August 2000; *Guardian* 30 August 2000
46. *Sunday Times* 3 September 2000
47. *Observer* 27 August 2000
48. *Evening Standard* 14 December 2000
49. *Scotland on Sunday* 29 October 2000
50. *Daily Express* 11 September 2003
51. Turner, *The Old Boys* p. 247
52. *Daily Telegraph* 12 October 2012; *Daily Mirror* 24 February 2016
53. Bennett, *Keeping On Keeping On* p. 190
54. *Daily Telegraph* 28 March 2013
55. *Guardian* 15 September 2011
56. Marr, *Children of the Master* p. 41
57. *Observer* 25 June 2000
58. *Independent on Sunday* 3 July 2011
59. Ibid. 7 December 2003

5: Cameron and Blair

1. *Guardian* 12 April 2005
2. O'Farrell, *Things Can Only Get Worse?* p 107
3. *Daily Mirror* 2 February 2005
4. *The Times* 31 January 2005
5. *Daily Telegraph* 20 May 2005

6. Horrie and Matthews, *True Blue* p. 25
7. *Edinburgh Evening News* 27 April 2005
8. *Observer* 15 May 2005
9. *Daily Telegraph* 1 June 2005
10. *The Times* 17 June 2005
11. *Guardian* 11 July 2005
12. *The Times* 1 October 2005
13. *Sunday Mirror* 3 July 2005
14. *Daily Telegraph, Guardian, Daily Star* 5 October 2005
15. Clarke, *Kind of Blue* p. 427
16. *Guardian* 3 December 2005
17. *Financial Times* 1 October 2006
18. *News of the World* 9 July 2006
19. *Daily Telegraph* 26 December 2005
20. Cameron, *For the Record* p. 92
21. *Sunday Times* 17 September 2006
22. Hansard 7 December 2005
23. Cameron, *For the Record* p. 48
24. *Sunday Times* 22 May 2005
25. *The Times* 18 November 2005
26. *Independent* 16 February 2007
27. Bennett, *Keeping On Keeping On* p. 124
28. *Daily Telegraph* 6 October 2005
29. *Sunday Express* 16 July 2006
30. *Daily Telegraph* 3 December 2005
31. *Daily Express* 10 October 2005
32. *Observer* 14 May 2006
33. Ibid. 23 February 2003
34. *Daily Mirror* 5 October 2005
35. *Sunday Times* 3 June 2007
36. Cameron, *For the Record* p. 76
37. *The Times* 5 October 2006
38. Ibid. 10 December 2005
39. *Daily Telegraph* 3 August 2005
40. *Observer* 27 August 2006
41. *Daily Mirror* 21 September 2006
42. Cable, *Free Radical* p. 287
43. *Guardian* 21 October 2007
44. *The Times* 17 October 2007

45. Blair, *A Journey* p. 655
46. Mandelson, *The Third Man* p. 416
47. Richards, *Whatever It Takes* p. 396
48. Young, *The Hugo Young Papers* p. 740
49. Blair, *A Journey* pp. 657, 583, 600, 600
50. Straw, *Last Man Standing* pp. 488, 489
51. *Guardian* 2 January 2006
52. Prescott, *Docks to Downing Street* p. 324
53. CommunicateResearch for *Independent* 1 May 2007
54. Hansard 27 June 2007
55. *Evening Standard* 27 June 2007; *Australian* 28 June 2007
56. Harris, *The Ghost* pp. 142, 76 and 78
57. *Guardian* 27 September 2007
58. *The Times* 9 February 2006
59. See for example *Western Daily Press* 20 May 2005
60. *Daily Echo* (Northampton) 6 November 1925
61. *Daily Mirror* 17 November 1997
62. *Daily Mirror* 11 January 2007
63. *Sun* 7 September 2010
64. *Evening Standard* 8 September 2010
65. *The Times* 10 September 2010
66. Asian News International 3 September 2010
67. *The Times* 29 October 2008
68. *Daily Telegraph* 14 April 2009
69. Mandelson, *The Third Man* p. 265
70. *Guardian* 6 January 2014
71. Blair, *A Journey* p. 650
72. *Daily Mirror* 16 November 2006
73. *Observer* 29 April 2007
74. Blair, *A Journey* p. 660
75. Ibid. p. 686
76. Rachel, *Don't Look Back in Anger* p. 179
77. Blair, *A Journey* p. 579
78. ibid. p. 488
79. ibid. p. 649
80. *Evening Standard* 19 September 2005
81. Blair, *A Journey* p. 550
82. Prescott, *Docks to Downing Street* p. 311
83. Blunkett, *The Blunkett Tapes* p. 408

84. Cook, *The Point of Departure* p. 242
85. Rachel, *Don't Look Back in Anger* p. 444
86. *Mail on Sunday* 2 April 2000
87. *Guardian* web edn 27 June 2007
88. *Sun* 27 June 2007
89. *Sunday Sun* (Newcastle) 4 April 2010
90. *Daily Record* (Glasgow) 1 October 2008

6: Bust and Broken

1. *Observer* 8 August 2004; Blunkett, *The Blunkett Tapes* p. 744; Bennett, *Keeping On Keeping On* p. 19
2. *Daily Express* 5 January 2005
3. *The Times* 10 September 2005
4. *Observer* 4 April 2010
5. Ibid. 8 October 2000
6. *Sunday Times* 4 March 2007
7. Young, *The Hugo Young Papers* p. 788
8. Ibid. p. 761
9. *Sunday Times* 10 September 2006
10. McBride, *Power Trip* p. 286
11. Ibid. p. 264
12. *Observer*; *Sunday Times* 28 May 2006
13. *Sun* 6 June 2007
14. *Yorkshire Post* 11 September 2007
15. news.bbc.co.uk/1/hi/uk_politics/7010664.stm
16. *Sunday Times* 4 November 2007
17. *Daily Mirror* 12 July 2007
18. *Guardian* 25 July 2007
19. *Financial Times* 19 February 2007
20. Ibid. 15 January 2007
21. *Daily Telegraph* 27 January 2007
22. *The Times* 4 April 2007
23. *Guardian* 14 September 2007
24. *Daily Express* 19 September 2007
25. *Evening Standard* 14 September 2007
26. Cable, *Free Radical* p. 331
27. *The Times* 16 November 2006
28. *Sun* 1 October 2007

29. *Guardian* 8 October 2007
30. Cable, *Free Radical* p. 328
31. *Daily Mirror* 3 December 2009
32. McBride, *Power Trip* p. 307
33. Straw, *Last Man Standing* p. 509
34. Brown, *My Life, Our Times* p. 223
35. *Daily Mirror* 17 October 2009
36. Ibid. 3 April 2010
37. *Guardian* 3 April 2010
38. *Daily Star* 4 April 2010
39. *The Times* 8 May 2008
40. O'Farrell, *Things Can Only Get Worse?* p. 134
41. Mandelson, *The Third Man* p. 451
42. Hain, *Outside In* p. 391
43. Richards, *Whatever It Takes* p. 277
44. Agence France-Presse 22 November 2007
45. *Evening Standard* 22 November 2007
46. *Guardian* 30 August 2008
47. Brown, *My Life, Our Times* p. 300
48. Cable, *Free Radical* p. 339
49. *Daily Star* 9 October 2008
50. *Financial Times* 28 January 2009
51. *Daily Mirror* 22 October 2009
52. *City AM* 15 October 2008; Carl Barât and Pete Doherty, 'What a Waster' (Rough Trade, 2002)
53. *Observer* 21 December 2008
54. Ibid. 4 January 2009
55. *Sunday Times* 9 November 2008
56. Blair, *A Journey* p. 664
57. Peston, *Who Runs Britain?* p. 8
58. *Financial Times* 4 June 2007
59. Hernon, *The Blair Decade* p. 188
60. James, *The Murder Room* p. 68
61. *Sunday Times* 11 January 2009
62. *Daily Telegraph* 6 October 2008
63. *Sunday Herald* 5 March 2006
64. *Sun* 17 December 2004
65. Cameron, *For the Record* p. 117
66. *Edinburgh Review* June 1831

67. Spicer, *The Spicer Diaries* p. 596
68. *Daily Telegraph* 30 May 2019
69. Spicer, *The Spicer Diaries* p. 598
70. Cable, *Free Radical* p. 312
71. *Daily Telegraph* 14 May 2009
72. *The Times* 22 April 2009
73. Mullin, *A View from the Foothills* p. 242
74. *Guardian* 22 April 2009
75. *Sun* 24 April 2009
76. *Financial Times* 28 April 2009
77. Richards, *Whatever It Takes* p. 407
78. *The Times* 2 May 2009
79. *Financial Times* 5 June 2009
80. Straw, *Last Man Standing* p. 524
81. Populus for *The Times* 12 January 2010
82. Clarke, *Kind of Blue* p. 438
83. Agence France-Presse 10 December 2008
84. Brown, *My Life, Our Times* p. 344
85. *Sunday Telegraph* 9 January 2011

7: Grooming and Abusing

1. *Independent* 13 April 1994
2. *The Times* 2 April 1997
3. Ibid.
4. Ibid.
5. *Sunday Times* 23 November 1997
6. West Yorkshire and North Yorkshire Counties Publications 21 September 1998, 12 December 1998
7. *The Times* 2 April 1997
8. West Yorkshire and North Yorkshire Counties Publications 12 January 2001
9. *Guardian* 16 August 1999
10. *Independent* 20 July 1998
11. West Yorkshire and North Yorkshire Counties Publications 12 July 2001, 31 August 2001
12. *Guardian* 14 July 2001
13. *Independent* 30 August 2001

14. West Yorkshire and North Yorkshire Counties Publications 19 July 2001, 26 October 2001
15. *Birmingham Post* 16 July 2001
16. Ali, *Brick Lane* pp. 19, 45
17. West Yorkshire and North Yorkshire Counties Publications 31 January 2003
18. Ibid. 29 August 2003
19. *Daily Express* 23 August 2003
20. West Yorkshire and North Yorkshire Counties Publications 29 August 2003, 28 August 2003
21. *Guardian* 22 May 2004
22. Ibid. 9 August 2004
23. *The Times* 21 August 2004
24. *Guardian* 9 August 2004
25. Ibid. 22 May 2004
26. *Independent* 21 May 2004
27. *Observer* 5 May 2002
28. Blunkett, *The Blunkett Tapes* p. 278
29. *Independent on Sunday* 5 May 2002
30. *The Times* 4 May 2002
31. *Prospect* June 2002
32. *Observer* 5 May 2002
33. Lancashire County Publications 6 May 2002
34. *Observer* 5 May 2002
35. *Daily Telegraph* 2 May 2003
36. West Yorkshire and North Yorkshire Counties Publications 13 January 2005
37. *Guardian* 24 May 2004
38. *Irish Times* 18 January 2006
39. Jay, 'Independent Inquiry into Child Sexual Exploitation in Rotherham 1997–2013' p. 35
40. *The Times* 15 January 2011
41. *Manchester Evening News* web edn 15 May 2017 and 14 Jan 2020
42. *Guardian* 7 January 2011
43. *The Times* 10 May 2012
44. *Independent* 11 May 2012
45. Ibid.
46. *Rochdale Observer* 28 March 2008
47. *The Times* 6 January 2011

48. *Daily Mail* 9 May 2012
49. *Guardian* 30 August 2014
50. Mullin, *A View from the Foothills* p. 502
51. *The Times* 24 October 2012
52. *Daily Mail* 9 May 2012
53. *Guardian* 21 May 2013
54. *Daily Telegraph* 26 July 2014
55. Ibid. 29 October 2011
56. *Daily Mirror* 9 November 2011
57. Ibid. 10 November 2011
58. *Yorkshire Evening Post* 8 November 2011
59. *Daily Mail* 18 July 2013
60. Savile, *As It Happens* p. 172
61. *Daily Telegraph* 4 October 2012
62. *Daily Express* 2 October 2012
63. *Daily Express* 4 October 2012
64. *Evening Standard* 1 October 2012
65. *Sunday Times* 5 August 2012
66. *Sunday Mirror* 13 January 2013
67. *Sun* 15 October 2012
68. Ibid. 4 November 2012
69. *Independent* web edn 31 January 2014
70. *Herald* 9 March 2018
71. Surrey Live 30 August 2018
72. *The Times* 9 April 1992
73. *New Standard* (London) 16 March 1981
74. *Independent* 23 February 2013
75. *The Times* 25 March 1993
76. *Sunday Times* 24 April 1988
77. *Daily Telegraph* 1 October 2009
78. *Sunday Telegraph* 14 October 2001
79. *Daily Telegraph* 25 October 2012
80. *People* 2 December 2012
81. *Sunday Mirror* 25 January 2015
82. *Daily Telegraph* 26 August 2015
83. *Daily Mirror* 8 August 2015
84. *Independent* web edn 10 October 2015
85. *Daily Telegraph* 19 December 2014
86. *Guardian* 6 July 2014

87. Ibid. 14 March 2019
88. *The Times* 22 January 1976
89. *Guardian* 12 January 2013
90. KingOfHits.com 27 February 2015
91. Jay, 'Independent Inquiry into Child Sexual Exploitation in Rotherham 1997–2013' p. 94

8: Coalition and Cohesion

1. *Independent on Sunday* 9 May 2010
2. Sky News 29 April 2010
3. *Herald* 17 April 2010
4. *City AM* 18 May 2010
5. *Guardian* 18 May 2010
6. *Daily Mail* 1 June 2008
7. *Guardian* 1 November 2001
8. *Independent on Sunday* 16 May 2010
9. *Evening Standard* 17 May 2010
10. *Daily Record* 27 September 2010
11. *Observer* 25 July 2010
12. *Daily Star* 30 September 2010
13. *Observer* 23 May 2010
14. Young, *The Hugo Young Papers* p. 740
15. *Sunday Mirror* 16 December 2007
16. *Guardian* 1 January 2011
17. *Daily Telegraph* 27 February 2010
18. Cable, *Free Radical* p. 351
19. Haddon, *The Red House* p. 143
20. *Guardian* 24 April 2009
21. *The Times* 22 June 2010
22. Cameron, *For the Record* p. 183
23. *Independent on Sunday* 3 October 2010
24. BBC website 5 October 2010
25. *Independent* 11 November 2010
26. Rowling, *The Casual Vacancy* p. 366
27. *Guardian* 2 April 2013
28. *Liverpool Echo* 28 August 2015
29. *Evening Standard* 4 October 2010

30. BBC website 3 February 2014; *Guardian* 25 September 2013; Huffington Post 13 August 2013
31. *Sunday Times* 7 March 2010
32. *Sunday Mirror* 31 October 2010
33. *Daily Telegraph* 16 June 2011
34. *Daily Mirror* 10 September 1968
35. *Sunday Telegraph* 10 October 2010
36. *Daily Express* 11 October 2013
37. *Evening Standard* 4 October 2010
38. *Daily Record* 17 October 2012
39. *The Times* 28 August 2009
40. *Sun* 28 August 2009
41. *Independent* web edn 28 September 2011
42. *Guardian* 26 March 2012
43. *Independent* 20 May 2012
44. *The Times* 9 September 2014
45. *Independent* 24 September 2003
46. *Daily Record* 22 March 2010
47. *Sun* 28 March 2012
48. *Sun* 2 April 2012
49. *Guardian* 24 April 2012
50. Cameron, *For the Record* p. 359
51. *Daily Express* 28 April 2011
52. *Daily Star* 30 April 2011
53. *Sun; Daily Mirror* 2 May 2011
54. *Sun* 2 May 2011
55. www.ipsos.com/ipsos-mori/en-uk/attitudes-hung-parliament
56. *Independent* 27 January 2007
57. *Guardian* web edn 9 July 2009
58. Bennett, *Keeping On Keeping On* p. 253
59. Figures from inquest.org.uk
60. *Evening Standard* (London) 10 November 2010
61. lbc.co.uk/politics/parties/labour/uncovered-john-mcdonnell-praises-2010-riots/
62. *Telegraph* blogs 28 March 2011
63. *Daily Star* 9 August 2011
64. *Daily Mirror* 9 August 2011; *Daily Telegraph* 8 August 2011; *Sun* 10 August 2011; *Daily Star* 9 August 2011; *Sun* 9 August 2011
65. *Daily Record* 10 August 2011

66. *Deutsche Welle* 11 August 2011
67. *Daily Mirror* 8 August 2011
68. *Liverpool Echo* 9 August 2011
69. *Evening Standard* 8 August 2011
70. Cher Lloyd, Autumn Rowe, Jermaine Jackson, Andre Davidson, Sean Davidson, the Strangerz, 'Swagger Jagger' (Syco, 2011)
71. *Daily Telegraph* 10 August 2011
72. *Event* 15 January 2013
73. *Mail on Sunday* 29 July 2012
74. *Daily Herald* 7 July 1958
75. *Daily Telegraph* 11 January 2008
76. Quoted *Birmingham Daily Post* 31 July 1964
77. Lawson, *The View from Number 11* p. 613
78. *Guardian* 39 May 2007
79. *Sunday Telegraph* 20 July 2008
80. *Yorkshire Post* 21 March 2013
81. *Derby Telegraph* 28 June 2008
82. *Telegraph* web edn 12 August 2012

9: Europeans and Europe

1. *Stage* 15 August 1968
2. *Edinburgh Evening News* 6 February 2004
3. *Daily Post* (Liverpool) 9 February 2004
4. *Guardian* 7 February 2004
5. Lewycka, *Two Caravans* p. 117
6. *Independent* 30 March 2007
7. Lewycka, *Two Caravans* pp. 133–4
8. Agence France-Presse 29 June 2008
9. *The Times* 6 June 2003
10. Blunkett, *The Blunkett Tapes* p. 613
11. *Daily Express* 18 August 2003
12. Blunkett, *The Blunkett Tapes* p. 386
13. *Independent* 22 February 2004
14. *Daily Express* 19 February 2004
15. *Guardian* 5 February 2004
16. Ibid. 12 September 2006
17. Mullin, *A View from the Foothills* p. 502
18. *Scotsman* 15 May 2006

19. Hansard 18 March 2003
20. Straw, *Last Man Standing* p. 423
21. All figures from the Office for National Statistics
22. *Evening Standard* 23 October 2009
23. *The Times* 29 June 2006
24. Imbeciles, 'Cool T-Shirt' (Only Lovers Left Alive, 2004)
25. *Hull Daily Mail* 7 December 2011
26. *Sunday Telegraph* 5 August 2007
27. *Daily Telegraph* 16 May 2013
28. *Gloucester Citizen* 28 March 2016
29. *Lancashire Telegraph* 29 November 2007
30. *Daily Telegraph* 18 May 2007; Agence France-Presse 29 June 2008
31. See Veličković, *Eastern Europeans in Contemporary Literature and Culture* p. 156
32. *Prishtina Insight* 14 September 2016
33. Quoted *Observer* 30 June 2013
34. *Daily Telegraph* 10 May 2013
35. *Guardian* 11 December 2012
36. Ibid. 7 July 2004
37. *Sun* 15 June 2004
38. *Guardian* 30 June 2004
39. Ibid. 24 January 2007
40. *Independent on Sunday* 4 November 2007
41. *Sunday Times* 4 November 2007
42. *Independent on Sunday* 4 November 2007
43. *Observer* 27 August 2004
44. *Daily Telegraph* 5 February 2009
45. *Boston Target* 23 January 2013
46. *Question Time* (BBC TV) 17 January 2013
47. *Boston Target* 23 January 2013
48. *Lincolnshire Echo* 24 January 2013
49. *Boston Standard* 13 June 2014
50. *Independent on Sunday* 4 November 2007
51. Ibid. 5 July 2015
52. Ipsos-Mori, quoted *Sunday Times* 4 November 2007
53. *Coventry Telegraph* 12 March 2007
54. Benn, *More Time for Politics* p. 16
55. *Daily Express* 2 December 2008
56. ipsos.com/ipsos-mori/en-uk/european-union-membership-trends

57. *Independent on Sunday* 6 January 2002
58. *The Times* 2 October 2006
59. MacShane, *Brexit: How Britain Left Europe* p. 113
60. Hansard 27 June 2007
61. *Financial Times* 14 May 2003
62. *Scotsman* 14 November 2000
63. Mandelson, *The Third Man* p. 382
64. YouGov for *Sun* 19 April 2004
65. Straw, *Last Man Standing* p. 428
66. Ibid. p. 424
67. Blunkett, *The Blunkett Tapes* p. 790
68. *Observer* 25 April 2004
69. *Sun* 15 May 2003
70. *Independent* 21 April 2004
71. *Guardian* 22 April 2004
72. *The Times* 22 June 2004
73. Blair, *A Journey* p. 530
74. Blunkett, *The Blunkett Tapes* p. 790
75. Straw, *Last Man Standing* p. 421
76. Hain, *Outside In* p. 273
77. Quoted *Northern Echo* (Darlington) 28 February 2008
78. *Sun* 5 November 2009
79. *Observer* 16 September 2007
80. Spicer, *The Spicer Diaries* p. 600
81. Farage, *Flying Free* pp. 75–6
82. BBC website 24 January 2014
83. *Financial Times* 9 March 2013
84. *Evening Standard* (London) 4 April 2006
85. Populus for *The Times* 27 June 2009
86. *Telegraph* blogs 1 March 2013
87. *Sunday Telegraph* 24 November 2013
88. *Guardian* web edn 12 June 2012
89. *Guardian* 1 January 2012
90. *Daily Telegraph* web edn 23 January 2013
91. *Daily Mirror* 23 January 2013
92. ICM for *Guardian* 2 April 2014
93. Clegg, *Politics* p. x
94. *The Times* 17 May 2014
95. *Telegraph* web edn 18 May 2014

96. *Sun* 17 May 2014
97. Ibid. 20 September 2007; 12 December 2011; 28 February 2013
98. *Independent on Sunday* 18 May 2014; *Guardian* 15 December 2014; *Daily Mirror* 17 May 2014
99. *Sunday Times* 25 May 2014
100. Cameron, *For the Record* p. 560
101. *Daily Mail* 26 May 2014
102. *Financial Times* 9 March 2013

Epilogue: Democracy

1. *The Times* 20 March 1998
2. Marr, *Children of the Master* p. 270
3. *Sunday Times* 9 November 2014
4. Mullin, *A View from the Foothills* p. 510
5. Brown, *My Life, Our Times* p. 204
6. Cameron, *For the Record* p. 226
7. *Independent* 28 May 2002
8. *Financial Times* 14 August 1998
9. Cameron, *For the Record* p. 318
10. *Sunday Times* 16 November 2008
11. *Scotsman on Sunday* 27 January 2008
12. *The Times* 29 December 1998
13. *Sunday Mail* (Glasgow) 26 December 2004
14. Blair, *A Journey* p. 651
15. *Herald* (Glasgow) 29 August 2014
16. Ibid. 16 September 2014
17. *Daily Mirror* web edn 17 September 2014
18. *City AM* 15 September 2014
19. Cameron, *For the Record* p. 555
20. Farage, *Flying Free* p. 282
21. *Independent on Sunday* 7 July 2002
22. *Sun* 10 April 2009
23. *Hindustan Times* (New Delhi) 9 October 2015
24. *Sunday Times* 19 October 2008
25. *Evening Standard* 19 November 2008
26. *Sun* 13 November 2008
27. *Sunday Express* 23 November 2008
28. *Scotsman* 20 November 2008

29. *The Times* 19 November 2008
30. Prescott, *Docks to Downing Street* p. 362
31. *Guardian* web edn 13 August 2009
32. *Daily Post* (Liverpool) 21 April 2010
33. *Evening Standard* 29 March 2010
34. *Observer* 17 January 2010
35. *Guardian Unlimited* 6 April 2010
36. Farage, *Flying Free* p. 278
37. *Guardian* 5 May 2015
38. Quoted *Daily Telegraph* 22 November 2019
39. James, *The Private Patient* pp. 42–3
40. *Sunday Herald* (Glasgow) 21 September 2015

Sources

As will be apparent from the list of references, much of the material comes from contemporary newspapers. The following works, however, have also been of assistance.

Books – non-fiction

Paddy Ashdown, *The Ashdown Diaries: The Ashdown Diaries Volume I: 1988–1997* (Allen Lane, London, 2000 – pbk edn: Penguin, London, 2000)

Lukas Audickas and Richard Keen, 'Membership of UK Political Parties' (House of Commons Briefing Paper, London, 2016)

Tony Benn (ed. Ruth Winstone), *More Time for Politics: Diaries 2001–2007* (Hutchinson, London, 2007 – pbk edn: Arrow, London, 2008)

Alan Bennett, 'Diaries 1996–2004' in *Untold Stories* (Profile, London, 2005)

Alan Bennett, 'Diaries 2005–2015' in *Keeping On Keeping On* (Profile, London, 2016)

Cherie Blair, *Speaking for Myself: The Autobiography* (Little, Brown, London, 2008)

Tony Blair, *A Journey* (Hutchinson, London, 2010)

David Blunkett, *The Blunkett Tapes: My Life in the Bearpit* (Bloomsbury, London, 2006)

Gordon Brown, *My Life, Our Times* (Bodley Head, London, 2017)

Vince Cable, *Free Radical: A Memoir* (Atlantic, London, 2009 – pbk edn: 2009)

David Cameron, *For the Record* (William Collins, 2019)

Alastair Campbell (ed. Richard Stott), *The Blair Years: Extracts from the Alastair Campbell Diaries* (Hutchinson, London, 2007)

John Charmley, *A History of Conservative Politics, 1900–1999* (Macmillan, London, 1996 – pbk edn: 1998)

Ken Clarke, *Kind of Blue: A Political Memoir* (Macmillan, London, 2016)

Nick Clegg, *Politics: Between the Extremes* (Bodley Head, London, 2016 – pbk edn: Vintage, London, 2017)

Max Clifford and Angela Levin, *Max Clifford: Read All About It* (Virgin Books, London, 2005 – pbk edn: 2006)

Nick Cohen, *What's Left? How the Left Lost Its Way* (4th Estate, London, 2007 – pbk edn: Harper Perennial, London, 2007)

Robin Cook, *The Point of Departure: Diaries from the Front Bench* (Simon & Schuster, London, 2003 – rev. pbk edn: Pocket Books, London, 2004)

Dan Davies, *In Plain Sight: The Life and Lies of Jimmy Savile* (Quercus, London, 2014)

Emily Duggan, *Finding Home: Real Stories of Migrant Britain* (Icon Books, London, 2015)

Larry Elliott and Dan Atkinson, *Fantasy Island: Waking Up to the Incredible Economic, Political and Social Illusions of the Blair Legacy* (Constable, London, 2007)

Larry Elliott and Dan Atkinson, *The Gods that Failed: How Blind Faith in Markets Has Cost Us Our Future* (Bodley Head, London, 2008)

Nigel Farage, *Flying Free* (orig. title *Fighting Bull* – pbk edn: Biteback, London, 2011)

Hyman Frankel, *Socialism: Vision and Reality* (Arena Books, Bury St Edmunds, 2010)

Peter Hain, *Outside In* (Biteback, London, 2012)

Peter Hennessy, *Winds of Change: Britain in the Early Sixties* (Allen Lane, London, 2019)

Ian Hernon, *The Blair Decade* (Politico, London, 2007)

Peter Horrie and David Matthews, *True Blue: Strange Tales from a Tory Nation* (4th Estate, London, 2009)

Alexis Jay, 'Independent Inquiry into Child Sexual Exploitation in Rotherham 1997–2013' (Rotherham Metropolitan Borough Council, 2014)

Nicholas Jones, *Campaign 1997: How the General Election Was Won and Lost* (Indigo, London, 1997)

John Kampfner, *Blair's Wars* (The Free Press, London, 2003 – rev. pbk edn: 2004)

Nigel Lawson, *The View from Number 11: Memoirs of a Tory Radical* (Bantam, London, 1992)

Ken Livingstone, *You Can't Say That: Memoirs* (Faber & Faber, London, 2011)

Norman Lowe, *Mastering Modern British History* (Palgrave, London, 1984 – 5th edn: 2017)

Denis MacShane, *Brexit: How Britain Left Europe* (I. B. Tauris, London, 2015 – rev. edn: 2016)

Peter Mandelson, *The Third Man: Life at the Heart of New Labour* (Harper Press, London, 2010)

Damian McBride, *Power Trip: A Decade of Policy, Plots and Spin* (Biteback, London, 2013)

Andy Medhurst, *A National Joke: Popular Comedy and English Cultural Identities* (Routledge, Abingdon, 2007)

Charles Moore, *Margaret Thatcher: The Authorized Biography – Volume Three: Herself Alone* (Allen Lane, London, 2019)

Chris Mullin (ed. Ruth Winstone), *A View from the Foothills: The Diaries of Chris Mullin* (Profile, London, 2009 – pbk edn: 2010)

John O'Farrell, *Things Can Only Get Worse? Twenty Confusing Years in the Life of a Labour Supporter 1997–2017* (Doubleday, London, 2017)

Robert Peston, *Who Runs Britain?* (Hodder & Stoughton, London, 2008 – pbk edn: 2008)

John Prescott (with Hunter Davies), *Prezza: My Story* (Headline Review, London, 2008 – pbk edn: *Docks to Downing Street: My Story*, 2009)

Daniel Rachel, *Don't Look Back in Anger: The Rise and Fall of Cool Britannia, Told by Those Who Were There* (Trapeze, London, 2019)

Steve Richards, *Whatever It Takes: The Real Story of Gordon Brown and New Labour* (4th Estate, London, 2010)

The Royal Liverpool Children's Inquiry: Summary & Recommendations (Stationery Office, London, 2001)

Anthony Sampson, *Who Runs This Place? The Anatomy of Britain in the 21st Century* (John Murray, London, 2004)

Jimmy Savile, *As It Happens* (Barrie & Jenkins, London, 1974)

Anthony Seldon with Chris Ballinger, Daniel Collings and Peter Snowden, *Blair* (Free Press, London, 2004 – pbk edn: 2005)

Clare Short, *An Honourable Deception? New Labour, Iraq and the Misuse of Power* (Free Press, London, 2004)

Michael Spicer, *The Spicer Diaries* (Biteback Publishing, London, 2012)

Jack Straw, *Last Man Standing: Memoirs of a Political Survivor* (Macmillan, London, 2012)

Norman Tebbit, *Upwardly Mobile* (Weidenfeld & Nicolson, London, 1988)

Margaret Thatcher, *The Path to Power* (HarperCollins, London, 1995)

Robert Tombs, *The English and Their History* (Allen Lane, London, 2014)

David Turner, *The Old Boys: The Decline and Rise of the Public School* (Yale University Press, London, 2015)

Vedrana Veličković, *Eastern Europeans in Contemporary Literature and Culture: Imagining New Europe* (Palgrave Macmillan, London, 2019)

Geoffrey Wheatcroft, *The Strange Death of Tory England* (Allen Lane, London, 2005 – rev. pbk edn: Penguin, London, 2005)

Hugo Young (ed. Ion Trewin), *The Hugo Young Papers* (Allen Lane, London, 2008)

Books – fiction

Monica Ali, *Brick Lane* (Doubleday, London, 2003)

Kate Atkinson, *Started Early, Took My Dog* (Doubleday, London, 2010)

Alan Bennett, *The History Boys* (Faber & Faber, London, 2004)

Mark Billingham, *Scaredy Cat* (Little, Brown, London, 2002)

Jonathan Coe, *Number 11* (Viking, London, 2015)

Michael Dobbs, *The Lord's Day* (Headline, London, 2007)

Sebastian Faulks, *Engleby* (Hutchinson, London, 2007)

Mark Haddon, *The Red House* (Jonathan Cape, London, 2012)

Joanne Harris, *Gentlemen and Players* (Doubleday, London, 2005)

Joanne Harris, *Different Class* (Doubleday, London, 2016)

Robert Harris, *The Ghost* (Hutchinson, London, 2007)

Paula Hawkins, *The Girl on the Train* (Doubleday, London, 2015)

Nick Hornby, *How to Be Good* (Viking, London, 2001)

Sandra Howard, *A Matter of Loyalty* (Simon & Schuster, London, 2009)

P. D. James, *The Murder Room* (Faber & Faber, London, 2003)

P. D. James, *The Private Patient* (Faber & Faber, London, 2008)

Peter James, *Not Dead Enough* (Macmillan, London, 2007)

Boris Johnson, *Seventy-Two Virgins* (HarperCollins, London, 2004)

Carolyn Jess-Cooke, *The Boy Who Could See Demons* (Piatkus, London, 2012)

David Lodge, *Deaf Sentence* (Harvill Secker, London, 2008)

Hilary Mantel, *The Assassination of Margaret Thatcher: Stories* (4th Estate, London, 2014)

Marina Lewycka, *Two Caravans* (Fig Tree, London, 2007)

Ian McEwan, *Saturday* (Jonathan Cape, London, 2005)

Andrew Marr, *Children of the Master* (4th Estate, London, 2015)

Lance Price, *Time and Fate* (Polperro Heritage Press, Clifton-upon-Teme, 2005)

Peter Robinson, *Friend of the Devil* (Hodder & Stoughton, London, 2007)

J. K. Rowling, *The Casual Vacancy* (Sphere, London, 2012)

Leigh Russell, *Killer Plan* (No Exit Press, Harpenden, 2015)

Iain Duncan Smith, *The Devil's Tune* (Robson, London, 2003)

Linda Smith (ed. Warren Lakin and Ian Parsons), *I Think the Nurses Are Stealing My Clothes: The Very Best of Linda Smith* (Hodder & Stoughton, London, 2006)

Adam Thorpe, *Between Each Breath* (Jonathan Cape, London, 2007)

Sue Townsend, *The Woman Who Went to Bed for a Year* (Penguin, London, 2012)

Television and film

Alexander Armstrong's Big Ask (Dave/So Television, 2011–13) wr. Dan Gaster, Will Ing, Paul Powell and Steve Punt

The Amazing Mrs Pritchard (BBC, 2006) cr. Sally Wainwright

Apparitions (BBC, 2008) cr. Joe Ahearne and Nick Collins

The Armstrong & Miller Show (BBC/Hat Trick Productions, 2007–10) dir. Dominic Brigstocke

Ashes to Ashes (BBC/Kudos Films, 2008–10) cr. Matthew Graham and Ashley Pharoah

Atheism: A Rough History of Disbelief (BBC, 2004) wr. Jonathan Miller

Believe Nothing (ITV, 2002) cr. Maurice Gran and Lawrence Marks

Benidorm (ITV/Tiger Aspect Productions, 2007–18) cr. Derren Litten

Borat: Cultural Learnings of America for Make Benefit Glorious Nation of Kazakhstan (Four By Two Films, 2006) dir. Larry Charles

Bremner, Bird and Fortune (Channel 4/Vera Productions, 1999–2010) cr. Rory Bremner, John Bird and John Fortune

Broken News (BBC, 2005) cr. John Morton and Tony Roche

Demons (ITV/Shine Productions, 2009) cr. Johnny Capps and Julian Murphy

Doctor Who (BBC, 1963–89, 2005–) cr. Sydney Newman, C. E. Webber and Donald Wilson

Downton Abbey (ITV/Carnival Films, 2010–15) cr. Julian Fellowes

Endeavour (ITV/Mammoth Screen, 2012–) cr. Russell Lewis

Fallen (ITV, 2004) wr. Steve Griffiths

Foyle's War (ITV, 2002–15) cr. Anthony Horowitz

Gavin & Stacey (BBC/Baby Cow Productions, 2007–10) cr. and wr. James Corden and Ruth Jones

The Girl in the Café (BBC/Tightrope Pictures, 2005) wr. Richard Curtis, dir.
  David Yates
Grantchester (ITV/Lovely Day, 2014–) cr. James Runcie, wr. Daisy Coulam
Harry and Paul (BBC/Tiger Aspect, 2007–12) cr. Harry Enfield and Paul
  Whitehouse
Have I Got News For You (BBC/Hat Trick Productions, 1990–) cr. Harry
  Thompson
Hustle (BBC, 2002–12) cr. Tony Jordan
The Inbetweeners (E4/Bwark Productions, 2008–10) cr. Damon Beesley and
  Iain Morris
Inspector George Gently (BBC/Company Pictures, 2007–17) cr. Peter
  Flannery
Jamie's School Dinners (Channel 4/Fresh One Productions, 2005) pr. Jamie
  Oliver
Jonathan Creek (BBC, 2007–16) cr. and wr. David Renwick
Kilroy: Behind the Tan (BBC, 2005) pr. Emeka Onono
Last Rights (Channel 4/Touchpaper Television, 2005) wr. Clive Bradley
Lewis (ITV, 2006–15) cr. Colin Dexter, dev. Chris Burt and Stephen Churchett
Life on Mars (BBC/Kudos Films, 2006–07) cr. Matthew Graham, Tony Jordan
  and Ashley Pharoah
Love Actually (Working Title Films, 2004) wr. and dir. Richard Curtis
Luther (BBC, 2010–) cr. Neil Cross
Misfits (E4/Clerkenwell Films, 2009–13) cr. Howard Overman
Mock the Week (BBC/Angst Productions, 2005–) cr. Dan Patterson and
  Mark Leveson
Mrs Brown's Boys (BBC/RTÉ, 2011–) cr. and wr. Brendan O'Carroll
Murder City (ITV/Granada Productions, 2004–06) cr. Robert Murphy
My Family (BBC/Rude Boy Productions, 2000–11) cr. Fred Barron
Nathan Barley (Channel 4/Talkback, 2005) cr. Chris Morris and Charlie
  Brooker
New Tricks (BBC/Wall to Wall/Headstrong, 2003–15) cr. Nigel McCrery and
  Roy Mitchell
Outnumbered (BBC/Hat Trick Productions, 2007–16) cr. Andy Hamilton and
  Guy Jenkin
Party Animals (BBC, 2007) cr. Robert Jones and Ben Richards
Peep Show (Channel 4/Objective Productions, 2003–15) cr. Andrew
  O'Connor, Jesse Armstrong and Sam Bain
Rebus (ITV/STV, 2000–07) cr. Ian Rankin
QI (BBC/Talkback, 2003–) cr. John Lloyd

Rev (BBC/Big Talk Productions) cr. and wr. Tom Hollander and James Wood

The Revolution Will Be Televised (BBC/Hat Trick Productions, 2012–15) cr. Heydon Prowse, Jolyon Rubinstein and Joe Wade

Robin Hood (BBC/Tiger Aspect Productions, 2006–09) cr. Dominic Minghella and Foz Allan

Roy Chubby Brown: Britain's Rudest Comedian (Channel 4/Spun Gold TV, 2007) dir. Will Yapp

The Second Coming (Channel 4/Red Production Company, 2003) cr. and wr. Russell T. Davies

Secret State (Channel 4/Company Pictures, 2012) wr. Robert Jones

Shafted (ITV/Initial, 2001) pr. Phil Parsons

Shameless (Channel 4/Company Pictures, 2004–13) cr. Paul Abbott

Skins (E4/Company Pictures, 2007–13) cr. Bryan Elsley and Jamie Brittain

Spooks (BBC/Kudos, 2002–11) cr. David Wolstencroft

Taggart (ITV/STV Productions, 1983–2010) cr. Glenn Chandler

That Mitchell and Webb Look (BBC, 2006–10) cr. David Mitchell and Robert Webb

The Thick Of It (BBC, 2005–12) cr. Armando Iannucci

The Trial of Tony Blair (Channel 4/Daybreak Pictures, 2007) wr. Alistair Beaton

Trinity (ITV, 2009) cr. and wr. Kieron Quirke and Robin French

A Very Social Secretary (Channel 4/Mentorn Television, 2005) wr. Alistair Beaton

W1A (BBC, 2014–17) wr. and dir. John Morton

Wimbledon (Working Title Films, 2004) wr. Adam Brooks, Jennifer Flackett and Mark Levin, dir. Richard Loncraine

Picture credits

Acknowledgements

I've never had occasion to thank my agent before, having not had an agent, so I'm very excited to thank Euan Thorneycroft of A. M. Heath, whose confidence was crucial to this project and is very much appreciated.

Euan introduced me to Profile, where Helen Conford commissioned this book and where Ed Lake edited it with tact, insight and a habit of being right. It was then brought it to fruition by a host of fine people: managing editor Graeme Hall, copy editor Hugh Davis, proof editor Graham Coster, art director Steve Panton and publicity director Valentina Zanca, as well as Niamh Murray and Flora Willis in marketing, and Claire Beaumont and Lisa Finch in sales. And Tony Lyons did a fabulous job on the cover design. They have all been extraordinarily enthusiastic and helpful, particularly since the process has been hampered by the restrictions occasioned by the Covid crisis. The book is much the better for all their contributions.

I benefited from talking about various aspects of the period with – among others – Dan Atkinson, Jennie Bird, Ben Blackwood, Adenike Deane-Pratt, Ben Finlay, John Flaxman, Brian Freeborn, Thamasin Marsh, York Membrey, Anthony Teague, Martyn Turner and Peter Webster. And, of course, Sam Harrison, who continues to edit my thoughts long after he ceased being employed as my editor.

During the period covered here, Hugo Frey invited me to deliver a lecture at the University of Chichester. That started an association with the University that has brought me much pleasure and taught me some academic discipline, though how much of the latter is on display here is debatable. I'm endlessly grateful to him.

My parents died during the course of writing this book. Even in their absence, I continue to rely on the memory of their support, encouragement and love.

Index

Page references for notes are followed by *n*